Praise for Sean McManus and the Irish National Caucus

"This is a hugely important book. It is probably the most significant memoir in the historiography of Irish-American nationalism since *Recollections of an Irish Rebel* (1929) by John Devoy."

Washington Irish Committee

"No one has done more than Father McManus to keep the U.S. Congress on track regarding justice and peace in Ireland. Indeed, I believe historians will record that no one since John Devoy (1842–1928) has done more to organize American pressure for justice in Ireland."

Congressman Ben Gilman (R-NY)
Chairman, House International Relations Committee

"Fr. Sean knows the history of the struggle for justice in Northern Ireland as well as anyone – he lived it. A very important book."

Ray Flynn, Former Mayor of Boston and U.S. Ambassador to The Vatican

"As Chairman of the Ad Hoc committee for Irish Affairs, I ... commend the Irish National Caucus for your steadfast advocacy on behalf of human rights ... Fr. McManus is 'The Apostle of Human Rights for Northern Ireland'."

Rep. Mario Biaggi (D-NY) 1980

"Fr. Sean McManus has spent a lifetime leading the fight to achieve a peaceful solution to the conflict in Northern Ireland. That so many Americans and, particularly those in American government leadership roles, joined in the effort to achieve a peaceful resolution of the conflict is a credit to his courageous and inspiring leadership."

Bill Flynn, Chairman Emeritus, Mutual of America
Chairman, National Committee on American Foreign Policy

"[Fr. McManus] stood out against powerful forces in a fight for justice and fairness. I didn't always agree with the causes he supported but I admired his persistence, his courage, his relentlessness. And admiration that one person, almost alone, could make such impact on public policy in the United States."

Noted journalist and broadcaster, Vincent Browne, Dublin

"Fr. McManus, from his Capitol Hill office, has been a prominent and influential figure in the quest for progress and peace with justice in Northern Ireland, blending knowledge of his native land with experience drawn from his years of dealing with the intricacies of the political system in his adopted one. His has been a unique role. Long may it continue."

Ray O'Hanlon. Editor, *The Irish Echo*. New York

"Fr. Sean McManus is a man to be reckoned with when it comes to advocating causes. His espousal of the MacBride Principles back in the 1980s caused fits for the British government ... McManus has also been a constant watchdog in Washington on Irish affairs and has been hugely successful in setting the Irish-American agenda over the past 30 years."

Niall O'Dowd. Editor, *Irish Voice*, New York

"The master ... in publicity terms, is Father Sean Mc Manus, a burly, plausible charmer whose Irish National Caucus has taken center stage ... the good Father has made himself expert in congressional lobbying techniques ... I spent a long and, to be perfectly frank, rather enjoyable afternoon with Father Mc Manus in his Capitol Hill office ... and it became clear that he hadn't been raised as a clerical apologist for nothing."

Christopher Hitchens, Public Intellectual, Author of *God is Not Great* and
The Missionary Position: Mother Teresa in Theory and Practice

"As a writer, singer and performer of Irish ballads, I know the value of voice, words and thoughts that expose injustice. Over the last 40 years Fr. Mc Manus has been the powerful voice that has kept the U.S. Congress involved in the struggle for justice and peace in Ireland."

Derek Warfield, (Young) Wolfe Tones

"I am a Protestant (which normally I would not mention). However, I had to turn to a Catholic priest, Father Sean Mc Manus, to seek justice for the murder of my son, Raymond Jr. Father Mc Manus helped me get a powerful Congressional hearing into young Raymond's murder and expose state collusion in his murder."

Raymond McCord Sr., Belfast

"The intrepid Fermanagh-born battler for justice, Fr. Sean Mc Manus, has published the definitive book on Irish-America's fight for justice in the North of Ireland, including the epic Mac Bride Principles campaign."

Máirtín Ó Muilleoir, Belfast Media
President, Irish Echo

"Thank-you [Fr. Mc Manus] for your gracious invitation to become a 'Congressional Friend' of the Irish National Caucus. The warm welcome that I have received from the Irish people on my visits there has gladdened my heart and made me always hopeful that people throughout Ireland will live in a climate of peace and nonviolence."

Senator Hillary Rodham Clinton (D-NY) 2003
(appointed U.S. Secretary of State by President Obama in 2009)

"So from Kinawley to the halls of Congress, your story – which I thank you for – is hard to put down. May this year be one of deepening justice and peace for Ireland."

Jim Douglass, noted author on nonviolence

"I support the Irish National Caucus because it represents a compelling voice for fair employment, legal justice, and lasting peace in Northern Ireland."

Rep. Joseph P. Kennedy II (D-MA) 1988

"I support the Irish National Caucus in its important work for justice and peace in Northern Ireland and would be proud to be associated with this worthy organization."

Rep. Peter T. King (R-NY) 1994

MY AMERICAN STRUGGLE FOR JUSTICE IN NORTHERN IRELAND ... AND THE HOLY LAND

Fr. Sean McManus

Fr. Sean McManus, President of the Capitol Hill-based Irish National Caucus, was born in 1944 in County Fermanagh, one of the six counties in Northern Ireland – in a parish, significantly, divided by the British-imposed Border.

In 1972 Church and State exiled him from Britain to the U.S. because he refused to be silent about injustice in Northern Ireland.

In 1974 he founded the American-based Irish National Caucus: "Thus McManus became Britain's nemesis in America, the driving force that would eventually erode Britain's influence within the U.S. government." (American Policy and Northern Ireland. Professor Joseph E. Thompson.)

My American Struggle for Justice in Northern Ireland is widely acclaimed. It has been declared a classic, a masterpiece, a must-read, and a hugely important book.

It is the perfect tool for replenishing, reinvigorating and recharging the Irish cause in America.

And with this new Edition, the book will, please God, prove an effective tool for promoting fairness by American companies doing business in The Holy Land. ... That the Holy Land Principles will do for The Holy Land what the MacBride Principles did for Northern Ireland .

Dedicated to the memory of my patriot brother
Patrick McManus (1929–1958)

In him it seems the ancient clans combined
In pagan strength and Holy Rood;
The unsheathed swords of proud and bitter kings,
Marched and mingled in his blood.
Brave Spirit, when of you Freedom sings
At the exultant gates of God,
Your passing serves to illumine the Cause;
You are not dead, but lack a mortal robe.

EPITAPH for Patrick McManus by P.J. Madigan. 1958.

MY AMERICAN STRUGGLE
FOR JUSTICE IN
NORTHERN IRELAND
... AND THE HOLY LAND

FR. SEAN McMANUS

* Holy Land Edition *
Irish National Caucus Publications
Washington, D.C.

To JOHN HARRINGTON
— A GOOD AMERICAN
WHO BELIEVES IN
JUSTICE FOR ALL

FR. Sean McManus
FEB. 14, 2014

MY AMERICAN STRUGGLE FOR JUSTICE IN
NORTHERN IRELAND ... AND THE HOLY LAND
Published by
Irish National Caucus Publications
P.O. Box 15128
Washington, D.C. 20003-0849
www.irishnationalcaucus.org
202-544-0568

ISBN-13: 978-1481080385
ISBN-10: 1481080385

Library of Congress Control Number: 2012902123
CreateSpace, North Charleston, SC

Cover Photographs
Front and Spine: Author photo (Belfast Media Group)
Capitol Hill: (iStockphoto)
Back: Hillary Rodham Clinton with author (courtesy of author)

Contents

Foreword to The Holy Land Edition

This book was first published in Ireland by Collins Press, Cork. 2011.

The Irish Edition told the story up to 2009. The American Edition brought the story up to 2012. However, there were many additions throughout the book – including 50 additional pages and 22 more photos.

The Holy Land Edition joins The Holy Land and Ireland, and recounts my recent visit to The Holy Land. But most of all, it launches the Holy Land Principles – a corporate code of conduct for American companies doing business in The Holy Land. These Principles were modeled on our famous Mac Bride Principles, which I also launched on November 5, 1984.

This book covers a lot of ground, and many years, so it is impossible to thank everyone who should be thanked.

In the first place, I want to thank my brothers and sisters who read the early chapters that dealt with our entire family.

I also want to express my heartfelt and humble gratitude to all those good and decent Irish-Americans who made my work for Irish justice possible. Without them, there would have been no Irish National Caucus – and no book either. God bless each and every one of them. While all their names cannot be recorded in this book, they surely will be recorded in The Book of Life.

I am grateful also to all the fine people I have met in the process of launching the Holy Land Principles. I am greatly impressed by their deep commitment to justice in The Holy Land, and I deeply appreciate their wise counsel and support.

As always, I must thank my colleague Barbara Flaherty, who makes so much of my work possible. She has been a tower of strength and a constant inspiration to me. She has played an indispensable role in every aspect of the production of this book – and in the launching of the Holy Land Principles.

Her daughter Barbara Maureen provided invaluable legal help and advice.

Any mistake or error is my own.

Introduction

The letter, dated Friday April 15, 1972, from my Religious Superior got right to the point in the very first sentence:

> "Will you please pack up all your own belongings & leave everything ready to be sent on later without your having to return to Scotland. When this is done, I would like to see you here in Clapham [London], please, as soon as possible afterwords [*sic*], and not later than Thursday night [April 21]."

Even if he had not said anything else, I knew the writing was on the wall (not just in his typed letter). But he continued and, after the polite, very proper English opening, he let loose:

> You will understand that we cannot any longer tolerate the harm you are doing to yourself, the Church, and the Congregation through your stupid and stubborn persistence in writing to newspapers. I do not want anyone to know your immediate destination, nor your proposed transfer from Perth [Scotland]. I once again forbid you to make any communications to the Press or Media either per se or per alium, or to call on anyone en route or before departure. You have had just enough public notice and it is time you thought about your own confreres and your apostolate. Please inform your superior, present or future, when you leave, of my permission for you to do so, and ask them for the time being to regard it as confidential.
> With sincere regards,
> Yours JMJA
> Charles Shepherd, CSsR[1]

There was a train strike at the time so I phoned Fr. Shepherd to let him know. "Then fly down," he huffed and slammed down the phone. In those days it would have been most unusual for a young Redemptorist to fly from Scotland to London, so I knew I was in serious trouble.

And what was my offense? Had I mistreated people, preached heresy, denied the Real Presence of Christ in the Holy Eucharist? No, none of these. But worse still, in the eyes of some, I had broken about the only remaining taboo in Britain, especially for a young Irish priest: I had the temerity to criticize what Her Majesty's government and army were doing in the North of Ireland. Never from the pulpit, mind you, but just a few times in the press and on TV.

As I packed my bag (singular) I knew my life would never be the same again. But I also knew, come what may, I would be true to my conscience or else something would die in my soul. I would not, through my silence, collaborate with England's oppression of my country. I prayed for a steady hand and a true heart. I was worried and anxious, with no idea I was embarking on the first leg of my journey to America. But now, almost forty years later, I can smile and "with malice toward none, with charity for all",[2] thank God that instead of silencing me, they – the Church and State – sent me to the one place on the planet where I was better able to work for justice and peace in Ireland. Charlie Shepherd, from his now high place in Heaven, must be echoing the famous words of Margaret Thatcher, when her Party ousted her from office in 1990, "It's a strange old world."

But more importantly still – and the thing that has given me the most peace of mind and spiritual consolation over all these years – is that I was able to carve out a way to reconcile my struggle for justice and peace in Ireland with my vocation as a Redemptorist priest. And what would provide me with the solid theological foundation for my work in America with the Irish National Caucus was the official teaching of the Catholic Church: "Action on behalf of justice [is] ... a constitutive dimension of the preaching of the Gospel" (*Justice in the World*, Synod of Bishops, Rome, November 30, 1971).[3]

This groundbreaking document could not have come at a more providential time for me. Unfortunately, it is still very little known and certainly the Bishops of Ireland, Britain and the United States[4] never seemed to stress it in regard to Northern Ireland. But for me it was "a lamp to my feet, and a light to my path" (Psalm 119: 105). And later, when I became more familiar with the "Social Gospel"[5] as preached and practised by the great Reverend Martin Luther King, Jr., I knew nothing was going to turn me around.

> "Ain't gonna let nobody turn me 'roun'
> Turn me 'roun'
> Ain't gonna let nobody turn me 'roun'
> I'm gonna wait until my change comes."
> (Old Negro Spiritual)

1

Bonny Banks of Lough Erne

And for all this, nature is never spent;
There lives the dearest freshness deep down things.

"God's Grandeur", Gerard Manley Hopkins

American Catholics who were very proud of their "historic" parishes used to be astonished whenever I told them that I came from a parish that had essentially existed since the sixth century – the parish of Kinawley in Fermanagh.

I was born on February 6, 1944 in the townland of Clonliff, which is about three miles from the village of Kinawley, which in turn is about two miles from the Cavan border near Swanlinbar. The historic parish of Kinawley is actually divided by the British-imposed border. So I grew up extremely conscious that the British government had partitioned not only my country but also my own ancient parish. The name in Irish, "Cill Naile," means Church of St. Naile, a famous saint who ministered in the area in the 6th century.[1]

I was the tenth child in a family of twelve. Our parents owned a small farm of 23 acres, on which our father, Patrick Sr., was born (January 28, 1877 – January 21, 1962). Our mother,

Celia McMullen-McManus (September 30, 1903 – June 28, 1991) came from nearby Carn Mountain. When they got married, my father was forty-nine and my mother twenty-two. The back of the farm is lapped by the waters of Upper Lough Erne and the front is bounded by the Cladagh River, which empties into Lough Erne. Our home was a small thatched house. Because Clonliff Lane was entirely Catholic (nine families then) it was not provided with running water or electricity until 1960.

No memoirs of mine would make sense without full acknowledgement of my brothers and sisters, for it was my whole family that shaped me. All that is good in me, I owe, under God, to them. My faults and sins I owe to myself alone: Mary Kate (born 1927), twins Patrick and Terence (born 1929; Terence died before he was three years old), Celia (born 1931), Thomas (born 1933), Alice (born 1934), Terence (the second, born in 1937), Jim, who also became a priest (born 1938), Frank (born 1942), and finally, my two younger brothers, Myles (born 1948) and Arthur (born in 1949, died in May 1950).

My father was sixty-seven when I was born so obviously I never knew him as a young man – indeed none of us did. Yet I never felt I missed out on that account – probably because there were so many of us and because our father was always there. He would never have been absent or away from home overnight in his entire life. Because my father was himself old, I grew up revering old people and that reverence has never left me. For me, God is almost tangibly present around the very old and very young. I don't suppose any father was loved more by his children. And that is still evident fifty years later when we all get together to reminisce. A smile always breaks out when we talk about him.

Your Father Was a Saint

About 20 years ago, when I was home from America on vacation, I was chatting to one of our nearest and dearest neighbors, the late Matthew McHugh, who was 28 years older than I. He, therefore, would have known Daddy (as the family always called him, and still does) when Daddy was still fairly young. So I asked Matthew what was the thing he most remembered about Daddy, as a younger man. I was expecting him to say, he was strong, funny, or something like that: to mention some such physical quality that stood out. But Matthew took me totally aback by saying, "Your Father was a saint." I asked him why he said that. He told me that whenever he worked with Daddy in the fields, at the end of the day when they would walk up to where the spades were kept, Daddy would bless himself with the Sign of the Cross (invoking the name of the Holy Trinity – Father, son and Holy Spirit) and say Three Hail Marys for a good day's work. It was the first time I had ever heard that, and I was touched by the sweetness of it – and the grace of it. My father knew that humble work blessed by God was "more precious than rubies." And he certainly knew that that was even truer of his bride, the fair Celia McMullen-Mc Manus: "Who can find a virtuous woman? For her price is far above rubies. She opens her mouth with wisdom: and in her tongue is the law of kindness. Her children rise up and call her blessed; her husband also, and he praises her." (Proverbs 31:10, 26, 28). My mother was a remarkably strong, independent and resilient woman – patriotic to the core with a profound trust in God. This will become very evident later in the story. In later life, she really blossomed and enjoyed her old age immensely.

There were a lot of us for a small house. Yet I don't ever remember feeling crowded and needing my own space. But of course not all of us lived in the house at the same time. You can see the closeness in age of some of the children, and the great age difference between the youngest and oldest. In that sense, as far as growing up together, we were like three different families. Mary Kate, Patrick, Celia, Thomas and Alice grew up together. Terence and Jim were the second crop. And finally Frankie, I and Myles sprouted up. There is a seventeen-year difference between Mary Kate and me, and twenty-one years between her and Myles.

Mary Kate left home for Omagh, Portadown and later England when she was nineteen (when I was only two years old). Alice went to school in the convent when she was thirteen (and I was three) and stayed in Enniskillen with our Aunt Lizzie, Daddy's sister, who had inherited a house in the town. Essentially she never lived full-time at home after that. Thomas left for England at nineteen (when I was eight) and in the same year Jim left (aged fourteen) for the Presentation Brothers in Cork, only to defect later to the Redemptorists; Terence left at seventeen (when I was ten) to work and stay in Enniskillen.

So for most of my growing up, the only permanent dwellers in Macs were my parents and Patrick and Celia, who were both adults. Frankie, Myles and I were the cubs. But we cubs also grew up with another almost-brother – our first cousin Patrick Maguire who is two years younger than I am.

Patrick with his parents, John James and Maggie, lived nearby. Maggie was my mother's older sister and they were very close. Patrick hung out with us a lot and is still like a brother to this day. In 2002 – inspired by showing the old McMullen ruins on Carn to long-lost cousins from America – Patrick crafted a moving poem (part elegy, part paean), "The Carn Lintel", the only thing left standing:

Tired and hungry fields, receding, as the gorse reclaims its space,
Our ancestral tracks have vanished, footprints faded beyond trace.
Vengeful bramble, angry briar, that for long were held at bay,
Boldly colonise the meadow where my mother trampled hay ...
Nettles, tall as were my uncles, stretch up from the strewn floor
And yet, the stubborn lintel sullenly protects the door.
Persevering through the decades, resolutely standing fast,
Tireless, it maintains the portal; guards this entrance to our past.
(See full poem on page 388.)

I guess I knew we were not rich but again I don't remember feeling deprived although I was conscious that Francie Reilly across the bog had a bicycle and I didn't. But then none of the

McManus children ever had a bike so it was no big deal.

Country poverty, at least as I experienced it, is vastly different from city poverty. We had 23 acres of our own land to roam, not to mention the entire countryside, in perfect safety – as long as we stayed away from the river because the monster, Terry McGrath, lived there. Nobody seemed to know the origins of the story behind this bogeyman but it certainly kept us away until we were big enough. Amazingly, although we were surrounded by water, hardly anyone in our area could swim. But then, how could they? They were all scared of Terry McGrath!

Ironically, one time the river did not seem to hold fear for any of us, not even for Mother. It was during the Big Snow of 1947 from the end of February well into March when the Cladagh River was frozen over (and therefore presumably keeping Terry McGrath frozen below). I remember clearly holding Mother's hand and walking on the ice with a group of people. I can also still see in my mind's eye the little snow house that my Father and older brothers built on the back street, as we called it, which was really sort of a back yard. I was only three at the time but my recollection is vivid.

Now by American standards, the Big Snow may not have been all that big, but for Ireland it was. Newspapers at the time reported "huge snow-drifts, some up to fifteen feet high were common in many areas." And *The Swanlinbar News* reported "that it had been estimated that over 1,000 sheep had been lost in the snow ..."[3]

Anyway, the Macs, as we were called locally, all survived The Big Snow, and without thermal clothing!

Fishing in the Blood

But when we were big enough, and no longer scared of Teddy McGrath, the Cladagh River became a beloved fishing spot – especially "Murphy's hole."

The Murphys lived one field across from us to the left. Charles (always pronounced "CHARL-es") 1877-1967, was a colorful and legendary figure and a lifelong friend of our Father. We got such a kick out him. He could be a quite fearsome spectacle as he supported Kinawley against Derrylin. But he was always kind and gentle to us – unless we just went too far in annoying him. Even then he would just chase us away for awhile. He never hit me. He had been a good footballer in his day but when I was growing up, he was in his late 70's. He was a fanatic fisherman, fishing almost every morning during fishing season, and at the ungodly hour of 5 AM. Clonliff Lane and indeed all of Kinawley was a late-starting zone. People stayed up late and got up late. Not the intrepid Charles. He would be in bed before nine o'clock at night, and by dawn's first light, the fish better watch out. He always fished with three rods (cut out of the hedge), and he would land the roach and perch on the river-bank with amazing rapidity.

Charles would feed "Murphy's hole" each night with all sorts of stuff: wheat, bread, anything at all. He didn't keep pigs, so all sorts of slops went into the fishing hole. And boy, did his strategy work. The fish practically begged to be caught. Pike would be caught by leaving a line out overnight. Bream were also in the river but not as abundant as perch and roach.

Charles would waken us at that ungodly hour, and we would fish to our hearts' content – with rods also cut from the hedge and string for our lines. I often think of that now when I'm using my fancy fly rod and all my sophisticated tackle. Charles would not have been impressed by any of it. Indeed, one day my brother-in-law, Michael Ferguson (Celia's husband), joined Charles at the river bank with a brand new spinning rod. Charles cast a suspicious eye on this new-fangled article and said, "That's a dangerous looking weapon."

One Sunday afternoon, Frankie and I went fishing with Charles in his boat, kept at the bottom of his land, which like our land, was on the edge of Lough Erne. Charles rowed to Kipping, a very small island about twenty minutes away from our adjoining farms. We stopped just off Kipping and in a few hours we had caught 13 dozen fish. I never forgot the number.

The fishing was so great that we could skim the hook/worm just above the water and the fish would jump up to grab it. I have never witnessed that phenomenon again. In those days, we could still actually see the fish a little bit under the water even though Lough Erne is naturally dark. One of my great laments is that the Cladagh and Lough Erne are so polluted. Like my own present day fishing-hole – the mighty Chesapeake Bay. In the 1600's, Native Americans could see a fish 30 feet below the waters of the Chesapeake. Now, one cannot see the tiniest fraction of an inch below the water. So much for progress. We have destroyed the waters of the world with "progress." It would have broken the stout heart of Charles Murphy.

Life on the Ranch

Out of the 23 acres of land, probably only about 15 were arable. The remainder was bog and bottomland along the edge of Lough Erne, and only good for growing bulrushes. Frankie, Myles and I used to pull the bulrushes and use them as a floatation device when we were trying to learn to swim in the shallow waters of the Lough (Terry McGrath did not inhabit Lough Erne). In fact the bulrushes were only an obstacle, a water-crutch that only delayed proper learning. Indeed, I could never really swim until at the age of sixteen I went to the Redemptorist junior seminary in Birmingham, England, in 1960. We were allowed out to go to the local public swimming pool once a week. And I was so embarrassed to see all the little English kids jump into the pool and swim like fish, and there was I, a big Paddy, standing at the edge of the pool like a proper eejit. I watched how they were doing it, and patriotic pride took over: "Says I to myself, if these English cubs can do it, so can I." And with that I dived in and swam, quite well. "Bulrushes, how are ye?" I thought to myself.

On the farm we grew potatoes, turnips, lettuce, carrots, cabbage and wheat – enough to keep us well fed, with chicken, hen eggs, duck eggs and bacon from our pigs that Johnny McCaffery, our neighbor out the lane, would slaughter in the backyard. Plus our diet was amply supplemented with fresh fish we caught and rabbits and hares we snared or caught with our dogs.

Not one of us was ever sick, apart from the usual stuff, except baby Arthur who had a hole in his heart – fatal in those days.

We made hay in the summer (and I never had hayfever until I came to Washington, DC) for our four to five cows, and cut turf, peat, to keep the home fires burning. Turf was our only fuel in the open hearth, and our only source of heat. The Macs were truly ahead of their time: green, all the way. No machinery of any kind. All farm work was done by shovel, spade, pitchfork and grape. Al Gore would have been proud of us.

When I was too small to spread fertilizer (a posh word for cow dung) with the grape, I spread it with my hands. Once you have done that, no job is beneath you and you come to know what holy men and women have taught from the beginning: that creation is sacred and all work has an inherent dignity.

School for all the Macs was Drumbroughas National School – one classroom, two teachers and a dry-toilet across the road. The younger children sat facing Miss McManus (no relation) and the older children sat in the opposite direction, facing Miss McHugh.

The school was about three miles from our house and, naturally, we walked there and back each day. In the summer we walked in our bare feet, not because we did not have shoes but because it was the custom. By the end of the summer the soles of our feet were as tough as leather.

Drumbroughas School was almost all Catholic, except for the odd Protestant. During religion class the Protestants got to go outside, and there were times I wished I were a Protestant.

GAA in the Blood

School never turned me on: that was the preserve of the GAA (Gaelic Athletic Association). All seven brothers were devoted to the game. Indeed, one of the family treasures is a photograph of all seven brothers togged out in football uniforms, posing proudly on the "hill" outside the house. We had, at least in our minds, our own seven-a-side team. The photograph was taken in 1956 when all ten children were home. Mary Kate remembers Mother saying it would never happen again that all ten of us would be home at the same time. Sadly, she was right.

Patrick had played a key role in reviving the Kinawley Football Club, the Brian Borus, for which he served as Secretary. The Fermanagh GAA County Secretary, Tom Fee, would later recall: "I remember making ... a number of trips to the [Kinawley] parish in 1950 in an effort to have the club resurrected ... We were fortunate enough to find the very man in Patrick McManus ... he was the vital part ..."[4] Patrick, however, did not play much himself but did occasionally act as referee. Thomas was a good player, although I never actually remember him playing. I do, however, clearly remember Celia cheering, "Come on our Thomas" at a game in the old field at Carron's Gap. Thomas played on the county minors, with his buddy across the field, Patrick Murphy, Charles' eldest son. But forced emigration cut short Thomas' football career. Terence, God rest him, was a strong player, if not the most genteel. Jim left too early to play for Kinawley and there was no Under-Fourteen team then. But while he was in Cork from 1952 to 1955, he got hooked on hurling. When he came home on holidays, I remember he would strut his stuff on the hill with his camán (hurling stick) and sliotar (the ball), probably thinking he was Christy Ring[5] or one of the famous Cork players. But hurling was a "foreign" game in Kinawley. Frankie and Myles played for the county, but I left for the Redemptorists just as I was beginning to peak: "I coulda been a contender" as Marlon Brando famously lamented in *On the Waterfront*.

However, I did have my share of glory playing on the Under Fourteens on a joint Kinawley–Swanlinbar team in the league. We won the cup for the Under-Fourteen County Cavan League in 1956 and 1958. Frankie was the captain in 1956 and I was captain in 1958.

It was a huge thrill for us Fermanagh boys to win in Breffni

Park – home pitch of the once-famed Cavan footballers. Also, I was the Kinawley captain when we won the Fermanagh Schoolboy Cup in 1959. When I left for the Redemptorists in Birmingham, England, in 1960, the only material things of value I had were the medals from those victories – and I still have them today.

While I was still under fourteen, I not only played for the Under-Fourteens, but also for the minors (Under-Eighteen) and the senior team. Which meant I was going up against big bruisers from Derrylin and elsewhere in their twenties and thirties. But I had a back-up strategy: while I played center-left, Terence was center-half, Frankie was center-right, and to top it off, my brother-in-law, Big Mick Ferguson, was full-back, so if "them Derrylin boys" wanted trouble, they had come to the right place.

Spirituality in the Blood

Our home was a devout one though we would never have been considered "churchy." Indeed, I never remember seeing the priest in our home until Patrick was killed. However, no night passed without Mother gathering us all around and saying the Rosary, with all the trimmings. She would recite the Litany of the Saints by heart without falter – unless one of us misbehaved and distracted her. Then she would have to stop, go back to the beginning and take another run at it. The only time my father ever "cuffed me in the ear" was during the Rosary when he wrongly blamed me for something Frankie or Myles would do.

The spiritual world – God, the Incarnation, Death and resurrection of Jesus Christ, The Word and The Sacraments, Heaven and Hell – was as real to us as the land and the sky. Even more real, because we knew the material world would pass but God's word would last forever. Our theology and cosmology may have been overly simple but compared to the shallowness and emptiness of much in today's culture we had the essentials right. And we have all been sustained by an unshakeable trust in God's abiding love for each one of us and the entire world.

"May God's holy will be done" was the constant refrain of my mother both in good times and bad – and bad times did come.

At the time, none of us would have seen that "worldview" as Celtic spirituality but today it's almost quite fashionably seen as that. Deacon Owen F. Cummings, a Professor of Theology in Oregon, frames the issue quite well: "[The second characteristic of Celtic spirituality] is the Celtic emphasis on the place of nature within the Christian revelation. The natural world has come from God and is, therefore, a place where God may be found. There is no principled dichotomy between nature and supernature, the world of nature and the world of grace, but rather they are best seen as a continuum. This attitude gives rise to a permeative sense of God's presence so that the Celt was very much a God-intoxicated man whose life was embraced on all sides by the divine Being. But this presence was always mediated through some finite, worldly reality. So it would be difficult to imagine spirituality more down to earth than this one'. For the Celt, there is no distance from the Divine."[6]

Religious vocabulary infused our culture. As a very young child, I used to think when the Gospel was read about Jesus being "wrapped in swaddling clothes" (Luke 2:12) that it meant "Swanlinbar clothing." You see clothing in Swad, as we called it, was much cheaper in than in the North. And Hugh Cullen, a draper in Swad, had a second-hand shop in Kinawley, from which we all were clothed. So naturally enough, being a budding theologian, I reasoned that just as we depended on Swad clothing, so did Jesus because He was poor just like us.

I guess almost every child in Ireland had a memory like that. The redoubtable Malachy McCourt, brother of Frank (*Angela's Ashes'* author) recounts in his book "A Monk Swimming" that he thought for a long time that, "amongst women" in the Hail Mary was "a monk swimming."[7]

I remember one day when I was about ten, I was all by myself clamping turf (building them in little criss-crossed blocks so they would dry) on Murphy's Bank. I was fed up and lonely. I lay down at the edge of the turf bank staring into the bog hole thinking,

"Badcest (bad luck) to Adam and Eve, if they had not sinned I would not have to work 'by the sweat of my brow.'" The Book of Genesis (3:19) says one of the consequences of sin is hard work.

And they say Catholic kids didn't know their Bible!

It seems fashionable these days for writers to deplore and complain about their Catholic childhood. I recognize that *Angela's Ashes* is a classic, but I must beg to differ with Frank McCourt's much quoted line: "Worse than the ordinary miserable childhood is the miserable Irish childhood, and worse yet is the miserable Irish Catholic childhood..."[7]. The *New York Times* loves that sort of thing. Frank may have said it tongue in cheek, of course, but it has perniciously promoted an ugly stereotype. I must confess my experience was totally different from McCourt's. I never had one ugly incident in my childhood, which was as Irish and as Catholic as any on the planet, and which I would not change for anything in this world. I was surrounded and protected by loving parents and devoted brothers and sisters, and the greatest neighbors in the world. I know that won't make any headlines but it is true – and its value is more precious than rubies.

That is why I was so deeply shocked and furious to read, it seemed like every day in the 90's, about all the sexual abuse of children in Ireland and America. I used to be scared to pick up a newspaper because I knew it would smash me in the face like a fist. It has forever harmed the Catholic Church. It is a demented sickness and a criminal betrayal of the worst possible kind. But I know that, after the victims and their families, the ones most outraged are the decent Catholic priests, ninety five percent of whom have never harmed a child.

2

The Day Celia Was Married and Patrick Was Killed

Your joy is your sorrow unmasked.
And the self-same well from which your laughter rises
was oftentimes filled with your tears.

Khalil Gibran, *The Prophet*

But my happy and carefree childhood would soon end, on July 15, 1958: the day Celia was married and Patrick was killed. Our lives would never be the same again. But let me go back to Sunday, December 9, 1956, to set the scene for Patrick's death, at the age of twenty-nine.

The family in general was not aware of Patrick's involvement in the IRA until the night before "he went on the run." That Sunday night there had been a parish bazaar. When the family came home (those who were still living there), Patrick sat us all down. Mother said she would stand but he insisted she sit down. He stood in the middle of the small kitchen and announced that he had something very important to tell us, which we had to keep secret – that in the morning he was leaving home as a soldier of the IRA, that we would not see him again until Ireland was free, that, if necessary, he was prepared to die for The Cause. He warned us that the police would harass us, that we could suffer reprisals and that we might be put under curfew. He stressed that the fight was against the British government, and that the family should continue to be friendly with our Protestant neighbors. He ended by explaining that nineteen-year-old Terence (the second), who had agreed in advance, would quit his job as barman in Enniskillen and work the farm. Terence's life and career was, therefore, drastically changed but no one ever heard him complain. To Terence, who died in 2000, it was something he had to do for his family and country. He, too, was an Irish patriot. (Jim, the next oldest at eighteen, was already in the Redemptorist Novitiate in Perth, Scotland.) Patrick then told us what reason to give to the police and indeed everyone as to why he had gone away: he had gone on a holiday to one of his uncles in Athlone (Mother's brother, Terence) and because war had broken out, he was afraid to return. What double irony! Patrick was fearless and never had a day's holiday in his life.

The family was shocked and stunned at Patrick's dramatic announcement, but amazingly, Mother expressed relief, as she was scared he was going to tell us he had done something bad that would disgrace the family. My father, then seventy-nine, only said one thing, "You will not be halfway out the lane until the police know" – expressing the age-old fear of informers.

The following morning, Monday, December 10, 1956, is still as clear in my mind as yesterday. Patrick was getting ready to take off. I remember him patching up his knapsack, putting in a blanket and ponger (tin cup). He told me to go and fodder the cows and followed me out. I had two armfuls of hay and let some drop. Patrick told me to pick it up, just like our father would have directed. I noticed he was wearing big boots and walking in a different way. I later understood he was in full military mode, marching along the street (the backyard of the farm).

Back inside, Patrick would say goodbye. Mother was standing behind the back door (which opened to the inside of the kitchen) to hide her tears and sobbing. He left quickly so as not to prolong the anguish. I followed him up to the top lane, and by the chestnut tree, tearfully watched him march out Clonliff Lane for the last time, his big boots stomping on the road. I felt I would never see him again, but I did, once. In the spring of 1958, I went to a football game in Swanlinbar, at which I was not playing. On my way, I stopped at a "safe house" in Swad to pick up a letter Patrick would leave there for our Mother. I was sitting in the room, waiting for the letter when, lo and behold, Patrick himself walked in. I couldn't believe it. I almost did not recognize him. He was looking fantastic, had put on about 14 pounds (which he badly needed) and he was dressed impeccably: sports coat, shirt and tie and slacks. I had never seen Patrick so spruced up and I was struck by how handsome he was, something of which I had never been aware. Being dressed in a professional manner was obviously the disguise that worked best for this country boy on the run.

Patrick bought me a lemonade and asked all about the family. He gave me his famous "big-brother talk"– study hard, look after my young brother Myles, then eight ... that Frankie and I should stay away from bad company and not give our parents any trouble, etc. And, of course, I was not to tell anyone outside the family that I had seen him. Mother would have seen him a number of times, at the same safe house but our father never did see him again – something which weighed very heavily on his elderly shoulders.

Patrick was quite right when he warned us we would be harassed by the police. They raided our home often. The typical tactic was to reverse their open-backed vehicles to both the front and back doors of our little house. So when we opened the doors, we would see them sitting with their guns pointing right at us. It was meant to frighten us but it never took a flinch out of us. I remember one evening they were up in the loft, where Patrick used to sleep, going through everything. One Special Branch man made a big show of carefully examining a stamp. My lovely sister Celia, normally the least combative of the entire family, said to him in exasperation, "What do you expect to find in that stamp – a machine gun?" Later when he went down the ladder from the loft, the same Special Branch man told us the next time we saw Patrick would "be when they carried him in, feet first and dead." Another Branch man in a gabardine overcoat told Mother the best thing she could do was to turn Patrick in, for his own good. Expecting our mother to be an informer was a hilarious notion.

Other times, the Royal Ulster Constabulary (RUC) would take Frankie and me off the bus at Montiagh Cross (a couple of miles from home), handcuff us and search us. Again, if it was meant to scare us, they didn't know the Macs. We never experienced one moment of fear. Patrick's own defiance had put steel in our backbone, and there was no way we would allow ourselves to be intimidated by servants of the Crown.

Patrick at Home

Let me now talk a bit about Patrick before he went on the run.

Patrick left Drumbroughas school when he was fourteen and worked the farm with Father. Being the eldest boy in a large family, and with an elderly father, Patrick assumed a lot of responsibility. Though not well educated in the formal sense, he became a knowledgeable man, especially in Irish history. He believed strongly that his much younger brothers should have the education he himself and the older members of the family were not able to have.

Patrick grew to be about 5 foot 9 inches, with a thin, wiry frame and flaming red hair. Years later, an IRA colleague would remember he "had a great smile", though of serious disposition. He had a healthy self-confidence and could turn his hand to many things. For example, the grandfather clock in the home had stopped for many a year. He believed that he could fix it. Without ever having seen the inside of a clock in his life, he took the inner workings apart, spread them out on the table, figured out what was wrong and restored it to perfect working order. And he went from clockmaker to boat builder. He felt a new rowing boat was needed, as the one our father had used all his life to row up and down the lough was no longer seaworthy. Patrick persuaded his father that together they could build a new and bigger boat. They worked at it for months. The maiden voyage of "Mac's new boat" was a major event for the family and the children in Clonliff Lane.

Patrick could even turn to poetry, using it years later to pay tribute to his two IRA comrades in arms, Seán South and Feargal O'Hanlon who were killed on New Year's Eve 1957, in an attack on Brookeborough Barracks, County Fermanagh:

> May God be with those noble hearts
> May Heaven be their home
> For they never feared the RUC
> Or B-Specials on patrol;
> In Brookeborough town they were shot down,
> In a cabin they lay cold:
> O'h-Annluain from old Monaghan town
> And Sabhat from Garryowen

The same analytical and practical mind that led him to mend clocks and build boats led him to accurately analyze and clearly discern the root causes of oppression, division and discrimination in the North of Ireland. He took his religion from Rome and his politics from Tone. With Wolfe Tone, Patrick believed in "breaking the connection with England, the never failing source of all our political evils."

He became active in the anti-partition campaign of the late 1940s and early 1950s. There were rallies in the parish hall and rousing speeches from local politicians including Cahir Healy, the MP for South Fermanagh at Stormont. The family always remembered with pride how Patrick defiantly flew the tricolor from a tree. The whole parish was talking about it. But then, as expected, the RUC arrived in force to tear it down.

Patrick remained "on the run" until the night he was killed, July 15, 1958, in a premature explosion of a bomb he was transporting. He was the Officer Commanding (OC) for South Fermanagh and in the spring of 1958 he was appointed to the Army Council.

Sean Cronin, future Chief of Staff, would later write, "He must have escaped death or capture a score of times. And it is ironic that when death came in the end it should come in the way it did to a man so wise, so cautious, so experienced. There was iron in his soul as well as in his body and he passed it on to those who came in contact with him ..."[1]

And J. Bowyer Bell, in his classic history, *The Secret Army: the IRA, 1916–1970*, describes Patrick as follows: "He was the only active IRA leader to escape arrest during the period. An intrepid guerrilla fighter, he preferred the mountains to the towns and disliked leaving his own area for meetings in strange places. Operating mostly from dugouts – a string of which he had built right across Fermanagh – he rarely slept in a house. His death was a major blow to the struggle ..."[2]

But the family now knows that Patrick did, in fact, go to "strange places," even openly campaigning, under the pseudonym of Tumulty, for a Sinn Féin Abstentionist Candidate, Pádraig Kelly, in County Galway in the spring of 1957. He was, in fact, safer away from his home base, where everybody would have recognized him.

Killed in Action

Patrick was killed at around 9:45 p.m. while handing over a bomb to colleagues who were waiting on an isolated country road in the townland of Derryrealt, about two miles outside Swanlinbar. He had constructed the gelignite bomb himself – "in a five-gallon gas drum with the head cut off it." Patrick came across a field, carrying the container-bomb, stopping on the inside of the ditch below where the car was waiting. As he lifted up the container to hand it to his colleagues, the bomb went off. Patrick was killed instantly, blown to pieces. Two of his colleagues were injured. The Republican Movement would later build a fine monument on the exact spot where Patrick was killed.

To make his death even worse, Celia had been married that very day. She heard the tragic news when RTÉ announced it the following day on the radio, as she and her husband were on their honeymoon in Salthill, Galway.

The following morning after Celia's joyous wedding, the first in the family, I was woken by crying. I rushed into the kitchen and saw the local curate, Fr. Gilmartin, there. I knew immediately that Patrick had been killed. It remains to this day my most vivid, traumatic moment. Jim was rushed home from the Redemptorist Major Seminary in England, and he, Terence and Michael Ferguson had to go and try to identify the "remains," which did not really exist. No family could have been more devastated, yet no family could have been more defiantly proud. Patrick had died for Irish freedom and that, along with our deep faith, sustained us as a family and as individuals.

What the family remembers most about Patrick was his spiritual side. While never wearing his religion on his sleeve, he was deeply religious, never failing to get on his knees before he went to sleep no matter how late he came home. Patrick meditated daily through the rosary, on the incarnation, life, death and resurrection of Jesus Christ, his Most Holy Redeemer. His colleagues later in the Republican Movement all recall Patrick's devotion to prayer. One remembers: "He'd kneel down and give out the rosary to us. I'd have to recite the rosary along with him ... He was a religious man. He was a very great man ... he was loyal to his country and his people ... and the people were loyal to him."

Another IRA colleague recounts how one night he and Patrick were pinned down by the RUC and British Army in a field just inside the border near the village of Kinawley. While the police spotlight beamed all across the field, Patrick and his colleague were hugging the ground. The colleague tried to cover his cough with his coat-collar and Patrick whispered, "What are you doing?" The colleague explained about the cough, and then asked Patrick, "What are you doing?"

"I'm on my third rosary," he replied.

Patrick had made it clear that should he die, he did not want to be buried "under the Union Jack," i.e. buried in the North. So he was buried across the border in Swanlinbar, but still part of the parish of Kinawley. Even at the funeral Mass, Fr. Fox, the curate in Swanlinbar, commented on Patrick's deep faith and his devotion to Our Blessed Lady. Thousands attended his funeral and, after the Mass, the funeral cortège marched to Killaduff Cemetery, about two miles outside Swad. The cortège was led by a lone piper. It was the most heart-rending sound I had ever heard. To this day every time I hear the bagpipes, even see them played on TV or in the movies, I can choke up.

I distinctly remember, as the cortège passed through the village, a garda saluted Patrick's coffin. As a consequence of that gesture of respect, I always had a friendly attitude towards the gardaí – no matter what I may have thought of their political bosses.

After Patrick's death, I naturally assumed I would stop playing football for an extended mourning period as was the custom then. But Fr. Fox – backed up by Fr. Gilmartin – with great pastoral wisdom, convinced my mother that I should continue playing. Now, of course, one could say he also wanted to win the upcoming final in Breffni Park. Either way, it was sound advice as football helped me to cope with our devastating loss.

Shortly after Patrick's death I was playing in County Cavan on our joint Kinawley–Swanlinbar team. A fight started and a general free-for-all ensued, with spectators storming the pitch, bringing the game to a halt. Frankie and a big lump of a lad got into a punch up. As they were pulled and held apart, another fellow, a non-player, from the edge of the crowd that had invaded the pitch, shouted at Frankie: "Your brother thought he was a tough guy and see what happened to him." Well, that did it. Up till then, I had not been really involved in the fracas as I was more focused on winning the game. I rounded on the fellow, who was probably about nineteen or older, and charged with such fury that he took off running. I followed him to the corner of the field, where he was trapped. I let loose with the perfect upper cut (Rocky Marciano style against Jersey Joe Walcott) with my full body weight behind my punch, hitting him under the chin.[3] He went straight down on the flat of his back. Out for the count. Out cold.

I would hear much later that, ironically, his own family was very Republican so the poor guy probably caught hell when he got home for disrespecting the name of an Irish patriot. I often wonder what became of him, and I wish him well wherever he is. The "big lump of a lad" is now parish priest in Derrylin and he and Frankie are good friends.

Today, in his native parish of Kinawley–Swanlinbar, the esteem in which this Irish patriot is held is demonstrated by five public honors: the monument at his grave; a monument at the spot where he was killed; a monument at the end of Clonliff Lane, close to the Derrylin-Enniskillen road; a monument just across the border in Cavan; and the Kinawley GAA stadium, named "Patrick McManus Memorial Park". The stadium was officially opened on Sunday, August 26, 1984, and proudly attended by Patrick's mother, his six brothers and two sisters. Mary Kate, who was then in New Zealand, could not make it.

Our family has always remained very proud of Patrick, regarding him as the quintessential Irish patriot. And even fifty years later, when we are all together as a family, we can still get choked up and tearful when we talk about him.

3

The Call

An unfulfilled vocation drains the color
From a man's entire existence.

Honoré de Balzac (1841)

On Monday September 2, 1957, at age thirteen years and seven months, I began my less than illustrious career at St. Michael's School in Enniskillen, an all-Catholic school. Patrick Maguire started on the same date; Frankie had started in 1953. Myles, still only nine, continued at Drumbroughas. I would remain at that school until September 1960, when I went off to the Redemptorist Juvenate in Birmingham, England.

St. Michael's was run by the priests of the Diocese of Clogher and I certainly do not owe my vocation to them because I did not like any of them, except Fr. Sean Clerkin. He was the only priest who called me aside to inquire about how my parents were doing after Patrick was killed. Imagine that! The place was full of priests and yet they did not have the decency or pastoral concern to minister to a young boy deeply traumatized by his brother's death. They were more concerned about being politically correct – they did not want to be seen showing any sympathy to an "IRA family." If my faith had depended on those priests I would have become a crusading atheist or joined Paisley's emerging Church. But my faith was grounded on my parent's example, on the Word of God and on the tradition and doctrine of the universal Catholic Church.

I am the first to admit that I was not a model student. My entire focus, apart from football, was chasing the fair girls at the convent school and fighting the "townies."

Fighting Townies and Teddy Boys

People may think the big divide in Northern Ireland was between Protestants and Catholics, but to me in those days the big divide was between the townies and the country boys. The townies liked to see themselves as Teddy Boys – slicked-back hair, combed like Elvis, leather jackets and tight blue jeans. I felt a moral obligation to "modify their thinking." There was one period I could not walk through the town without Frankie, who was a fearsome and mighty fighter. All the Teddy Boys were scared of his deadly right hand.

There was one fellow who was the epitome of the Teddy Boy and fancied himself as something of a legend. He was older than I was (I never fought anyone younger than myself) and for some inexplicable reason, he did not seem to fully appreciate my fine Kinawley qualities. He was determined to give me the mother of all beatings and equally determined to let everyone know about it.

Anyway, I knew I was going to be back in town on a Saturday (to celebrate my birthday, February 6th, which fell earlier in the week). So in "High Noon" fashion, I made an appointment with my adversary in the Broad Meadows, then a public park by the water in Enniskillen. I had not told Frankie about it because I wanted to fight this battle on my own.

When I showed up, Mr. Teddy Boy was there with a group of townies all eagerly awaiting with evident relish the impending humiliation of this poor country boy form Kinawley. Mr. Teddy

Boy began with a great display of bravado and showmanship, ducking this way and that, bobbing and weaving, doing the Ali shuffle even before it had been invented by Muhammad Ali – but in a mishmash of judo and heaven knows what. He would swipe at me with his right hand and then when I countered his swipe, he would duck immediately and try to grab my legs. Big mistake. I let him try it a few more times and then finally let him grab me by the hips. Then I reached over his bent back, as his head was rammed into my stomach, and I hoisted him up and held him in that position for quite a while demanding that he give up. He refused. I then carried him – in the same locked position, backside and heels up in the air – to a barbed-wire fence, hoisted him above it and held him about a foot above the wire. "Don't drop me," he pleaded, "these are the only pair of jeans I have."

"You have only one pair (of something else) that you should be more worried about," I retorted (that's the cleaned-up version I use for my sisters). I had, of course, no intention of dropping him. But I found it hard not to laugh. There he was being held over a barbed-wire fence – his belly facing down close to the wire – and the only thing he was worried about was his blue jeans!

I asked him if he gave up; he said yes. I asked him to promise not to bother me again and he did. So I put him down, hurting neither him nor his blue jeans.

Another time, I was up on Fort Hill – a wooded town park in the middle of Enniskillen – standing up on a park bench waving to the girls in the Convent School. There was a hedge right in front of me. All of a sudden, I was pushed in the back and shot right into the hedge. When I got up I saw a group of townies, bursting for a fight. One small skinny guy squared up to me. I knew I could knock him into the middle of next week, but I was concerned about the five or six other townies – especially one much older guy, with a totally bald head (when shaved heads were not in fashion). Baldy had a bit of a reputation and he was sporting a studded belt, sure sign of a tough guy. I whispered to Patrick Maguire, "go and get Frankie," and I played for time. The moment I saw Frankie's head appear over the brow of the hill,

I said to my would-be slayer, "So you want a piece of me, eh?" Just kidding; Kinawley boys didn't talk like that, at least in my day. But I did immediately light into him, and by the time Frankie arrived, my unworthy opponent was lying bleeding under a tree.

Baldy then challenged Frankie. Big mistake. Baldy pulled off his prized studded belt and with deliberate and ostentatious slowness began to wrap it around his fist, all the while looking hard and menacing. He must have thought our Frankie had been born yesterday, that Frankie would stand idly by and allow Baldy to arm himself. No way. Frankie charged him with a body slam, flattened him, grabbed his bald head and kept bouncing it up and down on the ground like a basketball until Baldy begged for mercy. Then we went back to class as if nothing had happened. But the word did go out: Don't mess with the Macs. And from then on, the townies left us alone.

Out of all my fights, only one was with a Protestant and it had nothing to do with sectarianism. Years later, in 1968, that same Protestant was at Matthew McHugh's house, two fields below our home. I had just been ordained. He gestured up to our house and said, "So I hear Sean McManus got ordained?" Matthew proudly and enthusiastically affirmed it. And the Protestant man said: "He was the right cross hoor of a cub." Matthew, God rest him, would regale us with that story for years – and it got better with each telling. Our family loved Matthew. To us, he was the nicest and funniest man in Ireland. Yet he never told jokes, only "bits," – funny anecdotes, which may or may not have "gained in the telling." We loved to see him come up for a cheilde (social visit) where he would light up the room with his "bits," which were never unkind. When we saw him tilt his head back and say, " I mind the time…," we all knew we were in for a classic Matthew story.

All this took place before my conversion to nonviolence and none of it would have been approved by Martin Luther King, Jr. But even Martin himself in his early days – during the Montgomery, Alabama, Bus Boycott (December 1, 1955 – December 20, 1956) – had a gun. Bayard Rustin had to convince him to get rid of it, as it was a contradiction of Gandhi's nonviolence that Martin was propounding.[1]

I continued to be a poor student at St. Michael's. And continued to chase the bonny Fermanagh lassies (and some from Tyrone and Cavan). But I was never sectarian. I dated bonny Protestant lassies too. One of the girls would later join the Ulster Defense Regiment (UDR) and would be killed in an IRA attack on her barracks in the 1970s. I was deeply saddened to hear it.

Be Still and Know that I am God (Psalm 46:10)

As the summer of 1960 progressed, a "small, still voice" kept whispering in my soul. There must be more to your life, you must commit yourself to a cause greater than yourself. I kept shutting it out. But finally it got the better of me. I was coming home one night from Aunt Maggie's. My bike got a flat tire and somehow I didn't mind. It was a beautiful, starry night. I was walking along Graffey Lane, going up the brae at Phil Murphy's big house, staring at the stars. Suddenly, softly, sweetly, a feeling of transcendence swept over me. And in a split second I knew I was being called to be a priest.

My next immediate realization was, "Sean, that means you will have to give up marriage, playing football and you will not be able to join the IRA and finish the job Patrick set out to do." It was a moment of total clarity, no drama, no thunderclaps, no gnashing of teeth. Just the profound peacefulness that comes when God makes the way clear. And, fundamentally, I have never looked back since that moment outside Phil Murphy's. I don't mean that there have not been ups and downs, nor that I have led a perfect Christian life. But I have never doubted my calling, despite my sins and failures.

In the Catholic tradition – at least up to that time – when a person had such a religious experience, it normally was seen as a call to the priesthood or the religious life. In the Protestant tradition, it is seen as "being born again" – a deeper commitment to Christ, but not necessarily a call to Ministry. Well, of course, I had been "born again" at baptism, with water and the Holy Spirit, confirmed in the Spirit at confirmation and nourished on the "Bread of Life and the Cup of Eternal Salvation" in the Holy Eucharist. So to me the only next step was the priesthood. Today, however, I am sure that some Catholics have similar experiences as I had, but see it as a call to more closely follow Christ, but not a call to the priesthood or the religious life. I am sure there is a lot to be discussed and developed in this area of Catholic spirituality, but I will leave that to my big brother, Fr. Jim, the spiritual guru in the family.

I realized that I would have to give up Gaelic football because I knew I would naturally follow Jim and join the London Province of Redemptorists. Plus there was that tradition: Ireland had already too many priests (little did we know how that would change), and anyway, it was heathen England that needed priests!

I never said a thing to Mother when I got home that night. I slept on it and in the morning it was still as clear as ever. So I told Mother. She nearly fell off the chair with shock. My father seemed very pleased. I think Frankie took a pain in his side from laughing. But the transition period went very smoothly.

Jim, a student at this time in Hawkstone, the Redemptorist Major Seminary in Shropshire, made all the necessary contacts for me.

Off to England

On Wednesday, September 28, 1960, Fr. Joe Hanton, CSsR, Director of the Juvenate, the minor seminary in Birmingham, wrote to me: "I am happy to inform you that you have been accepted as a candidate for the priesthood and ... you will be welcome to come to Erdington (a section of Birmingham) as soon as you can make arrangements." Thus began a whole new phase in my life.

It says something wonderful about the tradition that I was raised in that despite our absolute opposition to English rule in the North of Ireland, we never held it against the English people and never hesitated to minister to them, working for them without pay of any kind. Equally, it says something wonderful about the British Redemptorists for never holding Patrick against Jim and me. Sure, my activities later on would cause Charlie Shepherd serious heartburn, but that is a different issue from the point I'm making here.

I will never forget my voyage from Belfast to Liverpool. It was my first time leaving Ireland and my first time on a ship. Although full of religious zeal, I was nonetheless homesick. On board I was so relieved to see a Kinawley man, John Anderson. He gave me great advice: "Don't be frightened if you think your stomach is going to come out of your body when the sea gets rough – and it always does." Man, did it ever. I got as sick as a dog.

The following morning I arrived in Liverpool, sleep-deprived and still sick, only to be confronted by what I thought was the terrible smell of Liverpool – my first sniff of a big city. My country nose could not take it. My spirits were buoyed when Jim met me at the train and accompanied me to Birmingham. Mary Kate,who was also in England, supported me by sending me money weekly.

My first culture shock in the Juvenate was the breakfast – fried bread and beans. Baked beans sloshed onto bread dipped in frying fat. The taste was abominable. And to make matters worse, we had to wash it down with coffee made from liquid from a bottle. Where were my porridge, my fresh egg and my fadge (soda) bread? What barbarians had I come among?

There were about forty boys in the Juvenate. I went into the senior class and for the first time in my life hit the books and studied hard. Fr. James Mythen would soon amaze me by complimenting me on my Latin. In English Literature we had to study Wordsworth. My teacher, Fr. Hanton, was not too good as he was just filling in and did not really know Wordsworth. But I knew who did – Master O'Shea back in St. Michael's, a lay teacher whom I liked. I wrote to him, told him I needed help to prepare for an exam and he wrote me a number of pages about how Wordsworth changed English poetry, by taking it out of its baroque setting into the open countryside, etc. I aced the exam and I have never forgotten Master O'Shea who later became a priest himself. And thus began my lifelong affection for Wordsworth, who after Shakespeare, is the most worthy of all the British writers.

I was delighted to discover in my Religious Knowledge class that I was far more advanced than anyone else.

I trained myself to wake up at night to say one rosary, thereby completing the goal I had set myself of three rosaries per day – the Five Joyful Mysteries, the Five Sorrowful Mysteries, the Five Glorious Mysteries. (Pope John Paul II would later add the Five Luminous Mysteries in 2002.)

I enjoyed the Juvenate, even though the change of lifestyle was quite dramatic. I knew the one thing that could quickly get me into trouble was my tendency to settle things with my fists. I was helped by the fact that I was one of the biggest and certainly the strongest boys in the Juvenate, and nobody would mess with me, and I knew I would never hit anyone younger or smaller than I.

Indeed, even when I was at home, I never hit anyone smaller, except if they had bullied Myles, when they were much bigger than he was. Then my self-imposed law did not apply. To this day, Myles still recounts his alarm at the fact that Frankie and I left home around the same time – he to Belfast University, I to Birmingham. Suddenly, Myles was without defenders. But he would soon develop a formidable right hand of his own.

The other drastic change was football – no longer Gaelic but soccer. Yet I quickly got to like it while never mastering it. I played right-full-back. Later in Hawkstone, I would play in goal and really come into my own, just as Jim did.

4

Kinnoull and Hawkstone Years

Prayer without study would be empty.
Study without prayer would be blind.

Karl Barth[1]

In September 1961, I went to the Redemptorist Novitiate in St. Mary's Monastery, high up on Kinnoull Hill, Perth, Scotland. I pulled up in front of the monastery in a taxi. Gave a packet of cigarettes to the driver, saying. "I'll never use these here," and I never did.

The Novitiate, in those years, was a "religious boot camp" – a year of unrelenting self-discipline, penance, prayer, religious training, religious lectures, long periods of total silence and manual labor.

The Novice Master (in charge of spiritual formation) was Fr. Shepherd – the aforementioned Fr. Shepherd, who would later pack me off to America,

The monastery had a small farm and, when needed, I had to do the milking as I was the only novice with that skill. Brother John was the farmer and I was utterly amazed to see him using gloves while making hay. My first thought was, "What would Daddy and Charles Murphy think of a man wearing gloves to use a pitchfork?" I was also amazed to see Brother John "ruck" the hay (build it in large cone-shaped stacks) while it was still damp. My father would have chased him out of the meadow, as you daren't ruck the hay until it was bone dry. "It will rot," I kept telling Brother John but, in fact, it turned out fine.

Once a year the novices were allowed a bus trip to St. Andrews, not to play at the famous golf course, but to spend a day at the gusty beach. As the bus took off from the Novitiate, the Rector of Kinnoull, Fr. Vincent Lucas, brother of the Provincial Fr. George Lucas, sat beside me and said, "So, Brother Mc Manus, what part of Ireland are you from?"

"From British-occupied Ireland," I defiantly responded. He collapsed in laughter, as he thought it was the funniest thing he had ever heard. It was my first insight into how little the average Englishman knows about Britain's involvement in Northern Ireland.

Despite the Spartan regime, I loved the Novitiate and experienced a deep sense of spiritual tranquility ... no angst, no turmoil, no anguish.

Father's Death

But there was great sadness because my father died in January 1962. I was reading in the refectory from the pulpit-like dais (at evening meals the novices would take turns at reading aloud from some spiritual book to the entire community – the other novices, plus the priests who were giving Missions throughout Scotland). The Novice Master came over and asked me to stop, so I knew there was bad news. I had been aware that my father was failing. The Novice Master asked me to come outside the refectory, and told me that my father was very ill, and that I should prepare to go home immediately.

When I arrived home in Clonliff, I found my father near death. But I took great consolation in the way his eyes brightened up when he saw me, as he clearly recognized me. The last conscious action I saw him make was when he raised up his mouth to kiss the small crucifix I held to his lips. If dying a holy death, after leading a good life, is the supreme Christian goal, then my father surely went straight home to the Father, through Christ, by the power of the Holy Spirit and into Eternal Life. I spent about a week at home and then returned to the Novitiate.

Hawkstone

In September 1962, after two weeks of intense retreat and total silence, which I never once broke, I took my First Vows with four others. My mother and a few of my family came for the event, and then it was off to the pleasant fields of Shropshire for seven years at Hawkstone Hall, then the Redemptorist Major Seminary. (Later, Jim would develop it into a major international centre for spirituality.[2])

There were about forty students at Hawkstone. I loved all my seven years there and went after my studies with gusto, especially logic, philosophy and theology. Most of the available books, of course, stuck rigidly to the abstract, non-historical, neo-Scholastic line. Neo-Scholasticism was the philosophical theology that was taught in seminaries from 1860 until Vatican II. The *Encyclopedia of Catholicism* explains: "Neo-Thomism in turn is a development within neo-Scholasticism, the revival of Scholastic, that is, medieval theology. Modern neo-Thomism (rarely discussed outside of Catholicism and mandated by papal documents like Pope Leo XIII's encyclical *Aeterni Patris* of 1879) sought to transcend the Enlightenment and Reformation by proposing that the thought-world of medieval Scholasticism, and particularly that of Thomas Aquinas, could hold solutions to contemporary problems."[3]

The American theologian, Fr. Thomas F. O'Meara, OP, wonderfully recreates the atmosphere of those seminary days: "During my first week in the seminary [the Dominican seminary near Chicago] the professor introducing us to philosophy made [a] startling observation[s]: Everything a priest needed to know was found in the writings of Aristotle [384–322 BC] ... During the first half of the twentieth century, most priests in America [and in Britain and Ireland, he could have added] received some neo-scholastic indoctrination in philosophy and theology. That simple philosophy with a black and white logic emphasized laws that had no exceptions: the laws of logic, administration of the church, abstract moral rules, and obscure rubrics for liturgy. The Church had somewhat exchanged the Gospel for Greek antiquity and its Aristotelianism held no interest for scientific America or ordinary Catholics."[4] Nonetheless, neo-Scholasticism taught me how to reason logically and think analytically. And I have maintained an abiding reverence for the great St. Thomas Aquinas, whom we now know should not have been pigeon-holed the way some neo-Thomists tried to do: "Many sought through Vatican power a monopolistic and dictatorial control over Catholic thinking, and, in the name of Thomism, warred against modern philosophy, science, and politics as well as ecumenism, vernacular liturgy and modern art. This monopoly of thought ended when Vatican II (1962–1965) affirmed modern biblical, patristic, systematic, and pastoral theologies, many of which were rooted in Aquinas' historical openness and positive depiction of God and humans."[5]

In time, I would come to realize that the best way to understand the change brought about by the Second Vatican Council was to see it in terms of a paradigm shift: a shift from classicism to historical consciousness – from a classicist to a historical conscious Weltanschauung (world view).

Classicism views reality in terms of the immutable, the never changing. It uses the deductive method of reasoning: from the universal to the particular. This is best illustrated by the following syllogism, which was taught in Scholastic logic to every student for the priesthood, up to the mid 1960s:

> All human beings are rational.
> Seamus is a human being.
> Ergo (therefore) Seamus is rational.

Classicism uses the *deductive method* of reasoning. It seeks conclusions that are always true, in all situations: if it was true in 1962, it is true in 2062. Historical consciousness uses the *inductive method* of reasoning: from the particular to the universal. The conclusions it reaches (from the ground up, so to speak) will be based on changing circumstances and history. It does not seek absolute, dogmatic certitude but settles for moral, practical certitude. Vatican II would attempt to explain the faith, not just hand down authoritarian decrees, as in the style of Vatican I (December 8, 1869 – October 20, 1870) – the foundational style of teaching as opposed to the apologetic.

My greatest regret is that the Scripture classes were so poor. Most of the teachers were inadequate. In fact, Jim was the only really good teacher, and that is not a matter of standing up for my big brother. Every student would agree with me. Jim had been ordained on January 12, 1964. Most of the family, many of our relatives and neighbors from home came to Hawkstone for his ordination. It was a most special day in the life of our family. After ordination, Jim went to Rome for further study for four years. He taught Moral Theology for my last year in Hawkstone.

Despite the poor quality of the teachers, Jim excepted, it was still a great time to be embarking on theological training. Vatican II started on October 11, 1962 and soon seminarians would no longer have to be taught in Latin or read the Divine Office in Latin, the Mass could be said in English, the "new theology" would emerge, etc. It was really an exciting time – the ecclesiastical version of the Sixties! But no long hair, no dope and no sex.

Eucharist, Luther and Pius IX

Eucharistic theology became my particular interest, and I have kept up my study of this subject over the years. While I have always been prepared to question Church teaching on a variety of subjects, I've always been very careful on Eucharistic Doctrine which is, in a uniquely special way, the ultimate responsibility of the Magisterium. Get the Eucharist wrong, and you get the Church wrong – and vice versa. The age-old maxim nails it: "The Eucharist makes the Church and the Church make the Eucharist."

But I also came to believe that every good Catholic needs a good dose of Protestantism. So I developed a great interest in Martin Luther and his "Justification by Faith alone." I soon came to believe that Rome and he were just talking at cross-purposes and that, as in all fights, as the rhetoric heated up, the positions unnecessarily hardened when a resolution was possible. Fr. Shepherd (yes, the same, now the Rector at Hawkstone, and the teacher of Church history) cautioned me about my enthusiasm for the heretic Luther. It was, therefore, a very happy and emotional day for me when, over thirty years later, I attended the National Cathedral (Episcopal) in Washington in 1999, to celebrate the signing of The Joint Declaration on Justification by the Vatican and the World Lutheran Federation. Yet, for me, the occasion was tinged with sadness as I reflected on how easy it is for leaders to change, leaving their followers hung out to dry: "Oops, it was all a misunderstanding, now let's move on."

I was also very disappointed that the historic Joint Declaration did not receive proper attention. For goodness' sake, here was the wedge issue, the leading cause of the Reformation being essentially agreed on by the Pope and the Lutherans, yet Northern Ireland, of all places, does not give it due attention. What's wrong with that picture?

Fr. Shepherd even taught the notorious Syllabus of Errors, issued by Pope Pius IX in conjunction with his encyclical *Quanta Cura* (How Much Concern) (1864) as if they were revealed truth, instead of being, in part, the paranoid fears of an emotionally unbalanced pope. Among other things, they condemned freedom of conscience, freedom of religion, freedom of speech and the separation of Church and State. And here Scottish theologian, Fr. Fergus Kerr, OP, is not far off the mark when he says, "The history of twentieth-century Catholic theology is the history of the attempted elimination of theological modernism, by censorship, sackings and excommunication ..."[6]

However, I have other issues with Pope Pius IX. On January 12, 1870 at the urgings of the British government and sycophantic Irish Bishops, Pius IX excommunicated the Fenians, not only in Ireland but also in America: "the American or Irish society called Fenian," as the decree of condemnation put it.[7] Had Pope Pius IX condemned the Fenians because he believed in the philosophy of nonviolence, that would have been a different matter. But that Pope did not believe in nonviolence. He had his own papal armed force, and he had earlier appealed to Irishmen to come and fight for his Papal States. Hundreds of Irishmen – including Fenians – answered his call. So it was OK for Irishmen to fight for the Papal States, but it was a sin for them to fight for Ireland. Years later in Washington, I would write to the Papal Nuncio objecting to the proposed canonization of this anti-Fenian, anti-Semitic and anti-freedom pope.

But my reading in Hawkstone was not just Scholastic. I set out to read all the great Irish writers, starting with Edna O'Brien. I read James Joyce's *Ulysses* three times in Hawkstone. These books were still on the forbidden index but a traveling library (a van) would come regularly to the end of the Hawkstone road, and I would go out there to meet it each week. No matter how hard I tried, I could not make head or tail of *Finnegans Wake*. William Trevor became one of my favorite Irish writers.

From GAA to Soccer

Life at Hawkstone was not just all spiritual and intellectual for me. We played soccer three times a week and had some fine players. After Jim left, I took his place in goal and was in my element. I could soar like an eagle and catch the ball knowing none of the other players could touch it with their hands (except the other goalie at the far end of the pitch), and that no big bruiser from Derrylin would be spoiling my catch. In this way, the Gaelic footballer was in heaven playing goalie in soccer. It spoiled you rotten. However, diving on the ball at the players' feet was a skill that had to be mastered. When I first saw Jim do it in Hawkstone, I was amazed and wondered how he could do it without getting his skull split open. But I soon got the hang of it. In the latter years, we were allowed to play "outside" (non-seminarians) teams.

I remember once a local team came to play us at Hawkstone. I could tell immediately that they had a condescending attitude to "us monks", that they thought we were a crowd of sissies ... and that they had an anti-Catholic attitude (my Northern Ireland background gave me an unerring nose for that).

They were several years older than we were and they clearly thought they were masters of the game.

In the first minutes of the game, the ball came into me and I charged out to get it. One of their forwards blatantly jumped into me with both knees. When I cleared the ball, I turned to him and for the first time in years I reverted to type – to the Kinawley footballer – and told him: "*do not come back like that again.*" He sniggered and replied, "Every time, mate."

The ball soon came back in at chest level. At this level, the goalie has a great advantage from the point of physical contact (although the invading forward has the opportunity to take a low ball away from you). I saw our friend charge me and as I grabbed the ball firmly to my chest I swung my left shoulder hard to meet him. I knocked him a couple of feet off the ground, landing him flat on his back. His fellow-forward roared at me, "You're supposed to be a preacher." I replied, "And I have given him a sermon he'll remember for the rest of the game." And he did too. He never came near me for the rest of the game.

Well, we went on to beat them in a ridiculous fashion, 7–nil. They were the worst team I had ever seen in my life – absolutely hopeless. All hat and no cattle. Now to be fair, they were probably up late drinking beer the night before and rejoicing how they would thrash "the monks." None of our team smoked or drank, we were young and fit and we sent them "homeward, tae think again."[8] One thing is certain; none of them was ever recruited by Manchester United.

From Pioneer to Poteen Maker

The students did not drink alcohol, except for a glass of very ordinary wine with meals on special and rare feast days. Ironically, I was a Pioneer (had taken the pledge not to drink) until I arrived in Hawkstone. When the newly professed novices arrived from the Novitiate at Hawkstone, the tradition was to give them a glass of sherry. I was told that my religious vows superseded all other pledges and that I could break my pledge. I would later come to see that as "religious imperialism" and always regretted breaking my Pioneer Pledge. (In 1988 I redeemed my pledge and stopped drinking completely.)

But while in Hawkstone, I became a winemaker, and a moonshiner – a maker of poteen!

There was an elderly couple that lived on the Hawkstone property in an old gatehouse to the former Victorian mansion that Hawkstone was. My mother used to stay there when she came to visit Jim and me. One day the man of the house served Mother and me a glass of white wine. It was delicious. I had never tasted anything like it. "What is that, Harry?" I enquired. "It's rhubarb wine," he replied, "and if you like it, wait till you taste my elderberry wine." I asked him where he had got it. "Made it myself," he said proudly.

I was instantly hooked. Not on the wine, but on vinification, the process of making wine. I picked Harry's brain and he was only too pleased to enlighten me. I went back to the monastery and immediately went to see the Rector, then Fr. Nolan, who was originally from Dublin. (He was a wonderful man and I had huge respect for him. Years later, he would pass on to me, through a trusted courier, Jim, an IRA belt that was used in the GPO in 1916. It is a brown leather belt with a heavy brass buckle, which is inscribed with Óglaigh na h-Éireann, "soldiers of Ireland." The other end of the belt, also brass, that inserts into the buckle has a harp embossed on it.) In retrospect, I now see that my visit to Fr. Nolan was my first lobbying job. I proposed to him that he give me permission to start making homemade wine to be used on Feast Days ... that there was a long tradition of monasteries doing so, that we had a very fine, classically built wine cellar. In fact, the wine cellar was so good that even Winston Churchill wanted to buy Hawkstone for that reason alone, but could not afford the taxes. (After the Second World War, a lot of the great mansions were bought by religious or educational institutions because individuals could no longer afford them.)

Fr. Nolan, in his great voice and with a trademark slap of his hands, said it was a splendid idea and told me to go right ahead. Thus my life as an oenologist (wine "expert") began. At that stage I had no idea of trying to make poteen and so had not mentioned it to Fr. Nolan. Anyway, there was no way he could give me permission to do something that was, ahem, well, not quite legal.

I began as I always begin: by studying the subject. I got dozens of books from my friendly traveling library at the end of Hawkstone lane, and boned up on the quite surprisingly popular English tradition of brewing homemade wine.

I scoured the countryside looking for the right containers. In an antique shop in Shrewsbury, I ferreted out three amazing five-gallon pottery vats, like something out of Sinbad the Sailor. The vats, wide at the bottom, tapered into narrow necks – perfect for my mission. I fermented (the science of which is called zymology) rhubarb and elderberries, separately, in my prized vats and after the allotted time, I drained the contents, put in isinglass to bring all the impurities to the top, and tied the opening off tightly with a heavy cloth.

At the appropriate time, I bottled the wine, put it safely away in one large cubicle in the wine cellar, built a little door and put it all under lock and key. I would occasionally check the door to make sure none of my brothers-in-Christ had been tempted. None of them was. In due time, the wine was served to great acclaim.

Now the great philosophers teach us that knowledge should always be progressing and advancing. So in that grand tradition, I says to meself: I wonder how poteen is made. Wouldn't it be a worthy project to make it, purely for the science of it, you understand?

So I wrote to Frankie and asked him to find out the recipe and to mail it to me. There was no tradition in Clonliff of making poteen. If you wanted it you had to go to the law-breakers across the river in Knockninny–Derrylin.

Frankie duly wrote back to me with the recipe, warning me to drink only the most "infinitesimal amount" (the actual words, I still remember). In fact, I drank only two teaspoonfuls.

Then began my second scouring of the countryside. How to find a "still" (the pot or container used for distilling poteen), without calling it that? Again, my Guardian Angel led me to a shop in Shrewsbury that had the perfect container: a five-gallon copper pot with an airtight lid. (One needs a copper pot to avoid the danger of poisoning. Even though the big bruisers in Derrylin used tar-barrels.)

Then I would need to solder a copper pipe or tube, with a small opening, into the still. That was no bother. But how to make the copper pipe into a "worm"– the coiled pipe, in which the vapor would be cooled and condensed, under cold running water? That stumped me. Now, bear in mind there was no Internet in those days, and I could not go around asking people for help in making a still. Only one other person knew about my secret project. Finally I turned to a man I admired and trusted – Eddie Corish. He had been a Brother in the Irish Province and as an older man decided to become a Redemptorist priest in the London Province.

Eddie was a man for all seasons, deeply spiritual but with a very practical mechanical bent. "How can I, Eddie, twist this copper pipe into a coil without closing the air flow?" "Very simple," responded the intrepid Eddie. "Fill it with sand and twist it around a metal bar, horizontal to the ground, then shake the sand out." "You are a genius, Eddie," says I.

My first attempts did not work out too well. I started with the normal Irish method, fermenting potatoes. But I soon discovered it was much easier and far better to distill the rhubarb wine. It was a real thrill to see the first bubble of distilled liquid shyly emanate from the end of the worm, linger a moment, then gently plop into the container below. To add to the thrill, I ran my still in an unused room next to the room of the Professor of Moral Theology (not Jim) who was totally unaware. Unlike the big bruisers from Derrylin who used a turf fire in the bogs to do their distilling, I used a little gas stove. I sent a bottle of the poteen to Terence in London and he told me it was the best he had ever tasted.

I kept four bottles of poteen in my room – and never touched it – waiting for Christmas. After Christmas dinner, I invited a select few whom I knew I could trust, and who regarded themselves as guys who could hold their drink, to a classroom at the back of the building. I produced a bottle, and quoting my older brother Frankie, cautioned them to only consume the "most infinitesimal amount." I demonstrated its potency by first putting some in a teaspoon and setting it alight. I poured each person less than half a shot. Some sipped it straight, some drank it with orange juice. I demonstrated my caution by only sipping two teaspoonfuls. Then they claimed I had exaggerated the strength of the poteen and called for a refill. I remonstrated with them again, but George said, "Enough of the Irish baloney [or some such word that implied the Irish like to exaggerate], Sean, give us more poteen." So I relented.

Now, the classroom that was doing double duty as a monastic shebeen was about three lengths of a football field – up a long corridor, past the individual rooms of the revellers – from the students' common room. We knew we had to be there before too long as that was the only night, Christmas night, that the Rector would visit our common room – which was very large, with a stage, billiard ball table, TV, etc. The Rector now was Fr. Shepherd (yes, *that* Fr. Shepherd). On the way up the corridor, I lost five of the lads who "could hold their drink." They went down like logs and I had to carry them to their beds.

I went into the common room and Fr. Shepherd was sitting in a large circle talking to the students. I took my place, wondering what had happened to Pat. He had not fallen down, so where was he? I didn't have to wait long. Pat was seen as an ascetic, who spent long hours in prayer. He had Bedouin blood in him. In a short time, the bold Pat burst into the common room, still dressed in his habit but with a white bath towel wrapped around his head, Bedouin-style, and without further ado exploded into a Bedouin dance for about ten minutes. I was sure our game was up, that Charlie Shepherd would be on to us, but there he was doubled over, convulsed in laughter, like everyone else, at the extraordinary spectacle.

When I was leaving Hawkstone, I destroyed the still and refused to pass on my esoteric skills as a moonshiner. I was scared if it was done wrongly it could poison someone. Thus ended my career as a poteen-maker, a bootlegger. I was about to say that I had never touched the stuff again, but I did.

In 1977, the American Ancient Order of Hibernians (AOH) was holding its convention in Killarney. I was traveling down from Fermanagh to it and stopped overnight in the home of a high-up Republican and teetotaller. I had a terrible awful cold, with my chest totally congested. I worried how I could make the convention. To my amazement, this teetotaller who was regularly raided and harassed by the Special Branch, produced a bottle of the illegal substance. Made me a very large hot toddy, told me to drink it all down, and in the morning I would be as right as rain. And, honest to goodness, when I woke up the following morning, it was if my cold had been a dream. It was gone completely, no congestion, no cough, and I felt terrific! No wonder poteen was the universal cure for farm animals in those days in my part of County Fermanagh.

Old-IRA Father Confessor

The Sam Browne belt that Fr. Nolan had passed on to me was not the only Hawkstone connection with IRA history. There was a much closer link – a living, breathing one: the students' Confessor, the saintly Fr. Liam Pilkington (1894–1977). "Pilkie" as we affectionately called him, had been the Commandant of the Third Western Division, IRA, who took the Republican side in the Civil War. In 1924 he joined the Redemptorists in the English Province. In his seventies, he became the Confessor for the students. We would line up at his door, and when my turn would come he would say, "Come on in, Brother McManus and I'll clean your skillet (absolve your sins)."

He never talked about his IRA years (1913–1924) except to Jim and me. When he used to talk to me, after a while his hands would shake, as is common with many old soldiers, and he would end the conversation. He knew Liam Mellows, who swore him into the Irish Republican Brotherhood (IRB), Michael Collins, Éamon de Valera, etc.

I think he was a bit prudish. He said he was appalled by Collins' bad language, "The foulest mouth of any man he ever knew." And he never politically forgave de Valera. On one occasion Dev went to Cape Town, South Africa, where Pilkie was stationed at the time. Dev went to the monastery to see him, but Pilkie refused to meet him. He always believed that they did not need to sign the Treaty (that lead to the partition of Ireland), that they could have kept fighting because they were at their very strongest. Yet he mentioned that, years later as a priest when he was some place in England, walking around "acres and acres of munitions" he thought to himself, "we must have been mad to think we could beat them."

He showed me a prayer book (which I wished I had got) that was given to him when he was a political prisoner by the Catholic chaplain, an English priest. Pilkie had told him that when Ireland was free he was going to become a priest. The Chaplain jokingly inscribed it: "May you achieve the goal you desire, instead of the gaol [deliberate old English spelling] you deserve." Pilkie still got a great kick out of that and would smile with delight.

Sometimes in Hawkstone, Pilkie used to preside at the "preaching academy" – weekly, a student had to preach a memorized sermon from an approved source, in front of all the other students, while an older, experienced priest would sit in to evaluate the performance. Well, one day it was my turn to "preach". I had memorized a sermon and had entitled it "The

Last Day by Father James Joyce." (In fact, it was my own editing of Joyce's famous "sermon" by the Retreat Master in *A Portrait of the Artist as Young Man* – hardly an "approved" source, as Joyce was still on the Index, the list of books banned by the Church.) My thinking was that these English blokes would not recognize Joyce's "sermon." But, ah man, didn't Pilkie come in to preside over my sermon? There was nothing, however, I could do but plough ahead as I had nothing else prepared. So I gave the sermon, announcing that the author was Fr. James Joyce:

> The last day had come. The doomsday was at hand ... And lo, the supreme judge is coming! No longer the lowly Lamb of God, no longer the meek Jesus of Nazareth, no longer the Man of Sorrows, no longer the Good Shepherd, He is seen now coming upon the clouds, in great power and majesty, attended by nine choirs of angels, angels and archangels, principalities, powers and virtues, thrones and dominations, cherubim and seraphim, God Omnipotent, God Everlasting. He speaks: and His voice is heard even at the farthest limits of space, even in the bottomless abyss. Supreme Judge, from His sentence there will be and can be no appeal ...

On the way back, I walked down the corridor with Pilkie and he told me it was the best sermon on The Last Day he had ever heard in his life. He then asked me about the "priest" who had written it (he clearly had not connected "Fr. Joyce" with *the* James Joyce). I certainly was not going to tell a lie to my Confessor, so I leveled with him. I thought he was going to have a heart attack. "That blackguard," he hissed. "He was as bad as Yeats, who couldn't believe in Jesus Christ but did believe in fairies." And with that he turned on his heel and strode off in righteous exasperation, his military step more pronounced than usual.

I was ordained on September 1, 1968. That was another very special day for our family, most of whom came to the Ordination with relatives and neighbors from Kinawley.

Our class stayed on in Hawkstone until the following summer, finishing our studies. Then it was off to Bishop's Stortford in Hertfordshire, southeast England, for our Second Novitiate – a six-month period for writing sermons for the parish missions. Even this quiet town had an IRA connection. In 1953, Cathal Goulding and Seán Mac Stíofáin, each of whom would later become Chief of Staff of the IRA, were arrested there with a van-load of weapons stolen from "the officers training corps armory of Felsted School in Essex."[9]

Our class then went to different areas. I first went to Birmingham, back to Erdington Abbey, and then to the Redemptorist House in Liverpool, as part of a Parish Missions team. I preached missions and school retreats in a number of places in England and Scotland, thinking this was what I would be doing for the rest of my life. I had no idea what lay ahead.

5

The Troubles Come Back to Haunt

But just as I thought I was out, they pull me back in.[1]

Meanwhile, I had been keeping an eye on the developing political situation in Northern Ireland. Civil rights marches had begun in 1968 only to be met, inevitably and predictably, by the brute forces of the deeply sectarian and anti-Catholic State that the British government had violently and undemocratically created in 1920.

This artificial State had a two-fold purpose: to ensure a continuation of Britain's foothold on the island of Ireland, and to place the Unionists/Loyalist/Protestants in a permanent position of supremacy. Protestant supremacy would be guaranteed by discrimination, repressive legislation and a deeply sectarian and bigoted police force, the RUC and their auxiliaries, the B Specials.

The "credit" for this masterstroke goes to Winston Churchill who in July 1920 posed the question, "What if the Protestants in the six counties were given weapons and ... charged with maintaining law and order and policing the country?" The British government then proceeded to set up the new police force and recruited the Ulster Volunteer Force (a fascist Protestant militia that had threatened armed rebellion against the Crown) wholesale into it.[2]

The peaceful, nonviolent marches were beaten off the streets by Protestant mobs, incited by the demagoguery of Protestant politicians and clergymen, and facilitated by the RUC and the B Specials. Think Bull Connors and his racist police "keeping uppity blacks in their place" in Birmingham, Alabama, 1963, and you've essentially got the picture. In 1969, Bombay Street, a Catholic street in Belfast, was burned out by mobs, while the police looked on and the B Specials participated in the burning.

From the outset, my brother Frank was in the thick of the civil rights struggle, becoming chairman of the Fermanagh Civil Rights Association. On June 18, 1970, he was elected, as Unity Candidate, MP for Fermanagh and South Tyrone. For the next four years he was hardly out of the news, and never out of danger. On January 18, 1971, he was jailed for six months for leading a proscribed civil rights march. In May 1971 there was a national census in Britain and Northern Ireland, and the Catholic community, including a number of priests and teachers, refused to comply with the census in order to protest against the corruption of the judicial process and the systematic violation of human and civil rights.

Meanwhile, I was tormented by all of this. I was safe in Liverpool and feeling guilty. Women and children were putting their lives on the line while I was safe and secure preaching from nice, cozy pulpits all across England – the country responsible for the injustices in Northern Ireland. But what could I do? Hadn't I abandoned all patriotic duty when I became a Redemptorist? Wasn't there the cardinal Redemptorist rule, that a young priest did not rock the boat – on anything?

Some may find it hard to understand why it was so difficult for a young priest to speak out in those days. As I look back now, I even find it hard to believe it myself. But the ecclesiastical, religious climate then was almost cult-like in its control on individuals and in the blind obedience it demanded. "Blind obedience" was seen as following the will of God. But what if God was not blind to injustice? (God "is a God of justice", Isaiah 30:6 and "hates injustice", Isaiah 61:8).

What if God demands of all his followers, especially priests, to work for justice? ("This is what Yahweh asks of you: only this, to do justice, to love tenderly, and to walk humbly with your God." Micah 6:8.)

How could the Catholic Church wash its hands of "the Irish problem"? What if silence in the face of injustice is complicity with that very injustice?

Lone Protest in Britain

I knew I could not live in denial. After much prayer and the most serious reflection I had ever done since my decision to become a priest, I decided not to comply with the census. I released the following statement (which, on reading now, does not seem that much of a big deal but it was for me at that time):

> I have refused to cooperate with the census. I have refused to fill in the form sent to me. I have done so as a means of protest against the general injustices perpetrated by the Unionist Government in the North of Ireland. More specifically, it is a protest against the Northern Ireland judiciary who blatantly apply a double standard in the administration of justice: one of ridiculous leniency for the Unionists; and one of vigorous severity for the non-Unionists. The latter is exemplified not only in the well known cases of my brother, Frank Mc Manus, M.P. and of Frank Gogarty, Vice Chairman of the Civil Rights Association, but also in numerous recent but less publicized convictions.

> I want this carefully considered gesture of mine to be an expression of solidarity with those priests and teachers and others in the North of Ireland who have taken similar action. The fact that I live in Britain and received a somewhat different census than the one issued in the North of Ireland does not negate or diminish the intelligibility of my protest, because – to state the painfully obvious – Britain and the North of Ireland are not unconnected. Moreover, the above mentioned people in the North of Ireland are not opposed to the census in itself; they are, like me, simply using it as a means of protest.

I want to make it perfectly clear that I am not opposed to the census. I neither resent nor do I object to any single question asked in the census form which I received. I find it perfectly reasonable. In fact, I consider it a social necessity, and I truly regret that I am forced to refuse my cooperation.

Furthermore, because I am a priest, I find it embarrassing that I should have to make such a public protest ... but then a Christian conscience or sense of justice is not always a comfortable commodity.

I was the only priest in Britain – indeed, the only person in Britain, period – to make such a protest. The papers gave it small coverage. But poor Charlie Shepherd reacted as if I had called for the abolition of both the Papacy and the Monarchy. He telephoned me in utter panic and told me to pack my bag and go immediately to Kinnoull. I did.

On May 18, Frankie was released from prison, saying defiantly that it didn't do him "a damn bit of harm" – in the sense that it had not intimidated him in the slightest, as the authorities had hoped.

Frankie then set his wedding to the fair Carmel Doherty of Lisnaskea, County Fermanagh, for August 11, 1971, and asked me to perform the ceremony, as Jim had a few years earlier performed Terence's wedding.

Two days before the planned wedding, on August 9, 1971, the British government reintroduced their favorite weapon for keeping uppity Catholics in their place: internment, imprisonment without charge or trial.

Frankie was sure he would be interned, but he was determined to get married first. I drove him over the border to a safe house in Swanlinbar the night before. He came back the following day for his wedding in Lisnaskea. The British did not arrest him – perhaps they thought it would be stretching it a bit, even for them, to intern a Member of Parliament. Frank left for London on his honeymoon, and to attend parliament to condemn the introduction of internment.

Anti-Internment Protest and Arrest

On August 13, a large march was quickly organized in

Enniskillen to protest against internment. Naturally, Terence, Jim, Myles and my brother-in-law, Michael Ferguson, attended. And I attended.

The RUC and British Army were clearly out for blood. They bullied and harassed the peaceful crowd and inevitably the young men were not going to take it. A riot broke out. Tear gas was fired into the crowd. I did my best to calm things down, even pulling a brick from the hand of a very agitated young man from Kinawley, whom I knew very well. Then I spotted a group of RUC men flaying into another young guy. I went over and said, "Come on now, there is no need for that" and nonviolently interposed my body between the young man and his police attackers, as I had read the civil right activists in the American Deep South had been taught to do. An eyewitness to my arrest, Martin O'Brien, who would later become a reporter and producer for the BBC, recounted in the *Fermanagh Herald*: "Then, Fr. Sean McManus CSsR who had been trying to restrain the crowd, was arrested."[3] (Later in court the policeman who arrested me alleged I had broken his hold on a person he was arresting. That was not the case. Furthermore, had I wanted to use physical force, it is not his "hold" I would have broken!) I was immediately arrested, which I did not resist, and frogmarched to a police van. I was unceremoniously dumped into the van, landing on a young lad crying on the floor.

Immediately, another young man whom I could not properly see, as the inside of the van was dark, gave me a black beret and asked me if I would keep it because if it was found on him the police would use it as "proof" that he was in the IRA. I put the beret in my pocket.

The next thing, my young brother Myles was tossed in on top of me. Eventually the van took off for the nearby Enniskillen Barracks. It was somehow obstructed and had to stop and the two policemen jumped out of the front. Suddenly the back door of the police van was swung open with a mighty heave. Big brother Terence, always the rescuer of his younger brothers, commanded: "Out yous get."

With that, several young lads bounded like hares out of the

van. I grabbed Myles and stopped him from jumping out, in case it would only make matters worse for him. It is an action I have often questioned. Could he have got away, free and clear? Overall, I doubt it. It is almost certain the police knew who he was and that is why they had arrested him. Even if they did not know him, they would have quickly found out because of the informers and agents they had interspersed throughout the crowd. Then they would probably have put out a warrant for Myles' arrest for escaping from police custody, thereby increasing the seriousness of the charge. Myles then might have been tempted to slip across the border, and in no time would have been on "the most wanted list", not because he was a member of the IRA but because he was a brother of the local MP, Frank, whom they took glee in harassing.

And of course, had Terence been caught freeing the prisoners, he would have been in serious trouble. Eventually, the police van made it to the barracks. When I walked into the holding room there were dozens of young men lined up before a policeman sitting at a make-shift desk in the middle of the room, taking down statements. Now I was glad I had been arrested as I could see someone had to stand up for these worried young lads. In a very loud, commanding voice (well trained by years of elocution in Hawkstone) I said, "Do not tell them anything until you are first advised of your rights." That seemed to steady the young men and they all looked relieved, as the room fell silent. Then a short, mean-looking British soldier, in full infantry regalia (I think), got in my face and pulled me over to the corner of the room. He was the very embodiment of Synge's "loosed khaki cutthroat."[4] Sticking his finger in my face, and glaring up at me, he spat, "You have no rights and that's what's killing you." I told him that though he had no idea he was doing it, he had just summed up British rule in Ireland – we had no rights and it was killing us. He gasped and stared at me helplessly.

I then said, "Now you come with me," and motioned to him to follow me back to the policeman behind the desk. I said to him, "This soldier tells me we have no rights, is that right? Do you agree with him?" The RUC man had the decency to lower his head and not say a word. It was very clear who was in charge – the British Army, not the police. I had been told once before by another Englishman that I had no rights. In my last year in Hawkstone, while I was ordained, I went to see the Prefect of Students, Barty Meehan, to ask if we could stay up to watch an Irish film on TV (I think it was *The Informer* or *Shake Hands with the Devil*). Barty said no. I pressed the case and said we should have the right to watch it. "As a Redemptorist, you have no rights. You gave them all up when you took your vows."

I was beginning to get fed up with Englishmen telling me I had no rights.

At 2.00 a.m. the police tossed me out on the street, not caring that my home was 8 miles away. I would later learn from my study of the Black Freedom Struggle in the U.S. that it was a favorite tactic of the racist police – dump the blacks on the street late at night and tip off the Ku Klux Klan. But before I left the barracks, I got – or so I thought – the assurance from the Enniskillen RUC Chief Inspector, H. J. Currie, who had been previously stationed in Kinawley, that neither Myles nor any of the other young lads arrested would be mistreated. Nonetheless, after I left, the police would point their guns through the spyhole in the door of Myles' cell, and say, "Shall we shoot him now, or later?" They would keep switching the lights on and off, go into the cell and give him a good whacking. That went on throughout the night. Remember, this was only at the start of the Troubles. Can you imagine what the police did when the Catholic community really rose up in rebellion, and when they captured actual members of the IRA, which Myles was not? The following morning, Myles was brought to court, fined and released.

Meanwhile, while the rioting was still going on and while Myles and I were still at the barracks, Frankie got a telephone call in London from the wife of a local Catholic politician: "Come home, Frank, the town's in flames and ALL your family has been arrested." Hell of a way to begin a honeymoon.

One of my in-laws, an elderly lady, on learning that her priest-relative had been arrested by the hated RUC, flew into a righteous rage and declared that the arm of the arresting officer (a Constable Frederick Scott) would "rot from the shoulder down" and to back up her prediction she quoted Scripture: "Touch not my anointed ..." (1 Chronicles 16:22). Who says Catholics don't know their Bible? I hope Constable Scott did not lose his arm. I often wonder what happened to him and I wish him well.

The British soldiers and the RUC did not scare me, but Charlie Shepherd did. What would he do now that I had been arrested in a riot situation? He would certainly have no precedence to go on as I was almost certainly the only Redemptorist from the English Province to have been arrested.

I Refuse to Recognize the Court

I returned to Kinnoull and waited to hear from the police. I was summoned to appear in the Enniskillen Magistrates Court on September 6, 1971, charged with "obstructing a Constable in the due execution of his duty." When the Resident Magistrate, Mr. John W. Adams, asked me how I pleaded, I responded: "I do not recognize the authority of the court." Fighting words and a characteristic tactic of the IRA.

The Magistrate imposed a fine of £20 to be paid in fifteen days and, "in default of payment to be imprisoned in the Prison of Belfast for the period of three months unless the said sum be sooner paid." I also refused to pay the fine.

I had not told my brother Frankie, who sat with me, that I was going to refuse to recognize the Court. I did not want to implicate him so that he could truthfully tell the media that he was not involved in my decision. I was also concerned that there was some parliamentary rule in the House of Commons which the British could use to expel Frankie for being complicit in such "treasonable" language.

I had, however, given an advance copy of my statement to Sinn Féin's office in Dublin for release the moment the hearing was over.

My statement got wide coverage. *The Irish Times* not only wrote a report on the court hearing but also printed my lengthy statement, word for word, which, given the history of that paper, amazed me. My statement was as follows:

[I] refused to recognize the Court because it has no legitimate authority. But that is only the "tip of the iceberg." I do not, I never have and I never will recognize the colonial State of British Occupied Ireland. This State exists because of a morally and politically criminal action. It was illegally imposed by force, and it is illegally sustained by force, against the will of the Irish people. Therefore, its institutions, its laws, and its legal and political expressions are invalid.

The creation and maintenance of this State blatantly violates God's laws and the natural law, because its fundamental principle is "ownership by the right of conquest," i.e., ownership through violence and the gun, and by violence and the gun it is maintained. And those who created it, and those who sustain it, are the real men of violence – they are the gunmen, they alone are the terrorists.

This terrorist State I reject in its entirety. I reject in particular its judiciary. In principle it is illegitimate, in practice it has a despicable record of injustice, corruption and sectarianism.

Refusing to recognize the court is the policy of the Irish Republican army. I will immediately be suspected of being in sympathy with the IRA. Well, let's clear up this "suspicion." I want to state publicly and unequivocally that I am in sympathy with the IRA. Indeed, sympathy is too weak a word.

Many people may wonder why I should want to publicly proclaim my convictions. The answer is simple. My conscience forbids me to be silent, and if I did not now speak out, I could never live with myself because for the rest of my life I would know that I had been a coward ... no matter how hard I tried to justify my silence as prudence. I would know that I had been deceitful and treacherous to the patriots who were sacrificing their lives for the freedom of Ireland. I cannot join them in the fight for the freedom of my country, but the very least I can do is to speak up for them when they are being slandered and vilified by unscrupulously vicious propaganda.

The oppressors of Irish freedom call the IRA terrorists and murderers, but I call them by their proper titles: I call them freedom fighters, I call them heroes, and I venerate their dead as martyrs for Ireland. And I know that any true Irishman or indeed any informed, honest and fair-minded person thinks and feels the same way.

I could not live with myself, if by my silence, I traitorously stabbed these patriots in the back. I abhor the deceit and hypocrisy that condemns these men and women who are sacrificing their lives for the freedom of Ireland. I could not bear to be even remotely associated with such deceit and hypocrisy – and my silence would associate me. It is only expected that the violent men who are opposing Irish freedom should condemn the IRA freedom fighters, but it is unforgivable when many so-called Nationalist spokesmen also condemn them.

Yet, in the light of history, condemnation from the latter is not surprising for every struggle for Irish freedom has been traitorously condemned by this sort of people. (And yet our patriots, despite "this unkindest cut of all," still fought on because they were, and are, men and women of courage, integrity and dedication.) And of this I am certain: that when our patriots free Ireland, and free it they surely will, these very people will be the very first to jump on the bandwagon and salute the men and women they now condemn. They did it before and they will do it again.

To praise Tone, Pearse, Connolly, Sean Treacy and Cathal Brugha and all the others, on the one hand, while on the other, condemning those (and here I make no distinction between the Provisionals and the Officials) is treachery and deceit of the lowest kind. How I detest such chicanery. It revolts and disgusts me, and I will have no part of it.

I finalized my decision to speak out as I stood by a lonely grave. It is the grave of a man who was the personification of nobility, courage and integrity: a typical member of the IRA. He is a man whose memory I honor and of whom I am deeply proud: my brother Patrick who died for Ireland in 1958.

The day before the court hearing, I was being driven by the late Dave O'Connell, a top IRA man and political strategist, from Dublin to Monaghan. I read my statement out loud for him to hear. When I had finished, he pulled the car off the road, clearly very moved. "I never thought I'd see the day when a priest would have the balls to say what you have said." And with great embarrassment he silently sobbed for about five minutes. "If nothing else, it's worth it, just for this," I thought, as memories flooded back into my mind about how the priests at St. Michael's were so scared of being associated with the IRA that they would not even perform a basic act of Christian charity or human decency, except Fr. Clerkin. Dave pulled himself together and in his signature Cork accent – at once authoritative, yet almost roguish – said, "Don't tell anyone I cried. It would be bad for my image if the Brits knew." His secret was safe with me. Dave died in Dublin in January 1991, aged fifty-three. Sadly, Sinn Féin split in 1986 and Dave broke from Gerry Adams and Martin McGuinness, both of whom would go on to do truly historic work. However, no one can diminish Dave's stature, integrity and heroism. I had deep respect for him and held him in great affection. On my annual pilgrimage to Glasnevin Cemetery, "where the Fenians sleep," I always kneel and say a prayer at his grave in the Republican Plot.

When Frankie saw my statement, he told me I would be interned, which I was quite prepared for. In fact, I would have welcomed it, for as Thoreau said: "Under a government, which imprisons any unjustly, the true place for a just man is also a prison."[5] But I was neither interned for my statement, nor imprisoned for not paying the fine.

I knew that the British government and its whole intelligence operations would not stand idly by, even though they had not publicly moved against me. I knew they would exert huge pressure on the Catholic hierarchy in Britain and Ireland, and through them on Fr. Shepherd. After all, the British government had succeeded in 1870 in getting Pope Pius IX to excommunicate the Fenians, both in Ireland and America. No matter how badly the British treated Irish Catholics, the Vatican always listened to them on Ireland with the aid of the Irish Bishops. 'Twas enough to make a Kinawleyman a Protestant!

However, I continued to speak out but, again, never from the pulpit. Finally that letter, dated Friday April 15, 1972, with which this book opened, arrived from Fr. Shepherd telling me to pack my bag for Clapham in London. "I do not want anyone to know your immediate destination, nor your proposed transfer from Perth. I once again forbid you to make any communications to the Press or Media either per se or per alium, or to call on anyone en route or before departure."

I was blessed with the insight to see that for what it was: an unconscionable, almost racist missive, which in fact meant: do not fraternize with any Irish person on the way to your ecclesiastical house arrest, on behalf, in effect, of Her Majesty's government.

The racist implication become clear if one imagines a white Church superior telling Martin Luther King, Jr. (not that I'm comparing myself to that great man) that he must not associate with any black person, especially one engaged in the Black Freedom Struggle. James Joyce said of Ireland that "Christ and Caesar are hand in glove" but that applies even more so to England, as I was soon about to learn.

I felt no moral obligation to obey this patently unjust and politicized diktat. Charlie Shepherd was simply implementing that British soldier's ignorant decree: "You have no rights ..." I am sure Charlie saw himself as protecting the Redemptorist Order but the only way he could do that was by pleasing the British government. So the end result was the same.

Protestant Solidarity

But let me contrast Charlie's letter with the one I received on April 19 from a local Episcopalian priest in Perth. You be the judge as to which is the more Christian:

Dear Father,

Whilst I was at the altar celebrating the Liturgy this morning, I thought about you and the difficult situation in which you find yourself at present. I would like you to know that this vivid thought prompted me to include you in my prayers and intention in the Eucharist.

I would also like you to know that I think that I can sense – and to some extent share – the anguish which you feel about the situation in Ireland. I suppose it will always be difficult for the priest transfixed by the knowledge that he must be an [intermediary] representing God to his people and the people to God – and yet, burning within with a great desire to move into an area of what seems like worldly action for a cause which he knows in his heart of hearts is right. I use the word "transfixed" for it seems to me that in this kind of situation, the priest is nailed to the cross, a cross which is that well-nigh unbearable tension between his priesthood, as conceived of in spiritual terms, and his (dare I use the word?) priesthood as he sees it in worldly terms. But of course, this is what the priesthood is all about. It is surely more than offering the Eucharistic sacrifice and preaching the Word (though it is that too) – but a living of this tension between the spiritual and the physical, between this world and the "other" world. The priest who lives this tension in his own life is stretched on the Cross with his Master.

Take heart, Father. There are many who will understand and pray for you – as I do. I hope that when "things are blown over" you will be able to come to visit me and have another "natter."

On Friday, I will be celebrating the Liturgy at our cathedral at 8 a.m. I will pray especially for you. In our calendar and Ordo, it is the double feast of St. Maelrubha (Abbot of Applecross and Bangor) and St. Anslem,

Archbishop of Canterbury – a Celtic saint and one from an English See: perhaps there might be some significance in that – reconciliation – ?

With every prayer and blessing
Yours in Christ,
Reverend John Ross.

I flew down to London. Frankie was in Parliament and naturally I needed to talk to him about the whole thing. Incredibly even at that period (the week of April 16, 1972) I was able to check in my bag at the House of Commons cloakroom. Then I remembered that in my bag there was an alarm clock, set to go off at 5.30 a.m. and it was now nearly 5:30 p.m. and I was concerned my clock would not distinguish between a.m. and p.m. So I hurried back to the Clerk and told him not to worry if the alarm went off. "Don't worry, Reverend, that will be no problem," said the very nice Englishman.

It was there I met Bernadette Devlin, MP, for the first time. She had been elected the year before Frankie and he and she fought the good fight in "the belly of the beast". I had, of course, great admiration for her fearlessness, courage and eloquence. But I was not expecting someone with such a formidable public persona to be so charming and gracious. And thus she has been each time I've met her over the years. She and Frankie (and sometimes Gerry Fitt, MP for West Belfast) had to fight lonely battles. The day after Bloody Sunday (January 30, 1972 when British paratroopers killed thirteen innocents at a nonviolent march in Derry) Bernadette punched out the Foreign Secretary, Reginald Maudling, in the House of Commons for trying to cover up the act of State terrorism. Years later, in an interview with the London magazine, *The Big Issue*, Bernadette would recall: "I walked over and clattered Maudling ... Big Davison, a conservative, hit me and Frank McManus floored him."[6]

That evening I went to St. Mary's, Clapham, the Provincial's headquarters. Fr. Shepherd told me he wanted to see me first thing in the morning. At the appointed time, I went to his office (which, ironically, my brother Jim would later occupy as Provincial for three terms, 1990 to 1999). Charlie was in no mood for chit-chat. He got right to the point: "Unless you give a promise, without mental reservation or equivocation, never to criticize the government again on Northern Ireland, I will suspend you from all public priestly work."

I deliberately paused for a very long time before replying so that he would know that I was as serious as he was. My reply was slow and steady: "Father, in conscience and with all due respect, I cannot make such a promise. While I do not intend to speak out all the time, I cannot make a promise to be silent in the face of injustice because that would make me as guilty as the British government and British army." Then he lost it: "*You are in the English Province and you will not criticize the English government.*" Well, despite my intention to maintain a controlled demeanour, the Kinawleyman reasserted itself and I gave it back to him in kind: "For as long as your government oppresses my country, I will not be silent."

He jumped out of his chair, declared he had not called me in for a discussion and told me to pack my bag for Chawton (to Alphonsus House, the Redemptorist publishing house, which had no parish) in Hampshire, about 56 miles southwest of London.

As I headed for the door, I turned and said, "Does this mean I am being silenced [in the canonical sense of not being able to function as a priest]?" He snapped, "Nobody said anything about silencing."

Ecclesiastical Long Kesh

So that meant I could say a private Mass in Alphonsus House and, as there was no parish attached, the issue of public Masses did not apply.

I would come to refer to Chawton as "my ecclesiastical Long Kesh," after the prison of that name the British were operating in the North.

Charlie Shepherd would telephone me every week or so to see if I would recant. "In good conscience, and with all due respect, Father, I cannot ..." But he would often slam down the phone before I could complete my mantra.

The fact that Chawton had no parish seemed a logical place to sequester me, but it had one ironic disadvantage: it was only about nine miles from Aldershot. On February 22, 1972, the Official IRA had bombed the 16th Parachute Brigade headquarters at Aldershot in retaliation for the Parachute Regiment's murderous attack on the peaceful march on January 30, 1972 in Derry – the atrocity and act of State terrorism known as Bloody Sunday. Five women and one Catholic priest, a chaplain, were tragically killed in the IRA attack. The priest, Fr. Gerry Weston, thirty-seven, had been a regular visitor to Alphonsus House and was a good friend of all the Redemptorists there. So that made the situation very poignant for all of us. Yet I must say everyone in Alphonsus House treated me very kindly, though they must have wondered what they had done to deserve this turn of events.

However, my forced ecclesiastical quarantine gave me time for serious reflection and prayer. The library wasn't too bad. It had a copy of *Justice in the World* (mentioned in the Introduction). I went to the local library and got a copy of Martin Luther King, Jr.'s "Letter from Birmingham Jail" – his magisterial response to the top eight Birmingham Church leaders, including the Catholic Bishop of Birmingham, who had publicly censored his protest actions:

> "I have almost reached the regrettable conclusion that the Negro's great stumbling block in his stride toward freedom is not the White Citizen's Councillor or the Ku Klux Klanner, but the white moderate, who is more devoted to 'order' than to justice; who prefers a negative peace which is the absence of tension to a positive peace which is the presence of justice; who constantly says: 'I agree with you in the goal you seek, but I cannot agree with your methods of direct action;' who paternalistically believes he can set the timetable for another man's freedom; who lives by a mythical concept of time and who constantly

advises the Negro to wait for a 'more convenient season.' Shallow understanding from people of good will is more frustrating than absolute misunderstanding from people of ill will. Lukewarm acceptance is much more bewildering than outright rejection ... Before closing I feel impelled to mention one other point in your statement that has troubled me profoundly. You warmly commended the Birmingham police force for keeping 'order' and 'preventing violence.' I doubt that you would have so warmly commended the police force if you had seen its dogs sinking their teeth into unarmed, nonviolent Negroes. I doubt that you would so quickly commend the policemen if you were to observe their ugly and inhumane treatment of Negroes here in the city jail; if you were to watch them push and curse old Negro women and young Negro girls; if you were to see them slap and kick old Negro men and young boys; if you were to observe them, as they did on two occasions, refuse to give us food because we wanted to sing our grace together. I cannot join you in your praise of the Birmingham police department."[7]

I am still amazed, almost fifty years later, how comparable the Black Freedom Struggle is to the Irish struggle.

Pax Christi or Pax Britannica

I also decided to contact one of the priests who had taught me "the new theology" in Hawkstone. So on May 9, 1972, I wrote asking him for his guidance on the theology concerning the "conflict of conscience" – the possible conflict between conscience and authority. I stressed I did not want him to take a position on my stand, nor make judgments about the Irish situation, but to clearly explicate the theological principle. He wrote back saying that a good Redemptorist can never have a conflict of conscience! That was a total contradiction of both the new and the "old" theology. Not *Pax Christi*, but *Pax Britannica*. Rule Britannia. And I was supposed to be the one being political.

Because of my rather unique position, I had to make a serious study of the subject. I knew that first of all, one had an obligation to have an informed conscience – to seek out all the available teaching on the issue, to study it sincerely and objectively and, above all, pray that one was not deceiving oneself, because all of us can have a "self-serving" conscience. The Second Vatican Council, in its document *Gaudium et Spes* (Joy and Hope), told me that "conscience is the man's most secret core, and his sanctuary." So I knew if I betrayed my conscience, I would be betraying my truest self – the inner me who stands naked before the all-seeing eye of God.

I knew very well how the deal would go down: some good Catholic MPs (and I hoped it wasn't Frankie or Bernadette Devlin!) would contact Cardinal Heenan saying it was very bad for the Church to have a young priest accusing the British Government of such awful things and wasn't there something His Eminence could do about it? The Cardinal would then call Charlie. Indeed, Charlie admitted as much to me – well, he let it slip out and then couldn't take it back.

I also knew there was another fundamental principle involved in making a conscientious protest: you take your punishment without whining and you do not, after the fact, unfairly look to involve others in the consequences of your action. Again, I found solace in Martin Luther King, Jr.: "An individual who breaks a law that conscience tells him is unjust, and who willingly accepts the penalty of imprisonment in order to arouse the conscience of the community over its injustice, is in reality expressing the highest respect for the law."

I finally wrote to Fr. Shepherd on May 16, 1974:

I have thought things over – but, it was all well-charted ground. I am unable to see things in a different light. The actions I took were not impetuous: they were studied and calculated, and prayed about. I am totally convinced that what I did was right, and that I was bound to do it. Therefore, in principle I could never give an absolute unconditional promise never to speak out again ... Before God, I do not believe that my actions were motivated by anything base or ulterior. In fact, from the very nature of the case, I have patently nothing to gain but everything to lose. Indeed, from the way things look at present, I know that I may very well have (if I may speak like this for a moment) ruined my "personal career."

I went on to acknowledge that I had put him in a difficult position but stressed that any apparent clash between my loyalty to the Province and my conscience was only that, i.e. apparent: "... because when a man stands up for what he knows is right, then he is not being disloyal to any side: he is being loyal to the truth, which can never 'compete' against any value or good." But I knew the die was cast. There was no way I would be allowed to continue working in Britain or Ireland.

I would have liked for Fr. Shepherd to acknowledge the moral integrity of my conscientious protest, but he never did. He insisted as seeing it "formal disobedience," maybe because it was easier that way for him, or because he was just plain scared or because he was incapable of respecting a conscience that disagreed with his. Religious superiors can easily fall into the sin of thinking they speak for God at all times and in all ways. They don't. That's why we have this thing called conscience. No authority, no superior, can take its place.

Soon the whole world was my parish. Fr. Shepherd gave me all sorts of choices: go to Rome for further studies in Eucharistic theology, or any place in continental Europe, Canada or America. South Africa would have been the usual "dumping ground" for the English Province. But an Anglican priest had recently been deported back to England for speaking out against the apartheid system. And there was no way someone like me would be allowed into that country.

I chose America. I checked out which Redemptorist Province in America was the most Irish. If I was going to be "transported" (the very resonant word that was used for the exiling of political prisoners to Australia, up until 1868), then I might as well go to an area where I could do the most good. I chose the Baltimore Province, because that included New York, Boston and, most importantly of all, the nation's capital, Washington, DC.

Charlie now became very cooperative, doing everything in his power to facilitate my "transportation." On June 16, 1972, he wrote to the Provincial of the Baltimore Province, Fr. Joseph L. Kerins, at his headquarters in Brooklyn, New York.

"Fr. Sean McManus aged 29 [*sic*]. This young man is an excellent priest and a very promising missionary on the Parish Mission. Unfortunately, owing to his Irish origins, he has foolishly become implicated through newspaper articles & a TV appearance in the very sad political impasse in N. Ireland ... Would it be at all possible for you to take him and let him work on the Parish Mission band in the Baltimore Province? ... I am not trying to unload a bad priest on anyone, but one who has been foolish and stubborn in this particular Irish problem." (Notice here, the strange distancing, probably unconscious, but typically British ... "the Irish problem" – as if it had no connection to Britain or that the British Army was not in the North doing terrible things.)

I acknowledged earlier that the average British person knows little about Northern Ireland. But is that really a good enough excuse? How long can a well-educated people be excused for not knowing what their government, army and "tax dollars" are doing in another country? Is it ignorance or indifference? And how could the Churches in Britain ignore the mistreatment of Catholics in Northern Ireland? Is it because they did not want to become "involved in politics" or is it because they were being profoundly political? Was their silence prudence or betrayal?

How could ecclesiastical silence be reconciled with the clarion call of *Gaudium et Spes* issued by the Second Vatican Council in its very opening lines: "The joys and the hopes, the griefs and the anxieties of the men of this age, especially those who are poor or in any way afflicted, these are the joys and hopes, the griefs and anxieties of the followers of Christ. Indeed, nothing genuinely human fails to raise an echo in their hearts."

Attempt to Kill Mother

In August I went home to Clonliff to prepare for my exile to America. So far, 1972 was proving to be one of the worst years of the Troubles. Danger was palpable all over the North. And it visited Mother. She was home alone one night. A gunman blasted her bedroom window but mercifully she escaped injury. She was sixty-nine at the time. And to make it all the more painful, the man who tried to kill her was a local Protestant whom we had known all our lives, and whom we had always treated with friendliness and kindness (as we had treated all our Protestant neighbors).

Now let me tell you the follow-up to this incident in two parts. The first and most important part is about my Mother's forgiveness; the second is about the nature of the State of Northern Ireland.

About two nights after the shooting (while we still did not know who the shooter was) I was sitting home with my mother. There was a knock on the door, and as we were not expecting any visitors, I signalled to my Mother not to move and went to the door. Outside there was standing the tallest policeman I had ever seen in my life, indeed the tallest person I had ever seen. I then saw there was someone hiding behind him whom the policeman then brought forward. The policeman said: "[first and last name] has come to apologize for shooting at Mrs. McManus." The man then, sheepishly said, "Hello, Fr. Sean," casting his eyes down.

I brought them both into the kitchen and the Protestant gunman said, "Mrs. McManus, I am sorry for shooting at you. Will you forgive me?" Without hesitating a split second, Mother reached out, grabbed his hand in hers and said, "Of course, I will [first name]. God love you."

I have told that story to very few outside the family because it is so profoundly personal and precious, and also because it is difficult for me to get through it without crying.

And now to the second, less edifying, part of the story: can you imagine that, had a Catholic tried to kill the mother of a Protestant MP, the police would have brought him to that woman's house to apologize? Nothing can tell you more about the nature of the

State of Northern Ireland than this. Why would the police do such a thing? Certainly it had to come from the very top, as no local policeman would take it upon himself to do such an extraordinary thing. Local people immediately saw it as an attempt to get the court to go easy on the gunman. But the far more serious question was why would the police go so far out on a limb for an ordinary working-class Protestant? What was the purpose of their damage control? What were they trying to contain or hide?

We have never been given an explanation. But we all, like Mother, forgave the gunman, whom we felt had been used as a patsy, like so many other working-class Protestant gunmen.

The first night after the shooting, mother and I were alone in the house. She was asleep in her room upstairs. I was across the hall in my room.

I was woken by pounding on the front door. I sprang out of bed, fearing we were under attack again. I charged out of my room to the top of the stairs, thinking "if they have guns, we are done for." I braced myself at the top of the stairs in the dark as the front door was forced open. "If I hurl myself on top of them at least I will slow them down," I thought, as I prepared to jump at a shape at the bottom of the stairs. And then the "shape" began to scamper up the stairs yelping with delight to be inside. It was Judy, mother's big, much-loved black Labrador dog. She had learned the trick of pouncing on the front door until the simple "yale lock " eased open.

I was never so pleased to see any dog in my life.

A final note on this episode: Shortly after I arrived in New York, I learned more about the shooting incident. I discovered that a prominent IRA leader in the Leitrim-Cavan area had taken grave exception to the attempted shooting of "the mother of Patrick Mc Manus." He dispatched two men to cross The Border "to go looking for" the Protestant gunman. They spent two nights trying to find him but could not. That Protestant man never knew how lucky he was. Then again, the police would have expected the IRA to retaliate and would have taken the gunman into protective custody.

6

Bound for America

I know how men in exile feed on dreams.
Aeschylus

I have never met an emigrant from Ireland who did not know the exact date of their arrival in America. It is a big day in their lives – truly a transitional moment in every sense. My big day was October 2, 1972. I flew out from Dublin on Aer Lingus with a stop in Shannon Airport. At the airport I telephoned Celia to get the momentous news that Carmel, Frankie's wife, had just given birth to a lovely baby girl, Emer. I ran back to the plane, my homesickness abated by the good news. Needless to say, I never have a problem remembering Emer's birthday.

Ironically, I wasn't back on the plane ten minutes before the woman sitting next to me brought up Frankie's name, totally of her own accord, having no idea who I was. When she heard I was from the North, she immediately started talking about the Troubles. I knew immediately she had to be living in America because most people from southern Ireland did not want to talk about the North. She was a nice, middle-aged woman, originally from Dublin, who had spent most of her life in America but was now living six months in Ireland and six months in America. "God bless us," I thought, "she must be a millionaire." Anyway, she proceeded to tell me something which was not "generally known": that Frank McManus and Bernadette Devlin were secretly married; and there was nothing wrong with that; that they were properly married in the Church (an acknowledgement of my clerical collar); but the marriage had to be secret because a husband and wife could not serve in the British Parliament at the same time.

Keeping a straight face, I asked her the source of her information. She implied she knew some very well-connected people. "Well, now, I don't think that's quite right," I said, looking for a way to let her down gently. But she would have none of it, and dismissed my mild protestations with a wave of the hand and changed the subject. It was my first introduction to how some Irish-Americans (even Irish born) have very definite views about Ireland that may not be exactly correct.

I will never forget my arrival at JFK Airport in New York. I was a little apprehensive. I had never seen so many people, racing like crazy. I see some sort of uniform, a gun in a holster and instinctively I tighten. Then I see it is a black man in uniform and somehow that made it all right. It had been my first sight of an armed policeman, other that the RUC.

I got a cab and headed for the Redemptorist headquarters on Shore Road, Brooklyn. And, would you believe it? The cab broke down, in the worst looking area I had ever seen in my life. I immediately thought it was a set-up. I was relieved the driver was an African American, but what if the British had paid him to "break down"? That may all sound melodramatic now, and it may have all been in my head, but the reality was that the British were regularly setting up people for assassination in the North.

But my driver waved down a passing cab, and I made it safely to the Redemptorist headquarters. When I had settled in, I went to the common room where about five or six Redemptorists were watching TV news. They welcomed me kindly and offered me a seat. I took out a pack of cigarettes, and in my good mannerly way, offered one to each priest. They laughed and declined. I had learned my first etiquette lesson in America: it is not considered cheap if you do not offer a cigarette, as everyone smokes their own. (But you better unlearn that when you are back in Ireland.)

As we watched the news (each smoking his own cigarette), Kissinger comes on. He has just returned from the Middle East. He is asked if America has plans to take over the Arab oil fields. That would only be done if America's national interest were at stake, he droned. I wanted to shout back at the TV, but I was just off the boat, so to speak. I glanced around the room expecting a reaction to Kissinger's British-imperialist-type declaration but it hadn't even raised an eyebrow. I had learned my first political lesson: America is permanently in danger of making the same mistakes as the British – the hubris of empire.

My most vivid first impressions of America came the following morning as I jumped into the shower in my room. The water took lumps out of me. I couldn't believe its force. In the Redemptorists' showers in Britain, you almost had to beg the water to trickle out. When I grabbed the towel, I couldn't believe its size, softness and absorbency. The towels in the London Province, by contrast, were like glorified dishcloths that became soaked on the first contact with your wet back. When I stepped out of the bathroom, it appeared that my feet almost sank up to my ankles in the lush carpet. Coming out of the showers in Britain was always the worst part. You stepped on cold floor, covered with linoleum, if you were lucky, and froze until you had dressed again. Not in the good old USA. I could have been quite comfortable in my room with just the big towel around my waist. (Mind you, the rooms in the Redemptorist houses throughout the Baltimore Province were not as nice, and did not have their own bathroom.) After Mass and breakfast, I met with the Provincial, Fr. Joe Kerins. I knew immediately I was in the presence of a remarkable fine man. Things even got better when he knowingly said, "One of my uncles in Kerry was in the IRA." (Put that in your pipe, Charlie Shepherd, and smoke it, I thought to myself.)

Then he completely bowled me over when he said, "Here's your file."

"What do you mean?" I asked.

"It is a copy of all correspondence regarding you – including Fr.

Shepherd's letters," he explained.

"And do I get to keep this file?"

"Yes, in this Province, we have a policy of total openness. It is the right of every Redemptorist to see every letter that is written about him."

To me, this was extraordinary and revolutionary. I had been so used to Englishmen telling me I had no rights. God bless us, I thought, this is a great country altogether.

And that is how I got a copy of the letter from Charlie Shepherd, to Fr. Kerins, that I quoted earlier. Over the next few years, Fr. Kerins would keep sending me copies of letters Fr. Shepherd would write about me, as I kept denouncing the British government – the more I denounced, the more angry and personal Shepherd's letter became. And I'm sure he had no idea I was being given copies of his letters.

Fr. Kerins told me they badly needed a young priest in Sacred Heart of Jesus parish, in Baltimore, especially for youth work. I suspected that Baltimore was selected because it was not as Irish as New York or Boston. He told me to take some time for myself, and visit my brother Thomas in upstate New York and my sister Alice in Reading, Pennsylvania.

He also told me that he was sure I would want "to meet my many admirers in New York City." And with a big smile, he handed me a copy of the *Irish People*, which I had never heard of, but which announced to great acclaim there was "an Irish rebel priest" in town.

Ardent New York Irish

A delegation of ardent Irish men and women came to Shore Road to escort me into the city. I stayed in the apartment of a man from Ballinamore, County Leitrim, who had been in the IRA with Patrick, and had soldiered alongside him. He was a laboring man. Yet, when he showed me into my room, he pulled out two drawers from a cabinet, and said if I needed any vests (T-shirts), there were plenty there. And was there ever! I had never seen so many gleaming white T-shirts, all neatly folded, maybe even pressed. Now, I had come to America wearing one T-shirt and one in my bag. "God bless us," I thought, "this man must be rich indeed."

My Ballinamore host could not wait to take me to meet Seán Cronin, who was Chief of Staff of the IRA after Patrick was killed. He was then a journalist in New York City. Seán was very pleased to meet me as he had great respect for Patrick. He told me I could do a lot of good work for the Cause, but to watch my back, as both the London and Dublin governments would try to bring me down. I soon met all the leaders and activists in Irish Northern Aid, AOH and general Irish organizations in New York City. They were fiercely anti-British and furious at the quisling attitude of the Free State government. Suddenly, I felt very much at home.

When I arrived at Sacred Heart of Jesus, in the section of Baltimore called Highlandtown, the first thing that struck me was that there were absolutely no people on the streets, although it was mid-afternoon. The next thing I spotted were the famous marble steps that lead up to each row house, and which the housewives kept as clean as their own very white teeth. Highlandtown was mostly German and Polish, hardly any Irish.

After the Masses on Sunday, my reaction was that apart from superficial differences, Sacred Heart could have been like any city parish in Belfast, Dublin or London. I was sad, however, to see only a few black faces – the great weakness in the American Catholic Church. How often over the years would I reflect on that telling quote of Martin Luther King, Jr. about eleven o'clock on a Sunday morning being the most segregated hour of the week!

Right away, I arranged a meeting with the officers of the parish CYO (Catholic Youth Organization) – a group of lovely young girls, aged fifteen to seventeen, I guess. They were delighted to have a young priest for their group. The TV show *Charlie's Angels* was very popular at the time, so they took to calling themselves "Fr. Sean's Angels." When I told them I was from Ireland, they nodded their heads. But at the end of the meeting, the president, a very bright young lady, said, "Fr. Sean, where is Ireland, near Canada?" My first lesson about Americans and geography. And there was I thinking Ireland was the center of the world, with everybody knowing about it.

I quickly got the run of the parish, and did my work with gusto. There was hardly any Irish activity in Baltimore and none on the

North. But I was determined to quickly change that. The word got out that I was in town and a group wanted me to speak to them. I made them feel guilty that they were ignoring their homeland and told them they were aiding British oppression in Ireland by their silence. Soon there was an active chapter of Irish Northern Aid in Baltimore and Washington.

As the only young priest, I was doing a lot of good work in the parish. All the other priests were over fifty, with most in their seventies. I loved the people. I had never met any nicer people than these German and Polish folk – all patriotic Americans and deeply committed Catholics. I was humbled by their devout Catholicism and surprised at how strongly Catholic this big country was.

I was getting on with my work, reinvigorating the parish with no thought that I would see Ireland in the near future. But just as I thought I was out, they pulled me back in.

Mac Stiofain Hunger Strike

A month after I arrived in Baltimore, Seán Mac Stíofáin, Chief of Staff of the IRA, was arrested in Dublin on November 19, 1972, and immediately began a hunger and thirst strike. On November 25, he was sentenced to six months imprisonment. The previous day, Irish Northern Aid leaders in New York had appealed to me to come and speak at protest meetings in New York, and to go to Ireland because Mac Stíofáin had asked for me.

I tried to reach both my Rector at Sacred Heart and Father Provincial in New York. They were unavailable so I left a message for them that "I had presumed permission" (the theological principle that states one can, in an emergency, legitimately and in good faith presume the superior would grant permission if he were present). I traveled to New York and spoke at the hastily called public meeting at the Irish Institute. The other two speakers were Seán Cronin and Congressman Biaggi. The meeting was followed by an all-night vigil outside the Irish Consulate.

Jack McCarthy, the crusty but admirable leader of Irish Northern Aid, arranged my flight to Dublin.

When I picked up my luggage at Dublin airport, I asked the

luggage handler if Mac Stíofáin was still alive. "Unfortunately, he is. It would be far better for the country if he died." He clearly thought because I had a clerical collar on that I would be supporting the Dublin government. I gave him such a withering look he scurried off. I stayed at the home of friends, a fine elderly couple from Kerry. Their house was a veritable hotel for IRA leaders like the late Joe Cahill.

I spoke at a massive rally, which my brother Frank also attended. On Sunday afternoon, November 26, I visited Mac Stíofáin in the Mater Hospital, to which he had been transferred from prison because of his deteriorating condition. As I walked into the hospital ward, a group of Special Branch men grabbed me and pinned me with my back to the wall. I had never seen such fury or hatred in anybody's eyes as the man who held me by the throat. I said, "You fellows are worse than the British Army. Why are you doing this?" The lead guy hissed, "One of you f**kers tried to shoot me." "What do you mean one of us f**kers tried to shoot you?" I demanded.

Then I learned why they were so (understandably) agitated. A short time before I had arrived, an IRA team, disguised as priests, had tried to rescue Mac Stíofáin and had got into a shoot-out with the Special Branch. Two IRA men were wounded and four caught. I had been oblivious to all of this, and had innocently blundered into an explosive setting. IRA leaders had known in advance that I was going to be visiting Mac Stíofáin but had not said a word to me – and I guess that was also understandable.

Finally – with bruised neck, but none the worse for wear – I got into Mac Stíofáin's room. I was stunned to see how terrible he looked on his eighth day of hunger and thirst strike. The last time I saw him he was a vigorous, strong man. But now he was a shadow of his former self. It was evident he was in a most critical condition.

That night or early morning the following day – to avoid any further rescue attempts – Mac Stíofáin was transferred by helicopter to the Irish Army's main barracks in the Curragh, about 30 miles from Dublin. Dave O'Connell, a top IRA man, told me it was vital that I got into the Curragh to see Mac Stíofáin, as the Republican Movement would have no other point of contact.

Friends drove me to the Curragh and I tried to see Mac Stíofáin the evening of Monday, November 27, as it was getting dark. The Free State Army had the entire area cordoned off. I asked to speak to the lead soldier, a surprisingly young man. He was absolute: It didn't matter if I were the Pope. I was not getting through, he told me with just too much relish. "How does it feel to be doing England's dirty work?" I blasted. Sticking out his chest he boasted, "It feels great. It feels great." I think if I had not been a priest, I would have decked him on the spot.

The following morning, I returned to the Curragh military hospital and waited outside with Mrs. Mac Stíofáin and her daughter, Marie. They were eventually allowed in.

Then I went to a soldier guarding the door and asked him if I could use the bathroom. He refused. I told him it was an emergency and if I could not use the bathroom, I would go behind the trees at the bottom of the field. He then earnestly pleaded, "Father, please don't. We have orders to shoot anything that moves down there." At least he's a decent sort, I thought, compared to the blackguard from the night before.

Sometime later, the top brass summoned me in: "It's an emergency." They rushed me to where Mac Stíofáin was caged, literally: his bed was inside a huge cage. From inside the bars, Mac Stíofáin's daughter was screaming, "Fr. Sean, Fr. Sean, my father is dying." Mac Stíofáin was having some sort of seizure, shaking violently. However, he survived and came off his thirst strike, and afterwards off his hunger strike.

Later on, when the emotion and high drama had subsided, I slipped up to Fermanagh to see my mother. In retrospect, it was probably a risky thing to have done as the Orangemen were out for my blood.

When I was returning to America, Dave O'Connell drove me to the Dublin airport. He assured me he had given a full report to Irish Northern Aid leaders in New York about all the details of my efforts.

The same luggage handler was there. I had been on TV so much that he could not fail to recognize me. A look of sheer terror came over his face, scared that I might have passed on his vicious comment about Mac Stíofáin to the IRA. I had not, of course, as I did not want him to suffer any retaliation. I went over to him and assured that I had not told anyone. "Oh, thank you, Father, thank you, Father. I didn't mean it. I'm a good Republican meself." You've never seen a more relieved man.

Years later, a Redemptorist friend told Jim and me this story in Washington. He was based in Clapham with Charlie Shepherd during the Mac Stíofáin hunger strike. They were in the common room watching the TV news and the hunger strike was covered. Charlie turned around and intoned to all in the room, "Thank goodness Sean Mc Manus is safely in America." And at that very instant, I appear on the TV, large as life, not safely in America but in Dublin. Charlie got such a shock he almost fainted.

When I arrived back in Baltimore, I wasn't sure of the reception I would receive at Sacred Heart of Jesus. The national and Baltimore media had covered my activities and everyone in the parish had been excited to read about their "young new Irish priest." I did not receive one negative comment from the parishioners, only, "right on, Father, way to go" from those lovely German and Polish Catholics.

Parishioners are one thing, but what about the powers that be?

Fr. Kerns – the noblest of them all – would provide me with another file of all correspondences relating to my Irish visit. God bless us, I thought to myself yet again, this is a great country altogether.

On December 1, while I was still in Ireland, the Rector of Sacred Heart had written to Fr. Kerins: "My reaction about this whole affair [the Mac Stíofáin hunger strike] is that Sean is welcome back here at Sacred Heart, as far as I am concerned. My motives for saying this perhaps are not unselfish in that he is filling a need here for someone in the younger age brackets ... I honestly don't think he has caused any serious embarrassment or problem to us here."

Fr. Kerins replied on December 6: "I certainly would have no objections to his return to our Province. I would agree with you that he had a valid reason for going to Ireland ..." And then this splendid human being instructs the Rector: "It might be well if you ask [Sean] if he had to borrow the money for his travels. I would not want him to be saddled with a debt or have to approach his own Provincial [Charlie Shepherd] for funds in this situation ..."

Then on December 10, (ironically, International Human Rights Day), Charlie Shepherd wrote a letter to Fr. Kerins decrying my disobedience in "presuming permission" and the harm I had done to both the English and Irish Provinces. I did not mind his attack on me. I was fair game. But Shepherd – abandoning even the slightest pretense at objectivity and fairness – took out his anger on my brother Jim. He complained: "I have heard his brother, Fr. Jim ([at] Hawkstone) has been in touch with Baltimore [Sacred Heart]. He is just as politically minded as Sean, but more cautious in the way he goes about things. The point of the matter is that at least 75% of this Province are heartily fed up with the two of them, especially with Sean, in the complete disregard they show for the feelings of the people of this country, where they received the opportunity of their priesthood and the chance of exercising it."

Let's examine the bit about England being "the opportunity of their priesthood". A bit like telling Martin Luther King, Jr., a native of the State of Georgia, that if he wanted to exercise his ministry in Alabama or Mississippi he would have to be silent. The analogy is even more apt if one accepts, for the sake of the argument, Maggie Thatcher's dictum "Northern Ireland is as British as Finchley."

And there you have it, the classic blackmail. You must not oppose England's injustice in Ireland lest you upset the feelings of the English people. So forget human rights. Forget democracy. Forget even the teaching of the Catholic Church on justice. Anything that disturbs order in Her Majesty's realm is sinful, inconsiderate and to be crushed. Remember that quote, given earlier, from Martin Luther King, Jr. about how the greatest stumbling block to justice is the nice, respectable "moderate, who is more devoted to 'order' than to justice; who prefers a negative peace which is the absence of tension to a positive peace which is the presence of justice."

Contrast Fr. Shepherd's myopic moral view with that of the greatest Redemptorist moral authority, after St. Alphonsus, the famed German moral theologian, Fr. Bernard Haring: "One of the most important criteria for determining a genuine priestly vocation is a deep rootedness in, and practice of, the virtue of nonviolence. If strength and resolve to become witnesses to justice, peace and nonviolence do not flow from our Eucharistic celebrations, then we must fearfully and sadly conclude that far too many priestly and lay Christian vocations are not sufficiently authentic."[1]

As regards Fr. Shepherd's gratuitous swipe at my brother: Jim was and is one of the most respected and productive members of the London Province and would go on to be himself elected Provincial, not just once but three times for a total of nine years (1990–1999).

The ever unflappable Fr. Kerins replied to Shepherd on December 18: "Despite your own evident displeasure at this development in his life, I would have to frankly let you know that in my judgment the presumption on his part was valid." Still Charlie Shepherd would not let it go. He must have thought the natives in the former colony (these United States of America) were getting uppity. On January 17, 1973 he replied to Fr. Kerins: "I do understand that in your country you have learned to live with protest, especially made in the name of conscience, which over here is still something of a novelty." A novelty? Charlie was here personifying what Thomas Merton (1915–1968) – the Trappist monk who was at the time one of the most incisive spiritual thinkers and prophetic voices – deplored: "One of the grave problems of religion in our time is posed by the almost total lack of protest on the part of religious people and clergy in the face of enormous social evils. It is not that these people are wicked or perverse ... but simply that they are no longer fully capable of seeing and evaluating certain evils as they truly are: as crimes against God and as betrayals of the Christian ethic of love."[2]

Fr. Shepherd concluded his letter with a parting shot: "Let us hope that Fr. Sean won't want to dash over – on the grounds of conscience – to console other leaders of the IRA if the Dublin legislation puts more under restraint."

This from the man who was supposed to be non-political! This from the man who warned me never to express political opinions!

Status Quo Clericalism – Brits' Best Friend

The "Dublin legislation," so blithely referred to, allowed the imprisonment of any suspected IRA member just on the word of a senior policeman.

This type of double-standard has unfortunately a long history in the Catholic Church, and ranks, in my mind, as almost a heresy. It is the belief that the politics with which the religious superior agrees – i.e. the status quo – is not politics at all but in effect, the divine order. Therefore, the Churchmen conclude (and always on behalf of God) that a person is only political if he opposes this "order."

To give another perfect example, jumping ahead some years: Two members of the Irish National Caucus from Kentucky, a nun and a social worker, made a fact-finding trip to Northern Ireland. They called on the bishop of Derry, Edward Daly, and he, too, is an honorable man. When my name came up, the good Bishop said, "but you realize he's from a VERY POLITICAL family?" He failed to point out (or, I guess the point here is that it never occurred to him) to mention that so was he himself from a very political family. For at that very time, his brother was Chairman of the SDLP in County Fermanagh, while my brother Frank was Chairman of the Irish Independence Party ... Frankie was of course "political," the Bishop's brother was not!

I have often heard authors say that they had no idea where their writing would take them. I never fully understood that until I started writing this book. All these years, I have been giving Charlie Shepherd a pass – making excuses for him, that I had put him in a difficult position, that it was impossible for him to understand, that he was timid and scared, etc.

But now as I read these letters almost 40 years later (and it's at least 20 years since I've gone into my files), I think the objective reader would find it hard to recognize the spirit of The Gospel in any of Charlie's letters: no concern for justice (only "order"), no charity, no compassion, no solidarity with brother Redemptorists. Just personal spleen that his hectoring-will is not enforced, and that his personal comfort zone is disturbed. No thought of the sufferings of Catholics in North of Ireland. No mention that the British Government was running a racist, sectarian undemocratic regime there. No concern for "the poor and abandoned" for whose sake the great St. Alphonsus founded the Order... I had not expected my writing to take me there, but it has. And so be it. That, however, is not to say I think my own actions were always without fault. And yet I still retain affection for Charlie. He was a prisoner of an introverted system, which can rob some clerics of true freedom.

Charlie also suffered from the all too common "Irish in England syndrome" – the anxiety that because they are Irish and Catholic they will not be fully accepted as loyal Brits. This can apply particularly with certain types of Catholic priests. And I think Charlie is a good example of this because he had the extra "burden" of having being born in Dublin. Had Charlie been of impeccable English heritage, with unquestionable patriotic credentials, he would have been much better able to deal with the issue.

For example, Fr. Edward Lumley-Holmes, with whom I was stationed in Liverpool, was such a perfectly credentialed Englishman. His sister had been Churchill's personal secretary. Lumley used to type my anti-British government letters. I would always apologize for asking him to do that but he shrugged it off, merrily announcing he had always known England had treated Ireland badly, and that he always believed Ireland should be free. Then he would chuckle that whereas his sister was secretary to Churchill, he was secretary to the IRA.

But I am lead to this somber reflection: How often have Churchmen practiced the abuse of authority over the centuries? How often have they used the "voice of God" for their own comfort and agenda? My own case is very minor and I will never play the victim. But what about those priests (in all sorts of different contexts), who were not as strong as I, who were forced into silence and their spirits crushed because it was "the will of God"? After all, I had the example of my brother Patrick's heroism to sustain me, and the desire for Ireland's freedom to steel me. What resources did they have to withstand the capricious, often bullying, tactics of superiors claiming to speak for God?

If a priest, as a sacrifice/penance/fast to God, obeys his superior then such obedience is pleasing to God. But he must always remember the words of the Prophet Isaiah: "Is not this the fast that

I have chosen? …to loose the bands of injustice, to undo the heavy burdens, and to let the oppressed go free, and that you break every yoke?" (58:6). "God's will," therefore, can never be invoked to cover up injustice. It can never be for the good of the Church to cover up injustice, no matter what "prudent" Churchmen say.

But the priest can never just resort to blind obedience: "No one can or may delegate this responsibility in a 'blind' obedience – so to speak – to the official Church and her teaching office. Obedience of faith against one's own understanding would be an immoral act." That is how the renowned theologian, Walter Kasper, later Cardinal, in 1969, stressed the importance of conscience.[3]

And an even better known theologian, explains the central role of conscience in this most unequivocal way:

"At the same time … conscience represents the inner complement and limit of the Church principle. Over the pope as the expression of the binding claim of ecclesiastical authority, there still stands one's own conscience, which must be obeyed before all else, if necessary, even against the requirement of ecclesiastical authority."

That young theologian was Joseph Ratzinger, the future Pope Benedict XVI, speaking immediately after Vatican II (October 11, 1962 – December 8, 1965).

I thank God (the real God, the God of justice, the God who "hates injustice") that I was able to distinguish the will of God from the will of the British Government. What if Martin Luther King, Jr. had listened to what white Churchmen in the Deep South were telling him "the will of God" was? Again, I am not trying to compare myself to that great man, just holding him up as a model for all who work for justice.

And what about all the Irish-American priests, especially the Irish-born? Why were ninety percent of them silent? Some from Southern Ireland were even known to tell Americans that Northern Ireland is an internal matter for the British Government! What pathology is at work there? What explains such self-loathing gombeenism? It was enough to make a man become a Protestant. History will not forgive them – neither will biblical theology.

7

Formation of the Irish National Caucus

*The imagination, courage and energy of an
immigrant Northern Ireland Catholic priest made the
dream of an Irish-American lobby a reality.*

Joseph E. Thompson[1]

Once the hullabaloo over my visit to Ireland for the MacStíofáin hunger strike died down, I was back to my good work in the parish. I said Mass, preached, administered the sacraments, visited the sick, comforted the dying and instructed the young – all the ordinary, wonderful work of any parish.

But the Baltimore media kept me in the news. I gave interviews on TV, radio, spoke at colleges and to all sorts of groups.

The months sped by and it was soon the summer of 1973. I was entitled to go home on vacation, but gave it up to go on a speaking tour for Irish Northern Aid. On July 8 I went to Cleveland, Ohio; July 10 to Detroit, Michigan; July 12 to Chicago, Illinois; July 14 to St. Paul, Minnesota; July 15 to Portland, Oregon; July 17 to San Francisco, California; July 18 to Los Angeles, California; July 19 to St. Louis, Missouri; July 21 to Dayton, Ohio; July 23-27 back to New York to speak all over the city and state. I was so impressed and touched by the dedication of Irish-Americans. And that feeling has never left me.

The Long March: Baltimore to Washington

I wanted to put Baltimore on the map as an Irish city. All the publicity I had received greatly helped. But I wanted to get the Irish on the move. What better way than a march to the nation's capital, 45 miles away? So I announced we were going to have "An Irish Freedom March" and then set to organizing it with a small group of very enthusiastic men and women. The bets started immediately on who would be able to walk the full 45 miles.

And here is when I established a principle that would be the guiding one for the rest of my work with the Irish National Caucus. Others immediately thought I would be leading them to the British Embassy. No, I insisted, Irish-Americans have no influence with the British Embassy but they do have with their own government. The proper role of Irish-Americans is to change American foreign policy, to end the historic "hands off Northern Ireland" policy. So the march would be to the White House to protest the silence of the American government about British oppression in Ireland. I immediately got opposition. The intrepid Jack McCarthy, who by now was a good friend, was on the phone in high panic: "Fr. Sean, Fr. Sean, we cannot be seen to be criticizing America. We should only criticize England."

I explained that if we only criticized a foreign government, we would be giving a pass to all politicians in America, and they need never listen to us: "Jack, if you were still living in County Cork, you could criticize England. What is the point of being an American unless you mobilize America to put pressure on England?" But Jack was really scared that the march would be seen as anti-American. And of course, he would be right, if marching on the White House was anti-American. (In the same way Jack was right to tell Republican speakers from Ireland not to confuse Americans by mentioning "socialism" as they would be branded communist.) "Jack, there is nothing more

American than petitioning your government for help, and for having input into its foreign policy. We will march from Fort McHenry, birthplace of the star-spangled banner and site of a famous victory against the Brits, with both American and Irish flags flying proudly for 45 miles. I will be the only one with the bullhorn, calling out the question: 'What do we want?' And all of you will respond: 'England out of Ireland.' What better message, Jack, to carry to the White House?"

I could feel Jack was softening up. And I clinched it by asking him to be in charge of supplying American flags. He was delighted. It was as if he was back in his youth, and being given his first assignment to go and fight the Black and Tans, "like the boys from the County Cork." And that great-hearted Irish patriot went on to deliver two busloads of people for the last leg of the march to the White House.

I invited Bishop Thomas Drury of Corpus Christi to attend one of the planning meetings – a small group of about ten. He urged us to see the march as a pilgrimage that the Irish should be proud to march in, "even with pebbles in their shoes." Years later, when I got my FBI file, through the Freedom of Information Act, the exact quote from the Bishop is filed in the report, by the informant at the meeting. Needless to say, with my background, I was totally conscious that there would be informers everywhere – FBI, British government, Irish government, etc. I was equally aware that there was nothing I could do about it, except to make sure they would never gain control of my work.

The plan was to split the journey into two. We would stay overnight in Laurel, Maryland, the halfway point, in St. Mary's church hall, sleeping on the floor in sleeping bags. The pastor, an Irish-born priest, insisted that I would use the spare room in the rectory. I was a bit concerned about this, as I did not want it to affect the morale of the "troops" – seeing the leader defecting to a comfortable bed while they slept on the floor. But once they all assured me that I should accept the courtesy of the parish priest, I agreed I would.

We had invited my brother Frank to speak at the rally outside the White House. One morning my sister Alice woke me with a phone call: "Frankie has been shot." Alice had forgotten how back home when people said someone was shot, it meant shot dead. And for one terrible moment, that's what I thought she was telling me. "But, he's okay, just a slight wound in the leg," she added. I'll let Frankie tell the story himself:

> At about 10.30 p.m. on the night of September 18, 1973, I was travelling home alone. I was not paying any particular attention to road users behind me. As I turned left off the main road, I heard my car being hit. Road works were taking place at the time, and I immediately thought that I had hit loose stones at the side of the road, and I did the one thing that I should not have done, I stopped and got out of my car. It was only then that I realized that I had been shot. As I turned left, the car behind me carried on, effectively creating the two long sides of a triangle. The gunman was obviously an expert. He fired three shots, two of which hit the car and one of which hit the front of our new home. One of the shots pierced the driver's door, and shot me just where my right thigh made contact with the seat, causing an unpleasant but essentially a superficial flesh wound.[2]

I assumed that Frankie would not be able to travel to Washington. But he did, marching a good distance, with limp and walking stick, which added to the urgency and drama of what we were about.

The Washington Post gave the march reasonable coverage under the headline "Irish-Americans Urged to Enlist Aid of Countrymen Against British": "With sore feet and soaring enthusiasm, 250 persons ended a 45-mile 'Irish Freedom Walk' at Lafayette Park yesterday, where they were urged by [Frank McManus] a member of the British Parliament to enlist the support of other Irish-Americans in their quest to oust British troops from Ulster." (Sunday, October 15, 1973).

The following year, as promised, we had another Irish Freedom March, this time to the British Embassy. The Embassy sent word that they would receive a delegation, but I refused to accept their offer, which was meant to co-opt the march and show how reasonable they were.

Why No Irish Lobby?

Any chance I could get I would go into Washington to speak to Members of Congress to tell them about the great injustices Her Majesty's government was inflicting on the Catholics in Northern Ireland. As I walked through the Halls of Congress, I would run into all sorts of ethnic groups lobbying for their homelands – Jewish Americans, African Americans, the Poles, the Greeks, etc. But there was one group noticeably absent. And they were one of the largest, best educated, affluent and politically connected: Irish-Americans.

I just could not believe it. There was no Irish lobby or office on Capitol Hill. I knew that would have to change. In the meantime, my immediate priority was to get Congress to officially show concern for the violation of human rights in Northern Ireland.

One of the very first people who offered her help and expertise was Bernadette O'Reilly (later McAuliffe) whose parents were from County Cavan. Bernadette was the personal secretary for Silvio O. Conte (R-MA) and, therefore, was very familiar with the workings of Congress. Fred O'Brien, an attorney with U.S. Customs also offered to help.

My First Congressional Hearing

One of our first efforts was to arrange for brother Frank to be called to testify before the House Foreign Relations Subcommittee on Human Rights, chaired by Congressman Donald M. Fraser (D-MN). We met with the Director of the Subcommittee. He explained that the practice was not to have someone testify for a foreign government: "Don't worry," I said, "Frankie will not be testifying for, but *against*, the British government." That sealed the deal. Then we convinced him to

invite Ruairí Ó Brádaigh, then president of Sinn Féin (like Dave
O'Connell, Ruairí unfortunately would split from Gerry Adams
in 1986 and form Republican Sinn Féin, of which he is now
president. Ruairí was in the IRA with my brother Patrick and
they soldiered together so I have always had respect for him).

The hearing took place on October 9, 1973. Frank and
Ó Brádaigh gave powerful testimonies – much to the shock and
chagrin of both the British and Irish Embassies. Congressman
Conte and Tip O'Neill, then Democratic Majority Leader, held
a reception in their honor, which Bishop Drury also attended.
Before the reception, Tip chaired a press conference with
Frank and Ó Brádaigh. He complained bitterly that he never
got information about the Troubles from the Irish Embassy and
promised "if the good Father [yours truly]" kept him informed,
he would do everything he could to help. That, of course, was
further proof to me that an Irish lobby had to be launched on
Capitol Hill.

By now I was getting to know Tip quite well. He was very
friendly, in the way all Catholic Boston politicians are to priests.
I remember later when he called a number of Congressmen
together in his office for a publicity photograph for the Irish
National Caucus, he put his hand on my right shoulder and
said to the late Congressman Joe Moakley (D-MA): "Look at
those big shoulders, Joe. He's got them from loading guns in the
coffins they ship to Ireland." And they had a great laugh at that.
Personally, I resented it but did not say anything. I have always
hated frivolous stereotyping of the Troubles – a sure sign of
superficiality, with no sensitivity for the deep pain and anguish.

But I would quickly learn a basic Washington law – "For
every action, there is an equal and opposite reaction." It may
be Newton's third law of motion, but it is Capitol Hill's first
law. Our initial successful foray in Congress would now force
the Irish Embassy to organize against us. Isn't that ironic? They
had not been lobbying to get the Congress to put pressure on
the British, but they would lobby against us. And of course, so
would the British Embassy, but it would let the Irish Embassy

lead the public charge, as would be later admitted by Ambassador Peter Jay, son-in-law of James Callaghan, Britain's Labor Prime Minister from 1976 to 1979.

Tip would later, as Speaker of the House, give me the cold shoulder but in the meantime, the Irish Embassy provided him with the perfect cover. He would put that big hand on my shoulder and say, "Fr. Sean, how can I be more patriotic than the Prime Minister of Ireland?" My response was always the same, "That wouldn't be hard, Tip."

Caucus Launched on My Birthday

But anyway, buoyed up by the success of the Congressional hearing, I knew I had to give a name to the work I was doing, which was simply not being done by any other Irish group, no matter how worthy. My basic conviction was that the primary role of Irish-Americans should be to influence American foreign policy on Ireland – to change the long-standing "hands off Ireland because we must not offend the British." My operating principle was: "Human Rights for Ireland is an American Issue." It became one of the first mottos of the Irish National Caucus. Our job would not be to raise funds for Ireland or to relate to a particular group, party or government in Ireland. And we would most certainly not be controlled by any entity in Ireland, North or South. In other words, we would have "no foreign principal."

My initial thought was to get others to head up the new organization, but I quickly realized that if I did not do it, it would not be done. So on my birthday, February 6, 1974, I founded the Irish National Caucus and signed up, as officers, Bishop Drury, Bernadette O'Reilly and Fred O'Brien. Bernadette did invaluable work for us until the opening of the Caucus office on Capitol Hill on December 10, 1978.

Amazingly, some books have said the Caucus' origins were unclear, yet no organization ever had such clear origins. I founded it, and put out a press release announcing it. The late Jack Holland in his book *The American Connection* states,

"Though the Caucus' beginnings are a matter of dispute, even among its own members ..." Strangely, Holland, who had taken up residence in the U.S. by that time, never called me to ask how the Caucus started. Even more oddly, in over thirty years of writing about Irish-American activity, Holland never called me except once – on the death of Seán Mac Stíofáin in 2001. Holland then proceeds to make the ridiculous claim that, "Mike Flannery, the founding father of Irish Northern Aid ... was among those involved in its formation."[3] Nothing could be further from the truth. Indeed, Flannery was always opposed to the formation of the Irish National Caucus, feeling that there was no need for any other Irish organization because Irish Northern Aid could do it all – something that most evidently was not true. Also, he seemed to be always concerned that I might overshadow him – a silly fear that seemed to motivate some others in Irish groups. Petty jealousy was always something I could not abide – especially since we were supposed to be about a noble and selfless cause.

I then turned my attention to the AOH (Ancient Order of Hibernians), which by this time was very familiar with me. Up until 1974, the AOH was only nominally involved in the Northern Ireland issue. It followed the Dublin government line, which was "do not support the IRA and do not criticize the British lest it give aid and comfort to the IRA." A non-policy, which in fact aided and comforted the British government.

But there were many members of the AOH who vehemently disagreed with this appeasement of the British government, and they wanted me to "convert" the AOH. In 1974, two AOH stalwarts, the late Dave Burke from Massachusetts and Liam Murphy from New York, arranged for me to address the AOH National Board meeting in Washington, DC in advance of the National Convention in Anaheim, California. I spoke very strongly, denouncing the weakness of the Irish government and urged them as proud Americans to stand up for American values in Ireland. "I believe," I told them, "that Ireland too has the right to be one nation under God, indivisible, with liberty and justice for all."

Dave Burke and Liam Murphy were ecstatic – they could see the AOH change before their eyes as I spoke. Jack Keane, who was running to be the new AOH president, was particularly moved, and immediately proposed that I would be invited to give the keynote address at the National Convention. His proposal was unanimously accepted.

Reminiscing on those days, Jack Keane, on May 30, 2008, said: "At that time I was trying to get the AOH to take a firmer stand on the North of Ireland. The perfect instrument came along in the person of Father McManus. He electrified the National Board Meeting and then the entire Convention. From that moment we made sure the AOH would be intensely involved."[4]

Jack Keane was elected president. He appointed Bishop Drury to be the National Chaplain and appointed me Deputy National Chaplain. It would be safe to say that now the AOH had indeed been officially converted. Liam became the editor of the AOH paper, *Hibernian Digest,* and kept up a steady Irish Republican drumbeat. Dave went on to become, without doubt, one of the most dedicated and productive leaders the AOH ever had. Tom McNabb, New York, would follow Jack Keane as president. Tom was as good as Jack, and both men have been the two most important National Presidents the AOH has had in the past 100 years. I feel a particular debt of gratitude to these two fine Irish-Americans. They deserve great credit. They showed real courage and leadership, setting the proper course for the AOH. Since that time, the AOH has retained an activist and excellent position on Northern Ireland.

On September 28, 1974, Jack, in keeping with a promise made to me if he were elected AOH president, called a meeting in New York of all the major Irish organizations and they unanimously endorsed the Irish National Caucus.

However, while I appreciated their endorsement, I made it clear that the Irish National Caucus would continue to be an independent organization – that they had endorsed us but we had not endorsed them, and we would not be getting involved in their internal business (or feuds). I also made it crystal clear that while they could have reasonable input, they could not control us in any way. I knew, of course, there would be immediate attempts to destabilize and marginalize us – by the Irish and British governments, and maybe the American government. I knew what to expect – agents, informers, "useful idiots" (those who would be helping the British without even knowing it), malcontents, people who simply did not like me or people whom, through my own fault, I rubbed the wrong way. But hey, welcome to Irish-American politics!

Later the following year, on February 18, 1975, the Executive Council of the AFL-CIO (American Federation of Labor and Congress of Industrial Organizations) endorsed the Irish National Caucus after I addressed a luncheon meeting of about 300 Union members in Bal Harbour, Florida. The then president, the famed George Meany, sent Lane Kirkland, Secretary Treasurer, to deliver the endorsement.

8

Caucus Baptized in Blood at British Embassy

To sin by silence when they should protest makes cowards of men.
Abraham Lincoln

Organizing politically did not mean that I would cease my activist "street politics." Both were needed – and necessitated by developing circumstances. I decided that the first action of the Irish National Caucus should be symbolically at the British Embassy.

In Baltimore, I got to know the late Phil Berrigan (1923-2002), the former Josephite priest and anti-war activist, and his wife Liz McAllister who had founded Jonah House. Phil was one of the most remarkable men I have ever met. He was a bigger, better-looking version of Paul Newman. I've never known a man with such physical presence. I confided in them that I wanted to do a nonviolent action at the British Embassy in Washington, and I needed their advice on how to pour blood all over the premises, and how to contain things in a nonviolent manner so that nobody would get hurt – except the pride of Her Majesty's government.

I could not have consulted a more wise or seasoned source than Phil. He tutored me in the technique – and nonviolent resistance is most certainly a technique as well as a principle. He explained it was vital for me at all times to maintain control of the situation – through the unique calmness that descends on one if nonviolence is done correctly. I had explained to him that the British tended to lead with their fists, and I was concerned that things could spiral out of control, and lead to one of my group being shot by Embassy security or the many British agents housed there. Phil explained that the more I knew about the layout of the British Embassy the better, so as to minimize surprises or confusion.

One of his group, a mother of a four-year-old boy, kindly offered "to case the joint" – to visit the British Embassy and give me an intelligence report. When she visited the Embassy, she would prod her son to send him to different corners of the embassy so that she would have an excuse to follow him. What a gal! And she didn't have one drop of Irish blood. She then drew a perfect sketch of the layout of the inside of the Embassy.

Now about the blood. How were we to get it? "Leave that to me," said Phil, "I know a doctor who does that for us when needed."

The doctor drew two pints of blood from me, on two separate occasions. A local man gave another pint. And the late Mitch Snyder (1946–1990) gave one pint. Mitch, a Vietnam vet, had been converted (back to active Catholicism) in Danbury Prison, Connecticut, by Phil Berrigan and his Jesuit brother, Dan. And he would go on to dedicate his life to the poor and homeless in Washington as the driving force in the Community for Creative Nonviolence (CCNV). In a celebrated hunger strike he forced President Reagan to hand over a federal building for the homeless, now called Mitch Snyder Place. In 1986, Martin Sheen, also a disciple of the Berrigan brothers, would make a TV biopic about him, *Samaritan: The Mitch Snyder Story*. Sadly, this great man who had "given his blood for Ireland," hanged himself on July 5, 1990.

I decided I needed only three colleagues, as anything more than four people would be a bit unwieldy. I felt there should be two men and two women. And I knew I would have to pick carefully and diligently. They would have to be totally reliable and prepared to go to prison, maybe for several years, without regrets or recriminations. I was proud of my choice: the late Maureen Armstrong of New York, from County Monaghan, a grandmother in her late fifties; Joe Mitchell, sixty, a warehouseman of Queens, NY, from County Meath; and Mary Baggarly, twenty-eight, of Maryland, a housewife and mother of two, from the Bogside, Derry. Mary was a "Stickie"[1] when I met her, but I converted her from the error of her ways.

We were all set. But there was no point in having a protest in the British Embassy if nobody knew about it. So I alerted trusted reporters, telling them they could enter a few minutes after us.

At exactly 11.58 a.m., Friday April 24, 1974, Jack O'Brien[2] of Maryland (who also had been a Stickie until I converted him), drove the four of us to the front of the British Embassy (Chancery, technically; the Embassy is the residence of the Ambassador, a bit further down Massachusetts Avenue, NW).[3]

In the Belly of the Beast

I jumped out of the car, and immediately a young man headed towards me. I thought he was on to us. In an exaggerated display of coolness I looked up at the sky and said, "What a beautiful day." "Indeed," the young man replied with a smile. We headed for the big glass doors, and again I was alarmed as another young man hurried to the door – but only to open it. "Good morning, lovely day," I said and with that all four of us made it safely in.

Phil Berrigan had drilled it into me to immediately "disarm" the first point of contact – to engage the guy at the security desk in a friendly, one-to-one, eye-to-eye dialogue. I headed straight for the desk, while the other three remained by the inside of the door. "Good afternoon," I beamed, "'Tis a grand day."

"Indeed it is," he replied.

"My name is Father Mc Manus."

"Oh, yes, Father."

"I'm based in a parish in Baltimore."

He folded his arms and looked very interested.

"I have come with some friends to the Embassy ..."

"Yes, good."

"To express our concern about Northern Ireland."

That changed everything. He unfolded his arms, shot up in his chair and grabbed the telephone. He had the phone up to about his shoulder when I positioned our statement right in front of his face, and urged, "Please read this" – never once breaking the eye contact that Berrigan had warned me was so crucial.

He put the phone down and read the opening sentence: "Our action – the pouring of blood ..." His mouth fell open. He jumped to his feet, put one foot up on the chair behind him and held the arms of the chair with both hands and sank back staring at me. "Just a moment, just a moment," he gasped and grabbed the phone. I leaned over towards him and in my best Confessional manner I whispered: "Look, it is very important that you remain cool, otherwise you will cause panic. Remain calm. Do not be afraid. We are nonviolent people. We will not hurt anybody, I assure you."

I gently motioned with both hands for him to sit down and he did, never taking his eyes off me, in sort of a trance. Berrigan and his people told me to be prepared for that to happen. I then told the man I was going to open my coat and for him not to be afraid. "In this pocket," I said, "there is a bottle, which I am now going to slowly take out." His eyes followed my hands. "In the bottle is some blood. My friends and I are going to pour blood all over the Embassy. But stay calm and do not scare people."

I then turned to Joe, Mary and Maureen and gave them the signal to begin pouring blood.

Spilling Irish Blood

And then for the first time, I think, the man realized what was happening. He jumped up and shouted: "Stop there, sir. That is forbidden. I am sorry I cannot allow you. This is an Embassy." As

I turned away from him, he shouted, "Get someone. It's the Irish."
(You're damn right, I thought to myself. It is the Irish.)

It is amazing how quickly blood diffuses and spreads. Squirted methodically from "squeeze" bottles, Mary and I had the entire front of the glass building covered in no time. (The night before I had called Mary to express concern that we did not have enough blood and asked her to make some blood-substitute – ketchup, etc. – and that we would explain to the media that we had made some extra blood substitute as a backup.)

Meanwhile Maureen and Joe were doing their thing, as planned. The *Baltimore Sun*'s reporter, whom I had brought with us, would describe Maureen as, "... neat as a pin, no make-up, and no nonsense grandmother." Joe, he wrote, was "a soft-spoken law-abiding ... man with a steady hand and a narrow tie."[4]

Both stood in the middle of the Embassy holding a Union Jack, and proceeded to pour blood all over that flag, which for centuries has been soaked in Irish blood.

Cowardly British Assault

Suddenly, the head of the chancery, John Graham, probably in his fifties, charged Maureen from the back, bowled her over, grabbed the flag and ran part of the way up the stairway, stopped and turned around, clutching the flag to his chest. It was a cowardly, violent British assault on a nonviolent Irish grandmother.

As Maureen lay moaning on the ground, we knelt beside her and I grabbed hold of all of them and said, "Remember, we had vowed nothing would make us retaliate. If we do, we will destroy our entire protest." We had role-played and mentally disciplined ourselves that no matter what happened we would not be violent. We helped Maureen to her feet, and continued our business, calmly and serenely.

Mary and I opened the glass doors and poured blood on the outside and on the doorsteps. As I stepped back in, a distinguished grey-haired man came towards me to usher me out. "You can't, you can't possibly ... this is the British Embassy," he said. I gently patted him on the shoulder and ever so soothingly said, "You do not understand. This is a nonviolent protest and it is precisely to do this that we came." He stared at me in complete astonishment. Then he saw that Mary was still outside, so he ran and held the doors closed against her. I tapped him on the shoulder, and with complete authority in my voice, ordered, "Excuse me, let the lady into the Embassy." And incredibly, he did. He looked at me apologetically and said, "Okay, okay," and then walked away. Again, the amazing power of nonviolence!

When we had finished pouring the blood, we calmly reassembled in the middle of the Embassy. We quietly stood there while all around us the Embassy was in chaos. A feeling of complete harmony and tranquility descended upon me. It was a beautiful moment, which the Berrigan people had told me to expect if our motives and techniques were pure. The other three, I could tell, were experiencing the same serenity, although flushed and smiling from our success.

We waited for the confrontation. It had been agreed that I alone would do the talking, no matter what happened, so we could contain the situation in a disciplined manner – another essential ingredient of the successful nonviolent action. If each of us were tricked into speaking to different members of the Embassy the coherence of our protest would be shattered.

While we waited, Embassy people started pouring out from everywhere. Employees were hanging over the banisters of the big spiral staircase in the lobby, staring down. Dozens of people began forming a semicircle around us. In a calm but loud voice (well trained in Hawkstone for the parish missions in Britain) I called out. "Would you all be quiet, please?" There was instant silence, a palpable hush. "Please do not be alarmed. This is a nonviolent protest. We come in peace. We will not do you any harm." They all stared in astonishment. Then a pompous little man in a dark suit pushed his way through the crowd. His face was deathly white and he was bubbling with venom, "Mister, are you in charge?" He fairly spat at me. I calmly demanded, again with authority, "Who are you?" It had the expected result. He was astonished at the temerity of this intruder asking him who he was. He prodded both hands to his chest and in complete exasperation spluttered, "Who ... who am I? I'm the head of security."

"Fine," I replied, "I will talk to you. My name is Fr. McManus. This is Joe Mitchell, this is Mary Baggarly, and this is the lady whom one of the Embassy officials assaulted, Maureen Armstrong." The three courteously nodded.

"There was no assault here," shouted an official to my left. "Yes, there was," said a reporter, "and we have a photo to prove it." Then an Embassy official tried to grab the camera. "Take your f***ing hands of my camera, buddy," the reporter said with explosive force and for a moment I thought there was going to be a fistfight. I remember thinking: wouldn't it be ironic if, after all our nonviolent role-playing, the press starts a riot in the Embassy?

I turned back to the little security man who was wailing away, "I have got a responsibility ... I have got to do my duty." I said reassuringly and softly: "We understand; no need to give explanations. Of course, do your duty and we will do ours." He just could not handle it and was going to start wailing again. "No, no," I said, "it's all right, be calm, there is no need to worry. This is a nonviolent protest and we will not harm anyone."

He made an obvious effort to control himself, then very officiously pulled out a little notebook and said to Mary, "Okay, madam, what's your address in Ireland?" Do not answer that, Mary," I directed. He almost pleadingly said, "But I've got to have ... I've got to have ..." I gently leaned towards him and said, "We are not answering any of your questions like that. We will answer all questions at the appropriate time and place." The poor guy just gave up. He put his little book into his little pocket and walked off, dejected and defeated.

An ashen-faced individual was hovering around the periphery of the semicircle going nuts. "He is sheltering behind his collar," he was screaming. I turned to him and demanded, "Do you want to speak to me?" It stopped him dead. Then he started up again, arms flailing: "He's a priest. He does not have to tell the truth."

"Do you work here?" I asked. "Yes," he hissed. "It appears

you are giving vent to religious prejudice, which ill becomes the British Embassy. And how could I be sheltering behind my collar when I'm completely at your mercy?" He stared at me in total exasperation and then darted off.

Have You Been to Ireland?

Then I began to address the crowd again: I realize that we have caused you embarrassment," I began. "We are not embarrassed," someone shouted from my right. I turned around. A tall, well-groomed young man was glowering at me. "What nationality are you?" he asked. I quietly stared him in eye, and wondered if the same tactic would work again. "Who are you?" I asked. The simple question stunned him by its impertinence. I could see he was trying to regain his poise. "I am Baker Bates, the Embassy information officer," he said. "What are you doing here?"

I replied we were conducting a nonviolent protest against British mistreatment of political prisoners and the assassination campaign of the British Army. Thinking he had a trump card, he shot back, in a perfect English accent, "I am from Northern Ireland. Have you ever been to Ireland?"

(There was I thinking the British Embassy would know all about me!) "My home is in British-occupied Ireland," I conversationally replied. He was not expecting that. "Well, it's a pity you just missed John Hume," he sniffed. "Was this done to offset the good John Hume did here? Did you know he was here?"

We, of course, had no idea Hume had just been there and I told him so. He very illogically responded, "So you're saying this was not a planned protest?" I replied, "Not at all. It was a very planned protest."

"Yes, indeed," he shouted. "You even brought your own hired press." Then whirling on his heels, he snapped, "Okay, Jack, you have made your point."

"Thank you," I replied, "you are most courteous."

Then I turned to the next official, a young man with fairly

long, well-styled hair, who clearly wanted to have a go at me. "Now it's your turn," I said to him. He let loose, "I suppose you also brought rubber bullets with you, Fr. McManus?" (I had shown rubber bullets on TV all over America to illustrate that they were not harmless little pellets but six-inch projectiles of hard rubber that had killed children and blinded people in Northern Ireland.)

"So you know me?" I said.

"Yes, I've seen you on TV and I read the *Irish People* every week," he said. Then he, too, started up about John Hume: "John Hume says that all the money of the Irish Northern Aid Committee goes to the IRA. It all goes direct to Joe Cahill." I asked, "What has the IRA and Northern Aid got to do with this protest?" He replied, "This is an Irish Northern Aid protest."

"Please don't speculate. Read our statement and you will see what it is." He would have none of it. "You are the spokesman for Irish Northern Aid," he persisted. "No, I am not," I said. "But I've heard you speak on their behalf," he shouted. "Yes, I have spoken on their behalf, but I'm not their spokesman," I tried to reason.

He finally agreed to read our statement. When he came to the part about political prisoners, he went on again about John Hume. (The British Embassy for years always paraded out John Hume to cover up their misdeeds.) "John Hume says there are no political prisoners in Northern Ireland." I looked him straight in the eye and earnestly said: "I am prepared to discuss Northern Ireland with someone in the Embassy who knows something about it, but you quite obviously know nothing about it." The gentleness with which I said it puzzled him, I could tell. I kept calmly looking him in the eye until he felt uncomfortable and finally walked away.

Baker Bates came back, a little bit more in control of himself: "Fr. McManus, you have made your statement. Now why don't you leave?"

This was unexpected. And the Berrigan people had warned me about the unexpected, as that is when things can unravel.

We had expected to be immediately arrested, and clearly the Embassy did not want that. I needed to play for time so as to be able to talk to my three colleagues. I glanced admiringly around the fine building, and said to Baker Bates, "I've never been in the British Embassy before. I think I will stay a while."

"So it's a sit-in, is it?" he snapped, and took off like a scalded cat.

Standing Up – By Sitting Down

I huddled with Joe, Mary and Maureen and explained we would have to do a sit-in, which we had not planned, because they were not going to have us arrested. I told them to do exactly as I did.

The Executive Protective Service, the uniformed branch of the Secret Service, soon arrived. The moment the lead officer saw me he smiled broadly. I immediately knew he was Irish Catholic. I told them that we were concluding our nonviolent protest by a sit-in. We would not resist in anyway but they would have to carry us out. I then signaled to Maureen, Joe and Mary to sit down. The smiling officer said to me as he and another lifted me off the floor, "I had a nice pint of Guinness in your country, Father, a few months ago."

"Which part?" I asked. "Mayo," he grunted as he held me. "My mother is from Mayo and my father is from Galway."

It was only in the police station that we realized the extent to which Maureen had been hurt. Her left arm and back were badly bruised by the body-slam of the Embassy official. She did not want to go to hospital and leave Mary in prison by herself. But we insisted.

We refused to sign the "citation form," which would have entitled us to get out. Instead, in solidarity with the political prisoners, we spent the night in prison – Mary in the Women's House of Detention and Joe and me in the DC Central Cell Block.

I got on the metal bed, no blanket, put my shoes under my head and slept soundly throughout the night. The following morning, I was handed a sandwich through the bars of my cell. It was just a piece of ham between dry bread but no food ever tasted so good (I had not eaten for several hours before being arrested and was now starving).

Afterwards I was moved from my cell to a holding area – a huge cage-like structure with dozens of young black men. I think I was the only white man in the cage (although I never think of myself as white, just Irish). They were astonished to see me, in my black suit and clerical collar: "Hey, Preacher-man/Rev./ Father what you in for?", as they swarmed around me all excited. I was in high spirits so I decided to have some fun with them: "Well you see, I work in a poor all-black parish in Baltimore. I just got tired and angry at the poverty of the poor people so I go and rob a bank and I give thousands of dollars to the black parishioners." Well they went crazy, cheering and whooping and giving me high fives. When I told them I was just kidding they were visibly disappointed.

More Protestant Solidarity

Before arraignment, I was greeted by a nice surprise, a Press Release form the Fellowship of Reconciliation, one of the oldest Christian nonviolent movements. It read:

The following is the text of the statement that two leading representatives of the organization Fellowship of Reconciliation (F.O.R.) issued in response to the nonviolent blood-protest that Fr. Sean Mc Manus led at the British Embassy on Friday, April 24. The statement was hand delivered to Fr. Mc Manus while he was in prison. "We British visitors to Washington welcome such dramatic nonviolent protest against the military policy of the British Government in Ireland."

"Blood given for justice in Ireland is a supremely good investment."

This statement was released by Rev. David Harding, a Methodist Minister, who is Secretary General for Fellowship of Reconciliation in Britain; and by Mr. Guy Otten who is a member of the International Executive of Fellowship of Reconciliation.

Later that morning, we were arraigned, charged with "protesting within five hundred feet of an Embassy." The British Embassy did not press charges and the judge told us we were free to go.

We were well pleased by our good work. It sublimely confirmed to me the transcendent power of nonviolent action – and demonstrated that the British Government cannot simply handle it, as Gandhi knew so well.

I will be eternally grateful to Phil Berrigan and Mitch Snyder. May God rest their noble souls.

9

All the News That's Fit to Print – Or Not

*In wartime, truth is so precious that she should always
be attended by a bodyguard of lies.*

Winston Churchill

My arrest at the British Embassy – plus all the previous
publicity and consciousness-raising my activity had
generated – gained huge support for my work all across the
United States. Therefore, when I stressed the need for the new
approach of the Irish National Caucus, people listened and
trusted my judgment. Furthermore, the new approach could not
be dismissed as being "soft" because, as the action at the British
Embassy proved, we were prepared to go to prison. I was, of
course, aware that my actions could be seen as "radical" – a real
taboo among many Irish-Americans. Being "radical" was almost
as bad as being a communist. So I had to walk a fine line, which
some very conservative folk believed I crossed often.

But without resources and money, I knew of no other way to
spread the word. One had to break the unbelievable conspiracy
of silence in the media and U.S. Congress.

To give one passing example of media bias: After my brother
Frank was shot, *The New York Times* reported that he had been

shot by the IRA because he was not sufficiently militant. Now, how do you suppose they got that ridiculous piece of information? I called the *Times* from Sacred Heart in Baltimore and asked to speak to one of the editors responsible for publishing the item. I began by protesting the story and he countered by saying, "What would a priest in Baltimore know about the incident?" I told him I was Frank's brother. He countered by saying their information was good and that they were standing by the story. If such a prestigious newspaper as *The New York Times* can be so obtuse on Northern Ireland, what could one expect from the general American media that simply kept churning out the same old British line?

In fact, my very first letter to the American media was to the Baltimore Archdiocesan newspaper, *The Catholic Review*. The well-known priest, sociologist and novelist, Fr. Andrew Greely, had written in his column that the IRA was in business for the thrill of killing and being killed. This from a man who prided himself on his Irishness and knowledge of all things Irish. Just how do you suppose he came by that conviction? Years later, Greely would become an outright defender of the IRA. A few years ago, I met him on two occasions at the White House for St. Patrick's Day celebrations. On both occasions I reminded him of his ridiculous letter and each time he totally ignored what I said, making absolutely no response.

And in speaking of *The Catholic Review*, I recently checked its website where it reviews its own history and its "campaign against the Ku Klux Klan in the 1920s or its calls for justice in Central America in the 1980s. What about justice for Catholics in Northern Ireland? No campaign for them! So it was not just the secular media that was complicit in British oppression of Catholics, so were the Catholic media, with some exceptions – and so were the U.S. Catholic bishops, with very few exceptions. More of that later.

So with that sort of media indifference, what could one do? If the American media were not going to announce the news, I would have to announce it myself. A case in point: on October 15, 1974, the political prisoners – incarcerated without charge or trial – burnt Long Kesh to the ground in protest at the inhumane conditions. That did receive media attention, but the resulting British punitive action, including forcing the prisoners to sleep in the open air, covered only by sheets of polythene did not. I tried, to no avail, to get the media to cover that inhumanity. So I decided if they were not going to announce it, I would do it for them.

At that time, ABC nationwide news was announced live, at least in part, from its studio in Washington, D.C. by Howard K. Smith. I decided to interrupt the live newscast and tell America, all 100 million of the estimated viewers, about the mistreatment of prisoners in Long Kesh.

Again, I decided four was a good number for the action. I selected Mary Baggarly and a young woman from Baltimore, Cathy Fogarty, who, with her father, had become very active. The third person was Sean Walsh of Washington who had recently joined the Irish National Caucus. Naturally, we had to "case the joint." In particular I had to know exactly when Howard K. Smith was broadcasting live otherwise my protest would not be carried.

Days well in advance, I went to the ABC studio and introduced myself to the appropriate persons. I told them that I was visiting from Ireland, where I was in religious broadcasting, and I wanted to learn from the real professionals of ABC, and could I perhaps come back and observe from within the studio how these great experts did it? They graciously accepted. While I was talking to them, Sean Walsh was casing the joint, even using his credit card to slip the lock to enter the broadcasting room, then not in use. He even made a date with the young receptionist who would have to buzz us in when we came back for our action. He took her to dinner the night before the action.

Announcing the News Ourselves

On Tuesday, October 22, 1974, the four of us headed to ABC News. They recognized Sean and me, and brought us in. At first I was escorted into the glass control booth, with all the TV monitors, etc. I was initially concerned because it cordoned me off from the actual studio where Howard K. Smith was seated. But I quickly realized it was a blessing as it enabled me to know exactly what was going on, with the very helpful control-team giving me a blow-by-blow account. Otherwise, I would have no idea when Smith was going out live. The control team told me there was a commercial break coming up and that right after it, Howard K. Smith would be broadcasting. I made my move, quickly telling my three colleagues to follow me. I walked into the actual broadcast room. A technician looked momentarily alarmed, I put my finger to my lips, in the silence gesture, and nodded reassuringly that I was just going to stand nearby. He nodded back, understandingly.

I was now in a perfect position to see and to interrupt Howard K. Smith. I had given the others the exact same sentence which each of us would say, knowing we would have only a split second to get it out before we were cut off.

At exactly 6:16 p.m. I mounted the raised dais from which Howard K. Smith was reading the news live. I walked right behind him (and felt guilty at the way the poor man jumped off his chair in real shock) and proceeded to say my lines: "Will someone please help? The British are torturing political prisoners in Northern Ireland." Every word went out as clear as a bell, all across the United States. I then moved on, as planned, to let the three others walking behind in single file, say the same words. But they were cut off, as I feared they would.

The allegedly unflappable media went flapping like crazy. These folk, who demand that others keep their cool under the most trying circumstances, were like headless chickens. I walked out of the main newsroom, to wait for the police, reassuringly holding out my hands saying, "Don't worry. This is nonviolent protest. We will cause no harm."

A small guy with longish hair, in his late thirties, and obviously in some position of authority in ABC, tried to confront me, saying he was not going to let me leave. I told him not to worry: we were not leaving but waiting for the police because we wanted to be arrested in completion of our nonviolent act.

He then got a bit hysterical, screaming at me that I was

protected by my collar. I quietly asked him if it did not occur to him that my collar might be protecting him. "What do you mean?" he incredulously asked. "Well, if I were not a priest, I might have punched you out for your abusiveness," I gently responded. That seemed to steady him up.

Then a group gathered around, all complaining about our action. I asked which of them were reporters as opposed to technicians, producers, etc. A few indicated they were. I then made the point that the first question a real newsperson should be asking is "Why did we do it?" not just berating us for doing it.

I further explained that we were fed up with the news always presenting the problem in Northern Ireland as a senseless conflict between Protestants and Catholics with no explanation of the vicious role of the British government. One newsman defiantly said ABC did not present the problem in simple Protestant–Catholic terms. And just as he said it, Howard K. Smith stormed among us, incandescent with rage. He roared at me: "What are you – Protestant or Catholic?" I gave a knowing sweep of my hand to the previous newsman who had just been speaking and said: "The top ABC man has just confirmed my point." Smith rounded on me, "What the hell does that mean? What are you talking about?" I explained to him that the other newsman had denied my charge that ABC presents the Northern Ireland problem as just a religious squabble. "And Mr. Smith," I said, "you just proved my argument." Then he spluttered that he gave money to both Protestant and Catholic charities. "Very commendable," I said, "but that is not the point. You have not exposed British government violation of human rights in Northern Ireland." He waved his hands dismissively and stormed off to his inner sanctum.

The police finally arrived, a hefty black officer of about forty in the lead. He immediately gave me a huge smile. He's Catholic, I said to myself. "Okay, okay, settle down, you all. What's going on?" I waited for ABC to explain what happened. The officer then inquired if the intruders had a knife or anything or attacked anybody. No, he was told. Then he burst into a huge smile and asked what all the commotion was about.

He then turned to me, "Father, what's going on?"

"Well, Officer, in the tradition of Martin Luther King, Jr. (here he broke into the biggest smile I had ever seen), we have done a nonviolent action to protest ABC covering up British oppression in Northern Ireland. We interrupted Mr. Smith's live broadcast. And in the spirit of Martin Luther King, Jr., we waited for you to come and arrest us."

It was clear that the officer was enjoying all of this. "Do you want me to arrest the good Father?" he asked the ABC officials. They huddled for a moment. "No," was their firm answer. "Okay, Padre," said the smiling cop, "you and your friends are free to go." And so ended my stint as an ABC newscaster.

I got hundreds of letters, even three marriage proposals! For years later people would say to me, "Oh, you're the priest that made Howard K. Smith jump out of his chair."

Richard Harris – Movie Star and Irish Patriot

One of the last things I did in Baltimore before moving to Boston was to organize with Ed Brady and others an Irish Testimonial Dinner on June 21, 1975 for Irish Northern Aid with Limerick-born movie star, Richard Harris, as the guest speaker.

About a year before the event, I had met Harris for the first time after a live performance at a local university. After the performance, I waited for him to come out from the stage area. Out he comes, with the longest overcoat I had ever seen on a man – down to his heels – and with a stunning lady on his arm, Ann Turkel. She was the most glamorous woman I had ever seen, almost as tall as Richard and with a smile as wide as the ocean. I gingerly approached this super-couple, excused myself for interrupting, but explained I was desperately trying to help the North, and if he was interested, as rumored, I would like to meet with him. "I'm fiercely interested, absolutely, passionately," he declaimed in his best King Arthur voice. "Annie, let's cancel our appointments for tomorrow and meet with Fr. Sean for breakfast."

Richard was intensely patriotic. And we got on very well. Before the Baltimore Dinner, I had him as the guest speaker for the big Irish Northern Aid Dinner in New York. He recited the poem, "The Fool" by Patrick Pearse and concluded by singing, without any accompaniment, "Kevin Barry." Needless to say, that brought the house down. Ann was especially pleased as she told me she had never seen such an outpouring of love and respect for Richard.

Ann was a lovely lady and, though not Catholic, had an exaggerated respect for priests, as is shown by the following story. At the time, the horror movie *The Exorcist* was all the rage. I had seen it in Baltimore. One evening I called Richard from Sacred Heart at their New York apartment. Ann answered the phone. "It's Fr. Sean, Ann," I said. Well, she let out a bloodcurdling shriek. I heard Richard shout, "Annie, Annie, it's all right." Richard then came on and said he would have to call me back as Anne was almost fainting.

I was really worried and didn't know what to do. Anyway, a short time later Ann called back, very apologetic. "Don't worry," I said. "What happened?"

She explained that they had just come in from seeing *The Exorcist*, which had deeply troubled her, and on the way back Richard was increasing her fear by telling her even worse stories that happened in Ireland – bigger and scarier, of course. Ann kept fretting that if diabolic possession could happen to anyone, might it happen to her? By the time she was walking in the door she had worked herself into somewhat of a frenzy. She says to Richard, "I've got to call Fr. Sean or I will go insane." She grabbed the phone to dial my number, and at that very split second, I said, "It's Father Sean". It scared the living daylights out of the poor woman.

Off to Mission Church, Boston

In the summer of 1975, the Baltimore Province of Redemptorists was making the periodic new appointments. I was assigned to Mission Church in Boston. That surprised me. Had my Superiors been unduly concerned about my escalating activity, they would have hardly sent me to the most Irish city in the most Irish state of all.

I was given the same room that de Valera used when he visited Mission Church to meet with his half-brother who was stationed there, Fr. William Wheelright. (That was during the period 1919–1920.) Down the street from Mission Church was the funeral parlor owned by Gene Sheehan, an old IRA man who was a close friend of Dev and the last man on the run in the Civil War (according to Gene).

I loved Boston. What a city! No Irishman could feel unwelcome there. However, the Irish in Boston were not as militant as the New York Irish regarding Northern Ireland.

I had spoken several times in Boston so I was already well known by all the Irish with an interest in the Troubles. Mission Church parish itself was no longer strongly Irish. The neighborhood had changed and was now predominantly black and Hispanic. I welcomed the chance to work for them, as there had been no blacks or Hispanics in Sacred Heart in Baltimore. I got to know many of them, especially those involved in social work and community activism. Some were really radical, in the good sense. And boy, did they stand by me when the Irish Consulate in Boston tried to have me silenced or moved! More of that later.

Shortly after I arrived, an old Irish-born man came to see me. He said it was great to have a young Irish priest again in the parish, that it would be like old times and that I should use the parish halls for Irish dances – not the newfangled stuff, mind you, no bands, just a man sitting in the corner, playing a fiddle.

I was touched by the wistfulness of the moment, but acutely conscious of how he was living in the past. That day was gone. The parish would never be like that again – when 50,000 people attended the Masses on Sunday during the Second World War and practically every newly arrived Irish person in Boston wanted to get married at Mission Church. I have since used this as a parable to illustrate how Unionism in Northern Ireland has changed forever: no going back to the big house on the hill where Unionists rule supreme. That day, too, has gone forever.

But I did have some Irish dances in the hall. And I took the theatre – yes, the theatre – out of mothballs. It had the best acoustics in all of Boston and a local Irish drama group put it to fine use. One of my jobs was looking after the parish's primary school, which was run by Notre Dame Nuns – all of them walking saints. All except one was over fifty. They were a group of dedicated, loving and joyful women, so totally different from the often ignorant, cruel and sexist stereotype of nuns in the media. It was a terrific school, totally integrated, black, white and Hispanic. And I loved the kids. I became good friends of the Sheehan family, who had three girls at the school. The father, Mossie is an ardent Kerryman who loved to sing and was GAA mad; the mother, Pat (Patricia) is a wonderful Irish-American lady.

Tricia – Little Kerry Angel

Their youngest girl, Tricia, was out sick for a while. One day I was walking back to Mission Church from my hospital-chaplain rounds, and as I passed the local pharmacy I spotted a cute teddy bear in the window. And a strange thing happened, which I've never been able to explain, and which has never happened since. I found myself thinking: "Why should I rush to New York to meet a politician (some politician had asked to meet with me) when little Tricia is sick?" I decided to cancel my New York visit, bought the teddy bear, and went to the Sheehans and gave it to a delighted Tricia. It was on her hospital bed the day she died. In a heartbreakingly short time we discovered Tricia did not have the flu, but leukemia. I was in her hospital room with her parents when her heartbeat started to fail. The doctors swooped into the room and practically lifted the parents out, leaving me inside as they desperately attempted to revive her. I could feel death descend on the room almost like a wind, while Tricia's soul soared to God.

Even now, after all these years, I tear up as I write this. My sorrow at Tricia's death was made all the more acute because my sister Celia and her husband, Michael, had lost their young daughter Caroline to the same dreaded disease. Tricia was a special child, with beautiful, golden-blonde hair and a personality that lit up the room. I preached at her funeral Mass, and I think it was the most difficult thing I have ever done. But I made it through without breaking down, buoying up the grieving congregation with my tribute to Tricia, aged eleven. The power of the funeral Mass, with its message of hope and resurrection, remains one of the most visible sacramental graces of the Catholic Church. It has healed and helped millions to recover from the most awful human suffering and bereavement.

Lobbying the Vatican

My campaigning for justice and peace in Northern Ireland did not appear as sensational as it had in a German–Polish parish in Baltimore. I continued to speak and organize chapters of the Irish National Caucus all across the United States. And then we made a surprise move. I organized an Irish National Caucus delegation to the Vatican.

Through the assistance of an Irish nun from Belfast, I was put in touch with a priest involved with the Pontifical Commission for Justice and Peace at the Vatican, Monsignor Maurice Bonneric, who felt it would help to raise the profile of the Troubles if an American group was to visit specifically for that reason. He guaranteed a meeting with Archbishop Giovanni Benelli, Substitute Secretary of State. The *Sunday Telegraph* said the Archbishop had "in effect become the Pope's [Paul VI] chief executive."[1] He was made a Cardinal in 1977. He was also on most *papabili* lists – shortlists of likely future Popes. But he died suddenly in 1982 at the age of sixty-one.

We traveled to Rome during the week of December 7, 1975. The delegation I headed up was composed of Bishop Drury, Jack Keane (president of the AOH), Brendan Mc Cusker (chairman of

Irish Northern Aid Committee), Sean Walsh and Fred O'Brien of the Irish National Caucus. Cardinal Wright of Boston welcomed us to the Eternal City by giving us dinner in his apartment. Wright, who was the Prefect of the Congregation for the Clergy, was the highest-ranking American in the Roman Curia.

Archbishop Benelli gave us a very attentive and gracious hearing. I spoke very strongly and urgently, but very respectfully. The Cardinal seemed to be very sympathetic, and emphasized the importance of America putting pressure on Britain. As we were leaving, he grasped my hand and whispered earnestly, "The Irish National Caucus must be nonviolent. In the Lord's name I beseech you to follow the path of nonviolence."

When a top Vatican official, so close to the Pope, and in the Vatican to boot, says that to a young priest, it has to register. And it did. The fact that the Archbishop listened carefully and did not automatically take the side of the British made his appeal more authentic. He was preaching *Pax Christi*, not *Pax Britannica*. In that instance, I just knew the Irish National Caucus would have to formally adopt the position of nonviolence. The Caucus was, in fact, nonviolent, as our actions showed, plus we had no foreign principal, but we had not formally taken a position of nonviolence. I knew it was one thing for me as an individual to say the IRA had as much right to fight for freedom as the British or Americans had, but if I were to head up an organization as a priest, then I would have to formally adopt a policy of nonviolence. This became even more compelling later on when I realized I would have to go full-time into a special ministry of justice and peace if the Irish National Caucus was to succeed in its mission. I issued a press release saying we were well pleased with our visit.[2]

After the Vatican visit, we went to Dublin. Ruairí Ó Brádaigh and Joe Cahill met us at the airport. And the Special Branch went crazy. They were scurrying about the place as if aliens had arrived. We filled in Republican leaders on our Vatican visit. I gave interviews to the Irish media and told them that since the Caucus was now well established, we would be making Ireland an issue in the 1976 presidential elections. I slipped up to Fermanagh to see my family and then returned to the United States.

10

The Caucus and Jimmy Carter

*The Irish National Caucus ... achieved its first major mark
... when it obtained an "Irish justice statement
from candidate Jimmy Carter."*

Professor Paul Power[1]

As mentioned in the previous chapter, I was determined that the Irish National Caucus would flex its muscles in the 1976 presidential election. The first Democratic candidate who made contact with me was Senator Henry "Scoop" Jackson of Washington State. I traveled to meet Jackson in New York. The first thing he said to me was, "Well, Father, I'm of Viking stock, so the Irish cannot be mad at me." With a totally straight face, I said, "You guys killed Brian Boru in 1014 and we haven't forgotten it." He almost fell off his chair thinking he had made the classic and much dreaded candidate faux pas. Then I laughed and told him I was kidding. I urged him to make a strong statement, no wishy-washy nonsense, condemning the violation of human rights, internment and calling for British withdrawal. He did exactly that in January 1976.

Then one of Jackon's top operators made contact with me during the hunger strike of Frank Stagg (1942–1976), who died in a British prison on February 12, 1976, after sixty-two days on hunger strike. I explained that Stagg's hunger strike was making a huge impact on the Irish in Massachusetts and that Jackson should campaign vigorously among them on his Irish position. Finally, when Stagg died, I invited Jackson's man to the public Mass I was saying at Mission Church for Stagg. We had put on a special effort to have a suitable turn-out for the Mass. Thousands flocked to honor and pray for that young Irish hero who sacrificed his life for Irish freedom.

I preached a moving tribute to Stagg. I was careful not to be "political" as this was the Mass, not a political rally. I have always been scrupulously correct in this matter. Nonetheless, I could not preach a proper funeral Mass homily unless I properly explained who Stagg was, what his values were, and why he had sacrificed his young life.

After the Mass, Jackson's man told me I was "a master" at presenting a difficult subject, expressed amazement at the size of the congregation and how they responded to my words. I replied that it "was the song, not the singer" that the Irish felt deeply about, i.e. the Troubles, and all politicians ignored that at their peril. "I bet you're now glad that Senator Jackson put out that strong statement," I added.

Jackson went on to win the Massachusetts Democratic primary on March 2. On March 16, he wrote me a personal letter of thanks: "Let me personally thank you and the Irish National Caucus for your efforts with the Irish voters on my behalf ... Let me reaffirm my commitment to the cause of Irish Freedom so closely related to the founding of our great nation. As stated previously, I support a declaration of intent from the British Government regarding their withdrawal from Ireland, and I believe that will be a concrete step towards peace with justice in Ireland, a cause for which an Irishman, Frank Stagg, died recently in a nonviolent, peaceful protest in an English prison."

That from a Cold War anti-communist senator! You knew it had to get the attention of the British (and that of the Irish government). But more importantly, it got the attention of the man who beat out

Jackson for the Democratic nomination – Jimmy Carter. (Jackson won the New York primary on April 6 but dropped out on May 1 after Carter beat him in Pennsylvania.) I sent the Jackson letter to the Carter people through Senator Joe Timilty of Boston, a good friend of mine and an ardent Irishman, who was a key man in the Carter campaign. I told Joe we wanted to meet Carter, and that we would not support him unless he met with us.

Irish "Welcome" for Queen

But here let me digress a bit, to take care of the Queen of England. She visited Boston on Sunday July 11 and I had to make sure she got an Irish welcome. Tommy and Agnes Clifford, two good friends, and I organized the protest. Tommy drove me around the city for weeks so that I could speak to every possible Irish grouping. We had a pretty good turnout for the protest. *The New York Times* carried a photograph of Her Majesty surrounded by placards saying: "America 1776. Ireland?", "Ireland Unfree Shall Never Be at Peace", "Tyranny is Not Easily Conquered, But We Will Conquer" and "England Out of Ireland."[2] To my own astonishment, I was able to get right up beside the Queen – only Mayor Kevin White was between us. Sometime later when I arranged for the Mayor to meet Nora Connolly O'Brien, daughter of Irish patriot-martyr James Connolly, when she visited Boston, he smiled and said, "Seems like I always see you, Father, when we greet famous ladies from across the Atlantic."

Carter Meeting

Just when it seemed that a meeting was in the works, Carter's people got nervous and admitted that the British were going crazy and putting a lot of pressure on them to cancel the meeting. "How is it going to look if Carter is seen to back down because he is scared of the Brits ... how many votes will that get him?" I retorted. Then Al Stern, First Assistant to Stud Eizenstat, Carter's top adviser, sent a telegram to us: "Urgent ... Trying to reach you. Please call."[3]

I called Stern and he assured me that Carter was not scared of the British and that the meeting was still on, even though the Irish Embassy was also opposed to the meeting. The meeting was finally and hurriedly scheduled for Wednesday, October 27, 1976 in Pittsburgh – just six days before the presidential election. I discussed with Stern, line by line, the opening statement I would make on behalf of the 34-member Caucus delegation. And I had sent him a copy well in advance of the meeting; with the assurance not a syllable would be changed:

Irish National Caucus statement to Governor Jimmy Carter,
Pittsburgh Hilton Hotel, Pittsburgh, Pennsylvania
October 27, 1976

Governor Carter,

On behalf of the Irish National Caucus, may we say that it is an honor to meet the next President of the United States.

The Irish National Caucus represents all the major Irish-American organizations in the United States, and is their official voice on justice and peace in Ireland.

We are deeply saddened by the ongoing tragedy in Ireland; and as Irish-Americans, we are deeply hurt by the stonewalling silence of the Nixon-Ford Administration. But we are greatly encouraged by the Irish plank in the Democratic Platform which states: "The voice of the United States should be heard in Northern Ireland against violence and terror, against the discrimination, repression, and deprivation which brought about that civil strife and for the efforts of the parties towards a peaceful resolution of the future of Northern Ireland ...

The United States should encourage the formation of a united Ireland, pertinent alliances such as NATO and international organizations such as the United Nations should be fully apprised of the interest of the United States with respect to the status of Ireland in the international community of nations."

We are even more encouraged, Governor Carter, by your words in your recent address at the University of Notre Dame: "We have watched passively as human rights are violated in Ireland. We should begin by having it understood that if any nation, whatever its political system, deprives its people of basic human rights, that fact will help shape our people's attitude towards that nation's government. If other nations want our friendship and support, they must understand that we want to see basic human rights respected."

We welcome this, Governor Carter, as a reinforcement of the Democratic Party Platform which also states "a primary object of American aid, both military and economic, is first of all to enhance the condition of freedom in the world. The United States should not provide aid to any government – anywhere in the world – which uses secret police detention without charges, and torture to enforce its power. Exceptions to this policy should be rare, and the aid provided should be limited to that which is absolutely necessary. The United States should be open and unashamed in its exercise of diplomatic efforts to encourage the observance of human rights in countries which receive American aid."

Governor Carter, in a recent letter to the National President of the Ancient Order of Hibernians, you stated: "I am sympathetic with those who seek to promote a stable and free Ireland with full civil and human rights for all citizens."

"... A stable and free Ireland with full civil and human rights for all citizens", Governor Carter, is precisely what we in the Irish National Caucus stand for. We thank you for meeting with us and we look forward to meeting you again as President of the United States.

Not only did Stern have a copy in advance but he also suggested I would add the word "stonewalling" before "silence" in the third paragraph.

Then Jimmy Carter made his statement. And for the record,

here it is, word for word:

> President-Elect Jimmy Carter's Statement to Irish National
> Caucus in Pittsburgh, on Wednesday October 27, 1976.
>
> It is a great honor to me to come here this afternoon to
> be with you who come to meet with me from a major part
> of this nation.
>
> I don't disavow my own Irish heritage. As I said, in a
> speech earlier today, it does not matter when our ancestors
> came here, two years ago or twenty years ago or two hundred
> years ago or more ... It is why we came here and what we do
> after we arrive to make our nation great.
>
> It would be a mistake for all of us to forget that we have
> a dual commitment; first and foremost, of course, to our
> country, here, the United States. But then secondly, and very
> importantly, to the nations from which our families came.
>
> When I was in Notre Dame two weeks ago last Sunday
> with Father Hesburg and just a few moments ago, as a
> matter of fact, with Cardinal Cooke in New York, we talked
> about the need for the establishment of a Commission on
> International Peace, to pursue in the multitude of places
> around the world, the concept of our country's standing firm
> in its commitment to human rights.
>
> We see, or come on the evening television news and in
> the national headlines every now and then, specific instances
> where human rights are subjugated and where quite often
> our nation as was pointed out by Father [Mc Manus], stands
> mute and doesn't speak.
>
> The Democratic National Convention Platform Plank
> was written jointly, by my own staff and by Mayor Daley
> from Chicago, to be sure that the world knows that the
> Democratic Party understands the special problems in
> Ireland and that it is a mistake for our country's Government
> to stand quiet on the struggle of the Irish for peace for the
> respect of human rights and for unifying Ireland.
>
> I would like to say that I almost feel like I am a

member of the Ancient Order of Hibernians as well. For six years in a row, I was honored to go to Savannah on Saint Patrick's Day, and if any of you have ever been to Savannah on Saint Patrick's Day, you know that it is one of the fine and wonderful events in the life of a human being, and those who come there from Boston and other major cities in the world say that they have never seen anything like it. Although Savannah is a fairly small city, we have two hundred and fifty thousand people participating in the parade and the beer is green, the grits are green, the streets are green, everything is painted green; in fact, one year we dyed the entire Savannah River green. So Georgia has an awful lot of Irish settlers including my own family. To some degree, I know the heartache that you feel to see the bloodshed and the disharmony and deprivation in Ireland. And I am very honored that you come to let me feel a part of a hope that will never be extinguished that we can have a redressing of grievances, and a realization for hopes of our brave, unfortunate mankind in Ireland.

Needless to say, we were delighted by that statement. And needless to say, the British were not. The *Guardian*, supposed to be a moderate and reasonable paper, sniffed in an editorial: "And now, a few days from what may be his elevation to the Presidency of the United States, along comes Jimmy Carter, sharing a platform with Seán Mac Stíofáin's confessor and pledging himself to a United Ireland."[4]

Carter was roundly condemned by the British media and by British and Unionist politicians. Mr. Roy Mason, the British Secretary of State for Northern Ireland told the House of Commons that Carter was, "giving aid and succour to Ulster terrorists." Nothing surprising there.

FitzGerald Rallies to Brits

What would surprise many Americans (but not this

Fermanagh man) was the hysterical reaction of the obsequious Dublin government of that time. (*The Boston Globe* would later report: "Irish embassy officials protested vehemently to Carter aides. Carter, under pressure, agreed to send a telegram of clarification ... Carter, the next day, telegrammed Irish Foreign Minister FitzGerald": "... I have been informed that certain news reports concerning my meeting yesterday with Irish-American leaders have misrepresented both my position and my statements ... I do not favor violence as part of a solution to the Irish question."[5] No one, of course, had reported Carter had favored violence. But this was classic Dublin government tactic – scare people from speaking out for justice in Northern Ireland lest they be accused of supporting violence. It was unconscionable to do that to Carter. Yet the media establishment in Ireland never objected to FitzGerald's inexcusable and disgraceful actions. Years later, when candidate Bill Clinton, on April 5, 1992 in New York City, made promises to a group of us (some who also had been at the Carter meeting in Pittsburgh), the huge difference was that Taoiseach Albert Reynolds welcomed Clinton's statement – and the rest is history. I am haunted by this thought: had FitzGerald welcomed Carter's statement, how much sooner the peace process could have started, how many lives might have been saved and how so much suffering could have been spared? And I am not alone in thinking this way. Well-known author and journalist Tim Pat Coogan says in his memoirs, "During the 1974-7 coalition period the voice of the Dublin component of the Toffs" Brigade [pro-British elite] was particularly strong, powerful and continuous. I would blame Dublin's attitude in these years for helping to create a mindset that deepened the political vacuum and helped to prolong the Troubles."[6]

But I had inadvertently given some of Carter's people an opportunity to make specious excuses. In my hurry to prepare my statement for the Carter meeting, I quoted the Irish plank in the Democratic Platform, as given by the *Guardian*. But that paper quoted a previous draft that had been changed. The phrase, "The United States should encourage the formation of a united

Ireland" was not, in fact, in the final version. It was a genuine mistake, which even the Carter people themselves missed, even though they had an advance copy and had approved every word.

Al Stern quite disingenuously went on to allege that I had tricked Carter into talking about "unifying Ireland." My response was if a simple man from Fermanagh could do that, what would the Soviets do to him, for goodness' sake. But Stern in the same *Globe* article was forced to admit that I had made an honest mistake: "Stern said he telephoned Fr. Mc Manus after the flap and accused the priest of having tricked Carter into using the phrase [unifying Ireland]. The presidential aide subsequently accepted Mc Manus' explanation that it had been an honest mistake based on an incorrect version of the platform as reported in the Manchester *Guardian* ... But Stern added: 'I have reason to believe he (Mc Manus) was delighted.'"[7] Stern could also have added that he himself did not catch the error even though he was intimately involved in the drafting of my statement, and was in possession of an advance copy, and had approved every word – even adding one. Stern also told the National Catholic News Service, that he was satisfied that what happened "was not done deliberately or maliciously."

But in fairness to Carter, he himself never withdrew his words, which were recorded. And it's his words that count, not my misquote.

But FitzGerald's apparatchiks at the Irish Embassy were instructed to continue the misinformation campaign so as to discredit the Caucus and make Carter back off. The *Jack Anderson Column* – then one of the largest syndicated columns in the United States – regurgitated the FitzGerald misinformation: "At the height of the presidential campaign, Jimmy Carter inadvertently stirred up a tempest in Great Britain ... He met in Pittsburgh with Irish-American leaders, many of them dogmatically anti-British. A militant priest read Carter what purported to be a copy of the Democratic platform on Ireland and asked whether he supported it ... But the priest spiked the non-controversial platitudes with some language of his own ... The unsuspecting Carter, groggy from the gruelling campaign, overlooked the inflammatory sentence."[8]

Whitten, a writer for the *Anderson Column* had never contacted me and clearly allowed himself to be used to do a hatchet job. He came to realize that, and later he and the paper would do some fine pieces on British human rights violations in Northern Ireland.

Paul O'Dwyer Rallies to Irish Cause

Irish-Americans were appalled by the unfairness of it all, so they took their grievance to the ultimate court of appeal – the intrepid Paul O'Dwyer, then President of New York City Council, who had the zeal for justice of an Old Testament Prophet. On November 17, 1976, Paul wrote to President-elect Carter: "An article appearing in The Jack Anderson syndicated column ... has greatly disturbed members of the Irish-American community. It charges a most respectable clergyman with having played a vile trick on you ... Leaders of the Irish-American community have requested me to make my own inquiry into the facts ... I found the following to be the facts ... The Carter campaign leadership in Atlanta, very properly, insisted that the leader spokesman of the delegation, long in advance of the meeting, present a written script which would contain the delegation's position. The delegation adhered to the rules with meticulous care ... From the facts, and circumstances, I believe that the Anderson column is a garbled distortion carrying a scurrilous and unfounded accusation against a prestigious clergyman which has angered a whole community."[9]

With that letter Paul O'Dwyer – in his own right, an important figure in the Democratic Party – was steadying President Carter and at the same time "the Lion of Bohola", as I called him, was sending a message to the Irish government and Irish Embassy that he was on to them.

Despite the Irish Embassy's concentrated campaign to discredit me with the Carter White House, I was given about a dozen tickets to the Carter Inaugural Ball and continued to be invited to the White House – although the smear campaign against me did inevitably limit my access to Carter's policymakers.

Nonetheless, on February 24, 1977, I met for two hours with Marilyn Haft, Carter's Associate Director of Public Liaison, who specialized in advising the President on international human rights.

On March 16, 1977, Carter paid a visit to Clinton, a very Irish town in Massachusetts. Hours before, FitzGerald met with Carter and implored him not to refer to human rights in Northern Ireland, only to condemn IRA violence. Despite FitzGerald's plea, "The President defended his policies on human rights, and said he would speak out on human rights in Northern Ireland, without saying why."[10] Now you know "why" ... because FitzGerald tried to stop him, and Carter did not appreciate it.

Neither was the Irish Embassy able to stop my meeting with Andrew Young while he was U.S. ambassador to the United Nations (1977–1979). It was just after the State Department had made Young apologize for saying that if England had not actually invented racism, she had institutionalized it around the world. Despite his forced apology, Young was in high good spirits, and with delight showed me some of the irate letters he had received from people in Britain. Andy had no doubt about who was the oppressed and who was the oppressor in Ireland.

And in face of the ongoing campaign by the Irish Embassy to blackball me, I was still invited to the Carter White House on two occasions. On Friday April 11, 1980, I was invited "to join the President at a meeting for ethnic fraternal leaders."[11] When I met the President for a handshake and photograph, I smilingly asked him if he remembered me from Pittsburgh. "Oh, how could I forget?" he chuckled. I then said, "Please don't forget human rights in Northern Ireland." He replied, "I shan't. I promise you".[12]

But FitzGerald was obsessed by the success of the Caucus and was ridiculously concerned that the Caucus would be seen as having any influence with Carter. For example, he told *The New York Times* that "... the Irish Government had been anxious about

American policy involving Ulster in the aftermath of widespread publicity in Ireland and Britain that the Irish National Caucus ... had access to the White House. [The Caucus] has had a propaganda campaign suggesting that they had access to the White House, that they were influential."

Apparently, according to FitzGerald, Americans should not have the right to free speech or the right to petition their government. But even FitzGerald cannot rewrite history. It was the Irish National Caucus that first got Carter speaking about the Troubles, and that nobody can deny. As Professor Paul Power says, "The Irish National Caucus ... achieved its first major mark in October 1977, when it obtained an 'Irish justice' statement from candidate Jimmy Carter, providing the INC with a basis for claiming a seminal role in the later Carter statement on Northern Ireland."[13]

The significance of that assessment is all the more apparent when it is realized that in the 1970s, Professor Power of the University of Cincinnati was "the only American political science academic researching Northern Ireland affairs."[14] "The later Carter Statement" to which Power refers – also known as the Carter initiative – was made by the President on August 30, 1977.[15] Power states that it was "the first, explicit comment on Irish political issues of any kind ever made by an incumbent President". That is why it was so important to the Irish National Caucus – not so much for what it said, but that it was said at all.

But it did also contain the key points we had been pressing on the Carter White House. In fact, *The Sunday Press* (Dublin) on September 4 claimed that "some hours before the long-expected Carter initiative was finally announced ... the text of the statement was released word for word to an Irish newspaper [by the Irish National Caucus]."[16]

The key part of the statement said: "The United States wholeheartedly supports peaceful means for finding a just solution that involves both parts of the community of Northern Ireland and protects human rights and guarantees freedom from discrimination – a solution that the people of Northern Ireland, as well as the Governments of Great Britain and Ireland, can support. Violence cannot resolve Northern Ireland's problem: it only increases them and solves nothing."

The Irish Times, the day after the Carter statement was released, carried the following headline: "Irish Caucus cued Carter: McManus":

> The Rev. Sean McManus, of the Irish National Caucus in the United States, said yesterday that it was the Caucus that first initiated President Carter's involvement in Ireland by making human rights, justice and peace in Ireland an issue in the Presidential election. In so doing, he said, the Caucus made such matters an international issue for which it was criticized by the British Government, and the previous Coalition Government, and leading SDLP members. Ultimately, Father McManus said in a statement, the real significance of the President's interest was that it would formally, and at the highest level, "internationalize" British involvement in Ireland, thus making it clear to the world that Northern Ireland was not just a British internal matter.[17]

11

The Long Knives of the Dublin Government

*The Dublin Government will fight Irish-Americans
but not the Brits.*[1]

In the previous chapter, I quoted the thank-you letter that Senator "Scoop" Jackson had sent me with his very respectful reference to Frank Stagg who had died for "peace with justice in Ireland."

There you have a non-Irish, non-Catholic decent "Viking" paying deep respect to that young Irish martyr. What respect did the Irish government show this heroic young Mayo man? When his body was flown from England back to Ireland, the Irish government kidnapped the body, in a frightfully ugly fascist display, to stop Stagg being given a Republican burial, as he had requested. The Irish government, on February 21, 1976 had Stagg buried under six feet of concrete, in a grave 70 yards from the Republican Plot in Leigue Cemetery, Ballina, County Mayo. The grave was guarded twenty-four hours a day by armed Special Branch men to stop the Republican Movement from reinterring their martyred comrade. But on November 6, the IRA succeeded in burying Stagg's remains in the Republican Plot.

Mrs. Stagg, Frank's mother, had written me a beautiful letter to thank me for the Mass we celebrated for her son. I promised her I would visit his grave in Ballina and say a prayer there. In the summer of 1976, I went to his grave, not wearing my clerical collar. I started to take a photo, and was immediately surrounded by Special Branch men. "Stop, that's not allowed," they barked. "What do you mean, it's not allowed. Has the Irish Constitution been changed to forbid photos?" Then in that bullying way that seems special to the Special Branch, they told me if I took photos they would confiscate my camera and place me under arrest. "Am I allowed to say a prayer or is that, too, forbidden?" I snapped.

Can you imagine anything more guaranteed to recruit members for the IRA than the barbaric way the Dublin government treated the body of a dead hunger striker? Even the British did not do that to Bobby Sands and his nine comrades when they died in Long Kesh in 1981.

So you can imagine that when I returned to Boston, my condemnations of the Dublin government grew stronger. Then came the shameful sandbagging of Jimmy Carter by Garret FitzGerald and all my Fermanagh contempt for the Dublin government was mightily reinforced. There was simply no way of avoiding it: the Dublin government was collaborating with Britain in its dirty war in the North.

Now fast-forward again to March 1977. The St. Patrick's Day statement of Senator Teddy Kennedy, Speaker Tip O'Neill, Senator Pat Moynihan and Governor Hugh Carey further indicated proof that FitzGerald had tried to muzzle President Carter from speaking about human rights in Northern Ireland. To explain what I mean, it is important here to give their statement in full:

> Joint St. Patrick's Day Appeal for Peace in Northern Ireland
> For Release on Thursday a.m., March 17, 1977.
>
> The world has looked with increasing concern over the past eight years on the continuing tragedy that afflicts the people of Northern Ireland. Each of us has tried in the past to use our good offices to help see that the underlying injustices at the heart of the Northern Ireland tragedy are ended so that a just and peaceful settlement may be secured.

It is evident to us, as it is to concerned people everywhere, that continued violence cannot assist the achievement of such a settlement, but can only exacerbate the wounds that divide the people of Northern Ireland.

We, therefore, join together in this appeal, which we make in a spirit of compassion and concern for the suffering people in the troubled part of Ireland. We appeal to all those organizations engaged in violence to renounce their campaign of death and destruction and return to the path of life and peace. And we appeal as well to our fellow Americans to embrace this goal of peace, and to renounce any action that promotes the current violence or provides support or encouragement for organizations engaged in violence.

We make this appeal on St. Patrick's Day 1977, a day on which Irish peoples of all traditions everywhere should feel proud to rejoice in our common heritage. And a year in which peace should come at last to Northern Ireland.

Edward M. Kennedy
Thomas P. O'Neill Jr.
Daniel Patrick Moynihan
Hugh L. Carey

Not a word about British violence, repressive legislation, and mistreatment of political prisoners. Not a whisper about how British security forces and the RUC were colluding with, arming and controlling Protestant murder gangs. Not a scintilla of mention about the deep-seated, all-pervasive, anti-Catholic sectarianism – the State religion of Northern Ireland. The "Four Horsemen" (well versed in how the media, which had christened them thusly, operates) had to know how their statement would play. The headline in *The New York Times* makes my case: "Four Top Democrats Urge Halt in Support for the IRA."[2]

In fact, the statement did nothing to stop those who were supporting the IRA. I never met an Irish-American who stopped supporting the IRA because of Tip O'Neill or Teddy Kennedy. The statement just gave the British carte blanche.

My collision course with the Dublin government was further

escalated by a nasty development in Croke Park on Sunday, April 17, 1977, before the Kerry–Dublin National Football League final. Before the game began, a group of human rights activists ran on to the pitch with banners protesting the treatment of hunger strikers in Portlaoise Prison. Two of the Dublin team – David Hickey, a medical doctor, and John McCarthy, a Dublin-based garda – attacked the protesters in an unseemly and unnecessary manner. My brother Frank, a most ardent attendee of all matches in Croke Park, alerted me to the outrage, pictures of which were prominently carried in all the papers. I was especially offended that a doctor and a garda were involved. I lobbied the two American GAA governing bodies, the New York GAA Board and the North American Board, urging them to ban the two offending Dublin players from playing in upcoming games in America. I knew most of the key members of both boards who were also members of the Irish National Caucus. In no time both boards authorized me to make the following statement, which was carried in all the Irish newspapers:

> These two players [Hickey and McCarthy] will not be allowed to play in any part of the U.S.. They disgraced the uniform of the Dublin team and the spirit of the GAA by using Croke Park to violently express their political hostility to the hunger strikers. Hickey and McCarthy in the most sordid manner introduced politics into Croke Park. Therefore, the leadership of the GAA in the U.S. is banning Hickey and McCarthy from playing with the Dublin team on their upcoming tour.[3]

Well, as they say, all hell broke out. I was told by an insider that Seán O'Síocháin, GAA Director General, erupted wanting to know, "When the f*** did Father Mc Manus and the Provos gain control of the GAA in America?" There they go again ... Any time a stand for justice is taken, it has to be the IRA!

Anyway, the hunger strike in Portlaoise Prison was settled and we called off the ban. Prominent GAA writer Paddy Downey reported: "News that the ban had been lifted was announced by the

Boston-based priest, the Rev. Sean McManus, after his brother, Mr. Frank McManus, the former Westminster MP for Fermanagh and South Tyrone, had informed him that the Portlaoise prisoners had ended their hunger-strike ... The North American Board of the GAA is now expected to follow the lead of the Caucus – as they had followed it originally when imposing the ban."[4]

Boston Irish Consul Tries to Silence Me

But as I said, the GAA ban would speed up the Irish government campaign against me.

On April 18, 1977, *The Boston Globe* ran a front-page story on me, with photograph, "Hub priest denies he backs IRA,"[5] by top reporter David Nyhan. It told the story of how the Irish government, Irish Embassy in Washington and Irish Consulate in Boston were out to squash me. A month later, Nyhan had another front-page story on me, with a photograph of me without my clerical collar demonstrating at City Hall Plaza for political prisoners in Ireland, North and South: " 'Ireland putting heat on me,' says priest."[6] It reported how the Irish Consul in Boston, Carmel Heaney, had approached the Chancellor of the Archdiocese, Bishop Thomas V. Dailey, to try and get him to silence me. And how, in turn, Bishop Dailey, called my Rector, Fr. Jim Foley, to a meeting at the Chancery. Nyhan wrote: "Heaney said, 'I certainly have not made any approach of the kind described by Fr. McManus. I really can't discuss what I may or may not do ... Obviously, I have conversations with all kinds of people in the course of my job. In some cases they can be regarded as public, and in other cases as private.'" Heaney's words give her away.

Nyhan's story continues: "Last night Fr. Foley said in an interview that Bishop Dailey had 'mentioned his interest' in Fr. McManus' activities ... I told him what a wonderful priest Fr. McManus is. We had absolutely nothing but the highest regard for him here. Asked if Bishop Dailey had told him of being approached by Heaney, Fr. Foley replied, 'I don't want to comment on the various details. It was a private conversation.' Bishop Dailey was unavailable for comment."

Naturally, many other U.S. papers picked up the front-page story. The *Boston Herald American* ran with the headline, "Hub priest charges Irish consul with 'dirty trick'":

> A Mission Church priest yesterday accused Irish Consul Carmel Heaney here of "running for cover behind a wall of equivocation and diplomatic immunity" after working her "dirty trick" ... In response to his latest criticism of her, she said, "it would be counter-productive to get into a debate at second-hand or indirectly with Fr. McManus' ... The priest, who has been accused of terrorist activities by the Irish government in Dublin, said he learned of the "dirty trick" from the Mission Church rector ... Fr. McManus said, "I am opposed to violence, whether it be British or the IRA ... I believe the fundamental violence in Ireland is institutionalized by the British government with its army, its enforced unemployment, its sectarianism and its discrimination."[7]

The *Irish Post* in London – published by the late Brendan MacLua – went right to the source of the Heaney's dirty trick: "A few weeks ago the Irish Minister for Foreign Affairs, Dr. Garret FitzGerald, singled [Fr. McManus] out for special attention and condemned his activities in the U.S."[8] The National Catholic News Service (the news wire service of the U.S. Conference of Catholic Bishops) filed the following syndicated report:

> Boston priest will not be silenced on his Irish views, pastor says. "There is no danger of Father McManus being silenced – either by the Archdiocese or the Redemptorist Order." Father Foley told National Catholic News. "I'm not going to report on the details of a very private and cordial conversation with Bishop Dailey ... but I backed up Father McManus as a good priest and a good school prefect. As far as his priestly work, he's tremendous. He has every right to talk out on human rights violations as long as he's doing it nonviolently."[9]

There was huge outpouring of support for me, not only in the parish but throughout Boston. The principal of the local public school, Charles H. Gibbons, Jr., wrote to *The Boston Globe*: "I can personally attest to [Fr. Mc Manus'] commitment and humanitarian concern for the people of Mission Hill – black, white and Hispanic ... Perhaps the Irish government would suggest someone else to help us in Mission Hill. If not, I would appreciate their concerning themselves with other affairs since the most impressive priest I have seen operating in Mission Hill is Fr. Sean Mc Manus ..."[10]

A middle-aged black woman, not a Catholic, became a fierce defender. This lady was a social worker dealing with great deprivation in the area. She was a force of nature and as tough as nails. She phoned Carmel Heaney and bawled her out: "You [expletive deleted], leave Fr. Mc Manus alone. How dare you say he's collecting guns for the IRA? In Mission Hill we keep our own damn guns."

So there you have it. In Britain the government tried to have me silenced. In America, the Dublin government tried to have me silenced. And I am quite convinced that had it not been for David Nyhan, God rest him, and the other journalists, they might have got Bishop Dailey to move against me. Dailey never gave me any further trouble. He was scared of *The Boston Globe*.

But here's the rub, the moral, if you wish, of the story: the Irish Embassy and Consulates only really escalated their attacks on me after the Irish National Caucus formally adapted nonviolence and wrote it into our constitution. Instead of welcoming this development, the Embassy and Consulates were frightened by it. Why?

I have mentioned that after Archbishop Benelli's plea to me at the Vatican, I knew we would have to formally adopt a policy of nonviolence, even though I have been practicing it since I decided at sixteen to become a priest. That did not mean that I could no longer understand what made the IRA fight. It meant that I personally could not join them in that struggle. It meant that I personally had to accept nonviolence as a way of life. It did not mean I had to tell lies to cover up British injustice in Ireland, or to collaborate by my silence with that injustice. Nonviolence does not mean doing nothing. It is short for "nonviolent resistance" to injustice and oppression.

In 1976, I went home for Christmas. *The Irish Press* interviewed me on my position on violence: "In an exclusive interview with *The Irish Press*, Fr. McManus said he was convinced that the only long-term solution to the problem was one of nonviolence ... [He] said he disagreed with many things the Provisional IRA had done. 'I disagree with the whole broad use of violence, but I must honestly say, I understand why they turned to these acts.'"[11]

In 1977, I declared that the "subtitle" of the Irish National Caucus would be: "The nonviolent pursuit of justice and peace for Ireland." That appeared under our name in all our literature – and I should know, as I wrote all our position papers and announcements. "The Irish National Caucus is totally opposed to the use of violence to achieve political objectives in Ireland. It is, therefore, logically and necessarily opposed in the very first place to British policy in Ireland because the British government historically and currently and par excellence, uses violence to achieve political objectives in Ireland. But the Caucus is opposed to all forms of violence, whether it is British or Irish, State or civilian. It is an exclusively American-based organization and does not support any party or organization in Ireland. It has no foreign principal and it does not, and never has sent funds to any part of Ireland for any reason – least of all for violence."

Could anything be more clear and unambiguous? Why did the Irish government not welcome that unequivocal nonviolent declaration? Why were they not as happy as the IRA was unhappy about it?

Irish Embassy Out to Destroy Me

But there would be no let-up in the Irish Embassy's campaign of character assassination. In 1977, Doubleday published a book, *The Power Peddlers*, by Russell Warren Howe and Sarah Hays Trott. The book, about foreign-policy lobbies in Washington, had a section on the Irish National Caucus. On page 391 it says, "Father McManus' Irish Embassy file card bears the mention 'homicidal tendencies'."

Paul O'Dwyer's law firm initiated a libel lawsuit on my behalf against Doubleday and the authors. My Provincial, the admirable Father Joe Kerins, totally backed my lawsuit and offered to sign on as a co-defendant. He also wrote to the then Irish Ambassador in Washington, John Molloy, expressing outrage and demanding an explanation. On December 8, 1978, an embassy counsellor replied for the Ambassador, denying that such a file card existed and that "... no representative of the Embassy has at any time suggested ... that such a card existed or that Father McManus had such tendencies."

Howe, a British subject, was ordered by a Federal judge to reveal his source in the Irish Embassy. He refused: "He indicated," said *The New York Times*, "that the source could face retaliation by the Irish Republican Army because of the criticism of Father McManus."[12] He was threatened with contempt, and the Embassy official whom the Irish Ambassador had denied existed offered to appear before the judge "in camera" (in the judge's chambers, hidden from the public) so his identity could never be revealed, as he was allegedly scared the IRA would kill him and his family! In other words, they piled on the libel against me, making it even more outrageous.

Anyway, the case was eventually dropped. Later Howe would write about the case in an article, "Reveal the Name or go to Jail", in the *Washington Journalism Review*: "During an interview in New York, an Irish diplomat read me the priest's address and telephone numbers from an Embassy file card. He chuckled and cited a cheeky comment that someone had written on the card: homicidal tendencies."[13] Howe then continues: "My source felt wretched about my case ... He said his ambassador would not allow him to testify, in any case. He had considered bypassing me and 'going public' on his own (although he feared IRA reprisals against his wife and children or his family in Ireland). However, his Ambassador had rejected that, saying waiving immunity would set a bad precedent. The source appealed to Irish foreign minister, Garret FitzGerald; although sympathetic, the minister decided against overruling his envoy ... 'The irony of it,' said the source, 'is that I'm sure they've guessed it's me, because the IRA knows I'm the Embassy member who keeps tabs on them here.'"

All that from a person who did not exist, and from an Embassy that always denied it was spying on American citizens.

Howe then explains that when the "source" appeared In Camera before the judge, he "produced photos of his endangered wife and children. [Judge] Weinfeld looked at them and nodded sympathetically."

I hope all this shows I was not exaggerating when I say the Irish Embassy was conducting a character assassination campaign against me and was out to destroy

Formation of Ad Hoc Congressional Committee for Irish Affairs

But the Irish Embassy would have even more reason to be concerned by what *The New York Times*, in a front-page article, described was, up until that time, "the Caucus' boldest success" – the formation of the Ad Hoc Congressional Committee for Irish Affairs.[14]

On Tuesday, September 27, 1977, I chaired the press conference on Capitol Hill at which we appointed Congressman Mario Biaggi (D-NY) as chairman: "Congressman Biaggi was selected by us," Fr. Mc Manus said, "because he has truly distinguished himself by his consistent and outspoken concern for my country. Although his ancestry is not from Cork, Kerry or Fermanagh, the Congressman has shown more compassion than some congressional leaders with Irish names. On behalf of the Irish National Caucus, the National President of the AOH and all Irish-American organizations, it gives me great pleasure to appoint you, Congressman Biaggi, Chairman of the Ad Hoc Congressional Committee for Irish Affairs."[15]

Then I announced the Committee's threefold purpose: (1) To seek full Congressional Hearings on violations of human rights in Ireland; (2) to reverse the U.S. policy of refusing visas to Irish Republicans; and (3) to represent the views of Irish-Americans to the President of the U.S.

The one acid test that I had given Mario before we asked him to chair the committee was, "Are you prepared to stand up to the Dublin government?" Mario had responded, "Absolutely." Is it not it pathetic that we had to have this concern? Is it not shameful that this highly decorated police hero, and proud son of Italy, had to not only take on the British government, but to watch his back with the Irish government as well? But that's the way it was. One could see Dublin's real policy towards the North far more clearly in America than in Ireland.

Mario – born 1917 and still happily with us – deserves huge credit and must never be forgotten by Irish-Americans who are dedicated to justice and peace. He is a truly great man.

The Irish Embassy had been telling Members of Congress that Congress had no role to play in Northern Ireland – that it should be left to the British and Irish governments and to diplomats. In a very short time we had signed up over 100 Members – Republicans, Democrats, Liberals, Conservatives, Protestants, Jews, Catholics, etc.

On September 28, the Religious News Service filed a report: "In an interview [after the press conference] ... Father McManus said, "We are disappointed with Sen. Edward Kennedy (D-MA) and Rep. Thomas P. O'Neill, Jr. (D-MA) – the most powerful politicians in the United States, and both Roman Catholics. They condemn violence in Northern Ireland, but do not condemn British violence and torture ... The American Catholic hierarchy has made several comments about violence in South Africa, Rhodesia and Chile, and quite rightly so. But they are silent about British violence in Ireland – with only one honorable exception, Bishop Thomas J. Drury of Corpus Christi, Texas."[16]

Over the years certain elements would try to deny the Caucus' pivotal role in forming the Ad Hoc Committee. However, the intrepid Tom McNabb, who was actually present (as the photo shows) when I Chaired the launching of the Committee, would

set the record straight. As National Editor of the *Hibernian Digest*
Tom declared in an Editorial: "It was through the Irish National
Caucus that the important Ad Hoc Congressional Committee for
Irish Affairs came into existence within the National Congress."[17]

Jack Lynch Tries to Destroy Biaggi and INC
AOH Convention in Killarney

In February 1978, I was tipped off that the Irish Embassy
was planning something big against us for St. Patrick's Day. My
informant heard one of the Irish Embassy staff boast: "Come St.
Patrick's Day, only Mc Manus and Biaggi will be left standing."
So we braced ourselves for the gathering storm, and it came on
February 17, 1978. On that date, Taoiseach Jack Lynch wrote
to Congressman Mario Biaggi, denouncing him and the Irish
National Caucus. But before sending it to Biaggi, Lynch made it
public to *The New York Times*, *The Washington Post* and all the
major American media. The intention was clear: to put the Ad Hoc
Congressional Committee for Irish Affairs and the Irish National
Caucus out of business. The Irish Embassy genuinely thought the
Members of Congress we had signed up for the Committee would
resign en masse. When Lynch made his attack, we had 93 Members
of Congress signed up for the Committee for Irish Affairs. Only
two resigned, and we went on to recruit a total of 133 Members
of Congress. (Years later, I would discover that Mrs. Jack Lynch
had written to Fr. Sheperd. She urged him to silence me, and stop
me from criticizing her husband, whom she described as a great
Irish patriot!)

The conflict with the Irish Embassy would be carried across
the Atlantic to Killarney when the AOH held its annual convention
there from June 27-29, 1978. The Irish Embassy had engineered
Division 36 of the AOH in Shrewsbury, Massachusetts, to submit
a resolution to the convention: "... that the Convention record itself
as in favor of the goals and directions of the government of the
Republic of Ireland, and further, that the Convention repudiate all
groups advocating violence in Northern Ireland."

The Irish Embassy had simultaneously arranged for Teddy Kennedy to send a telegram to the convention supporting the resolution. Well, one did not need a degree in political science to know what was going on here. I made a statement to the convention that if Senator Kennedy and Division 36 would amend the resolution to include British violence – the violence of the British government, British army, RUC, etc. – I would support it. No such amendment was offered.

The chairman of the Resolutions Committee felt the pressure would be too much for him, so he called in sick and asked me to act as chairman. When the resolution came up, I ruled it out of order on the grounds that the AOH had no "foreign principal" and therefore could not support a foreign government. All hell broke loose and the establishment media went crazy.

The Irish Times screamed, "AOH refuses to back government."[18] I thought one journalist was going to assault me. "How the f**k is the Irish Government a foreign government?" he snarled at me. (And he was a "religious" reporter.) I patiently explained, "Any government outside the U.S.A. is a foreign government to an American organization." Then I really set him off by adding, "Besides it is not the government of Ireland, only of twenty-six counties." He would later write that there were angry scenes between Jack Keane (AOH president) and me, when, in fact, he was the one causing the angry scene. Jack only got angry because the reporter had used the F-word to a priest.

One of the most disappointing things for me about the Irish media was how they allowed themselves to be co-opted, with some honorable exceptions, by the Dublin and British governments. They were scared stiff of deviating from the party line on the North. Oh yes, they could take on the governments on all sorts of issues, but on the North they were docile.

The convention would go on to pass resolutions calling for "the absolute independence of Ireland and urged the U.S. government to work for the re-unification of Ireland." It also passed resolutions endorsing the Ad Hoc Committee and the Irish National Caucus, and our initiative for the Ad Hoc Committee to host an Irish Peace

Forum in Washington, to which "all parties could come without preconditions or compromise".

During the convention, I went to a private location for a meeting with Ruairí Ó Brádaigh, Dave O'Connell and Joe Cahill. They were clearly concerned about my emphasis on nonviolence and expressed great concern about Fred O'Brien (of whose affiliations they were suspicious). Each of them asked me a series of questions, and played a recording of an interview I had given to RTÉ radio on why I had ruled out of order the resolution calling for support of the Dublin government. At the end of the meeting, Ó Brádaigh very formally asked O'Connell and Cahill if they were satisfied with my answers and both said they were. Then he, again very formally, summed up the discussion and pronounced that he too was satisfied. Later, he told me I had been "in a Sinn Féin court."

Irish Peace Forum

After the convention, Fred O'Brien, Bob Bateman and I traveled up to the North to sound out all the groups and parties on the Irish Peace Forum. We checked into a hotel in a strong Loyalist part of East Belfast for three nights. The UDA put a guard outside our door so that no freelancer would "shoot the priest" – at least, while I was under safe passage. In one amusing incident, when a UVF man came into our room, he challenged me very aggressively about the armed guard. But he calmed down when I told him it was UDA, as he had suspected it was IRA.

One of the first things one of the Loyalists said to me was, "I've always wanted to see you, Sean – down the barrel of a gun."

"Isn't much nicer this way, at least from my point of view," I replied.

We met with all the Loyalist paramilitary groups – UDA, UVF, Red Hand Commandos, etc.

John McKeague, leader of the Red Hand Commandos, told me that he could always tell when Rev. Ian Paisley was going to tell a lie: he would remove his collar. He sent one of his top commandos to meet me so that "I could see his men were of better mettle than either the UDA or UVF." After I talked to that young man, he started to cry as he said goodbye. He said I was the first priest he had ever met, and that maybe he had been told lies about priests. I don't remember his name and I often wonder what became of him.

The late Paddy Reynolds, Northern Editor of *The Irish Press*, came to see me in a panic: "Fr. Sean, the only way you are going to get out of this hotel alive is if I call RTÉ to come over and cover your exit with their cameras." I appreciated his concern but told him I was in no danger. Years later, I tended to think he may have had good reason for his concern.

All the Loyalists were in favor of the Peace Forum and so was the Republican Movement, at first. They later turned against the idea because the British would not attend. The Dublin government, as expected, was totally opposed to the idea of giving "terrorists a platform."

However, although the forum did not happen, I believe it helped to further our concept that Washington held the key to unlocking the stalemate in the North. It also made nonsense out of the Dublin government's allegation that the Caucus was supporting violence when we were trying to organize a Peace Forum in Washington.

Back in Boston, I concentrated on making preparations for my move to Washington. But, before that, a couple of things should be mentioned. I began to finalize the naturalization process of becoming a U.S. citizen. When I went for my final interview, the official had a copy of *Trinity* by Leon Uris sitting on his desk. He was an Irish Catholic, and proud of it. He conducted all the questioning, and I got all the answers right – until he came to the part about my being prepared to bear arms in defense of the United States. "Catholic priests do not bear arms," I responded. He sat up in the chair and with obvious relish said, "So, Father, tell me where in the U.S. Constitution does it exempt Catholic priests from bearing arms?" I told him I had a problem with that. Then he told me that I would have to help him out because if I did not give the right answer I would be denied citizenship. So he said, "Father. I'm going to ask you that question again, and I can only ask it once. I am going to make it easy for you and ask, "If the communists invaded Boston would you bear arms to defend Boston?" I asked him not to say that but instead to ask me if the British invaded. He did, and I said yes.

When the interview was over, he confided that my file was the largest he had ever seen, indicating with his hands that it was about 3 feet tall. And me in the Land of the Free only five years! I became a U.S. citizen on May 8, 1979.

The Visa Issue

But back to the Peace Forum: if the forum was going to work, then Irish Republicans would have to be allowed to enter the United States, from which they had been banned for a number of years. Opposing the visa double standard had been one of our main campaigns: Loyalist paramilitaries were given visas to enter the U.S., Irish Republicans were not. I had asked my good friend Congressman Hamilton Fish (R-NY) to take the lead on the visa issue. Congressman Fish was the very first Member I had signed up for the Ad Hoc Committee in 1977. Of course, Mario Biaggi had also asked him to join, but as Mario stressed, it was important that the Members be invited to join by me as the Committee was meant to be representing the Irish-American community.

I had become very close to Fish. Indeed, before I had moved to Washington, he telephoned me in Boston to tell me that because I had spoken so highly of him in his Congressional District, the Irish groups wanted to honor him at an event. He told them he would accept, on one condition: "that Fr. McManus was the speaker." And he was telephoning me with that request. Needless to say, I agreed to speak.

Congressman Fish was the ranking Republican on the Subcommittee on Immigration, Citizenship and International Law (which came under the full Judiciary Committee).The Chairman of the Subcommittee was Joshua Eilberg (D-PA), also a good supporter of the Irish cause. Both of them got the Judiciary Committee Chairman, Peter Rodino (D-PA) – famous for chairing the impeachment proceedings against Richard Nixon – to commission them to investigate the issue. He directed them thus: "Respected members of the Irish-American community [i.e. the Irish National Caucus] have indicated that U.S. consular officers at posts in London, Belfast and Dublin have recently been more reluctant to issue non-immigrant visas ... I believe the interests of the Committee on the Judiciary would be well served if you would ... interview ... the officials ... to determine whether their decisions are arbitrary ..."[19]

Congressman Fish was really insistent that I travel with them, but I could not, so I sent Fred O'Brien instead. Their visit to Ireland and London took place from August 28 to September 1, 1978. It was a major coup for the Irish National Caucus, and their report of 675 pages totally exposed the double standard of the visa policy: "The delegation feels that the Department of State may have acted unfairly ... the delegation failed to understand the rationale of labeling only the individuals in the Provisional IRA as terrorists and exonerating individuals in Loyalist paramilitary organizations ..."[20]

The London and Dublin governments were furious at the report and, of course, they blamed me and the Irish National Caucus.

And how did the Republican Movement show their gratitude to me for orchestrating this major indictment of the visa policy that excluded them from the U.S.? On September 27, 1978, the IRA made a most unusual statement: "The Irish Republican Army would like to put on record that Dr. Fred Burns O'Brien is persona non grata. Signed, P. O'Neill."[21]

Because they had given me no advance notice, which would have been the decent thing to do, I knew the statement was a way of getting at me, and not really about attacking Fred. And sure enough, when I later met with Ruairí Ó Brádaigh, Dave O'Connell and Joe Cahill in the Sinn Féin office in Dublin in December 1979, I asked them if the statement was meant as much for me as for Fred. "About sixty:forty," said Ó Brádaigh, sternly. "Who's the sixty and who's the forty?" I asked. "You're the sixty, Fr. Sean,"

said O'Connell in his great Cork accent, but no twinkle in his eye
this time.

They obviously thought Fred was much more important to the
workings of the Caucus than he really was, and that without him I
would be handicapped. In truth, Fred did very little actual work for
the Caucus, and was mostly only seen in my company. The ironic
thing was that since they were trying to "crack the big whip and
keep me in line," there was no way I could be seen to accept that.
As a consequence, I kept Fred on much longer than I would have
otherwise done.

I made a public statement that, "My response is to simply
point out that it is irrelevant what group or party in Ireland finds
Fred O'Brien acceptable or unacceptable."[22]

Gerry Adams was also supposed to be at that meeting in the
Sinn Féin office. The other three leaders were noticeably concerned
that he did not show. And I realized something was wrong – my
first glimpse of the brewing problem between Ó Brádaigh and
Adams.

Later in the Caucus office on Capitol Hill, a BBC correspondent
from Belfast told me that a Republican spokesman was able to tell
him that the IRA could not be seen to be attacking a brother of
Patrick Mc Manus, so instead they had a slap at Fred O'Brien to
bring me into line. But that, too, would change – soon the IRA
would have no scruples about attacking me.

There is, however, a peculiar corollary to Fred O'Brien being
formally declared "persona non grata" by the IRA. Years later –
after I got rid of him – he re-emerged as a hysterical critic of mine,
in an interesting capacity, on an interesting platform. He is "the
Washington Correspondent" (even though it's years since he lived
in this city) for the Dublin newspaper, *Saoirse*, under the name,
Peadar Mac Fhínín. *Saoirse* is the organ of Republican Sinn Fein,
which has until recently been led by Ruairí Ó Brádaigh, former
president of Sinn Fein. Ó Brádaigh – along with the late Dave
O'Connell – would have been in key positions of influence when
the IRA declared Fred "persona non grata." And yet Fred is now
given this platform. When Ó Brádaigh was asked what happened

to the IRA's declaration, he simply replied: "It lapsed."

But can such a declaration simply lapse? Must it not be lifted? And who decided it lapsed? Now, remember here that Republican Sinn Fein split from Sinn Fein and the IRA in 1986. It sees itself as the true Irish Republican Movement.

Why would Ó Brádaigh have an interest in giving O'Brien a platform from which to attack me? For example, O'Brien in the July and October 2011 issues of *Saoirse* makes the bizarre and crazy charge that I did not even know Congressman Fish until a long time after Fish got involved in the Irish issue, and that I was opposed at that time to Irish Republicans getting visas!

Ó Brádaigh first used O'Brien as an excuse to attack the Irish National Caucus; now he is using O'Brien himself to attack the Caucus. What is going on here? Who is pulling the strings? Furthermore, did *Saoirse* ever even inform its readers that the IRA had declared their "Washington Correspondent" "persona non grata?"

Furthermore, O'Brien is now in cahoots with a malcontent in New Jersey who has opposed the Irish National Caucus virtually from the beginning. This individual has never built up, just torn down, and I never trusted him. From the moment I met him, my Kinawley antenna went into overdrive. He has allegedly done Ó Brádaigh's bidding for many years (or could it be the other way around?). Ironically he is the same guy who plotted to have the IRA declare O'Brien persona non grata. And now they are both plotting together. For what ends and for whose benefit? Again, what is going on here? Perhaps *Saoirse* can enlighten its readers.

I will return to this subject (who was really behind the attacks on me and the Irish National Caucus?) later on in this book.

12

Move to Washington

*Thus Mc Manus became Britain's nemesis in America,
the driving force that would eventually erode Britain's
influence within the U.S. government.*

Joseph E. Thompson[1]

I mentioned previously that while at the Vatican I felt I was being drawn to the ineluctable conclusion that if we were going to get the job done (whatever that might eventually be), I knew I would probably have to "go full time."

When we had finished our business at the Vatican, Bishop Drury and I broke away from the rest of the delegation to pray in St. Peter's. When we finished praying, I told the Bishop I wanted to talk to him in confidence. We sat in the pews and I told him about a recurring dream I was having: "I am rushing back from some Irish activity to the Redemptorist rectory to check the assignment board only to discover I'm late for some assigned duty. I wake up in a panic."

Bishop Drury listened very sympathetically. And, of course, one didn't have to be a dream interpreter to see what was going on. "You shouldn't have to feel so torn," he said. "I must see how I can help."

With that I knelt down and asked for his blessing. When I got up, it was as if a huge weight had been lifted off my shoulders. Bishop Drury was seen in his Diocese of Corpus Christi as a very conservative man. And he certainly would have eschewed all talk about charismatic blessings or healings. But something happened to me when he blessed me there in St. Peter's. I was confirmed in the peace of Christ – I don't know how else to put it. And man, would I need that peace as the attacks from all sides would keep escalating: from the British, the Irish government, SDLP and finally from the IRA and Sinn Féin – almost as if directed by the same hand.

Over the next two years the Bishop and I talked about how I could be less "torn." He then made the remarkably generous offer that if the Redemptorists would agree, I could come under his jurisdiction and he would appoint me to a Special Ministry of Justice and Peace for Ireland. What a courageous gesture from a conservative Bishop! And here is where praxis trumps theory every time: the Bishop was born in 1902. His experience of the Black and Tans was real. And he had not forgotten.

With Vatican II, the Catholic Church had begun to recognize the validity and importance of the "Special Ministry." And with the new stress that "action on behalf of justice was a constitutive dimension of the preaching of the Gospel" (*Justice in the World*), why should there not be a Special Ministry for that? Bishop Drury was not scared of the British government. And so in December 1978 he appointed me to a full time Special Ministry of Justice and Peace for Ireland.

Before I left, I met with the Archbishop of Boston, Cardinal Medeiros, to ask for his blessing on my new Special Ministry. He provided me with a warm letter of introduction to Cardinal Baum of Washington, so despite the efforts of the Irish Consul in Boston to get me silenced, the Cardinal was giving me his blessings. Indeed, I am firmly convinced – and so was Bishop Drury – that one of the main reasons why the Irish Consul escalated her attacks so strongly was to sabotage my appointment to the Special Ministry. The word had somehow leaked out, leading the Bishop to wonder, "Sean, do you think the buzzards have our phones tapped?" "Buzzard" was the strongest word I ever heard him use for the British government.

In a press release announcing my appointment, dated December 11, 1978, Bishop Drury said: "I have been deeply impressed by [Fr. McManus'] dedication to human rights, justice and peace in Ireland. The Catholic Church teaches that certain priests are given special charisms, or 'gifts' for special work. I recognize that Father McManus has been given by God a 'charism' for this work. He has truly distinguished himself by his total commitment to peace in his country. Anyone who has met Father McManus or has heard him speak must have been deeply impressed by his determination and zeal. He is uniquely suited for this Special Ministry. For the past several years, in the face of disappointments and frustration, he has worked with true Christian Charity. Father McManus is committed to nonviolence, reconciliation and freedom in Ireland. I ask people to pray hard that his work will be blessed."

Opening of Capitol Hill Office

On December 10, International Human Rights Day, 1978 the Irish National Caucus opened its National Office on Capitol Hill. December 10 was also the date Patrick went on the run in 1956. This would be first time in Irish-American history that the Irish had an office on Capitol Hill to lobby for justice and peace in Ireland. (The Friends of Irish Freedom opened an office in 1919, not on Capitol Hill but downtown. It lasted only a few years.)

I had moved down to Washington without a red cent to my name. But I had called a dear old friend, Howard Smith (not the Howard K. Smith, whose broadcast I had interrupted) and he gave me $5,000 for the first month's and last month's rent of the office on Capitol Hill.

Now we were perfectly positioned to increase our influence on Capitol Hill. The Washington Bureau of *The Boston Globe* predicted that, "with the arrival of McManus here, one thing is certain, [Tip] O'Neill will probably feel at least two thorns on that issue." The other "thorn" was Congressman Biaggi.

Now that I had moved to Capitol Hill to lobby full time, the roles of Bernadette O'Reilly-McAuliffe and Fred O'Brien petered out. Rita Mullan, who had arrived in the U.S. from Belfast in May 1977, became Executive Director. She did a lot of fine work until she became ill in 1983.

I immediately went to work on an eighteen-hour daily schedule. I knocked on the door of virtually every Member of Congress, building up goodwill for the Irish cause, signing them up as members of the Ad Hoc Committee for Irish Affairs, putting pressure where needed, but always politely and respectfully. I made sure I would never mislead the Members or give them wrong information. I immediately leveled with them that the Irish government was bitterly opposed to me, not to mention the British. I acknowledged that I had in the past, as a private individual, expressed support for the IRA but that the Irish National Caucus was nonviolent, and that we would never compromise them – that we would only seek to get Members of Congress to support nonviolent projects. I also emphasized that we would not seek any special favors for Ireland, only for America to apply a single, not a double, standard in its policy of promoting international human rights; that the "hands off Northern Ireland lest we offend the Brits policy" had to end; that left to the triangle of Belfast, Dublin and London, no solution could emerge; that an outside catalyst was needed, and that it was only possible and proper for America to be that catalyst.

Knowing that we could not depend on Senator Kennedy and Speaker O'Neill, whom the Irish Embassy, working in cahoots with the British Embassy, had scared off, I concentrated on non-Irish and non-Catholic Members of Congress. And to further broaden and "mainstream" the Irish issue, I made a point of enlisting the support of Republican Members of Congress. The Washington correspondent for *The Irish Times*, Sean Cronin, would write, "The 'Irish question' was almost exclusively a Democratic Party matter up to recently when the Irish National Caucus ... began to make inroads in Republican ranks."[2]

As we began to make impact on Capitol Hill, the media in Northern Ireland sent reporters to check us out. The well-known journalist David McKittrick would describe our approach thus: "The Caucus has done some effective lobbying in the past few years, achieving its propaganda successes simply by doing it the American way – playing the lobbying game according to Washington's rules, making contacts and friends in Congress, presenting the human rights case convincingly. It has become the Madison Avenue of Irish Republicanism ..."[3] And another equally well-known journalist, Barry White of the *Belfast Telegraph*, wrote, "from there [the Caucus office] Fr. Mc Manus is just two and a half minutes from the Capitol building, where he is becoming one of the best known faces among the lobbyists ... the way the British and Irish Embassies react to what they see as the twin menace of the Caucus and the Ad Hoc Committee of Congressman Biaggi demonstrate its potential."[4]

One of the first signs that we were beginning to have an impact was – according to a senior *Boston Globe* writer – the change in tone of Teddy Kennedy and Tip O'Neill.

On March 15, 1979, *Boston Globe* journalist Ken Harnett telephoned me and told me he had no hesitation in believing the Caucus was responsible for the change in the upcoming St. Patrick's Day statement critical of the British. I immediately told him that I never even had a meeting with Kennedy. Harnett persisted, explaining he had checked it out and because of the pressure the Caucus was putting on Congress, Tipp and Kennedy had been forced to move to "cover their asses."

Two days later, Harnett would write:

> The leader of the Irish National Caucus listened as the long statement from the "Big Four" – Senators Kennedy and Moynihan, Speaker O'Neill and Gov. Carey – was read to him over the telephone, and for a moment, Fr. Sean Mc Manus was almost at a loss for words. "I'm a little inarticulate right now," said the Ulster-born priest. "God, I'm elated. I welcome that statement enormously." ... The conventional

wisdom, as reflected in the "Big Four's" earlier statements, was to stress the responsibility of the Irish Republican Army for the violence in the North, and to warn Irish-Americans against giving either financial or psychological support ... [McManus] felt frustrated trying to get across the idea of British culpability for the violence and stalemate in the North ... But suddenly, this year, someone listened ... It was not that McManus had changed, or the IRA, or the perception of the IRA ... Rather, it was a variety of changes in the Irish situation itself, not the least of which was the growth in the awareness of the human-rights violations ...

And so, the annual St. Patrick's Day proclamation had its obligatory condemnation of sectarian violence again this year but it had much more. It had a scolding of the British government, not just for its political lassitude but for its acquiescence in "official brutality and violation of human rights." The pressure on the British was being raised by several degrees and Sean McManus couldn't hide his great enjoyment. "Everyone was saying we were terrorists last year for saying these things. Now it's the popular respectable thing."[5]

But not everyone would be pleased with our success, as my first St. Patrick's Day Parade in Washington would show.

Sean Donlon – FitzGerald's Protégé

The late Matt Hannon, an ardent Irishman and very active member of the Irish National Caucus, was the Chairman of the Parade. Matt insisted that I would lead the Caucus contingent seated in a fancy limousine, with the name Irish National Caucus emblazoned on both sides. When the limousine arrived at the reviewing stand, Matt announced me with great theatricality and with aplomb escorted me up on the reviewing stand. I was seated next to a local bishop, so naturally I stood and shook his hand. Then I realized that Sean Donlon, Irish Ambassador to Washington (1978–1981) was seated next to the bishop. I knew he was hostile to me, but I did the well-mannered thing, held out my hand and said: "Happy St. Patrick's Day, Mr. Ambassador." With the entire reviewing stand looking on, Donlon burrowed himself deeper in his chair and refused to shake my hand. I kept my hand extended for a long while, until everyone could plainly see what was happening.

Donlon was a protégé of Garret FitzGerald. FitzGerald claims he had got Taoiseach Jack Lynch to appoint Donlon as Ambassador to Washington.[6]

Donlon would go on to be a bitter and hysterical opponent. The ever-colourful Con Howard, at that time an official of the Irish Embassy, recounted this story to me: Donlon was speaking to him in the Irish Embassy, giving out about us. "In six weeks I will have stomped out the Irish National Caucus," he said as he stomped the floor with his foot.

Mind you, the same Con Howard did not hesitate to attack us when so directed. On the night of that same St. Patrick's Day, I was in his home for a party. He hoisted a glass of champagne, drank it down and then with great flourish smashed it into the giant fireplace, vowing with patriotic fervor never to say a bad word about the Caucus, no matter who ordered him. A few days later, he had a letter in *The Washington Post* charging the Caucus with supporting violence. That evening I ran into him at an event in the Library of Congress and I said, "Con, what happened to your dramatic vow never to attack us?" He replied with a sheepish smile, "Orders from the Captain." I was never sure who he meant.

The strange thing about Donlon is that years earlier, while I was still in Boston, and he was head of the Anglo-Irish Division of the Department of Foreign Affairs, he called me from the home of a mutual friend in New York City. He told me there was no interest in a united Ireland by anyone in the Irish government. And that if "Ó Brádaigh and O'Connell were to take over in the morning", he would be working for them (Ó Brádaigh was then President of Sinn Féin and O'Connell the most visible IRA leader in Ireland).

As Ambassador, Donlon disgusted Irish-Americans by his silence about British violence and human rights violations.

He seemed only concerned about IRA violence, and he had a particular animus for me. One former member of an important Fianna Fáil national organization amazed me by suggesting that one of Donlon's problems with me could be explained by the "spoiled priest" syndrome, i.e. that Donlon had been studying for the priesthood but left the seminary. Therefore, according to the former Fianna Fáil apparatchik, when Donlon arrived in Washington, he was really incensed to find a priest (me) saying, "Don't listen to the Irish Embassy, listen to the Irish National Caucus instead."

But whatever explained Donlon's problems, he seemed to be obsessed with destroying the Irish National Caucus. So much so that we launched a campaign to have him recalled as Ambassador, and it almost worked, too. This is how it came about.

The veteran Donegal politician, Neil Blaney, TD and MEP, was on a speaking tour for the Irish National Caucus. He was in our office on December 7, 1979 when Charlie Haughey called him with the dramatic news that he, Haughey, had just been elected Taoiseach. Before hanging up the phone, Blaney said, "Fr. Sean McManus is right beside me. Why don't you say hello?" There was silence. I knew very well Haughey would not speak to me. Then Blaney hung up, and said Haughey could not speak then, but that he said he would call back. "Yeah, right," I skeptically thought to myself.

But, nonetheless, it did represent the possibility of an improvement. Taoiseach Jack Lynch was gone. Blaney was now in a position to influence Haughey, at least to some degree. Maybe he could convince Haughey to issue a new policy directive to the Irish Embassy, like stating that British injustice was the enemy not Irish-Americans.

Blaney became convinced Donlon had to go after we told him about how Donlon had sabotaged an effort to free the Birmingham Six.

A month earlier, November 1979, the Caucus had brought Fr. Raymond Murray from Armagh to Washington to help promote our campaign to free the Birmingham Six. We brought him along to meet our dear friend, the late Congressman Hamilton Fish (R-NY) whom I held in great affection and esteem. Ham, as he was known, was the great grandson of U.S. Secretary of State Hamilton Fish who, having slapped the Fenians on the wrists for one of their invasions of Canada, urged that they be released. On August 16, 1870, Secretary Fish wrote to President Grant: "I always supposed that you would deem it wise to release the prisoners convicted of participation in the Fenian raid. Purely political prisoners are the worst kind of birds to keep caged."[7] I always kidded Congressman Fish that the reason he was so good on the Irish issue was that he had to do penance for his great grandfather locking up the Fenians in the first place.

I remember thinking it was a special symbolic moment when – in Fish's office, right in front of his great grandfather's photo – I introduced my colleague Bob Bateman to the Congressman. Bob is the great grandnephew of the famed Fenian, Captain Timothy Deasy, who was rescued from the Fenian prison-van in Manchester, England (1867) and who – according to Bob – also participated in one of the Fenian invasions of Canada, as had also Bob's great grandfather.

Anyway, one of the results of bringing Fr. Murray to meet Ham Fish was that the Congressman promised to try and get the law faculty of some prestigious university to examine the entire case of the miscarriage of justice that the Birmingham Six represented.

Donlon Moves Against Birmingham Six

Fish, an officer in the American Consulate in Dublin in the 1950s, being a very diplomatic man, met with Donlon at the Irish Embassy to inform him of his plans. Donlon went berserk. Fish told me that he had never been talked to in such a disrespectful fashion. Donlon followed up the meeting with a letter on November 6, 1979:

Dear Mr. Fish,

In view of our recent conversations and correspondence, I thought it might be useful to let you have the attached recent reports from *The Irish Times*.

The report dated October 27 describes a recent interest of yours in the Birmingham bombings case as "the fruit of the work of Fr. Raymond Murray of Armagh ..." In the report of October 22, Fr. Murray is criticized by the leading elected representatives of both sections of the divided Northern Ireland community..."[8]

The two "elected representatives" were Gerry Fitt and Martin Smyth, the head of the Orange Order, who was not then an MP.

So here was the Irish Ambassador in Washington using the head of the Orange Order to discredit a Catholic priest of the calibre of Fr. Murray, all with a view to stopping the campaign to free the Birmingham Six! Neil Blaney was outraged and embarrassed that, in his name and in the name of the Irish people, Donlon would dare pull that stuff. He began to privately urge the new Haughey government to replace Donlon. Haughey agreed but Donlon rallied Tip O'Neill, Teddy Kennedy and other important Americans to intervene on his behalf (not what one would expect from an ambassador). Haughey backed off. *The Washington Post* reported that "Irish Prime Minister Charles Haughey decided today to keep Sean Donlon as Ireland's ambassador in Washington after being warned that replacing him would harm relations between Haughey's seven-month-old government and leading Irish-American politicians. Haughey was told that he would upset Sens. Edward M. Kennedy (D-MA) and Patrick Moynihan (D-NY), House Speaker Thomas P. O'Neill (D-MA) and New York Gov. Hugh Carey if he removed Donlon in response to complaints about him from the Washington-based militant Irish nationalist lobby, the Irish National Caucus, and its ally in congress, Rep. Mario Biaggi (D-NY), according to well-informed sources."[9]

Later Brian Lenihan, Minister for Foreign Affairs, told us on the phone, "maybe we will have another stab at Donlon and send him to Tehran" (which was then in the midst of the American hostages crisis).

But even when Donlon was eventually replaced in 1981, it did not really change the bad attitude of the Irish Embassy. That only changed with the beginning of the Irish peace process and the IRA ceasefire of August 31, 1994.

In November 1985, Donlon's opposition to the campaign to free the Birmingham Six resurfaced in the Irish newspapers. *The Irish Press* reported: "In yesterday's *Sunday Press*, Mr. Donlon said any action he had taken had been on the instructions of the Irish Government. But last night, the then Foreign Minister, Mr. O'Kennedy, to whom the diplomat was answerable, rejected the claim ... Mr. O'Kennedy said ... he did not give Mr. Donlon any authority to write such a letter."[10]

As I had expected, Haughey himself would go on to condemn the Irish National Caucus on July 27, 1980. But he did so under threat from FitzGerald: "A threat to end the bipartisan policy on Northern Ireland is contained in a letter which will be sent from the Fine Gael leader, Dr. Garret FitzGerald, to the Taoiseach today calling on Mr. Haughey to spell out his attitude to IRA front organizations in the United States."[11] And FitzGerald, eager to claim the credit for the condemnation, released a copy of the letter he had sent to Haughey on July 21, demanding such condemnation:

> You will have seen that John Hume, Frank Cluskey and myself speaking independently ... urged on the 9th July, that you clarify at once your Government's position with respect specifically to Congressman Biaggi, and to organizations such as Northern Aid and Irish National Caucus ... Failure to re-state in unambiguous terms the position of three successive governments on this matter can only confuse the issue in the United States, as may be seen by the statement on RTÉ news programme last week by the Rev. Sean McManus, speaking on behalf of the Irish National Caucus, that he presumed that they were "right in thinking that there is a difference between the policies of Mr. Haughey and Mr. Lynch – it is our general impression and hope that Mr. Haughey's policies will be quite different ..."[12]

In his autobiography, FitzGerald crows: "My letter achieved its purpose ... the Taoiseach provided belatedly the necessary clear repudiation ... The Caucus' leader, Sean McManus, responded that the Taoiseach's statement was a response to "threats and blackmail from me", and that I had "once again dictated policy to Mr. Haughey" – a statement that I did not feel it necessary to deny."[13]

But here it must be noted, as FitzGerald makes clear, that John Hume was in full collusion with the Irish government's policy of marginalization of any group that wanted the British embarrassed and pressured. John would later go on to do great work on the peace process, but for too long, he, in effect, gave the British a pass, as will be seen when I give the history of the MacBride Principles.

Donlon was the first person who ever refused to shake my hand. The second and only other person ever to do so, was Donlon's master, Garret FitzGerald. It happened this way: on August 2, 1979, the State Department announced it had suspended the sale of U.S. weapons to the RUC. (This was one of our greatest victories and I will explain it in a moment.) I was back in Belfast at the time so naturally the media was very interested in what I had to say about the arms ban. As a consequence, I was constantly in the news. When my press work was over, I noticed that Garret FitzGerald, now no longer in government, was due to give a lecture at the Corrymeela Reconciliation Centre on the north Antrim coast. I decided to attend. And so did, it appeared, the entire Supreme Council of the UDA, including Andy Tyrie, Glenn Barr, etc. FitzGerald spoke eloquently about the need for both parts of Ireland to come together (albeit not in a united Ireland) in mutual understanding and forgiveness. During the question-and-answer period, he warmly addressed the UDA leaders by their first names, clearly making great play for the UDA. Now remember, at that very time, the UDA, with the cooperation of the British government and security forces, were slaughtering hundreds of innocent Catholics. After the speech, FitzGerald, his wife and a core group went into a private room. The Rev. Ray Davey, founder of the Centre, then came and invited me to join the "inner circle."

FitzGerald Refuses to Shake My Hand

When I entered the room, the group was sitting in a semi-circle, facing the entrance, with FitzGerald and his wife sitting in the middle. The Rev. Davey announced, "This is Fr. Sean McManus, president of the Irish National Caucus." Of course, all of them knew me anyway, even though I was not in my clerical collar but in a suit and tie. As I approached the semi-circle to the right, they started to stand and I shook their hands. Out of the corner of my eye I noticed FitzGerald was still sitting down with his eyes resolutely fixed on the floor. "This is going to be interesting," I thought, suspecting what was going to happen. I pleasantly shook the hands of all the polite Ulster folk, as I approached FitzGerald. When in front of him, I held out my hand and said, "I enjoyed your lecture, Dr. FitzGerald." Like a clocking hen he fluttered in his seat. I kept my hand extended, it seemed forever. He finally hissed, "Please go away, you are creating a disturbance." I calmly responded that the Rev. Davey had invited me. Davey was standing by my side and he nodded in assent.

I finally moved on, skipping over Mrs. FitzGerald, to shake the hand of Glenn Barr who was sitting next to her. With a smile, I expansively said, "Maybe you guys are right, after all, Glenn, that there are two nations in Ireland." He laughed loudly. (The UDA at the time were advocating an independent Northern Ireland based on the alleged premise that Northerners and Southerners were two distinct peoples.)

So there you have it. That's the Blue Shirt's version of reconciliation in Ireland. I had shaken the hands of ex-Black and Tans, B Specials, RUC, British soldiers, and leaders of every Protestant paramilitary group in Northern Ireland. But FitzGerald, in best Blue Shirt tradition, refused my hand, after waxing eloquently about reconciliation.

Of course, FitzGerald, apart from his long antipathy for me, was seething in particular about our success in stopping the sale of U.S. weapons to the RUC, and about all the publicity the media was giving me. Because, you see, the obvious issue it raised was why did the Caucus have to do it? Why had the Dublin government not done it?

RUC Gun Ban

But it was not just the likes of FitzGerald who resented the Caucus victory. *The Irish Times* clearly had a problem with it. I spoke to a young male and female reporter in the Belfast office of *The Irish Times*. The male reporter, whom I had never met before, could barely hide his hostility. He pompously told me that his sources in Washington told him that the Caucus had nothing to do with the ban.

Months later, *U.S. News and World Report* would write: "high among the concern of the Irish National Caucus is human rights in Northern Ireland. When members protested the issuance of a license to ship machine guns and magnum pistols to the Ulster police, the shipment ceased."[14] And on May 28, 1980, *The New York Times* ran an editorial, "What's a Boycott Between Friends?" Referring to the RUC ban, it said: "What should have been a routine transaction aroused the opposition of the Irish National Caucus, whose leader, the Rev. Sean Mc Manus, has been an open supporter – and occasional critic – of the Provisional wing of the Irish Republican Army. The Caucus has its ardent partisans in Congress, and House Speaker O'Neill was moved to oppose granting an export license for guns ..."[15]

I duly sent both articles to the male *Irish Times* reporter in Belfast with a letter suggesting that he might want to reconsider his position. I also sent copies to Douglas Gageby, then Editor of *The Irish Times*, and to Sean Cronin, the Washington correspondent. I never heard back from the reporter in Belfast. Cronin emphatically denied that he was that reporter's alleged "source." Later a well-established reporter from another newspaper told me that *The Irish Times* liked to indulge in the conceit that it was not only the paper of record, but that it also shaped and influenced national events – and that it had to give its stamp of approval before a person was considered a "player."

The Washington Post would also refute the pompous young man from *The Irish Times* when it wrote: "British officials believe the Caucus and Biaggi's ad hoc committee are responsible for influencing the Carter administration to hold up the sale of American-made guns to the police in Northern Ireland ..."[16]

But the Rev. Paisley had no doubt who was responsible. He said it was an insult, but said that clearly it was seen as a triumph for the Irish National Caucus in America and the Ad Hoc Congressional Committee for Irish Affairs, led by Congressman Mario Biaggi.[17]

Notice in that *New York Times* editorial it says, Speaker O'Neill was "moved." It uses more parliamentary language than Ken Harnett of *The Boston Globe*, but it amounts to the same thing: O'Neill was bounced into taking that position because we made the pressure irresistible. Tipp did not want to take that position, but he had to. Why do I say that? Because O'Neill, and indeed Teddy Kennedy, only took anti-British positions when forced to because the Dublin government had pressured them into silence: criticize the British, and you will be seen to be pro-IRA and anti-Irish government.

Perfect proof that the Irish government did not want the RUC to be blacklisted by the United States is that when we got dozens of Members of Congress to co-sign Congressman Mario Biaggi's letter of protest to the State Department, Matthew Nimetz, Counselor, replied in a letter, defending the weapons sale to the RUC: "The Royal Ulster Constabulary is the legally constituted police force in Northern Ireland ..." He then plays his trump card: "In this connection I would note that Irish Foreign Minister O'Kennedy, in a May 31 foreign policy speech to the Dail, pledged the continued cooperation of the Irish police and army with the Royal Ulster Constabulary in the fight against violence in Northern Ireland."[18]

Who do you think provided Mr. Nimetz with that speech? Do you think he just happened to have it in his hip pocket? Congressman Biaggi responded to that *New York Times* editorial. As a matter of respect, I quote The Great Man at length:

"It was my amendment to the fiscal 1980 Department of State appropriations bill which led to the decision by the State Department to suspend further sales or shipments of United States arms to the RUC pending a full review of our policy.

My initial reason for raising this issue in Congress was the incomparability of the sale of arms to the RUC and our foreign policy philosophy – respect for human rights. Section 502 (b) of the Foreign Assistance Act of 1961 bars the sale or export of any U.S. arms to nations or organizations that engage in persistent patterns of human rights violations ... Finally, the leadership provided by the Irish National Caucus on the issue of suspending arms shipments is fully consistent with their role as the leading Irish-American organization working for peace, justice and human rights for Ireland."[19]

Caucus' Growing Influence

It was clear to all by now that the Irish National Caucus was beginning to have significant influence in changing American foreign policy on Northern Ireland – despite the opposition of both the British and Irish Embassies.

The secret of our success was in hammering away on the theme of the single standard: America must apply a single standard, not a double standard, to human rights in Northern Ireland. I zeroed in like a laser beam on all double standards. For example, we had long opposed the policy of refusing visas to Irish Republicans who wanted to come to the United States to denounce British policy in Northern Ireland, yet the Rev. Ian Paisley was allowed into America. Because he was an MP, I knew it would be all the more difficult to frame the double standard issue. But when the State Department refused a visa to Owen Carron MP, a Fermanagh neighbor of mine, who was elected to fill the seat of martyred Bobby Sands, I struck like lightning. Now I knew we could have Paisley's visa revoked, and we did, on December 21, 1981.

I will let the late David Nyhan of *The Boston Globe* tell

the story: "The State Department yesterday revoked the visa of militant Northern Ireland Protestant leader Rev. Ian Paisley, who had planned a visit to the United States next month, because of the "divisive tone" of his recent speeches ... The campaign to revoke Paisley's visa was launched Dec. 2 by the Irish National Caucus ... [which] devised a strategy of asking conservative Republicans to lead the fight in congress, instead of the Irish-Catholic Democrats ..."[20]

We got 125 Members of the House and 22 Senators (including Senator Joe Biden, now U.S. Vice President) to co-sign a letter by Congressman Bill Carney (R-NY) and Senator Al D'Amato (R-NY) to Secretary of State Alexander Haig demanding that Paisley be refused entry. And that number did not include Tip O'Neill and Teddy Kennedy who again were forced to take action. When they saw that the two arch-fundamentalists, Senator Strom Thurmond (R-SC) and Senator Jess Helms (R-NC), had signed on, they simply had to get on board. In a previous article Nyhan pointed out that, when O'Neill and Kennedy finally wrote to the Secretary of State, "the letter from the two Massachusetts Democrats followed by several hours a speech on the floor by Rep. William Carney ..."[21]

In the lead-up to the visa denial, Paisley kept saying that "priest Mc Manus would never stop me going to America." When he was stopped, he then started blaming Prime Minister Margaret Thatcher and President Ronald Reagan. Of course, it was not lost on him that U.S. Secretary of State Al Haig was Catholic, with a Jesuit brother. Paisley's benefactor, Bob Jones III, attacked Haig as "a monster in human flesh" and publicly prayed that God would "smite him hip and thigh, bone and marrow, heart and lungs."[22]

1981 Hunger Strike

The year 1981, of course, was the year of the Irish hunger strike. We had been trying to move heaven and earth to get America to put pressure on Margaret Thatcher to grant the hunger strikers' demands. I had asked Congressman Hamilton Fish (R-

NY) to work on his good friend Vice President George H. Bush. When Fish called me to tell me that Bush had gotten back to him with a final decision that President Reagan would not intercede, I knew Bobby Sands was going to die. Twelve days before his death I embarked on my own hunger strike right outside the British Embassy. Because I did not hold any poster, and because I was by myself, I did not have to remain at the mandatory distance of 500 yards. Prince Charles was staying at the Embassy and each time he left in the car, he had to drive right past me. I could see him peering out of the darkened car windows – not without empathy, or so I thought. Certainly he was not glaring with hostility. I stayed on hunger strike for twelve days, only drinking water, losing 25 lbs. When Bobby died I came off the hunger strike, knowing I had to continue the work.

But I felt disgusted that although two of the most powerful men in the world, President Reagan and Speaker O'Neill, had Irish roots, they did not lift a finger to save Bobby Sands and his nine fellow-patriots who went on to die, "hungering for justice." I could never think the same way again about Reagan and O'Neill.

On May 12 Francis Hughes (twenty-four) was the second Irish martyr to die on the 1981 Hunger Strike. Francis is commonly regarded as being one of the most fearless soldiers the IRA ever produced. On May 30, the Irish National Caucus brought his brother, Oliver, from Bellaghy, County Derry, to Washington. Oliver – one of the most dynamic and charismatic speakers I have ever heard – declared in that unique Bellaghy accent: "I came to the United States to give a simple message. My brother, Francis, was not a criminal. He was an Irish patriot."[23] Later we would bring out Mrs. McElwee, the mother of Oliver's first cousin Tom, who would also die on the hunger strike. I marveled at the fortitude of this woman as she went around Capitol Hill speaking to politicians and the media, trying to save the life of her son. I would later attend Tom's funeral, and have my heart broken at the sight of his eight beautiful sisters carrying his coffin. I would also attend the funerals of hunger strikers Ciaran Doherty and Kevin Lynch.

13

The Old Sow that Eats Its Own Farrow

Loyalty is the sister of Justice – Horace[1]

James Joyce, through his alter ego, Stephen Dedalus, famously quipped, "Ireland is the old sow that eats her farrow."[2] That, of course, could be said of any institution. But maybe it can apply to the IRA with particular force.

The *Sunday World* carried the headline, with a photograph of President Carter and me, "Provos Fall Out With Caucus Priest" (March 21, 1982). The unsigned article described me as having been "long a painful thorn in the flesh of British Embassy officials in Washington" and reported on the increased attacks by the Republican Movement and Irish Northern Aid on the Caucus: "changed times indeed, when it's realized that Father McManus probably did more than any single individual to publicize the provisionals' political aims among influential people in the United States." Its conclusion was that "... the present fall-out between the Provisionals and McManus is probably due to the fact that, having built up a powerful Irish-American support lobby in the U.S., McManus doesn't want it sabotaged by heavy-handed interference ..."[3]

That certainly, in part, explained my attitude, but what were the Provisionals' reasons? I always put it down to the age-old fear of Irish leaders (whether Parnell, de Valera, IRA, Dublin government, SDLP, whoever) of the "tail wagging the dog" – that Irish-Americans would end up dictating to Ireland. It was a fear I was always sensitive to. I knew from my study of the history of Irish-American nationalism that the "home group" only fully trusted the Irish-American group to the degree it totally controlled them. I often say (half-jokingly) that that mistrust goes back to December 1866 when the American Fenians deposed James Stephen in New York at gunpoint. Stephens, the "Fenian Chief," had been trying to yet again postpone the Fenian Rising; the Americans wouldn't stand for it anymore, so they took over the Movement in both America and Ireland."[4]

But as the years have passed, and as revelations of British infiltration of the Republican Movement continues to mount, I now begin to wonder who really was behind the attacks on the Irish National Caucus. Now nothing is as simple as it once seemed.

Gerry Adams, then Vice-President of Sinn Féin, was the first to launch a personal attack on me. In a question-and-answer interview in *Hibernia Review,* he said: "The [Irish] National Caucus and especially people like Fr. McManus have been using Republicanism as a justification for what they've been involved in. They started off by calling for a United Ireland and now they're into human rights ... I think to a large extent Fr. Sean McManus is an opportunist."[5]

It was Sean Cronin, Washington correspondent for *The Irish Times*, who first alerted me to this article. "If you were an opportunist, you have picked a funny way to opportune," he laughed. Then he went on to point out that the IRA always accused priests for not speaking out because they were scared of the British and that it would damage their career, and now there was I being accused by Adams of speaking out to advance my career!

I had never met Adams, nor spoken with him, but I was struck by the unfairness of his attack. I recognized that it was the beginning of a calculated plan to put the Caucus out of business – just as the British and Irish Embassies were committed to doing. But I could not miss the irony of Adams thinking there was a contradiction between human rights and national self-determination. It was so reminiscent of de Valera's infamous dismissal of labor and social concerns in 1918, when he said "labor must wait."[6]

Adams' charge was all the more patently false since we had made our paraphrase of the Pledge of Allegiance quite famous all across America: "The Irish National Caucus believes that Ireland, too, has the right to be one nation under God, indivisible, with liberty and justice for all." The injustice of Adams' attack was unworthy of a man who was supposed to be fighting for a just cause. Justice can never be served by injustice.

Attacks Don't Deter Me

Then like clockwork, attacks followed from Irish Northern Aid Committee (Noraid) and their paper, the *Irish People*, which once lionized me. In October 1980, the *Irish People* published an editorial, dictated by the Republican Movement, which declared, "... the Caucus is an anathema to the Republican Movement in Ireland".[7] Notice the exact same term as Jack Lynch used – "anathema." It was as if the attacks were written by the same hand. And, God knows, maybe they were, as it's now known that British agents had penetrated the Republican Movement. We still don't know the full level of penetration of the Dublin Government, but it would be utterly naïve to believe it did not happen. If the Brits could "turn" Republicans with their fierce commitment and discipline, can you imagine what they could do to many of the spineless weaklings in the Dublin establishment of that time?

But I can honestly say the attacks did not really upset me too much. Because I had a clear vision of the absolute need for an Irish lobby on Capitol Hill long before others realized it, I was not going to let anything deter me from my mission – not the British or Irish Embassies, not the IRA or Gerry Adams. Years later, the *Sunday World* would reflect on this: "political observers in America say he was light years ahead of his time when he set up the Irish National Caucus to fight for justice and rights for nationalists back home in Northern Ireland."[8]

Gerry Adams went on to order a spokesman for Irish Northern Aid and editor of the *Irish People* never to mention me or the Irish

National Caucus in the *Irish People*, except to condemn me. In one absurd incident, the New York City Comptroller ran an election campaign advertisement in the *Irish People* that mentioned the Caucus, and the editor deleted the name of the Caucus. When the Comptroller's office called to demand by what right he had censored a paid advertisement, the editor plaintively pleaded he had no choice as he was under strict orders from Adams.

Years later Adams would tell someone I considered a friend that, "the big mistake Irish-Americans made was to allow Fr. McManus to seize control of the Irish National Caucus"… As if the Caucus had been built up by others, and then I pulled a coup! As if there were a long line waiting to do my job: to move to Capitol Hill with no money, and to work non stop for no real salary, for forty years! (It apparently did not occur to my friend that in telling me this he was also revealing that Adams clearly considered him to be in the anti-McManus camp).

Now, in fairness to Adams – for whom I would develop great respect – it could be said that the only thing he knew about what was happening in America was from what he was being told second-hand through Irish Northern Aid, or from other Republican leaders who had visited America.

And let me here mention one such visitor.

While I was in Boston, and after the Caucus had formally and constitutionally espoused nonviolence, Belfast Republican Jimmy Drumm came to see me at Mission Church. He had been sent to the United States to make a formal report for the Republican Movement on the state of Irish-American activity vis-a-vis The North. He was accompanied by another Belfast man.

Drumm was very unhappy about my statement on nonviolence that declared the Caucus is opposed to all violence: "Therefore, we are, logically and in the first place, opposed to British violence, the root cause of violence in Ireland." I explained my position, clearly and precisely. And I pointed out that the phrase, "no foreign principal" – which we used in all our documents from the very beginning – meant that we could not be directed by any group outside the United States, whether violent or nonviolent.

Sometime later, the sister of the man who accompanied Drumm telephoned me from New York. She told me she had to, "in conscience," tell me something: That when Drumm returned to Ireland, he gave the leadership of the Republican Movement a totally false report on what I had said. He outrageously charged that I was trying to take over the leadership of the Irish Republican Movement in America. After my telling him that the Caucus had to be nonviolent and that we could not have a foreign principal! Now here he is mendaciously reporting to the Army Council of the IRA that I was plotting to be the IRA leader in America. (The only time I ever saw Drumm again was at the funeral of hunger-striker Tom McElwee. He acted as if I were his best friend!)

Now I can well understand that often the Irish Republican Movement had to misinform the public – they are, after all, a secret movement. But how were the interests of the Republican Movement served by that false report? Who benefited? In whose interest did Drumm tell that appalling lie? What was going on here?

The late Jack Mc Kinney, columnist for the *Philadelphia Daily News*, who was sympathetic to the IRA, told me that Drumm, "on behalf of the Army Council asked him not to give any publicity to Fr. Mc Manus." Wouldn't you think the IRA had more to do than to worry about my getting publicity – especially when that publicity was causing huge embarrassment to both the British and Irish Embassies? Shouldn't the IRA have been pleased I was exposing British torture of political prisoners, British shoot-to-kill policy, anti-Catholic discrimination, etc., etc? How would silencing me help the IRA? It could only help the British. So, again, it must be asked: What exactly was going on here? Did the Army Council actually want me silenced, or was this another outright lie by Drumm?

Over the years as I struggled to keep the Irish National Caucus from being put out of business by the British-Irish Embassies and the IRA, I had assumed that each one was making separate attacks on us. But now, with hindsight and dispassionate objectivity, I must ask: What if the attacks were not indeed separate, but guided all along by the same hand – by British agents inside both the Irish Government and the IRA? Wouldn't that make complete sense and be consistent with the modus operandi of the British Government?

This is only one of the many things that has surfaced through the writing of this book. Let me give another one.

As was previously mentioned, Neil Blaney, TD and MEP, came on a speaking tour for the Irish National Caucus in December 1979. Shortly before he left Ireland, he was telephoned from New York by a former Donegal neighbor of his. The caller was a woman very active in Irish Northern Aid. She implored him to cancel his trip because it would harm the Irish cause as the Irish National Caucus had gone down the wrong road. Neil, of course, told her to get lost. Now, for years I had assumed that Ruairí ÓBrádaigh had put her up to making that call, and maybe he did. But now I am forced to wonder, as nothing is as simple as it once seemed: What if the lady were making the call on behalf of some one else? Who? Well, who stood to be most embarrassed by the Blaney visit? The Irish Embassy, of course. Blaney was a powerful politician, bitterly opposed to what he saw as Dublin's quisling-like policy on The North.

His visit would cause severe discomfort to Sean Donlon, the Irish Ambassador... Cui bono (who benefits)? Who would most benefit from Blaney's cancellation – Irish Northern Aid or the Dublin Government? What was going on here?

It was not the first time I had witnessed surprising collaboration between the Dublin Government and Irish Republicans (if in fact they were Republicans).

I became very conscious of the "pincer movement" of the Dublin Government: To IRA folk, they would present me as not Republican enough; to anti-IRA folk, they would brand me as IRA. And if that did not cover the spectrum, to Irish-Americans who were scared of getting involved, they would imply I was CIA. To right-wing Catholics, they would present me as a "rogue priest" (as former Irish Foreign Minister, Peter Barry, liked to do); and to left-wing Catholics they would argue that I was a fundamentalist cleric.

Many Irish Northern Aid members were privately disgusted by the unfair attacks on me and would secretly call me to assure me they did not approve. They would admit to me that the IRA had sent orders that Irish Northern Aid were to infiltrate, disrupt and destroy Caucus chapters throughout the country – just as the British and Irish Embassies were trying to do.

The head of Irish Northern Aid, Michael Flannery, was especially resentful of the Irish National Caucus. Because he was an old IRA man, and because he lived to be a great age, Flannery had a certain credibility. And he let everyone know he went to Mass every morning. But he could be a mendacious old knave. He put me in mind of Cardinal Spellman of New York (May 4, 1889 – December 2, 1967), of whom it was said that he would tell any lie for the good of the Church. But in Flannery's case, he would tell any lie for the good of the IRA, only as long as the IRA agreed with him. He would tell members of Irish Northern Aid, and even journalists, that I had built "a mansion on the shores of Lough Erne with all the money I collected that should have gone to Irish Northern Aid." I sent a message to him that if he wanted to know when my parents' humble home had been "roofed" (that is, changed from a thatched house to a slated one), all he had to do was ask the chairman and vice-chairman of Sinn Féin in Fermanagh, who were both neighbors of ours and they would tell him it was in the 1960s, long before I came to America.

Flannery would also tell people that I had to be a front for the CIA because our office on Capitol Hill was so big. Many Noraid leaders would tell me that they had received specific instructions from the Republican Movement to oppose and obstruct the Caucus in every way possible. One Irish-born woman told me in 2010 that, much to her regret, she had believed the lies the Republican Movement/Noraid had spread about me. One absolute whopper of a lie was that I "owned a yacht." That was told to her by a "person in authority, and one that was respected."[9] However, some claim this woman herself was one of the main persons Irish Republicans used to spread disinformation about me, as she was one of the Irish Northern Aid leaders in the Washington area.

They say she was the one who invented the absurd story about the yacht. Indeed, only a short time after our telephone conversation – during which she pretended to be really friendly and supportive – I discovered she was still trying to undermine me. Even though I never had a cross word with her in my life! I have never been able to understand such two-facedness. This person has not lifted a finger for the Irish cause in almost twenty years but she has time to still oppose me. Whose agenda is at work here? And to think I was the one who first introduced her to Ruairí Ó Brádaigh!

I always feel there is something tragic about people who are supposed to be working for a just cause but who don't hesitate to tell malicious and malevolent lies. What does that say about their commitment to justice?

To some of the Noraiders I would give "a fool's pardon." Many of them were the salt of the earth – fine, decent Irish-Americans with an admirable dedication to Irish justice. But they naïvely thought that if the IRA wanted the Caucus out of business, they had a patriotic duty to oppose us. Later on, of course, they would come to be deeply embarrassed. Over the years, I have had dozens of calls or conversations that began with, "Now, Fr. Sean, I am very embarrassed I opposed the Caucus ..."

However, I was not willing to give a fool's pardon to those who were trying to sabotage us on behalf of the Irish, British or American governments.

Agents, Provocateurs and "Useful Idiots"

Professor Joseph Thompson would later reveal in his book that, "... the U.S. government singled out the INC for special surveillance."[10] I was fully aware there was a multilayered campaign to put us out of business. And it was often difficult to know which entity was behind it – though it made no difference to me since they all had the same goal: to destroy the Caucus.

For example, there was a very determined effort to infiltrate the Washington local chapter of the Irish National Caucus, and to use it to oppose the National Office. I moved rapidly and disaffiliated the chapter. The leader of the attempted coup then disappeared like snow off a ditch – clear proof that he was up to no good. If he had been committed to working for Irish justice, why did he not continue working in some other capacity? Clearly, his only function was to disrupt the Caucus. When he was thwarted in that, he had no longer any interest in working for the cause of Ireland. That, for me, is always a dead giveaway.

In another part of the United States, I had taken an Irish-born man "in from the cold" and put him in a leadership position in a local chapter. (This was before Noraid had started to oppose us.) He had been previously isolated in that city, and a local priest and Noraid leaders warned me he could not be trusted. Indeed, Tyrone-born Eoin McNamee, IRA Chief of Staff in 1942, called me in Boston from Chicago and urged me to get rid of him because he was too close to the Dublin government. I refused, but I should have listened to Eoin.

Many years later that individual let it slip that an official from the Irish Consulate for that region had visited him with the proposal that the Irish government would back the Irish National Caucus "if they dumped McManus." The same individual was involved with a new Irish grouping in the 1980s. A representative of this new grouping came to see me in my office. He said he would offer the Caucus $200,000 a year if we came under his umbrella. I asked him what I would have to do for such kindness. "Do as I tell you," was his arrogant response. I told him that he had not the slightest idea of who I was, and what I was about if he thought he could silence me with money: "All sorts of people in Church and State have been trying to silence me for years. Do you really think you can?" Then, when I discovered that he had been driven to the Caucus office by the Irish Embassy's car (which was parked around the block with the driver waiting), I hknew I had to keep him at a firm distance.

Years later, my old friend, the late Matt Hannon, would reveal something that would validate all my suspicions. For a while Matt and I had become alienated because the Irish Embassy had told him all sorts of lies about me. Later on, when he realized he had been deceived by the Embassy and by the IRA and its supporters, he sought to be reconciled with me. I gladly welcomed him back. He then proceeded to tell me that shortly after the visitor to my office attempted to buy me off, a top Irish Embassy official telephoned him, urging him go to a very important meeting in Chicago, which that same visitor was organizing. "Why is it so important?" asked Matt. The official responded that the meeting was going to get rid of McManus, and the new grouping was going to take over from the Caucus, and would be backed by the Dublin government.

Before the Chicago conference, there had been a lot of pressure on me to attend. I had a lot of calls from individuals who had no real history of involvement in the Irish cause, all stressing how important it was for me to attend. I knew something was up, so I had stayed away. Again, my Kinawley instincts had served me well. Also, at the actual conference, the Irish-born man told people from Boston (not realizing they were friends of mine) that, "the Irish National Caucus would be out of business in six weeks."

Once the Irish Embassy had in effect set up this new grouping to sabotage the Irish National Caucus, another peculiar development took place. The IRA and Sinn Fein instructed their American followers to support the new group. What sort of sense does that make? What was really going on here?

No wonder I said earlier that it almost appeared as if the attacks on the Irish National Caucus (by the London and Dublin governments and by elements in the Irish Republican Movement) were directed by the same hand.

I know that it is easy to become a bit paranoid in this area, yet it would be hopelessly naïve not to realize that this is how the British Government has manipulated Irish affairs for a very long time. As American history professor Michael Connolly says : "Nearly every Irish political group throughout history has split into factions, thus worsening their chances of success. This tendency, together with a highly effective network of British spies and paid informers, usually doomed these insurrections ... ."[11] So just who was pulling the strings, both in Ireland and America, in the coordinated attacks on the Irish National Caucus? Why were the attacks so systematic and intense? What were we doing that merited such opposition?

This is all the more relevant now that it is known that the late exposed British agent, Denis Donaldson, a key Sinn Fein operator, had been dispatched to New York to oversee the Irish Northern Aid Committee. Who made that decision? What was his mission? Why was his role in America brushed under the carpet? I never went public with any of this at the time because there are only so many fronts one can fight on at once. But I also knew that if all these people were going to defeat me, they would have to rise very early indeed and be prepared to fight for a very long time. I also knew that the rank and file of the new grouping had no idea what was going on, and that over time the Irish Embassy could not control them. So I just got on with my work, all the more convinced I was on the right tracks as so many were trying to sabotage me.

Mr. Deceitful

Then there is the peculiar case of a person I will call "Mr. Deceitful," an Irish-American who has kept up an almost 40-year campaign against me.

I first met him in the 1970s when I stayed in the Albany region of New York State in the home of the late Joe Dooly, Assistant Attorney General for the State of New York.

Joe was an ardent Irish-American who died far too young. He warned me to watch my back with Mr. Deceitful. I replied that he seemed nice enough. "Until you turn your back and then he will stab you," responded Joe.

That was the only time I actually had a conversation in person with Mr. Deceitful, and I made sure I would keep him at a distance from then on – apart from some telephone conversations. Even though I never had a cross word with him, his one obsession appears to have been to destroy me. He once urged a journalist for a top British newspaper to contact my Provincial in London and demand to know why he was allowing, "Fr. McManus to be involved in politics on Capitol Hill." He then threatened that the next time he himself was in London (he has English connections) he would go to visit my Provincial and make the same demand. All this from a guy who at the same time was condemning clergy for not speaking out about Northern Ireland!

Mr. Deceitful kept hopping from one Irish-American organization to another but his one consistent theme was "McManus must be stopped." He never, of course, had the guts to say anything to my face – only behind my back or using his position within one of the Irish organizations to attack me.

He would go to absurd lengths. In 2001, a Florida State Senator introduced a Bill that would repeal the MacBride Principles legislation, which was passed in 1988. I branded the Bill as anti-Catholic, wrote to all the Florida State Senators and effectively raised the issue in the Florida media. We killed the Bill almost immediately. State Senators, Protestants and Catholic, telephoned me to urgently assure me that they were no way associated with the "anti-Catholic Bill." Meanwhile, the individual – who sometimes used AOH as a cover – was lobbying members of the AOH to dissociate themselves from my campaign.

In another example, he went to see Seán MacBride in Dublin to get him to change the MacBride Principles to accommodate the Ford Motor Company, against whom the Caucus had a very effective boycott for their refusal to sign MacBride. I telephoned Seán MacBride to warn him about the impending visit and he replied, "Do not worry, good Father. People like that have been coming to see me all my life to get me to change my principles and they never succeeded."[12]

Mr. Deceitful's modus operandi was (and still is) to be publicly very anti-British, while secretly opposing any campaign that would expose British injustice. He rants and raves in print against the British, while trying to undermine those most effective against the British. For example, in the 70s he was insistent that I would condemn Irish Northern Aid. I never would. Lo and behold, he then somehow ends up involved with them. In the 90s, for the first time in over twenty years, I called the office of Irish Northern Aid to speak to the late Belfast Republican, Joe Cahill. I was astonished that Mr. Deceitful answered the phone. Later, of course, it emerged that the infamous British agent, Denis Donaldson, had been placed in that office. So what was going on here?

Mr. Deceitful's hand inevitably surfaced against our campaign to expose the inherent anti-Catholic sectarianism and discrimination of the British Constitution, because of the Act of Settlement, 1701 – as will be explained later.

In 2007, Mr. Deceitful emailed key people trying to sabotage my campaign, bitterly complaining: "Last month it was how Americans should be objecting to the 16th century Act of Settlement. I guess under the belief that it has something to do with the conflict in Ireland. It is quite possibly the most idiotic thing for Americans to be lobbying for."

In other words, British state-sponsored discrimination has nothing to do with discrimination in Northern Ireland. The classic British position: "Sorry old chap, the problems in Northern Ireland has nothing to do with us."

When other Irish organizations complained about his peculiar activity he justified it with: "The response was as much an attempt to separate us [AOH] from … McManus and to distinguish us from the Sinn Fein 'AMEN' crowd in America."

That from a guy who publicly presents himself as a Sinn Fein supporter.

How has he gotten away with such deceitfulness for so long?

And, predictably, Mr. Deceitful would continually keep trying to spread the lie that I was not in fact a priest, or a priest no longer.

So, for example, he sent this email to an east-coast attorney who has done a lot of good work for human rights in Northern Ireland: "Not sure what e-mail you are talking about. First, McManus may or may not be a priest, but my point was don't we have greater need for priests than to sit in Washington issuing fatuous press releases in his delusional world that anyone cares what he thinks … I still think he should be serving in a mission in Darfur or better still Afghanistan."

The attorney, an honorable and authentic man, replied: "No, [FIRST NAME] I do not see what you mean. But I do see an ugly and childish and envious streak in you. And I suggest that it is offensive to use Darfur and Afghanistan in your denigration of Fr. Sean. You should make better use of your time. Please don't send me any more of the hogwash." (Emails. November 7 and 8, 2007).

Mr. Deceitful had manipulated one southern Irish-born AOH leader to a really ridiculous degree. He would draft absurd letters that the AOH leader would send to me, making extraordinary demands. In one case, demanding that I send him a copy of "every letter/memo" I had ever sent to Members of Congress. I replied that the entire Library of Congress could not contain all those letters.

For years, I had regarded that as ridiculous nonsense. But what if there is another explanation – one that never even occurred to me until I started doing the research for this book? Demanding a copy of all my letters to Congress may seem, on the face of it, ridiculous. But what if it were an intelligence-gathering attempt? Wouldn't the British Embassy have loved to see all those letters?

Leaders of both the AOH and Irish Northern Aid have told me that they, too, found Mr. Deceitful to be deceitful.

Rogue AOH Man

And then there is the case of another prominent "former AOH leader." a close associate of Mr. Deceitful. He began by working closely with us, but then "they" (whoever they are) got to him. I knew he had turned when he telephoned to tell me he was going to open an office on Capitol Hill. When I asked him why, he replied, "To steal your thunder." Not to struggle for justice, not to promote the Cause, but to compete against me! How sad is that? Of course I knew that if that were his sole motivation, then nothing would come of it, and nothing did. But it spoke volumes about him. In 1989, the Irish National Caucus was leading a very strong campaign in the State of Pennsylvania to get the MacBride Principles passed by the State Legislature. The INC leader in Scranton, the late John Breheny, had done magnificent work. He had got the local Scranton bishop and the Governor of Pennsylvania to support the Principles. The Chairman of the Senate Finance Committee, State Senator Gibson Armstrong (R-Lancaster) had bottled up the MacBride Bill in his Committee, and we were having a hard time getting it out. Lancaster was heavily Amish, very conservative, with hardly any Irish connections. John and I went to see his staffers and convinced them to hold a hearing on the Mac Bride Bill.

Shortly after our meeting, I had a call in my office from one of the staffers expressing alarm because he had had visitors who demanded I should be taken off the Witness List, i.e. the list of people who were scheduled to testify at the hearing. I told him he should not be surprised as I had told him up front that both the British and Irish Embassies were very hostile to me. "But Fr. Mc Manus," this non-Catholic staffer said, "it was not the Embassies but someone we thought supported the Irish cause." And he named the former prominent AOH leader. I almost fell off my chair.

John Breheny almost cried when I told him. John was an ardent student of Irish history with a particular horror of the traitor. "This is treason," John exclaimed. "The man is a traitor to Ireland and the AOH."

Anyway, on September 19, 1989, the hearing on the Mac Bride Bill took place in Harrisburg, the state capital. When I had finished my testimony, the entire hearing room broke into applause even though Chairman Armstrong had opened the hearing by stressing that there should be none. When the applause ended, Chairman Armstrong said, "Fr. Mc Manus, your church must always be full. I'm glad I don't have to run against you in an election."[13]

The AOH in Pennsylvania went on to eloquently repudiate the rogue AOH member by electing me Grand Marshal of the Harrisburg St. Patrick's Day Parade for March 1990. Neil McGinley, prominent AOH leader and General Chairman of the Parade, said: "We chose Fr. Mc Manus to acknowledge the leadership of the Irish National Caucus on the Mac Bride Principles nationally and specifically in the State of Pennsylvania ... Having him Grand Marshal will effectively demonstrate that we want the Mac Bride Principles passed in Pennsylvania, to which end, we have dedicated the Parade."[14]

And so it came to pass. The Mac Bride Principles were passed and signed into law by Governor Robert Casey (D-PA). "The stain of 'treason' had been erased, and the noble John Breheny could sleep again at night." (In 2007, one of Governor Casey's sons, Bob, became U.S. Senator for Pennsylvania and he would write to me: "It is with great pride and honor that I ... join the esteemed Irish National

Caucus. Your organization's commitment to advancing the cause of peace, justice and equality among the Irish people have long inspired the support of the Casey family... .)

However, the rogue AOH member would just not quit. On March 10, 1993, there was a public hearing on the Mac Bride Principles Bill before the Baltimore City Council. The Bill had mistakenly been crafted as a disinvestment Bill but we had lined up the complete support of the City Council to have it changed and brought into conformity with our national Mac Bride campaign. Bill Hughes was my key ally. A fervent Irishman and an all-round justice campaigner, Bill was one of the first Irishmen I met when I had arrived in Baltimore in 1972. And by a very nice coincidence, the person who introduced the Bill, Council Member Perry Sfikas, represented my old parish of Sacred Heart of Jesus. The President of the City Council, Mary Pat Clarke, would write to me: "It is our family's honor to be counted among your Irish-American supporters. Best wishes for a Brit-free Ireland."[15]

Well before the Hearing, I discovered that the rogue AOH man was still lobbying against me and trying to ensure that the Bill would remain a disinvestment bill. Therefore, I telephoned the then National President of the AOH, George Clough, in St. Louis, Missouri. I urged him to write a letter to all members of the Baltimore City Council counteracting his rogue member. On February 11, 1993, George wrote to the city council:

"The Mac Bride campaign, from its inception, has never called for divestment or disinvestment. I would urge you on behalf of our entire membership, and, in particular our members in Baltimore and Maryland, to make certain that the legislation in its final form reflects this quite clearly. It would be counter-productive at this time if the campaign was seen as calling for disinvestment or for divestment."

When he was informed of Clough's letter, he responded: "It doesn't matter what Clough thinks. He's in Missouri and I am in Maryland. And furthermore, I used to be the leader of the AOH."

However, despite his arrogant response, I thought he would now back off. He did not.

At the hearing, the rogue AOH member was the very last witness and the first words out of his mouth were, "I am here to oppose Fr. McManus." Then in an incoherent rant, he proceeded to say that the MacBride Principles had failed, there was no point in getting American companies to sign the Principles, and the only effective thing was to get American companies out of Northern Ireland. I quickly squashed his nonsense. Maryland Attorney General, Joe Curran, backed me up, as did his son-in-law City Council Member Martin O'Malley, future Governor of Maryland – a most ardent Irishman, and a possible future U.S. president.

This AOH member's outburst played right into the hands of the British government – intentionally or otherwise. But he was routed and the day was saved for MacBride.

At first I was not going to mention any of this petty nonsense, but it is necessary for the authenticity of the narrative. While it would be nice to think that in struggling for a just and noble cause, one would only have to face the oppressor, it would be naïve and unrealistic. Sadly, one also has to watch one's back from some of one's own people – or those who would present themselves as your "own." I have not named some of these people, as I feel I must show them more charity than they showed me. Moreover, their names are insignificant and can be left out without weakening the historical record – but their actions and agendas had to be recorded.

The words my Father said to my brother Patrick when he announced he was going on the run back on December 9, 1956 have always echoed down the years: "You will not be halfway out the lane until the police know."

I used to think that informers and agents were few and far between. But over the years I came to realize that they were in fact heavy on the ground. The Governments had the ground well and truly covered – in both Ireland and America.

I knew I could not do anything about that, but I was determined they would never gain control of my work. And the only way they could stop me was by killing me.

For a long time I tended to dismiss some of the nasty opposition I received as petty jealousy and stupidity. However, reviewing files that cover forty years and doing intense research necessarily changes one's perspective. One can dispassionately and objectively follow where the evidence leads. I am now ineluctably forced to see that much of that opposition was neither petty nor personal but official and institutionalized. It was not random or ad hoc but carefully choreographed and directed.

One striking feature of it has been that none of the individuals concerned ever confronted me to my face and said: "I disagree with a, b, and c." That I could accept and respect. Furthermore, there is another criterion one must use in retrospectively analyzing the evidence. I can understand individuals holding a grudge for many years if one had a fight with them or insulted their family. But how would those persons hold a grudge for forty years if you never had a fight or a disagreement with them – nor even any contact with them? How could they hold a grudge if they cannot point to one bad thing they personally experienced from me?

So grudges or "the Irish fighting each other again" cannot be conveniently trotted out here to explain things away. It was not about "a failure to communicate." It was about intelligence operations of the British Government. And, gentle reader, you would be very naïve, indeed, to think such intelligence operations were confined to the Six Counties!

The sad thing is that many genuine Irish-Americans who thought they were opposing me on behalf of the IRA were, in fact, unknowingly following the agenda of the London-Dublin Governments. How ironic is that?

But enough of informers, agents and "useful idiots" (those being used by the British without even knowing it). For every scoundrel and charlatan, there were thousands upon thousands of honest, decent, patriotic Irish-Americans. Those were the people who made my work possible. And despite all the attacks on me, from the right and the left – from Garret FitzGerald to Gerry Adams – the *Times* of London had to concede: "The most influential group of all is the Irish National Caucus ... From an office on Capitol Hill in Washington, a few yards from the heart of the U.S. government, Father Sean Mc Manus, leader of the Caucus, can sit at his computer terminal and summon up the names of 50,000 supporters."[16]

14

Capitol Hill Struggle

If there is no struggle, there is no progress.
Frederick Douglass[1]

As indicated previously, our presence on Capitol Hill really rocked the boat. However, there is no doubt that without that presence, the issue would have been horribly neglected. Noted journalist and commentator Vincent Browne, in August 1979, stated in the Irish media, "The growing U.S. interest in the Northern Ireland issue is traceable almost entirely to the efforts of the Irish National Caucus."[2]

Our job was to get the U.S. Congress involved in Northern Ireland – the aim of the British and Irish Embassies was, in effect, to block that involvement. I know Irish Embassy officials at the time would publicly deny that. Indeed, Sean Donlon would later claim that he was responsible for creating Congressional pressure on the British. And I know the Irish government (like the Vatican) can pull out a document to prove it always supported or opposed something.

Sean Donlon and Irish Embassy officials had tried to persuade Members of Congress that there was no role for Congress in Northern Ireland. In his authoritative book *American Policy and*

Northern Ireland: A Saga of Peacebuilding, Professor Joseph E. Thompson, states it well: "The British Government and the congressional leadership stopped laughing ... when the Ad Hoc Congressional Committee membership went over the 100-member mark.[3] Thompson further explains: "Despite being ignored by the leadership ... the Ad Hoc Congressional Committee joined with the INC to successfully make the Northern Irish question a public issue."[4] And then, very revealingly, he states what I always knew but which the Irish media would never acknowledge: "To counterbalance the growing impact of the Ad Hoc congressional committee, Michael Lillis of the Irish Embassy masterminded Tip O'Neill's trip to Ireland in April 1979. This visit was to muster the Irish-American leaders behind the John Hume–Sean Donlon–Michael Lillis approach toward moderate nationalism."[5]

I would add this, however, so that the perspective is not lost: it is not as if the Irish National Caucus was advocating "immoderate" nationalism. And this is where Professor Thompson tends to fall prey to Irish Embassy propaganda. We never asked the Congress to support the IRA or anything radical or revolutionary. Indeed, the reason we were so effective was because our demands were reasonable: ending torture, human rights violations, unfair trials, anti-Catholic discrimination, unfair visa policy towards Irish Republicans, etc. – everything the American Constitution stood for. And we had an official policy of nonviolence to which we adhered totally.

So why did the Irish Embassy oppose us so bitterly? Because they did not want the British exposed, which, in turn, would expose the shameless, cowardly record and policy of the Dublin government on Northern Ireland.

Throughout his book, Professor Thompson refers to us as, the "republican Irish National Caucus." Well, we are certainly not monarchist, but I have never said the INC is republican. Indeed, I have always refused to use labels like that, and I've always stressed that the Irish National Caucus has no foreign principal – that is, it does not support any group or party in Ireland, North or South, nor do we take orders from there.

So when Thompson says the Irish Embassy was for "moderate nationalism" and we were "republican," he is echoing the Irish Embassy spin – unconsciously, I'm sure, as he is a professionally objective political scientist.

Again, let me stress, there was not one thing the Caucus was lobbying for that the Irish Embassy should have properly and legitimately opposed. I fully understand that governments and people in power have to be diplomatic and do a lot of stuff in private. And that's okay. But the Irish Embassy has absolutely no right to attack Irish-Americans for speaking out – has no business attacking Americans, period. And certainly no business spying on them or interfering with their constitutional right of petitioning their Government.

Irish-Americans, like all Americans, have a right, even a duty, to demand that the United States apply a single, not a double, standard in its foreign policy. And why should Irish-Americans not have demanded that their Congress denounce British violations of human rights in Northern Ireland? Why should the Irish Embassy seek to muzzle Irish-Americans and the U.S. Congress?

I know the Irish Embassy – remember here we are speaking of the 1970s and 1980s – welcomed American pressure, discreet and private, if it enhanced their own status (and the status quo), but just as surely they did not want a Catholic priest from County Fermanagh kicking the hell (nonviolently, of course) out of the British government all over Capitol Hill and across the United States. Seriously, could anybody in Ireland at that time dispute this?

Again, Professor Thompson provides suitable context: "As the republican INC and the Ad Hoc Congressional Committee grew in strength, so too did Dublin's commitment to lobby in support of Irish constitutional nationalism and Irish-American leaders in Congress."[6]

However, by this time, it was clear to the Irish Embassy that it could not make us disappear. Furthermore, their sterile policy of telling Members of Congress that they had no role to play was clearly in shambles. We now had 130 Members signed up. Taoiseach Jack Lynch's frontal attack on the Ad Hoc Congressional Committee had spectacularly failed, as previously explained.

Friends of Ireland

What could the Irish Embassy do to save face, and also take the heat off the British that we were so very effectively applying? ... Drum roll, please ... Enter the Friends of Ireland! Yes, indeed, the Irish National Caucus not only initiated the Ad Hoc Congressional Committee for Irish Affairs – the Friends of Ireland came into existence as a direct reaction to our forming the Ad Hoc Committee.

The Friends of Ireland was launched on St. Patrick's Day, 1981 by Tip O'Neill, Teddy Kennedy, Senator Patrick Moynihan, etc. As my good friend Congressman Gilman told me at the time, "It was a place for Tip to hang his hat." Desmond Rush would write in the *Irish Independent* that Speaker O'Neill's office had told him that its purpose was to put the Ad Hoc Committee out of business, and it would happen in six weeks. "That's what Jack Lynch thought," I told Rush. I then called Kirk O'Donnell, one of O'Neill's top people. O'Donnell would not deny Rush's story.

Former British MP, Kevin McNamara, in his book, *The MacBride Principles: Irish-America Strikes Back* (more of which later), says: "The Ad Hoc Congressional Committee was proving so successful that the SDLP supporters ... encouraged by the Irish Embassy established the Friends of Ireland ... The Embassy was alarmed by the activities and influence of the Ad Hoc Committee on the Hill and its closeness to the INC."[7] And even more tellingly, McNamara goes on to say that Werner Brandt, a key aide to future Speaker Tom Foley, would later authoritatively state that "The Friends of Ireland was formed to prevent Northern Ireland becoming 'an irritant' in Anglo-Irish-U.S. relations."[8] And there you have it, folks: the less than noble origins of the Friends of Ireland. However, I was careful not to condemn them, feeling that in time they could do good. Our aim was to have a strong Irish presence on Capitol Hill. And now there were two Congressional committees, where a short time ago there was none.

Congressmen Mario Biaggi, Ben Gilman and Hamilton Fish asked me to come over to meet with them regarding the formation of the Friends of Ireland. I urged them to immediately join and told them we would be urging all members of the Ad Hoc Congressional Committee to join. I knew that although Tip and Teddy would toe the safe Dublin line, there was no way large numbers of Congressmen would be content with a "do-nothing" policy. They were being pressured by their constituents to speak out against British violations of human rights, and there would be no use in their just saying "we can't do anything but Tip and Teddy are engaging in private diplomacy with the Dublin government." That was no platform to run on. So many of them became just as outspoken as the members of the Ad Hoc Congressional Committee.

In time our strategy would bear great fruit. When the Democrats lost power and the Republicans took over in 1995, Congressman Jimmy Walsh from Syracuse, NY, took over as chairman of the Friends of Ireland. He was an ardent Fenian, a good friend, and a strong member of the Ad Hoc Congressional Committee. He would go on, in effect, to merge the two Committees together – making the Friends of Ireland just as strong on the issue. (And by this time, the Irish Embassy had eased off from trying to demonize me.) When the Democrats came back into power in 2007, Congressman Ritchie Neal (D-MA) became the chairman – a most dedicated Irishman who had long been a member of the Ad Hoc Congressional Committee, and whom we listed on our letterhead as a Congressional Friend, as we did Congressman Walsh until he retired from Congress in 2009.

I should explain here that in 1982 we began the practice of listing on our letterhead the names of the Senators and Representatives who had become "Friends of the Irish National

Caucus" – those who sent us a signed written statement confirming their support of our "nonviolent work for justice and peace in Ireland." The list had to be updated every two years because of the elections for the House of Representatives. And the list got so long we had to put the names on both the front and the back of our stationery. Democrats, Republicans, Conservatives and Liberals wanted their names to be proudly displayed – from Congressman Barney Frank (D-MA), commonly seen as the most liberal, to Senator Strom Thurmond (R-SC), commonly seen as the most conservative (which made the Irish Embassy look a bit daft in trying to brand us as radical revolutionaries with old Strom on board!).

I should add a note of interest here about the development of the Friends of Ireland. Congressman Brian Donnelly (1979– 1993) was elected with the help of many of our supporters in Boston and pledged to them that I would be one of the first people he would meet with when he came to Washington. He kept his promise. I went to see him in his office, and the very first words out of his mouth were, "Father, I want to be briefed by you before I hear the bullshit from the Irish Embassy" – exactly his words. Brian would go on to attend our functions in Boston. He would, however, become a protégé of the future Speaker Foley, and one of the first chairmen of the Friends of Ireland. He always remained friendly, and did good work on increasing the number of Irish visas.[9] However, when Joe Kennedy came to Congress (1987–1999), the first thing he told me when I met with him was that I "should keep him involved with the issues with an edge, as Brian Donnelly had all the soft issues." And I knew I could count on this eldest son of the revered Bobby Kennedy to do the "heavy lifting." I was sorry Joe left Congress as I felt in time he could have become President. He had guts and charisma in abundance.

Struggle for Congressional Hearings

One of the mandatory ways for a human rights lobby to

frame its issue on Capitol Hill is through Congressional hearings. Nothing happens in Congress without the appropriate committee (Appropriations, Judiciary, Foreign Affairs, etc). Obviously, the committee for our concerns was Foreign Affairs. And the way to get real action by a committee is to have it hold a hearing, at which experts and concerned citizens are called to testify – like the hearing we arranged back in 1973 at which my brother Frank testified.

So with crusading zeal, we set out to have another hearing on human rights in Northern Ireland. But this time it would not be so easy. In 1973, we had snuck in under the radar, so to speak. We had pulled off the hearing before our opponents (all those who did not want the British embarrassed) could block it. After that, I knew there would be all-out opposition to further hearings.

On Ash Wednesday 1979, I was concelebrating Mass in St. Peter's, which is on the same side of Capitol Hill as the House of Representatives. Hence, Catholic Congressmen/women tend to go there (whereas Catholic Senators tend to go to St. Joseph's, on the Senate side of Capitol Hill). I "gave the ashes" to Tip: dipping my thumb into previously blessed ashes, I made the sign of the cross on his forehead, saying, "Remember, man, thou art dust, and to dust thou shalt return." I did the same for Congressman Clement J. Zablocki (D-WI), the Polish-American Chairman of the House Foreign Affairs Committee from 1977 to 1983. After the Mass, I cornered Chairman Zablocki on the steps of St. Peter's. "You've got to do the right thing, Mr. Chairman. You should not block our hearings on Northern Ireland," I said. He grasped me by the arm – looked over his shoulder to make sure Tip was out of hearing range – and pleadingly said, "Fr. Sean, I want to, but Tip won't let me." He then assured me that as a good Catholic he was deeply sympathetic to the plight of Catholics in Northern Ireland. "But Tip won't let me," he said again, ever so plaintively. I was sure he was telling me the truth.

I went back into the empty church and knelt for a long time to compose myself, and to pray for the grace to forgive Tip. (My head was pounding: here was a Polish American willing to hold hearings, and an Irish-American was blocking him.) But while I was prepared to forgive Tip, I was not prepared to give up my struggle for justice. I had come to adopt a motto as my spiritual compass: "fight like hell for justice, but always forgive like Heaven." As I knelt there, my mind went back to kneeling in the other St. Peter's in Rome when Bishop Drury blessed me. And, again, I experienced the same tranquility – and the same determination to fight on.

Tip, A Lost Cause

There had to be something about Ash Wednesday and my relationship with Tip. The previous time I had a meeting with him was the year before on Ash Wednesday, 1978. I was still in Boston at the time, and I had been trying for a long time to arrange a meeting with him. He had become Speaker in January 1977, and, understandably, it was difficult to get a meeting. I had got to know the wonderful John McCormack of Boston who was Speaker from 1962 to 1971. By then he was a very old man, having been born in December 1891. He used to take me to the famous Jimmy's Harborside Restaurant for dinner at 4.30 p.m. And he used to love it when I had him invited to Mission Church to join the other priests for dinner. Speaker McCormack had taken Tip under his wing when he came to Congress and Tip felt very indebted to him. Anyway, I told Speaker McCormack I was having difficulty in getting a meeting with Tip. He took care of it right away, and on Ash Wednesday, February 8, 1978, I brought a group of INC leaders into Tip's office. Tip greeted me with great charm and friendliness. As I introduced each of the others, Tip very openly refused to shake the hands of one, a judge from Pittsburgh (I later found out it was because Tip considered the judge to have been part of a group that had had sent him thirty pieces of silver – Judas' price for selling out).

Tip immediately began the meeting from behind his very imposing desk: "Fr. Sean, what is all this spying about?" he asked most sternly. I was dumbstruck and said I had no idea what he was referring to. He said, "Before this meeting the Irish Embassy called me to express concern and was able to tell me the names of the entire delegation. Did you give them the names of these people?" I told him I certainly had not. "That's what I mean about spying," he said.

I briefed Tip on the situation and urged him to speak out; nobody expected him to support the IRA, but his silence could give the impression that he was condoning British oppression. He shot back, "There's a long history of anti-English bigotry in my family." Tip then told me that Desmond O'Malley TD, of Fianna Fáil, had been in to see him recently and had told him that both main parties in the Irish Republic, Fine Gael and Fianna Fáil, supported the Sunningdale Agreement.[10] I just happened to have in my briefcase a copy of an article by Vincent Browne in the *Sunday Independent* that said the exact opposite: "The Government would not reiterate the Sunningdale declaration on the status of Northern Ireland, according to the Minister for Foreign Affairs, Michael O'Kennedy ... 'That declaration is merely part of the negative British guarantee to help the Unionists ...' "[11] As I read out the article, Tip got visibly angry at what he was hearing. He said he would demand an explanation of the Irish Embassy.

He then told me that the Irish Embassy kept insisting I was a front for terrorism. I told him exactly where I stood. Then he demanded: "I want you to write a letter to me, in your own hand, stating that you are not involved in violence, and I will keep it here in my drawer [and he pulled out the top drawer on the right of his desk to demonstrate], and when anyone tells me you are a terrorist, I will show them it." I promised him I would, and as we were leaving he said, "Don't forget your ashes, Father." Two days later, on February 10, I wrote him a three-page letter – not in my own hand, as he wouldn't be able to read it! But I spelled out exactly where I stood.

Sometime later, I went to see Ari Weiss in the Speaker's office. Ari was Tip's top policy adviser, and then only twenty-five. Kirk O'Donnell, then thirty-two, was the general counsel and chief political strategist. Ari was considered one of the most brilliant people on The Hill, and I had great regard for him. He was a straight shooter: "A strict orthodox Jew who won't ride in a car on Saturday [he] walked 22 miles in a torrential downpour to attend the Speaker's son's wedding."[12] I always felt I would get total directness from Ari, whereas not from Kirk who would dance and weave. He tended towards the elitist approach on Ireland. Furthermore, because he was Irish-American he was more susceptible to pressure from the Irish Embassy. Ari told me that Tip was very impressed with the honesty and openness of my letter and that he completely believed me. Ari himself tried to get to the bottom of the Irish Embassy's accusations and he called well-known journalist Jimmy Breslin to ask his opinion. Breslin told him that "there was likely more truth on the priest's side." But then Ari added that for as long as the Irish Embassy was insisting I was an IRA agent, the Speaker felt he could not continue to meet me – even if John McCormack called him again.

Now back again to Ash Wednesday 1979, and to what Chairman Zablocki had told me about Tip not letting him hold hearings.

Tip's Cover-Up

Of course, I was already well aware of Tip's conniving with the British and Irish governments. We had got the famed Jack Anderson Column – nationally syndicated and carried in nearly 1,000 papers – to expose it three times within one year, 1977/1978.

(1) "Speaker Thomas (Tip) O'Neill, the big beloved boss of the House, is as Irish as anyone who ever kissed the Blarney stone. But he quietly squashed a congressional hearing on alleged British outrages against the Irish ...To dig up atrocities, the speaker pleaded, would only inflame the already emotional issue. It would be an 'inappropriate' time to stir up trouble over Irish rights, he said."[13]

(2) "Under pressure from two foreign governments, President Carter is betraying a campaign promise to speak out against human rights violation committed by British authorities in Northern Ireland. He made the pledge to ... [the Irish National Caucus] in Pittsburgh six days before the 1976 election, in exchange for their endorsement. Shortly after Carter took office ... [the Irish National Caucus] supplied the White House with 10 documented cases of alleged torture perpetrated by British security forces against suspected IRA members or sympathizers ... A move to air the charges on Capitol Hill is being thwarted by House Speaker Tip O'Neill at the behest of the Irish government ... An aide told us that the Speaker, a Carter confidant, was told by prominent members of the Irish government that an investigation would be counterproductive. In Dublin's view, the Irish National Caucus is pro-I.R.A., and a congressional hearing would signal U.S. support of the terrorist IRA gunmen."[14]

(3) "Human rights violations, reported to us by a number of reliable sources, have put Northern Ireland on an unenviable par with some of the most barbarous regimes of communist commissars or tinhorn Latin American dictators. The British are trampling on the rights of Irish citizens in a manner reminiscent of Oliver Cromwell's iron-fisted rule more than three centuries ago ... An Ad Hoc Committee of 119 members has been formed in congress. But the committee's attempts to publicize the outrages being committed in Northern Ireland, along with the efforts of the Irish National Caucus, have been blocked by House Speaker Tip O'Neill and other congressional leaders who are reluctant to offend our British ally."[15]

What's wrong with that picture? A Mormon journalist, of Swedish-Danish descent (considered one of the fathers of modern investigative journalism) forced to outrage at an Irish-

Catholic Speaker of the House covering up British atrocities against Catholics in Northern Ireland. How profoundly sad is that!

But now – after all these years and many months of dispassionately reviewing the historical record – I am, again, forced to wonder about something which in the early years would never have crossed my mind. Why would Tip O'Neill, who was so concerned about his place in history, go so far out on a limb to protect British interests? He had to know that in years to come (i.e. the present time) nobody would dare try to defend his blocking and, in later years as Speaker, his banning of Congressional Hearings on human rights in Northern Ireland. It was indefensible, absurd and corrupt. What possible, conceivable pressure was he under? What would force him to so undemocratically corrupt the Congressional process? What hold had the British on him?

British-Irish Government Cover-Up

Despite all this, the Dublin government was not too eager, at the time, to admit its role. However, Professor Thompson in his previously mentioned book (published in 2001) tells us that "the Irish and British ambassadors to the United States, John Molloy and Sir Peter Ramsbotham, respectively, made a joint request to Speaker Albert [1971–1977] not to hold any official hearings on Northern Ireland." Professor Thompson explains he elicited this information in a personal interview with Garret FitzGerald in 1999. Thompson then says: "Speaker Albert did not hold any official hearings on Northern Ireland, but to combat the growing influence of the INC in congress, he followed Congressman O'Neill and Senator Kennedy's advice and requested that the Congressional Research Service (CRS) of the Library of Congress produce the report Developments in Northern Ireland 1968–1976." Professor Thompson continues with keen observation:

> The introduction to the 1976 CRS report spread the blame for Northern Ireland's increased violence among

several parties. The Nixon and Ford administrations were admonished for not offering to facilitate a solution to the crisis. The administrations were accused of hiding behind the pernicious policy of realism, which allowed the party inflicting the injury to decide if an outside party should come in and expose the injured party's grievances. Kissinger knew that Britain would never ask the United States to assist in UK domestic affairs ... The same excuse for inaction in Northern Ireland was used by the United Nations (UN) when it was confronted by the INC request for an investigation into British violations of Irish human rights. U.N. Secretary General, U Thant, said that he was waiting for the United Kingdom to ask for U.N. assistance, implying that this request would publicize Britain's ineptitude to control its domestic violence.[16]

As I write this, and as I go back over the record, I must confess to feeling that old righteous Kinawley anger stirring up within me. The cover-up was cynical, calculated, and cowardly. And the ever-compliant establishment media went along with it (with a few honorable exceptions). Shame, shame, shame on all responsible.

In an October 1986 interview with Niall O'Dowd, a well-known commentator on Northern Ireland, Tip said, referring to Irish activity in Congress: "it all started with Father McManus. When he came over here, we were all sympathetic to him. Then he started to bring over some of the terrorists from Ireland, and we didn't agree with their philosophy and basically their means to the end, which we didn't like. So, we broke away and started our own group, a more stable one."[17]

The British and Irish Embassy had done their job well. O'Neill would trot out the old nonsense that the reason he opposed a Congressional hearing on Northern Ireland was because it would provide a platform for the IRA. Yet he knew perfectly well that for years the IRA and members of Sinn Féin were denied visas to enter the US. Furthermore, even if they had been able to enter, they just could not turn up and testify because Tip had the power to veto the witness list. So his excuses were dishonest. Tip and the Irish government were not scared of the IRA – they were scared of the truth.

Tip Was Not Just Opposed to Hearings

My problem with Tip was that he was not just opposed to Congressional hearings on Northern Ireland. After he had been "re-educated" by the British and Irish Embassies, he refused to show any interest in individual human rights violations – the Birmingham Six, Guildford Four, etc. (The same, sadly, can be said about Teddy Kennedy. This is particularly ironic in the case of the Guildford Four, as one of them, Paul Hill would eventually marry Bobby Kennedy's daughter Courtney.)

Tip turned a blind eye to torture, and showed no interest in combating anti-Catholic discrimination. It is as if the little people did not count – the victims of London's oppression and Dublin's negligence – despite Tip's image as champion of the working class. Nothing seemed to matter but "the big picture," whatever that is. All that mattered was that Tip would, to use that famous phrase of Werner Brandt, "prevent Northern Ireland becoming 'an irritant' in Anglo-Irish-US relations." Of course he would occasionally raise a question about British practice, and in private he might nudge them, but always within the Brandt parameters. It is the typical elitist approach – again, despite Tip's image to the contrary. He may have been a working class guy from Boston, but like so many Irish before him, when it came to Her Majesty's government, Tip would doff his hat and become ever so "respectable and diplomatic." And, in the meantime, Irish-Americans were supposed to sit down and shut up. Oh, sure, let them talk about every issue under the sun, except their own homeland – that had to be left to the quiet diplomacy of himself, Teddy Kennedy, and the Dublin government. I recognize Teddy went on to do very important work in the Irish Peace Process, and I salute him for that.

Author's parents, Celia and Patrick, 1929.

Patrick Mc Manus, author's eldest brother, who was killed in 1958.

7-Aside Team. Back (l-r): Frankie, Patrick, Sean. Middle (l-r): Jim, Terence, Thomas. Front: Myles. Clonliff, 1956.

Six brothers. Back (l-r): Myles, Terence and Frankie; Front (l-r): author, Thomas and Jim. Enniskillen, 1984.

Author's Mother and three sisters (l-r): Alice, Celia, Mother and Mary Kate. Clonliff, 1958.

Author (far right) with his family (l-r): Myles, Frankie, Celia, Jim, Mary Kate, Alice. Kinnoull, Perth, Scotland, 2007.

Author with Sean Mac Bride. New York, 1976.

*Author at
Mac Bride funeral.
Dublin, 1988.*

Author with Irish Northern Aid Leaders (l-r): Matt Higgins, Jack McCarthy, Mike Flannery, Mattie Reilly, Tommy Enright, Danny Crawford. Sean Cronin is the figure partially cut out. New York, 1972.

Author with Tip O'Neill, then Majority Leader of the U.S. House of Representatives. Washington, D.C., 1974.

Tip O'Neill at the hearing regarding the International Fund for Ireland. Author (left) and Congressman Mario Biaggi (center) keep a close on him. Washington, D.C., March, 1986.

Author Chairs launching of Ad Hoc Committee (l-r): Tomm Mc Nabb, Deputy National President, AOH; Congressman Edward P. Beard (D-RI); Congressman Mario Biaggi (D-NY); and Congressman Leo C. Zeferetti (D-NY). Washington, D.C., 1977.

Author with Teddy Gleason, International President of the ILA and George Meany, President , AFL-CIO. Florida, 1975.

Author with Bob Blancato (left) and Mario Biaggi (right). Washington, D.C., 1987.

Author with Senator Edward Kennedy. Washington, D.C., 1980.

Demonstrating at the British Embassy in 1988, author greets Congressmen Joe Kennedy (center) and John Lewis (right), hero of the U.S. Civil Rights Movement.

Author with Presidential candidate Jimmy Carter. Pittsburgh, PA, 1976.

Author with ardent Irish advocate Congressman Richard Neal (D-MA). Washington, 2009.

Author testifying before Ad Hoc Congressional Committee. Washington, D.C., 1979.

Author testifying at Congressional Hearing on MacBride Principles. Washington, D.C., 1995.

Author with Congressman Hamilton Fish (R-NY). Washington, D.C., 1977.

Author with Congressman Joe Kennedy, Bob Bateman and Derek Warfield. Washington, D.C., 1987.

Author with human rights champion, Congressman Chris Smith (R-NJ). Washington, D.C., 2000.

Author with Presidential candidate, Bill Clinton. New York, 1992.

Author with Vice President Al Gore (right) and Congressman Walsh (center). Washington, D.C., 2000.

Author with
Secretary
of State,
Hillary
Clinton, St.
Patrick's Day.
White House,
2009.

Author with
Congressman
Ben Gilman.
Gilman would
later chair the
House Committee
on Foreign Affairs.
Washington, D.C.,
1989.

Author with
actors Richard
Harris and
Anne Turkel.
Baltimore,
MD, 1974.

*Author with
Muhammad Ali.
Washington, D.C.,
1998.*

*Author with
Gerry Adams
and
John Hume.
New York,
February,
1994.*

*Author with
Speaker
Gingrich, St.
Patrick's Day.
Washington,
D.C.,1995.*

Author with Speaker Nancy Pelosi. Washington, D.C., 2008.

Author with Raymond Mc Cord (left) in front of the White House. Washington, D.C., 2009.

Author with the Ballymurphy Massacre Committee on Capitol Hill, seeking a Congressional hearing on the British Army Massacre, 1971 (l-r): Alice Harper, author, Briege Voyle and John Taggart. Washington, D.C., December 2010.

Soon-to-be President of Ireland, Michael D. Higgins, congratulates author on Memoirs, as journalist Vincent Browne and artist Bobby Ballagh look on. Dublin, 2011.

Michael D. Higgins – now Irish President – promotes Fr. Mc Manus' Memoirs at the Dublin Castle book launch. April 5, 2011.

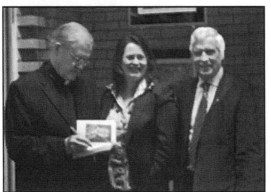

Author with Michelle Gildernew, Sinn Fein MP for Fermanagh/ S. Tyrone and the intrepid Donal Donnelly. Enniskillen, 2011.

Author with Sinn Fein leader Martin Mc Guinness MP, Deputy First Minister of Northern Ireland. Washington, DC, 2012.

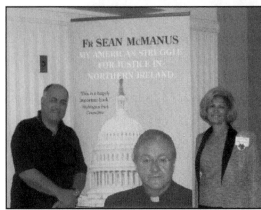

Ray O' Hanlon, Irish Echo editor and Barbara Flaherty, prime promoter of book. New York, 2011.

Author with Barbara Flaherty and her grandchildren, Joey, Adam and Sarah. Washington, D.C., 2011.

Tip and I would also clash over U.S. contributions to International Fund for Ireland (IFI), which was formed to support the Anglo-Irish Agreement of 1985.[18]

Like many, I had my problems with that Agreement, which gave the Dublin government a semi-formal institutional role – a right to have an opinion, so to speak – on the North. But it also obliged Dublin to accept that there could be no change in the constitutional position of Northern Ireland unless a majority there agreed. Because FitzGerald had such a hopeless record on the North, Nationalists/Republicans were very suspicious of the deal. To make matters worse, Garret FitzGerald had marketed it as the way to marginalize Irish republicans in the North, not to end British injustice and anti-Catholic discrimination. The words of T.S. Elliott immediately come to mind here: "The last temptation is the greatest treason: to do the right deed for the wrong reason."[19]

Anyway, we were determined that any U.S. money for the IFI would have conditions attached. On January 14, 1986, I wrote to every member of the House Foreign Affairs Committee (twenty-four Democrats and thirteen Republicans) saying: "The Irish-American community is deeply concerned that U.S. Foreign Aid to support the Anglo-Irish Agreement could in effect serve to bolster up British oppression and injustice in Northern Ireland or subsidize anti-Catholic discrimination. That is why we urge: (1) Foreign Aid should not be used by the British Government for military or security purposes or for the gathering of intelligence; (2) Foreign Aid should be tied to the MacBride Principles; (3) Foreign Aid should be tied to the human rights provisions of the Foreign Assistance."

Tip was furious – several sources informed me.

When the Foreign Affairs Subcommittee on Europe and the Middle East held its hearing on Wednesday March 5, 1986, Tip made a point of testifying in person. Although he did shake my hand, his look said, "I am going to blow you out of the water." And he certainly tried. "I believe," he thundered, "that Congress should make the aid subject to standard conditions for assistance and not make it contingent on a long list of political conditions. We need to express our unqualified support for the Accord [Agreement], not our doubts about it."

Beating Tip At His Own Game

However, we won the day. I had lobbied the Subcommittee so thoroughly that they were prepared to stand up to the Speaker. Congressman Lee Hamilton (D-ID) actually held up my letter, read out our conditions, one by one, and – looking directly at me – said all of them had been met and that should satisfy those who had concerns. It was a remarkable achievement, and of course, the British and Irish media played it down. However, an excellent reporter for the *Union Leader* newspaper, Manchester, New Hampshire, Tom Gorey would report: "The House Foreign Affairs Committee approved Reagan's aid proposal on Thursday, after attaching certain conditions that Mc Manus had lobbied for and were inserted by U.S. Rep. Ben Gilman (R-NY). Gilman's provisions restate an existing ban on the use of U.S. economic aid for military or security purposes, and insist that the aid be distributed "according to the principles of equality of opportunity" and that it promote "human rights." (As we shall see later, Gilman and I would finally succeed in getting the actual Mac Bride Principles tied to the International Fund for Ireland in 1998, when the Principles became part of U.S. law.)

Gorey's article then continues:

Mc Manus said O'Neill "wanted to come in and personally crush the campaign to add conditions. And yet we won this one ... We took him on – toe to toe – and we won. Mc Manus branded O'Neill's testimony to the subcommittee as "vintage British propaganda." His presentation was exactly how the British Government presents the Northern Ireland problem. Namely, that the British government is not at fault for maintaining an unjust, sectarian, oppressive system (in Ulster) in which violence is inevitable. But that the problem in Northern Ireland is the inability of two tribes – Catholic and

Protestant – to get along with each other. There wasn't one
condemnation of anti-Catholic discrimination, of repressive
legislation, of mistreatment of persons. There wasn't one
condemnation of British violence – military or institutional.
There was only a condemnation of IRA violence.[20]

That is fine journalism by Tom Gorey. He captured the story
perfectly, and accurately reported my long-standing grievance with
typical elitist misrepresentation of the Northern Ireland problem.

By this stage, I'd had it with Tip. I was always fond of him
– he was a hard man not to like – but I could no longer excuse
his actions. And it was not a matter of his being totally controlled
by the Dublin Government because when it suited him, he could
take a strong line. Remember in Chapter 12, when Tip thought
Taoiseach Charlie Haughey was going to take a stronger anti-
British line and remove Sean Donlon as ambassador, Tip very
"undiplomatically" and, some have argued, very improperly
intervened and made Haughey back off. Garret FitzGerald would
claim that by removing Donlon, Haughey was siding with IRA
supporters in America. Nonsense. Who would expect the Irish
Embassy, for goodness sake, to be pro-IRA? Haughey did not
want the Embassy to be pro-British, but apparently Tip did.

In celebrating that his protégé, Donlon, had been spared,
Garett FitzGerald would write: "Our American policy was back
on course ... thanks to the intervention of Tip O'Neill."[21] That
policy being, of course, that the Irish Embassy would continue
to shield the British government from really serious Washington
pressure. No self-respecting country should have tolerated the
Lynch, Cosgrave or FitzGerald governments. Their spineless
policy ensured that Catholics in the North would continue to suffer
needlessly, and that, in fact, the IRA would thereby increase, not
decrease.

Finally, regarding Tip's public record on Northern Ireland,
he may have argued that he was doing all sorts of good things
privately but one cannot judge a public figure by his private, secret
negotiations. Furthermore, what politician runs on a platform of

secret negotiations? What politician can get away with saying, "You don't know what I'm doing, and I can't tell you, but trust me anyway"? That certainly was not his policy on all the other issues he felt strongly about. On those – South Africa, El Salvador, etc. – he was vehemently outspoken, But on Northern Ireland, he had to be "diplomatic" and ever so careful in criticizing Her Majesty's government. Unqualified condemnations were only for the IRA. That was the double standard and dishonesty that drove me up the wall. I just could not take it, and never could. It is what forced me to get involved in the first place back in England, and it has kept me going all these years.

Now I recognize that Tip occasionally did apply some pressure, and the British reacted out of all proportion. One could argue that showed the British felt the pressure. Or one could argue that the British disproportionate reaction was their way of making sure that Tip would back off and not apply real pressure. I favor the latter argument.

Nobody wanted Tip and President Reagan to "nuke" London, send in the marines, or apply sanctions. But can you imagine what real pressure could have accomplished? Sadly, the two most powerful Irish-Americans in the world did not have the guts to do it – and the Irish governments at the time did not want them to do it. So we had to wait for President Bill Clinton, God bless his southern Baptist heart.

Speaker Tom Foley

The International Fund for Ireland (IFI) would also be the arena for another joust with one of Tip's successors, Congressman Tom Foley (June 6, 1989 to January 3, 1995) from the State of Washington. (Tip was Speaker from January 4, 1977 to January 3, 1987 and Jim Wright from Texas replaced him from June 6, 1987 to June 6, 1989.)

By this time there was growing concern about the performance of the IFI. Most of the funds were simply adhering to the systematic pattern of discrimination in Northern Ireland –

going to the Unionist/Protestant areas. The Second Annual Report on the IFI revealed, for example, that West and North Belfast and Derry received less than 6 percent of the 1988 budget: ".... the bulk of the money went to a variety of projects which had had no relation to northern violence: funding for hotels, tourist amenities, a skydiving club, golf courses and a $1.9 million gift of a fishing vessel to the British government ..."[22]

I had been inundating the Foreign Affairs Committee with documentation, and creating a lot of noise. I convinced Chairman Lee Hamilton that my concerns should be aired at a hearing, and that he should allow other Irish-American groups to testify, too. Gerry Coleman, an Irish-American from New Jersey, would represent eight Irish-American organizations, including Irish Northern Aid. I would speak for the Irish National Caucus.

On April 26, 1989, the Subcommittee for Europe and the Middle East held its hearing. In strode Tom Foley (Speaker-in-waiting) who proceeded to launch an attack, which clearly took the Subcommittee members by surprise: "We don't usually ask criminal organizations to come before the committee and recommend how to improve the law".[23] Sean Cronin of *The Irish Times* recorded that when asked to whom he was referring, Foley said, "Mr. Coleman has chosen to appear before you for Irish Northern Aid, the registered agent for the IRA ... Mr. Coleman ... looked startled."[24]

Then I would be given a blast but I wasn't a bit startled as I was well used to holding my own with Members of Congress. Significantly, Foley did not claim I was IRA. The worst he could come up with was that I "was on record of opposing the Anglo Irish Agreement." Then, clearly thinking he had the knock-out punch, pronounced: "Father Mc Manus has referred to Tip O'Neill, President Reagan, Pat Moynihan and Teddy Kennedy as lapsed Irishmen. Well, if that's a lapsed Irishman, I want to be included," Come on Foley, I thought, is that all you've got? My good friend Congressman Gary Ackerman (D-NY), a Jewish American, asked Foley what it meant to be a "lapsed Irishman." "It means that you do not agree with Father Mc Manus," was his reply.[25] First time I knew Foley had a sense of humor.

Struggle Against Extradition Treaty

Another major battle we fought on Capitol Hill, this time in the Senate, was against the Supplemental Extradition Treaty agreed between the British and the State Department in the summer of 1985. It proposed to remove the historic and venerable "political exception" to extradition – giving Britain the privilege of being the only country in the world without a political exception clause in its treaty with the United States, which meant that no Irish person who was wanted for a violent crime – and had escaped to America – could plead in a U.S. court that his or her offense was political. The British had hoped the Treaty would go through quietly, especially because of a recent Beirut hijacking. British Prime Minister Margaret Thatcher would also link to the Treaty her support for President Reagan's bombing of Libya on April 15, 1986.

However, the Treaty had to be ratified by two-thirds of the Senate. And I was determined to battle it for all my worth. I formulated three basic arguments, which became the accepted platform of all opposed to the Treaty: (1) it legitimized British rule in Northern Ireland; (2) it took away authority from the U.S. courts, which historically and properly adjudicated such cases; and (3) it surrendered an Irish person to a corrupt system of British law.

Although this Treaty was a terrible development, I pointed out to Irish-Americans all across the country that it provided us with the chance to bring our cause right into the U.S. Senate – an opportunity that rarely arises. We had to make the most of it. I extensively briefed the Minority Staff, i.e. the staff that worked for the Senate Democrats, whose ranking member was Joe Biden (who became Vice President in January 2009). We put out a press release saying:

It was a delight to hear Senator Biden right in the middle of the most prestigious committee state: "But I think this Extradition Treaty is an opportunity to do what we have been unable to do so far. There is an incredible reluctance on the part of this government to criticize one of our closest allies for what I believe to be an absolutely outrageous position which they have continued to maintain with regard to Northern Ireland, and an unwillingness on the part of the present government to do anything constructive about it, that is, the British government. So I want to make clear to you that I am going to do all that I can do to hold this up as long as I can to make the case."[26]

You know you have done your job when you hear your own words being repeated back virtually word for word in a Congressional hearing. The press gave our struggle considerable coverage. Even the British press was relatively fair with us this time. "Britain and Irish in battle on Capitol Hill", said the *Observer*, while displaying a photograph of the British Ambassador to Washington, Sir Oliver Wright, with whom I had clashed many times. The reporter, the well-respected Simon Hoggart, explained: "The British Government and the powerful Irish republican lobby are squaring up this week for their greatest fight ... Father Sean McManus is an affable and persuasive man who operates from an elegant office a few hundred yards from the Capitol ... [He] has sent a direct mail package to 250,000 people. The [outside] envelope says urgently: "The British are coming, the British are coming" – so cunningly associating their cause with the American Revolution."[27]

The Washington Post, national weekly edition, not usually a fan of those opposing Jolly Old England, was so taken with my direct mail package that it published a photograph of the outside envelope, with its entire graphics. In a lengthy article it proceeded to explain: "Inside the direct mail package the letter began: 'The British are indeed coming, this time into the United States Senate, and it's here we must meet and beat them.'"[28]

Even the brilliant curmudgeon Christopher Hitchens – who would go on to say bad things about God and Mother Teresa – did not bad-mouth me:

The master of these revels, in publicity terms, is Father
Sean McManus, a burly, plausible charmer whose Irish
National Caucus has taken center stage. In the years since
the Redemptorist order found him too much of a handful to
retain in Britain, the good Father has made himself expert
in congressional lobbying techniques ... I spent a long and,
to be perfectly frank, rather enjoyable afternoon with Father
McManus in his Capitol Hill office. He knew that I wanted
him to come clean about the Provisionals, and it became
clear that he hadn't been raised as a clerical apologist for
nothing ... Did he regard the Irish government (which
through its embassy is lobbying for the extradition treaty)
as the legitimate government of Ireland? A knowing smile:
"Do the Dublin government recognize Sir Oliver Wright as
the legitimate representative and envoy of Fermanagh and
West Belfast? If they do, they admit they represent only part
of the Irish people."[29]

I knew I had a massive task but I was committed. *The Sunday
Times* revealed just how committed: "The powerful Irish lobby
is ... working hard to kill the treaty. For example, Father Sean
McManus ... has even cancelled his annual summer holiday in
Ireland."[30] Now that's commitment – giving up a chance to go
back to Kinawley!

Our first task was to block speedy ratification, which we did.
The Boston Globe reported, "The committee originally intended
to hold one hearing last July 25. But opposition quickly developed
chiefly under the auspices of the Irish National Caucus."[31]
"Caucus blocks anti-IRA move: Irish group's pressure works on
U.S. Senate", was how Niall O'Dowd's article in *The Sunday
Press* heralded the story. "The U.S. Senate has baulked at quick
ratification of the proposed new extradition treaty ... following
a major lobbying effort by Irish-American groups headed by
the Irish National Caucus ... According to a spokesman for Sen.
Richard Lugar, head of the Senate Foreign Relations Committee,
pressure from Irish and concerned civil rights groups played a

major role in the postponement."[32] Margaret Thatcher lashed out: "The British Prime Minister, Mrs. Thatcher, yesterday criticized the delays, through 'a very effective Irish lobby' in the U.S. Congress, that have prevented the introduction of extradition for people accused of IRA activities."[33]

But despite our gallant effort, we did not win this one – but we were not beaten either. Although the "political exception" was rescinded, we, nonetheless, succeeded in getting some important conditions attached. Noted journalist Karen Tumulty – who covered Congress for the *Los Angeles Times* for fourteen years and would later join *Time* Magazine – assessed it this way:

> A compromise ... essentially allowed both sides to declare victory. Included in the compromise is a provision that permits a judge to deny extradition if he determines the accused could not get a fair trial because of "race, religion, nationality, or political opinions." Additional language in the accompanying report, not part of the treaty itself, would allow U.S. judges handling extradition cases to consider whether the British court system is fair. The language was added to answer criticism of the non-jury, single-judge courts, called Diplock courts, that are used to try IRA defendants.

As I said, we were not beaten either. And I think it may have been a pyrrhic victory for the British. An indication of this is that the British did not try to extradite Joe Doherty – who had been in prison for years in New York – under the terms of the new treaty. He was deported but not extradited.

I should note here that we not only briefed the Democrats on the Senate Foreign Relations Committee, but also the Republicans, as was always our bipartisan approach. Senator Orrin Hatch, a Mormon from Utah, whom we got to know quite well, became a strong opponent of the treaty. This deeply conservative man became an ardent supporter of Irish justice. Indeed, at that time, he was very critical of Teddy Kennedy's weak response. We proudly listed him on our letterhead as a

Congressional Friend of the Irish National Caucus for many years. But in 1991, I sent out a very large, direct-mail package in an attempt to stop Margaret Thatcher from getting the Presidential Medal of Freedom, and from being invited to speak at the Republican National Convention in 1992. As you can imagine, I told the truth about Thatcher's racist and anti-Irish Catholic record. Senator Hatch wrote demanding I take his name off our letterhead because of the "... offensive and intolerable language that was directed at Mrs. Thatcher ..." I responded in kind. "You shall, indeed, be removed because anyone who is prepared to condone and cover-up Margaret Thatcher's record of anti-Catholic bigotry and oppression in Northern Ireland has no right to be on our stationery."[34]

It was the end of a beautiful relationship. I never met with him again. But, still, he was a fine man, and I will always be grateful for what he did to oppose British violations of human rights – when some Irish-American Congressional leaders were too scared to take a stand.

Struggle Against Act of Settlement 1701

I must not neglect to mention one other campaign, which like so many others had not been attempted until the Caucus came along: repealing the anti-Catholic sections in The Act of Settlement 1701.

The Act of Settlement is an integral part of the unwritten and uncodified British Constitution. It determines succession to the Crown of England, and is, therefore, a fundamental constitutional statute, indeed, the very foundation stone of the Royal family. It contains provisions that decree a Catholic cannot succeed to the British throne, and that if the Monarch becomes a Catholic, or marries a Catholic, he/she forfeits the throne and "the people are absolved from their allegiance." (The ban on the Monarch marrying a Catholic was repealed in October 2011.)

Imagine had there been a provision in the U.S. Constitution forbidding an African American becoming President, or forbidding the President to marry a black person – think how that would have stoked the flames of racism and white supremacy.

While this statute may mean little to the average British man in the street, it has always been of the utmost importance to Protestant/Unionist/Orange extremists in Northern Ireland. It provides the ideological and philosophical underpinnings for their bigotry and sectarianism. For, you see, the spurious but deadly logic goes, if a Catholic by law can't get the top job, then Catholics are inferior to Protestants, and therefore, it's okay to discriminate against them.

But don't first blame extreme Orangemen – they did not create the Act of Settlement. Put the blame where it belongs: on the British monarchy and parliament – and on the Church of England and British Establishment for going along with this inherently sectarian Constitution. (The Constitution is also sexist and discriminates against women: if there is no direct male heir, a royal princess can succeed to the throne, but a younger brother takes precedence over an elder sister.)

It was a source of satisfaction to me that at long last the sectarian, anti-Catholic and undemocratic Act of Settlement 1701 was getting a public airing. For thirty years I had been "a voice crying in the wilderness" when I raised this issue. It astonished me that some Irish-Americans and indeed many Catholics in Northern Ireland failed to see that there was a causal connection between an anti-Catholic Constitution and anti-Catholic behavior by those extreme Orangemen who saw themselves as loyal upholders of the British constitution.

But now, in great measure due to the consciousness-raising done by the Irish National Caucus, there is a growing awareness in Britain and Ireland that those bigoted and sectarian provisions must be repealed.

One of the first Irish-Americans to appreciate the importance of exposing the sectarian Act of Settlement was a bright young attorney, Larry Downes, who was a leader of the Brehon Law Society in New York. Years later Larry, as Chairman of the Friends of Sinn Fein, would go on to raise millions of dollars for Sinn Fein. Few have shown more commitment to The Cause than he.

15

The Mac Bride Principles:
Genesis and History

*An Army of Principles Will Penetrate Where
an Army of Soldiers Cannot*

Thomas Paine[1]

I want to set out here for the historical record how the Irish National Caucus initiated, proposed, and launched the Mac Bride Principles. This is all the more important since there have been some attempts at revisionism. I will have to give an abundance of quotes from the press and other sources to document the clear and incontestable role of the Irish National Caucus. And the issue here is not the drafting of individual Principles, which are not particularly unique but generally modeled on the Sullivan Principles[2] and other such principles.

But first a statement of what the Principles are: the Mac Bride Principles – consisting of nine fair employment principles – are a corporate code of conduct for U.S. companies doing business in Northern Ireland and have become the Congressional standard for all U.S. aid to, or economic dealings with, Northern Ireland.

The Principles do not call for quotas, reverse discrimination, divestment (the withdrawal of U.S. companies from Northern

Ireland) or disinvestment (the withdrawal of funds now invested in firms with operations in Northern Ireland). The Caucus positively encourages non-discriminatory U.S. investment in Northern Ireland. The MacBride campaign is conducted on a three-fold level:

(1) Federal: the MacBride Principles became the law of the U.S. in October 1998. The U.S. House and Senate passed the MacBride Principles – as part of the Omnibus Appropriations Act for Fiscal Year 1999 – and President Clinton signed them into law. The MacBride law mandates that recipients of U.S. contributions to the International Fund for Ireland (IFI) must be in compliance with the MacBride Principles. (The U.S. has been contributing about $19.6 million per year since 1986 to the IFI.)

(2) State and cities: millions of dollars in State and city pension and retirement funds are invested in American corporations doing business in Northern Ireland. The MacBride campaign lobbies to have legislation passed to direct these funds to be invested, in the future, only in companies that endorse the Principles (again, note, not divestment or disinvestment). This is the first step. The second step – once the MacBride Principles investment law has been passed – is to get a contract compliance law passed.

(3) Shareholder Resolutions: the Campaign works to have shareholders pass resolutions endorsing the Principles.

The MacBride Principles did not suddenly appear from the sky like the Ten Commandments. They were the result of many years of hard and unrelenting work by the Irish National Caucus. The Principles were "conceived" in August 1979; "born" in June 1983; and "christened" in November 1984.

The MacBride Principles Conceived

One of the first objectives of the newly opened office of

the Irish National Caucus was to "stop United States dollars subsidizing anti-Catholic discrimination in Northern Ireland." To have impact on foreign policy you have to find the foreign policy nexus – that which connects Northern Ireland and the United States. The obvious "nexus" was the United States companies doing business in Northern Ireland. These companies could also be the "fulcrum" through which we could exercise leverage to oppose discrimination in Northern Ireland.

So these companies had to be held accountable to American legislators and investors. In July 1979, Congressman Ben Gilman (R-NY), a member of the House Committee on Foreign Affairs, and a member of the Subcommittee on International Economic Policy and Trade, commissioned the Irish National Caucus to conduct an investigation of the U.S. companies in Northern Ireland. We traveled to Northern Ireland at the end of July 1979 and the *Sunday News* announced our mission:

> Caucus in Jobs Blacklist Move: Americans probe workers' religions.
>
> American firms with production plants in Ulster are to be asked for a religious breakdown of local workers in a move to tighten up on United States equal opportunity laws. And some companies located in "sensitive" areas of the Province which do not have balanced Protestant–Catholic worker ratios could have a black mark against them in a report to an influential congressman in Washington.
>
> Later this week leading members of the Irish National Caucus from the federal capital will be touring Northern Ireland, knocking on the doors of American firms for details of their employment registers.
>
> The most significant of the credentials the team will present is a letter from New York Republican Congressman Ben Gilman, who sits on an international trade subcommittee with powerful controls on U.S. corporations operating overseas.

Fr. Sean McManus said the letter from Congressman Gilman gave their visit to American firms in the North a semi-official status. He added that the INC delegation would almost certainly be visiting the Ford-owned Autolite components factory at Finaghy and the management of the new DeLorean car assembly plant.[3]

The Irish Times said:

While in Northern Ireland the members of the Caucus will visit some American-owned companies to ascertain whether any discriminatory employment practices operate. The investigation is being carried out at the request of Congressman Benjamin Gilman, who is a member of the House Committee on Foreign Affairs and the Subcommittee on International Economic Policy and Trade. U.S. corporations, which are found not to reflect American respect for and protection of equal opportunities for all, could face withdrawal of tax concessions and trading licences.

One of the Caucus' recent achievements concerns the suspension of U.S. arms sales to the RUC, pending an investigation into the human rights situation in the north. They are also speaking of their determination to make Ireland an issue in the coming Presidential campaign.[4]

The Irish Press carried the story this way:

[Leaders of the Caucus] are in Ireland at present to investigate the behavior of American firms in the North. They are undertaking this mission on behalf of Congressman Benjamin A. Gilman, who is a member of the Congress Committee on Foreign Affairs and the Subcommittee on International Economic Policy and Trade.

This committee controls overseas aid, and if American firms locating outside the country are found to be discriminating against anyone on the basis of race, creed or color, their U.S. tax concessions may be cut off.[5]

The *Belfast Telegraph* said:

> The Irish National Caucus is investigating alleged discrimination at Goodyear's Craigavon factory. The Caucus has asked for a breakdown of religious affiliations of the 1,400 people employed at the Silverwood plant.
>
> Goodyear was one of many firms which signed the Fair Employment Declaration ... Prominent members of the Caucus are involved in the investigation – including Fr. Sean McManus.[6]

We made contact with most of the U.S. companies and asked them to submit a detailed breakdown of the religious composition of their workforce (in doing so we were years ahead of the British government's Fair Employment Laws, which did not make this demand until 1989).

Sean MacBride, INC Liaison Group

But the launching of the investigation into U.S. companies in Northern Ireland was not the only important initiative the Caucus took on its August mission to Ireland. There was another equally important initiative that would be full of significance and symbolism for the MacBride Principles later on. The Caucus established, in Dublin, the Irish National Caucus Liaison Group, chaired by Dr. Seán MacBride himself. The inaugural meeting was held in Seán's home, Roebuck House. *The Irish Times* reported:

> Mr. Seán MacBride, the Nobel Prize and Lenin Peace Prize winner, has become chairman of a new group in Ireland which aims to put forward the views of the Irish National Caucus, a United-States-based organization.
>
> Mr. Michael Mullen, general secretary of the Irish

Transport and General Workers' Union, is another member of the new group.

The Rev. Sean McManus, a leader of the Irish National Caucus, said last night in Dublin that the new group in Dublin would be called Irish National Caucus Associates. It would be based in the Republic and, besides Mr. MacBride, it would include Mr. Mullen and Mr. Kevin Boland, a former Fianna Fáil Minister.

The initial meeting, which was attended by 20 people, was held on Thursday, and another one would be held later this month.[7]

Back in the US, the *Irish World* told Irish-Americans of this initiative in the following way:

Sean MacBride, recipient of both the Nobel Peace Prize and Lenin Peace Prize, has announced his agreement to act as chairman of a new organization in the Republic of Ireland which aims to act as a liaison between the U.S.-based Irish National Caucus and the people of Ireland ... "The idea of our organization," MacBride said, "is to get across to the Irish public the truth about the United States organization and to emphasize the significance of the Irish-American dimension. The success of the Irish National Caucus was seen in the U.S. State Department policy review on supplying arms to the RUC." MacBride added that, in his opinion, the work of the I.N.C. had been somewhat misrepresented by a number of individuals in Ireland and that it is his hope that the work of the new organization will present a clearer picture of Caucus activities. "The Irish National Caucus is not a "front" for any group in Ireland. It is undoubtedly the most effective and widely-respected Irish-American Organization in the States and we hope to contribute to its goal of a just and lasting peace in the North of Ireland."[8]

It should be obvious to all that in these two Caucus

initiatives (investigation of U.S. companies in Northern Ireland and Seán MacBride becoming Chairman of our Liaison Group in the Republic of Ireland) were sown the seeds of the MacBride Principles. Since he had left the Dáil in 1958, Seán MacBride had established a policy of not belonging to any party or group dealing specifically with Northern Ireland. But he broke this policy to identify with the Irish National Caucus. He was attracted to the Irish National Caucus for the following reasons:

(1) It is nonviolent.
(2) It has no foreign principal – that is, it is neither controlled nor directed by any organization, party, or government in Ireland.
(3) It did not send funds to Ireland.

Seán MacBride particularly admired the Caucus' focus on stopping U.S. dollars subsidizing anti-Catholic discrimination in Northern Ireland. Paddy Harte, TD for Donegal, launched an appalling personal attack in the press on MacBride, calling him senile and other abusive things. (Harte never apologized for his attack.) The other Donegal TD, the late Neil Blaney, congratulated MacBride, joined the Liaison Group, and announced he was going to the U.S. to speak for the Irish National Caucus. Neil had a life-long record of concern for the North of Ireland. Paddy Harte would later become the founder of Irish-American Partnership that was launched by Taoiseach Garret FitzGerald in 1984.

We decided that a good way to "frame the issue" of U.S. dollars subsidizing anti-Catholic discrimination in Northern Ireland would be to have the Ad Hoc Committee for Irish Affairs, which we had initiated, hold a Hearing, and bring Fr. Brian Brady over from Belfast to testify about the hiring practices of U.S. companies in Northern Ireland. The hearing took place on July 22, 1981. It was the first time ever that discrimination by U.S. companies in Northern Ireland was raised in the United States Congress.

After the Ad Hoc Congressional Hearing, the Irish National

Caucus planned to have our principle, that United States dollars should not subsidize anti-Catholic discrimination in Northern Ireland, enshrined into law. We worked assiduously on this. In 1983, we succeeded at last in having a Bill introduced into Congress, HR 3465: "Requiring United States persons who conduct business or control enterprises in Northern Ireland to comply with certain fair employment principles." It was modeled on the Sullivan Principles and became known as the "Ottinger Bill", after its chief sponsor, Congressman Dick Ottinger (D-NY). Although the Bill did not pass, it was of singular importance because it perfectly framed our issue. We now had in place all the essential elements of what we would later call the Mac Bride Principles:

1) The ongoing investigation of the United States companies in Northern Ireland.
2) The high-profile involvement of Seán Mac Bride in our campaign.
3) A set of fair employment principles for those companies to serve as a corporate code of conduct.

The very first lobbyists against the Ottinger Bill were the Irish Embassy in Washington, DC, and John Hume. I issued the following press release:

> Irish Embassy Cover-up on Anti-Catholic Discrimination
> Washington, D.C., November 4, 1983
>
> The Irish National Caucus has reacted with anger to attempts by the Irish Embassy to sabotage legislation in Congress that would outlaw discrimination by American companies in Northern Ireland.
> The Caucus claims that it has been told by a number of Congressional offices that the Irish Embassy is advising them not to sponsor the Bill of Congressman Richard L. Ottinger (D-NY). One office reported in amazement to the Caucus that the Irish Embassy is saying that the Ottinger Bill would actually increase unemployment in Northern

Ireland.

Fr. Sean McManus, National Director, said: "The Irish Embassy is quite simply conspiring with the British Embassy to cover up anti-Catholic Discrimination in Northern Ireland. I call upon the Opposition Parties and Independents in the Dail to demand that this disgraceful sellout of the Catholics in Northern Ireland cease."

When Congressman Ottinger first introduced the Bill, Irish Embassy officials told him that they approved of it. Then John Hume and [the Rev. Ian] Paisley came to Washington. John Hume was quoted in the *Washington Times*, September 20, 1983, as saying, "There are 27 U.S. plants in N.I., and I have not heard one complaint about discrimination practices. We have a fair employment bill that makes discrimination illegal." That is an extraordinary thing for John Hume to say.

Paisley has leaned on John Hume, and the British Government has leaned on the Irish Government to oppose the Ottinger legislation. How can Garret FitzGerald possibly explain to the people of Ireland that it would be bad for the U.S. Congress to make it illegal for U.S. companies in N.I. to discriminate?

The greatest weapon the British have for oppressing Catholics in Northern Ireland is the Irish Embassy in Washington.

Whenever the Irish National Caucus succeeds in raising the Irish issue, the British always make the Irish Embassy jump to defend British interests,"concluded Fr. McManus.[9]

Niall O'Dowd – who would later become the publisher of the *Irish Voice* newspaper and *Irish America* magazine in New York – would report from San Francisco:

> The revelation that the Irish Embassy was actively campaigning against the Bill came yesterday from the offices of Congresswoman Barbara Boxer (D-CA) who

confirmed that in separate meetings representatives from both the Irish and British governments had asked her to oppose the Bill ... In response to Fr. Mc Manus' criticism, Michael Collins [later the Irish Ambassador in Washington], the Irish Government's press and information officer in the United States, stated that the embassy had "taken a long and detailed look at all aspects of the Ottinger Bill and that they foresee problems with it. We believe that this Bill could have a counter-productive effect."[10]

The MacBride Principles Born

The Ottinger Bill contained in essence the principles we would later call the MacBride Principles. That is why we say that the MacBride Principles were born in 1983. To promote the Ottinger Bill, the Irish National Caucus sponsored a visit to Northern Ireland by Congressman Ottinger in 1983. We hosted the Congressman's appearances at meetings and Press Conferences in Belfast. The visit received considerable press coverage in the Irish and British media. Bob Blancato, the Staff Director of the Ad Hoc Congressional Committee for Irish Affairs, was also part of the delegation, representing the Chairman of the Committee, Congressman Mario Biaggi (D-NY).

We could tell we were on to something very important by the way the press reacted. The *Daily Telegraph*, under the heading "Americans in Ulster Maelstrom," said:

Mr. Ottinger's mission is regarded with far more suspicion in the Protestant camp. At the moment, he is steering legislation through Congress to force American companies investing in Northern Ireland to employ more Roman Catholics.

In June, he introduced a Bill called the Northern Ireland Fair Employment Practices Act, which would require American firms with branches or other enterprises in Ulster to desegregate employees of different religions and eliminate religious discrimination in jobs.

The spotlight is being put on Short Brothers, the Belfast plane-makers, who are bidding to sell aircraft to the United States Air Force. The contract would mean an extra 600 jobs ...

Advising the Congressman, and helping him in the talks, was Fr. Sean McManus, the Washington-based Redemptorist priest ordained in England and now a scourge of the British Government. The lime-and-soda-drinking cleric is not liked by British diplomats in the American capital, where he leads the Irish National Caucus, a lobbying group aimed at influencing American foreign policy with the target of Irish unity, freedom and peace.[11]

The *News Letter* screamed the headline, "Anti-British to the Hilt", and said:

> The leading light in the delegation, Fr. Sean McManus, is a well-known republican sympathizer who rarely disguises his anti-British stance ... this fiery advocate of Irish republicanism did his utmost to embarrass British diplomats in Washington with a brief hunger strike outside the Embassy in support of Bobby Sands' death fast.
>
> He was instrumental in persuading the Carter administration to impose an embargo on American gun sales to the RUC in Belfast. And his latest campaign aimed at undermining the attempt by Shorts to secure a multi-million pound order to sell its SD-330 Sherpa freighters to the United States Air Force.
>
> It was back in 1979 that Fr. McManus told reporters: "The British thought they were getting rid of me in 1972, when they had me packed off to America. Little did they know I would be far more vocal on Capitol Hill".[12]

The *Daily Express*, August 18, 1983, however, really outdid itself. It devoted an editorial to our visit:

> Sean McManus, a rancid bigot loosely described as a

"priest," is campaigning to stop a £33 million order from the United States Air Force going to Shorts, the Belfast plane-makers.

McManus – born in Northern Ireland but now in Washington heading an anti-British pressure group – alleges there is discrimination against Catholics at Shorts: though the firm denies it.

Doubtless he is delirious at the calls from other pip-squeak Irish-American politicians urging President Reagan to appoint a special envoy to Northern Ireland.

Indeed, he probably has a hand in the setting up of the "Irish-American Presidential Committee" to push the issue of a unified Ireland into the 1984 presidential campaign."[13]

Shorts

While in Belfast, we took the occasion to pursue the other very hot issue – the question of the United States Air Force doing business with Short Brothers (Shorts had a notorious record of anti-Catholic discrimination). The Caucus had been raising this issue for quite some time. This was really one of our pivotal campaigns because it dramatically raised the whole issue of U.S. dollars subsidizing anti-Catholic discrimination in Northern Ireland. We met with Short's executives at the office of the Fair Employment Agency. Again, this meeting received considerable press coverage. Our Shorts campaign would eventually lead to Congressman Joe Kennedy (D-MA) getting an Amendment passed (1988, 1989 and 1990) in Congress to the U.S. Defense Bill. The Amendment required Shorts to submit an annual statistical report to the Defense Department on its subcontracting and recruiting practices.

At the meeting, I remember the Shorts' spokesman – with barely concealed hostility – telling me, "Shorts does not have to give any explanations to the Irish National Caucus or anybody in America." How their tune has changed. That same spokesperson would later have to go, cap in hand, to meet with the then

Comptroller of New York City, Elizabeth Holtzman, to assure her that Shorts was making attempts to hire more Catholics.

The Empire Strikes Back

Just before one main press conference was due to take place, Fr. Brian Brady called and told us that a high-ranking Catholic Church official in Belfast had asked him to ask us to meet with someone who had a special interest in the Shorts issue. We agreed.

The person arrived and asked to meet with us behind a big curtain in the room where the press conference would take place, in the Europa Hotel in Belfast. He did not want to be seen by the press. His name was James Eccles, a former Head of the Knights of Columbanus (a lay Catholic organization in Ireland. It is quite powerful and very "respectable"). Eccles' pitch was that the Knights had done a lot of investigation into anti-Catholic discrimination in Northern Ireland. We asked him to provide us with the results of the alleged investigation. He was completely taken aback. We knew the guy had an angle, to say the least. He said he agreed that Shorts was guilty of very bad discrimination, but ... "But," I cut in, "you still think they should get the contract with the U.S. Air Force?" Eccles said yes. He then promised if Shorts got the contract, the Knights would put pressure on them to end discrimination. We politely told him that we would keep up the pressure on Shorts, and showed him the door (or rather, the curtain).

While he was giving us this unbelievably disingenuous pitch, I couldn't help remembering that it was the Catholic Bishop of Belfast, Cahal Daly, who was among the very first to voice public opposition to our campaign against Shorts. There is a morning radio program in Northern Ireland called *Thought for the Day* on BBC Ulster. Bishop Daly instructed Fr. Gerry Patton – the media person for the diocese – to use the program to attack our campaign. Patton deplored the fact that there was a campaign in the U.S. to oppose Shorts getting an Air Force contract and wanted to make sure the people realized that the priest (myself) who was leading it had no connection with the Diocese of Down and Connor.

Mr. Eccles, about a year later, sent us an unsigned note identifying himself as the person who had met with us prior to the press conference and he wanted us to know that we had been right about Shorts – that they had only made promises to get the contract with the U.S. Air Force, and then it was business as usual.

The same Mr. Eccles would surface again in the U.S. as the main lobbyist against the MacBride Principles – assuring legislators that discrimination was a thing of the past, that the MacBride Principles would only hurt Catholics, etc. Eccles traveled all across the U.S. with the same message.

At one MacBride Hearing in Nebraska, on March 13, 1989, one of Eccles' prize statements was: "I was knighted by the Pope, and I'm very close to the workings of the Catholic Church in Ireland." I hung my head in shame and thought to myself, "Once again the Catholic Church is being used for British interests in Ireland."

I had many reports that while lobbying in the U.S. against the MacBride Principles, Mr. Eccles allegedly gave the impression that he was doing so with the blessing of the late Cardinal Tomás O'Fiaich, Archbishop of Armagh and Catholic Primate of Ireland. I made a statement in *The Irish Times* that I would be very surprised and deeply disappointed if Cardinal O'Fiaich was allowing his name to be used by the British government's anti-MacBride campaign in the U.S. The next day, I received a mailgram stating, "No one authorized to use my name in any way to oppose MacBride Principles. Northern Catholic Bishops have never made any statement on the MacBride Principles."[14] It was signed: Cardinal O'Fiaich, Ara Coeli, Armagh.

Mr. Eccles would later spread the word in the *Sunday News* that he was not paid for his anti-MacBride work: "... Mr. Eccles' son Jim said: 'My father does speak out against the MacBride Principles because he firmly believes that they will do more harm than good. But he has never received money for it, not even traveling expenses ... He visits America frequently. While he is there, he makes his views known on the Mac Bride Principles ... He sees it as an extension of the charity work he has been heavily engaged in for nearly 30 years.'"[15]

But former British MP Kevin Mc Namara in his book on the Mac Bride Principles would reveal – having had access to British government documents – that Eccles, "was expensive. He was employed for a maximum of 60 days a year at £220 per day plus expenses, and was in receipt of an annual retainer.'[16] Mr. Eccles was also a member of the board of the Fair Employment Agency (FEA) from 1985 to the autumn of 1989, when the Agency was replaced by the Fair Employment Commission (FEC). In May 1990, the FEC issued a report charging that the motor trade in which Mr. Eccles worked had a very serious imbalance – that Catholics were seriously under-represented. Indeed, the FEC said that the actual company for which Eccles worked – A.S. Baird Ltd – was only 18 percent Catholic. The FEC 1991 figures are 67 Protestants (73.6 percent); 24 Catholics (26.4 percent); 34 "unknowns"; in all, a total of 125 employees.

What did Mr. Eccles say in response to this very embarrassing exposure? He alleged he "had not come across any pattern of discrimination during his years in the trade. I was too busy trying to earn an honest pound."[17] Indeed.

Aer Lingus Cover-Up

By the way, the other very interesting "champion" that sprang to the defense of Shorts was Aer Lingus. One of our members had written to them complaining that they were using Shorts 330 aircraft. The Chief Executive Officer of Aer Lingus, David M. Kennedy, wrote back on June 23, 1983, saying, "We are satisfied there is no religious discrimination in recruitment or employment practices of Shorts." At that time, Short's percentage of Catholics was less than 5 percent out of a workforce of 6,300.[18]

I was outraged and issued the following press statement: "I simply cannot believe that any responsible spokesperson for Aer

Lingus – not to mention the chief executive – would make such an extraordinary statement. There is simply no other way to put it: This is a blatant cover-up. Whenever the British Government is in trouble, it seems it can always get some gombeen man to do its dirty work. Mr. Kennedy is but the latest example in this dismal tradition."

Aer Lingus is semi-state-owned and it is unlikely Mr. Kennedy would have made that statement without the explicit approval of the Irish government. Garret FitzGerald was Taoiseach at the time.

On May 3, 1983, I sent a letter to all 535 Members of the United States House of Representatives and Senate, outlining the case against Shorts. The following week (May 10, 1983), the British Ambassador, Oliver Wright, sent letters to all the same people – with a glossy brochure, specifically written by Shorts to refute our charges of discrimination. Two black-and-white photos were enclosed with the brochure: one of Garret FitzGerald standing beside a Shorts' aircraft, and one of the head of Aer Lingus receiving a Shorts' aircraft.

Dublin Government Cover-Up

But the plot thickens. In 1983, James Shannon was a Democratic Congressman from Massachusetts. He was very close to the Irish Embassy in Washington, DC, and would not make a move on the Irish issue without the blessing of the Embassy. One of our members – a constituent of his – wrote to the Congressman asking him to support the Caucus' campaign of opposing Shorts getting a U.S. Air Force contract. This was his response:

> The Irish Government recently reviewed the situation at Short Brothers in Belfast. It noted historical patterns of clear discrimination, and also noted recent efforts to correct that situation, including: the appointment of a Catholic personnel director, active recruitment in Catholic schools and in the Catholic press, and agreeing with the Fair Employment Agency to set up an affirmative action program. It also noted

that the prevailing opinion in both communities in the North was that the proper approach is to eliminate discriminatory hiring practices, and then to promote foreign investment and employment. The Irish Government recently contracted with Short Brothers for the production of aircraft for the national airline, Aer Lingus. This is the best evidence that progress is being made in correcting historical patterns of injustice.[19]

So there you have it. The first opponents of our campaign to stop the U.S. subsidizing anti-Catholic discrimination were John Hume, the Catholic Bishop of Belfast, the Knights of Columbanus, Aer Lingus and the Irish government. And you thought the British government ruled only through the Protestants of Northern Ireland! It would seem that the Irish Embassy was a wholly owned subsidiary of the British government. The architects of the Embassy's policy were Garret FitzGerald, Sean Donlon, Michael Lillis – and John Hume.

The Mercurial Mr. Devlin

It is also interesting to note here that on our visit to Ireland in 1979, we met with the late Paddy Devlin, former Social Democratic and Labour Party (SDLP) leader. He was very excited about our idea of making an impact on discrimination through the leverage of American companies. He kept saying he could not believe that he himself had not thought of this idea, and that nobody in the North even knew which were the American companies.

The next time I saw Paddy Devlin was in the U.S. at a hearing testifying against the Principles. He became one of the team of Catholics the British government (through its Department of Economic Development) recruited. Devlin would write later in his column in the *Sunday World*: "My personal view of the principles is that they will undermine our efforts to eliminate discrimination, deflect U.S. investment away and cause the withdrawal of U.S. companies by putting them into conflict with our labour laws."[20] The following year he said, "The Mac Bride Principles are a sham.

It is time we identified the primary issue of the hidden agenda that is the disestablishment of Northern Ireland society."[21]

Watershed

The Caucus/Ottinger visit to Northern Ireland served as a watershed in our campaign. After this, a number of elected officials contacted us, wishing to become associated with our campaign. Chief among these were: New York City Comptroller Harrison J. Goldin, Council Member Sal Albanese of the New York City Council, New York State Assemblyman John Dearie, New York State Senator John Flynn and Massachusetts State Senate President Bill Bulger.

The Caucus saw the need not only to involve United States legislators, but also institutional investors in our campaign. As New York City Comptroller, Mr. Goldin was one of the custodians of millions of dollars of New York City funds invested in a number of United States companies doing business in Northern Ireland. We eagerly welcomed him into our campaign. We worked with his office on issuing a new set of principles. For me, there could be no question as to the person after whom we should name these principles: Seán Mac Bride.

Mac Bride Principles Christened

But let me go back a bit. I first met Seán Mac Bride in New York City in the spring of 1976 when he was the guest speaker at an AOH function. At the time I was the Deputy National Chaplain of the AOH, and as such, I was seated at the head table, next to Seán. I was amazed and humbled he took such an interest in me and the work of the Irish National Caucus. I was used to the "great and the good" in Ireland not wanting to know me, which I took as a badge of honor.

The next time I saw Seán was at the previously mentioned AOH Convention in Killarney, June 27-29, 1978. When he spoke, he went out of his way to commend me and the work of the Irish National Caucus. A journalist commented to me that it was significant that he had done so, given the open hostility of the Dublin government to me. I kept in touch with Seán, and as explained earlier, in July 1979, I asked him to head up the INC Liaison Group in Dublin.

Then I invited Seán to be the guest speaker at the Fifth Annual Testimonial Dinner Dance of the Irish National Caucus on December 10, 1982 in New York City, attended by close to 1,000 guests. The following morning I picked him up at his hotel to bring him to speak to the Caucus chapter in Huntington, New York. "Did it [the dinner dance] end peaceably?" he smilingly inquired in his still partial-French accent. I asked him why he put the question. "Well, in my day, Irish-American events sometimes ended in a fight," he replied.

Later on I dropped him off at the airport. As we sat for a moment, before he left the car, I was deeply conscious of the history he represented, and felt in some inchoate way that I needed to do something to honor his family history. In truth, he was the only person in whose presence I felt overawed, indeed, a bit intimidated. I asked him if we ever came up with something – a document, proclamation, something – if he would lend his name to it. Without hesitation he consented.

So when the time came, I talked to Seán Mac Bride on the phone a number of times about naming the Principles after him. On October 18, 1984, I formally wrote him, proposing and enclosing, the Principles.

On Monday, November 5, 1984, the Irish National Caucus announced the launching of the Mac Bride Principles. Thus the Principles were "christened."

Our press release carried the heading, "Caucus' New Plan to Combat Discrimination" and went on to say: "The Irish National Caucus today announced a major new initiative to combat employment discrimination in Northern Ireland ... The Caucus has endorsed a set of Equal Opportunity Affirmative Action Principles for Northern Ireland that have been sponsored by Seán Mac Bride ... 'This approach,' said Fr. Sean Mc Manus, '... is the way for Americans to deal with anti-Catholic discrimination.'"

The Irish Echo (New York) captured the historic moment accurately with the headline: "Caucus Proposes New Initiative to Stop Discrimination in Northern Ireland."[22] The *Sunday Tribune* reported: "The nine-point employment code, which was drawn up by the Washington-based Irish National Caucus (I.N.C.) is sponsored by Seán MacBride S.C., leading Northern Ireland trade unionist Inez McCormack and Northern surgeon Senator John Robb and Father Brian Brady."[23] That was the very first occasion the MacBride Principles were mentioned by name in the Irish or American media.

Thus, a historic initiative was conceived, born, and christened.

We wanted to mention Comptroller Goldin's name in our announcement, but at that stage he was not prepared to associate his name with the Principles. In fact, he backed out at the last moment, after I had told Seán MacBride that he would join us in the announcement. The first New York politician, in fact, to publicly associate himself with the MacBride Principles was City Councilmember Sal Albanese (D-Bay Ridge). I had been advising Goldin to associate himself publicly with the MacBride Principles, otherwise other New York politicians would beat him to the punch. But he thought it was just a tactic to stampede him into supporting the Principles earlier than he wanted to.

Caucus Launches MacBride Campaign

The moment Councilmember Albanese read *The Irish Echo*'s report on the launching of the MacBride Principles, he contacted the Irish National Caucus with a view to introducing a Bill in the New York City Council. He and the Caucus worked on the drafting, and on December 19, 1984, a Bill was introduced: #878. This was to be the very first MacBride Bill in the U.S.

And so, the MacBride campaign had formally begun. The *New York Daily News* reported: "City Councilman Sal Albanese (D-Bay Ridge) will appear at City Hall tomorrow in a rally with Rev. Sean McManus, National Director of the Irish National Caucus, to seek support for the bill."[24] *The Irish Echo* announced: "Fr. Sean McManus, national director of the Irish National Caucus, will hold a press conference with Councilman Albanese at City Hall on Jan. 3 at 10:30 am calling on Irish groups to support Intro. No. 878."[25] The *Chief Leader* said: "The Irish National Caucus has chosen New York City to be the first where pension fund investments will be used to increase pressure for equal rights for Catholics in Northern Ireland ..."[26] The *Catholic New York* newspaper said: "Father McManus was present at City Hall recently to speak in favor of the [Albanese] legislation ... Father McManus said that proposed legislation is 'eminently reasonable ... One of the most effective ways for us to combat the situation is to get the investors involved and make them aware they are supporting anti-Catholic discrimination,' he told *Catholic New York*."[27]

The Sunday Times: "The [MacBride] campaign is being run by the Irish National Caucus ....The move, inspired by Father Sean McManus, who has been consistently opposed to British policy, is particularly well timed. For even if the law is never passed, it provides an opportunity to link, however, tenuously, the issues of South Africa and Northern Ireland. The MacBride Principles also call for the same kind of affirmative action programs for Catholics which American companies already use in the employment of women and blacks in the U.S.A"[28] This was the very first mention of the Principles in the British press.

In an interview with Niall O'Dowd in *The Irish Press* Comptroller Goldin said: "Moreover, having reviewed the MacBride Principles, I endorse this initiative."[29] (Notice: he speaks about "having reviewed," not having originated the Principles. It was only later that people associated with the Comptroller made the retroactive claim that he had developed the Principles.)

But in New York papers, Comptroller Goldin, unfortunately, came out very publicly against the Bill. The *New York Daily News*, under the headline "Koch & Goldin Oppose Ulster Investment Ban," said:

Mayor Koch and City Controller Harrison Goldin expressed opposition yesterday to a City bill that would prohibit city Pension fund investments in the U.S. owned businesses that discriminate against Northern Ireland. Their reaction came after the Rev. Sean Mc Manus, National Director of the Irish National Caucus Inc., a Northern Irish Catholic lobbying group based in Washington, appeared at City Hall to urge passage of the bill. The measure, sponsored by Councilman Sal Albanese (D-Brooklyn) [*sic*], is awaiting a hearing in the Council's economic development committee ... Goldin said the Council Bill was premature.[30]

A leading column in *The Irish Echo* stated:

Mayor Koch and City Comptroller Harrison Goldin are opposed to such tough measures on the grounds that the British have an official policy that is against discrimination, and the situation in Belfast is very different from South Africa where the government has an official policy of discrimination.

The "unofficial" nature of discrimination in Northern Ireland notwithstanding, it is still a fact that Catholics do not have equal opportunity in the North, and that New York City officials have every right to be concerned about it ...

It is for this reason Councilman Albanese should be encouraged ... and that Mr. Koch and Mr. Goldin – who I am sure are acting in good faith – should be asked to take another look at their position. Mr. Koch has the strong support of the majority of the Irish community in New York and I am sure he would like to maintain that support.[31]

The New York Times reported: "The Council measure is opposed by Mayor Koch, who sits on the boards of the four largest pension funds for city workers, and City Comptroller Harrison J. Goldin, the custodian for all five funds in the system and a trustee of the four largest funds."[32]

At this stage – and for a good while later – Goldin was

opposed to legislation on the Principles. He felt that shareholder resolutions would have sufficient leverage and his office did not want anything to overshadow his role. His office fought Albanese's office on this, so much so that Albanese and I had to call a meeting in New York City to push the need for legislation. About 400 Irish-Americans attended the meeting. I spoke very forcefully about the need for legislation – not just shareholder resolutions. Even at that meeting, Goldin's office opposed the idea of legislation. But the mood of the meeting was clearly in our favor, and soon afterwards, Goldin's office withdrew their opposition to legislation. That meeting was a key building block in the long construction of the Mac Bride campaign. At the meeting, Pat Doherty, Goldin's aide, was visibly shaken by the anger towards Goldin. Time and time again, I witnessed people say to him, "There has to be a law. There has to be a law," the adopted refrain of the Albanese–Caucus supporters. Indeed, I had to run interference several times to ask them to leave Pat alone. Goldin soon realized, however, that he had made a terrible mistake. The train was leaving the station, and he was not on board! He was in a position to play a key role in our campaign, but his public opposition to the New York City legislation had hurt him badly.

Comptroller Goldin had lost the high ground. How could he reclaim it? The Caucus wanted Goldin to be prominently involved because as the custodian of millions of dollars, he represented the vitally important role of investors in the Mac Bride campaign.

Caucus-Golden Visit

There is a well-known technique whereby American politicians stake claim to an interest in Irish issues – the highly publicized visit to Ireland. There is nothing wrong with this. Presidents Kennedy and Reagan did it; why shouldn't a non-Irish-American also do it? So Comptroller Goldin needed to visit Ireland. But how to go about it? Who would sponsor the visit? Who would set it up? And very importantly, who would have the resources to pay for it? The answer – the Irish National Caucus.

That the Caucus attached great importance to the role Goldin could play is seen in the fact that it was prepared to spend so much money on the trip.

Furthermore, the Caucus had already "covered" the legislative dimension of the Mac Bride Principles – we now needed to "cover" the investment dimension. The *New York Daily News* would give the Caucus–Goldin visit prominent coverage: "A U.S. based Irish lobbying group paid up to $12,000 so City Comptroller Harrison Goldin could visit Ireland – with his family and aide – to look into complaints of economic discrimination against Catholics in Northern Ireland ... A spokesman for the comptroller said it was official city business."[33]

The aide was Pat Doherty, who would go on to feature prominently in the Mac Bride campaign, and become a good friend.

Some Irish-American groups shortsightedly criticized the Irish National Caucus for "wasting money." But when they finally understood the significance of the Caucus strategy, they were very eager to associate themselves with the Mac Bride campaign. The Goldin visit received heavy coverage in the British and Irish media, thereby helping to establish the Mac Bride Principles firmly in the public mind. It was on this trip that Goldin met Seán Mac Bride for the first time – eight months after the Irish National Caucus had launched the Mac Bride Principles.

The Caucus arranged meetings with Charlie Haughey, the Fair Employment Agency, John Hume and various U.S. companies. It was ironic that the British government attempted to make great play out of the fact that Sinn Féin was the only political party in Northern Ireland to support the Mac Bride Principles. However, when Sinn Féin met with the Goldin group in Belfast, they expressed strong opposition to the Principles, saying they were not radical enough. But the real reason for their opposition was because the Principles were launched by the Irish National Caucus. (Sinn Féin opposed the Irish National Caucus because it is nonviolent, and because the Caucus does not allow itself to be controlled from Ireland.) But later, when Sinn Féin saw that the Principles were driving the British government up the wall, they reversed their position and began to express public support for them.

In the United States, the trip was also given considerable press coverage. *The New York Times*, the *New York Daily News* and the *New York Post* all devoted editorials to it. For example, the *New York Daily News* editorial said: "How did Goldin get involved with the so-called Mac Bride Principles? Although named for an aging Irish Nobel laureate Seán Mac Bride, they were actually drawn up in the U.S. by the Irish National Caucus. The Caucus organized and paid for Goldin's trip – at a cost of about $12,000."[34]

The New York Times editorial said: "A lofty but misguided proposition for opposing discrimination against Catholics in Northern Ireland has reared its head in Congress, three state legislatures and the New York City Council. Based on what are called the "Mac Bride Principles" ... The principal sponsor is the Irish National Caucus, a Washington lobby intent on getting Americans to pressure Britain to withdraw from Northern Ireland ... Comptroller Harrison Goldin, just back from Northern Ireland, is pressuring pension funds to act on their own."[35]

A *New York Post* editorial said: "City Controller Harrison Goldin says he recently visited Northern Ireland as a trustee of the city's $28 billion-plus pension fund. He wanted to see if employment discrimination exists, with an eye toward using the fund's considerable muscle to end it. It was official business, says Goldin. The Irish National Caucus – a private organization which lobbies politicians on behalf of Ireland – paid. It wasn't cheap, either. The Caucus estimates it cost upwards of $12,000."[36]

In a short time, the Irish National Caucus campaign would be featured in *The Wall Street Journal*, the *Philadelphia Inquirer*, *The Boston Globe*, and many other major newspapers.

Mac Bride Becomes State Law

At our urging, our good friend State Senator Billy Bulger used his influence to have Massachusetts become the first State to pass the Mac Bride Principles. I launched the Massachusetts Campaign in Springfield with a speech before the John Boyle O'Reilly Club – a very appropriate place – in February 1985. *The Sunday Republican* reported: "U.S. dollars mustn't subsidize anti-Catholic discrimination in Northern Ireland ... the Caucus is asking American firms to adopt the Mac Bride Principles ... "American businesses can have a profound effect," [Fr. Mc Manus] said. "You're talking about millions of dollars ... We're not calling for disinvestment. We are not trying to end American investment in Northern Ireland," he said.[37]

We worked closely with State Representative Tom Gallagher (D-18th Suffolk District). On October 1, 1985, he wrote to me: "I expect the Massachusetts House will shortly take up legislation applying the Mac Bride Principles to state pension fund investment. I believe the measure will reach the Governor's desk this session, and will make Massachusetts the first state to apply Mac Bride to its investments. I look forward to working with you in the future."[38]

The Massachusetts Mac Bride Bill was signed into law by Governor Michael Dukakis on November 21, 1985. It was the first Mac Bride law in America. Dukakis still supported the Mac Bride Principles as a presidential candidate in 1988 (despite the strong lobbying of John Hume). While I was still based in Boston, Governor Dukakis invited me to his office on St. Patrick's Day 1978, to present me with a proclamation he was issuing at our request, "Human Rights for Ireland Day." (That, of course, caused Irish Consul Carmel Heaney further fury.)

New York Assemblyman John Dearie and New York State Senator John Flynn initiated Bills on the Mac Bride Principles.

Soon afterwards, in May 1986, New York became the second State to pass the Mac Bride Principles. In 1992, New York State became the first State to pass a Mac Bride Principles Contract Compliance Bill.

The Irish National Caucus then initiated Congressional legislation on the Mac Bride Principles (the Fish-D'Amato Bill, introduced on October 1, 1986), just as we had done on the

seminal Ottinger Bill in 1983. And, as they say, the rest is history.
Virtually all Irish-American organizations, the AFL-CIO, many
religious groups (Catholics and Protestants) rallied behind the
Mac Bride Principles, making them the most powerful American
campaign on Northern Ireland since its creation in 1920.

Mac Bride's Death

After Seán Mac Bride's death on January 15, 1988, his son
Tiernan – with typical Mac Bride generosity – wrote to me: On
behalf of the late Seán Mac Bride I would like to thank you most
sincerely for travelling to Dublin to attend his funeral. He will
never be forgotten while the Principles drawn up by the Irish
National Caucus are named after him.[39]

And on June 28, 1993, Caitriona Lawlor in Dublin wrote the
following letter to Ken Bertsch, Investor Responsibility Research
Center:

> I understand that you are preparing an updated
> version of "The Mac Bride Principles and U.S. companies
> in Northern Ireland" ... During the years 1976 to 1988,
> I worked as Personal Assistant to Seán Mac Bride and
> witnessed the attention he paid to the causes in which he
> believed, in days when such causes were neither popular
> nor profitable. It amused me, therefore, to see the reference
> contained on p. 60 of the current edition, "Doherty and
> Mc Manus dispute exactly who should take credit for
> the idea of a fair employment code for recruiting Seán
> Mac Bride as Sponsor." My understanding always was
> that the fair employment initiative for Northern Ireland lay
> squarely with Father Sean Mc Manus and the Irish National
> Caucus in Washington, and it was to great advantage when
> the Comptroller of New York City, Harrison Goldin, and
> his office took up the cudgels. Indeed, Father Mc Manus
> was adamant even in the initial stages of preparation, that
> Mac Bride should be involved and should lend his name to

the Principles, based loosely on the Sullivan Principles for South Africa.

This is a very slight correction, but I feel in the interests of historical accuracy, due credit for initiating the code and recruiting Seán MacBride, should be given to Father McManus and the Irish National Caucus, and I hope you will feel able to do so ..."[40]

In 2009, former British MP Kevin McNamara released his book, *The MacBride Principles: Irish-America Fights Back*. In it he makes the remarkable statement about me: "What is not comprehensible is why he [McManus] should seek to exclude the important role played by Comptroller Goldin's office in the run-up to the launch, particularly as he takes great pains to credit him for his support once he came on board in 1985."[41] Of course, McNamara partly refutes his own accusation by pointing out that Goldin only came on board in 1985, whereas we had launched the Principles in November 1984. However, it is patently absurd to claim I tried to exclude Goldin when I went to great pains, and expense, to dig him out of the hole he had dug for himself.

Things admittedly became messy when Pat Doherty improperly made an issue of the drafting of the MacBride Principles. That was not expected, as staffers are not supposed to claim pride of authorship when assigned a project. And I have never known one to do so except for Pat. These were the MacBride Principles, not anybody else's. Just as, "Ask not what your country can do for you ..." is JFK's speech, not anybody else's.

That is also why I found it extraordinary when McNamara criticized me for saying the drafting of the Principles never concerned me too much: "This was a surprising statement to make."[42] There was nothing surprising about it. I was never too concerned about the drafting of the principles contained in the Ottinger Bill, the Fish–D'Amato Bill, or the Gilman legislation that became Federal Law in 1998. Nor did their staff make an issue of it.

But what had really forced me go public and set the record

straight was Doherty's bizarre version of events as reported by the iconic journalist, Mary Holland in *The Irish Times* in 1987: "Mr. Doherty researched the problem and drew up a set of guidelines for American companies ... Through Irish-American contacts, he then approached Seán Mac Bride and asked him to sponsor them."[43] Now that's chutzpah for you! Pat did not even really know who Seán Mac Bride was until I named the Principles after him – as Pat himself admitted to me at the time. Mary Holland was very upset when she realized she had got the story wrong. She apologized profoundly, writing in a personal letter to me: "I am really sorry that ... I misrepresented the genesis of the Mac Bride Principles ... I'm sure you'll understand that I was told the story as I recounted it."[44]

The historical reality is that the Principles only became the powerful force they did when they became the Mac Bride Principles. And the Principles would never have got off the ground with such a bang had they not been launched by the Irish National Caucus, which did all the initial publicity – framing the issue, briefing the media, educating the public, and lining up political support. As Mc Namara states, Goldin only "came on board in 1985."[45]

However, apart from the corrections forced on me here, I am the first to acknowledge the vital importance of Pat's contribution. In 2008, *The Irish Echo* asked me to rate his work. This is what I said: "Pat has played a key role in the campaign to stop U.S. dollars subsidizing anti-Catholic discrimination in Northern Ireland ... He is one of the most effective Irish-American campaigners since the time of the Fenians in 1858."[46] Pat just needs to be reminded occasionally that it was the Irish National Caucus that took him and Goldin to Ireland – not the other way around; and that we dug them out of the hole they had dug for themselves politically, launching Pat onto an excellent Irish-American adventure.

16

Anti-MacBride Campaign

*The Irish National Caucus have never seemed to us to have the
interests of the people of Northern Ireland genuinely at heart.*

British Embassy, Washington[1]

The Irish National Caucus launched the campaign for the
MacBride Principles. The British government launched the
campaign against the MacBride Principles. The battle lines were
as clearly drawn as that. For Irish-Americans, the moral clarity of
the campaign could not be more luminous.

The extraordinarily arrogant quote above is from N. E.
Sheinwald, First Secretary of the British Embassy, and current
British Ambassador to Washington. He wrote it in a letter in March
1985 to my good friend Tom Donahue, then Secretary Treasurer
of the giant labor organization, AFL-CIO. It strikingly personifies
the imperial attitude. He is concerned about the people of the
North and I, a Fermanaghman, am not! He then goes on to lecture
Donahue: "As always with this sort of thing, it is important to look
not only at the words used, but at the people and the organizations
promoting the initiative and the commentary they themselves
provide on the text. It is, in my view, instructive that the Irish
National Caucus is playing a prominent part in promulgating the
MacBride Principles."

But then, in the best imperial fashion and in the favorite British technique, Mr. Sheinwald conscripts the Dublin government by stressing: "The leader of the Irish Labour Party and Deputy Prime Minister, Dick Spring, said in January that the INC campaign may be designed at depriving the people of Northern Ireland of much needed investment rather than any concern about discrimination."

Well, thank you, Mr. Sheinwald and Mr. Spring: your opposition made us all the more determined to win – all across the United States and in the U.S. Congress, making the Mac Bride campaign one of the most successful Irish-American initiatives ever. Had those gentlemen supported me, I would have been examining my conscience.

Of course, neither Sheinwald nor Spring was calling the shots. That was the job of the Secretary of State for Northern Ireland, Douglas Hurd. On February 11, 1985 he laid down the marching orders: "We continue to brief U.S. companies and U.S. opinion to oppose the INC campaign ..."[2]

Now there's a perfect example of British government understatement and euphemism. When that government says it will "brief to oppose" – look out. What it really means is that it will vilify, demonize and resort to every dirty trick in the book. It means "crush the INC by any means necessary."

I can well understand some individuals in Northern Ireland being naturally opposed to the Mac Bride Principles, and I can respect their opinion. But there was nothing spontaneous about the campaign in the U.S. against the Mac Bride Principles. Someone in Northern Ireland did not wake up one morning and say to himself/herself: "There's a hearing on the Mac Bride Principles in Nebraska or Texas or Washington, DC. I'll get dressed, slip over and give my opinion."

Big Money

The anti-Mac Bride campaign was highly controlled, highly financed, and fiercely fought by the British government, the Dublin government and, sadly, by John Hume. The agencies the British government used to fight the campaign were the Department

of Economic Development (DED) and the Fair Employment
Agency (FEA) (now the Fair Employment Commission (FEC) of
Northern Ireland). The late Bob Cooper, former head of the FEA
and later head of the FEC was dispatched to lobby against the
Mac Bride Principles in California and Pennsylvania. How could
Irish-Americans, therefore, have had confidence in the FEC? In
the United States, the campaign was coordinated by the British
Embassy – the largest embassy in Washington. The Embassy hired
the top lobbyists, attorneys and Public Relations professionals.

I remember, during the Mac Bride campaign in Maine, meeting
one of the top lobbyists, Severin M. Beliveau. He told us that the
British Embassy called and asked to come and see him. He had no
idea what it was about. They came to his office, told him they wanted
to hire him to block the Mac Bride Principles from becoming law
in Maine, and offered him big money. "Sorry, gentlemen," he said,
"but my grandmother from Enniskillen would turn in her grave if I
were to work for you." (As he was telling me this, he had no idea
where I came from, until I shouted, "Up Fermanagh".)

But not all lobbyists were so principled – even ones with
Irish names. In fact, the British Embassy at the beginning always
tried to recruit Irish-American lobbyists. For example, one very
well established law firm in Washington is O'Connor and Hannan,
a big Democratic law and lobbying firm. Their home base is in
Minnesota. The Embassy hired them to lobby against the Mac Bride
Principles in Minnesota. When they were asked, "How could you?"
O'Connor replied, "Their money is green, also." Irish-Americans
in Washington and Minnesota were disgusted. But the Embassy
succeeded in getting an Irish-American lobbyist to work for them
in Maine: John Doyle of Doyle & Nelson in Augusta.

Another anecdote about a lobbyist hired by the British
Embassy is worth recounting. Someone – just for the fun of it –
told the lobbyist that other lobbyists were being paid far more than
he was and urged him to demand more money. He did, and the
Embassy gave it "without batting an eyelid."

So clearly, money was no problem when it came to defeating
the Mac Bride Principles. On their own admission, the British

government spent millions of dollars to battle the MacBride
Principles. A senior official in the Department of Economic
Development (DED) said, referring to myself, "We did not take
him very seriously at first but the MacBride Principles have caused
serious problems and cost millions to try and counteract."[3] Isn't it
too bad they didn't spend those millions of dollars creating fair
employment in Northern Ireland?

The MacBride Hearing

I wish everyone in Ireland could have attended a MacBride
Hearing. (To get the MacBride Principles passed into law in a
particular state or city, the legislature has first to hold a hearing,
taking witness from experts or concerned citizens.) The Hearing
Room was typically packed with enthusiastic Irish-Americans
and other supporters. The British Embassy officials were there
with one, two, sometimes three or four "castle-Catholics" whom
they had flown from Northern Ireland. Yes, it was nearly always
Catholics whom they recruited. I guess they thought it was the
clever thing to do.

The first thing those Catholics said when they testified was,
"I'm a Catholic, and the MacBride Principles will only hurt the
Catholics of Northern Ireland."

Legislators – especially African Americans – saw right
through that attempted subterfuge. At the MacBride Hearing
in Washington, DC, January 30, 1992, it was a delightful sight
to watch the Chairman of the Committee, and the author of our
MacBride Bill, Councilmember John Ray, systematically shred
the arguments of Sean Neeson, a leader of the Alliance Party, and
a Catholic from Northern Ireland. Ray told him that he was not
surprised (i.e. not fooled) that a Catholic should come before his
Committee to argue against MacBride, because he had seen blacks
from South Africa come to Washington to argue that U.S. pressure
could only hurt blacks in South Africa. Ray might not know all the
history of Ireland, but as a proud African American, he understood
discrimination. In fact, I have never met a politically aware African
American who does not intuitively know that Catholics are

oppressed in Northern Ireland. At the DC hearing I knew I had the game won when a friend of mine, African American Fr. Ray East, marched into the Hearing Room with about a dozen determined and formidable black women parishioners. Chairman Ray stopped the hearing and invited them all up to the front. Can you imagine the suppressed groans of Neeson's handlers from the British Embassy?

It had to be a very chastening experience for the British government to see themselves being beaten time after time in the Mac Bride campaign. (And, I confess, it warmed the cockles of my Kinawley heart. I took huge joy and consolation in it.) The constant defeats created much pressure, which sometimes showed itself. For example, at a hearing on Mac Bride in Minnesota, after the vote was taken and we had won handsomely, I turned to shake someone's hand in congratulations. As I turned, I saw a woman glare at me with unconcealed venom. I thought to myself, "My goodness, what's the matter with her?" I immediately asked someone who she was and was told that she was the British Consul from Chicago. On the way out of the Hearing Room, I happened to be walking right behind the same person. She slammed the door right in my face. So much for the British stiff upper lip.

One advantage, from the Mac Bride point of view, of the British government's practice of bringing out mostly Catholics to testify, was that it did not frame the issue in sectarian terms as it would had the people they brought out been Protestants. Then the press would be reporting that the Protestants and Catholics were clashing at hearings. But since it was, in general, only Catholics who came out, the issue was framed as Irish-Americans against the British government.

In the early days of the Mac Bride Campaign, I had stated publicly in the press that it was very interesting to watch the "body language" in the Mac Bride Hearing Room: "large numbers of enthusiastic Irish-Americans looking forward to inflicting another defeat on the ancestral enemy of their homeland. They take over the room ... And sitting at the back, looking very forlorn, are the few Catholics from Northern Ireland, along with their handlers from the British Embassy. Well, after I had said that, I noticed that at the next hearing the anti-Mac Bride forces occupied the front-row seats!"

Of course, there was another reason why the British recruited Catholics to testify against the MacBride Principles – they did not want to give Protestants a platform to attack the Anglo-Irish Accord. So for many reasons, the British government was very badly snookered by the MacBride campaign. If they did not oppose the MacBride Principles, they lost by default. But, on the other hand, in opposing the Principles, they alienated a lot of legislators. These legislators got very annoyed when they saw the British government coming into their state and city to oppose their legislation. But, by the same token, the legislators got a kick out of the British opposition. It showed them that their legislation was having an impact – that it was "tweaking the lion's tail."

Process As Important As Product

Why was the British government so opposed to the MacBride Principles? Well, the simple answer is that the discriminator always has to oppose a campaign against discrimination – whether it is South Africa, South America, the United States, or Northern Ireland.

But it is important to understand that when it comes to the MacBride Principles, the "process" is as important as the "product." The product is, of course, getting the Principles passed into law, with all their implications, both politically and economically. But consider what is involved in the "process."

For a MacBride campaign to begin in a state or city, legislators have to be "recruited" to introduce the legislation. They have to become familiar with the issue; their colleagues have to be lobbied; supporters have to be activated to make MacBride an issue. And then there has to be a hearing (which often lasts for hours).

When, without the MacBride Principles, would state and city legislators ever have focused on the Northern Ireland issue? The answer is never. And that was a huge reason why the British government feared the MacBride campaign, because it powerfully and nonviolently exposed – in a responsible and important setting (the Hearing Room) – the malicious record of British rule in Northern Ireland. Even though the hearing was about discrimination in Northern Ireland, inevitably, and very properly, all the other British government abuses of human rights got an airing – and I made sure they did. And that profoundly embarrassed the British government.

There is another thing that really frustrated the British government: knowing that time, for a change, was on our side. If we failed to get Mac Bride passed in a particular city or state, we would be back next year or the year after – more determined, better organized, and more experienced. And the harder they fought us, the better we liked it. So the British government was in a no-win situation.

The basic strategy of the British government was to use Catholics (and, of course the Dublin government) for their propaganda in the United States. That, of course, is nothing new. It is as old as British policy in Ireland. Uneducated and politically unaware Catholics can be excused for being used in such a manner. But what can one say about politically sophisticated Catholics? Surely, granting the reality of the anti-Mac Bride campaign, such Catholics could not argue that they just made statements in a vacuum, not knowing that their statements would be used by the British Government. The two Catholics whose names were most used (apart from the Dublin government) in British government propaganda were John Hume of Derry and the late Bishop Cahal Daly of Belfast, later Cardinal of Armagh.

John Hume

On December 10, 1982, International Human Rights Day, Seán Mac Bride spoke at the Caucus Testimonial Dinner in New York. The following day, I traveled with him by car from Manhattan to Huntington, New York. I was asking Seán all sorts of questions about international affairs. I finally asked him if John Hume and Garret FitzGerald had ever consulted him about the problem in the North of Ireland. Seán gave me a very emphatic "no." I asked him what he thought the reason was. "Because they know I'm implacably opposed to Partition" was Seán's equally emphatic answer. Significantly, neither Hume nor FitzGerald attended Seán's funeral in Dublin in 1988.

Hume was in a very strong position as leader of the Social Democratic and Labour Party of Northern Ireland (SDLP) and a member both of the British Parliament (MP) and of the European Parliament (MEP). He was committed to the Anglo-Irish Agreement of 1985, of which he was a key architect along with Garret FitzGerald. The quid pro quo for that agreement was "thou shall not criticize the British government." (In fact, Hume had long since stopped criticizing that government.) All problems could and must now be solved within the context of that Agreement. The MacBride Principles were outside the Agreement, and thus beyond the pale for John Hume.

Hume was to be one of the first and potentially most deadly opponents of the MacBride Principles. It is without doubt he blunted the cutting edge of the MacBride campaign. But in the process, he came out the worse – because the campaign was not significantly weakened by him. But he was weakened. His credibility and judgment were put into question. It is probably one of the few times John Hume has been wrong-footed in America.

His opposition to the MacBride Principles did not make sense to Americans – even to many of his own supporters and admirers. The Principles were, after all, what Americans would expect Hume to be for: a modern, progressive, enlightened way to address discrimination in this global economy. We must be responsible investors.

In *The Boston Sunday Globe* of March 8, 1987, Hume had a half-page interview, with photograph, under the headline, "Ulster Leader Assails American Supporters of MacBride Plan." And assail he did. "Those responsible for the campaign just don't know the damage they're doing. Discrimination against Catholics in Ulster had to be attacked on the ground, not in America," Hume said – missing the whole point of the MacBride Principles.[4]

The huge – and obviously orchestrated – interview was followed up three days later, March 11, 1987, by an editorial. In an appalling example of parroting British government propaganda, the editorial said, "Unless this long-term economic decline can be reversed, the only way the MacBride Principles could get jobs for the unemployed Catholics is if Protestant workers were fired." And then it continued with incredible fatuity: "If new investment arrives, pressure from the Catholic community, and from the Irish and British governments working together through the Hillsborough Agreement [Anglo-Irish Agreement] will see to it that jobs are fairly apportioned."[5] Yet everyone knew that the only pressure on the British government on the issue of discrimination was the MacBride campaign.

There is simply no way of avoiding it: Hume allowed himself to be used by the British government in their anti-MacBride campaign. He was, however, smart enough not to get his hands dirty. He never put himself through the indignity of testifying against the MacBride Principles. Hume was not prepared to be on the losing side at a hearing. But the British government used Hume's name as the main weapon in their arsenal, quoting him liberally in their anti-MacBride discrimination material. And when both the previous Governors of the State of California vetoed the MacBride Bill, they quoted John Hume to justify their veto.

The following month *The Boston Globe* ran an interview with Seán MacBride under the headline "Ex-IRA Leader Fights for Jobs" (even though MacBride had left the IRA in 1936). "When asked to respond to Hume's statement, 'Fairness will prevail but first get companies to invest,' MacBride replied, 'That's wishful thinking on his part. Ideological baggage. Without pressure there is no reason to believe Catholics would be hired ...'"

Seán MacBride then proceeded to give his ultimate assessment of John Hume. "Hume," he said, "has become an apologist for British rule in Northern Ireland," and "is in a position of defending the existing system in Northern Ireland."[6]

Hume's anti-MacBride campaign (in conjunction with that of the British and Dublin governments) did ensure that its main target, Senator Teddy Kennedy, would fall into line. Teddy never supported the MacBride Principles. But great credit must be given to former Mayor Ray Flynn of Boston, later Ambassador to the Vatican, for resisting Hume's pressure. Flynn has been a fearless and effective advocate of the Mac Bride Principles. Credit must also be given to former Congressman Joe Kennedy. He stood firm on his election pledge and supported the Mac Bride Principles – as did the vast majority of the Massachusetts Congressional Delegation.

Cardinal Cathal Daly

Another prominent Catholic from Northern Ireland who was perceived to have joined the British Government anti-Mac Bride campaign was Bishop Cahal Daly, later Cardinal Daly, Archbishop of Armagh and Primate of Ireland.

In November 1989, as the Bishop of Down and Connor (the diocese that includes Belfast) Cahal Daly came to the United States in what was widely perceived to be, at least in part, an escalation of the British government's campaign against the Mac Bride Principles. We were in the middle of fighting a very tough battle to get the Principles passed in the state of Pennsylvania. I got calls that one key supporter of the Principles was contacted to see if he would meet Bishop Daly so that the Bishop could show him the error of his ways.

Bishop Daly proceeded to confirm suspicions by an interview he gave to *The Boston Globe*, November 25, 1989, with James L. Franklin, who was a very experienced writer, having been the Religion writer for that newspaper since 1976:

> The Catholic bishop of Belfast yesterday opposed the adoption of the United States of measures to reduce job discrimination against Catholics ... He was reacting to a recent adoption by Boston and several states of the Mac Bride Principles. Such legislation is more likely to discourage companies from investing in Northern Ireland, said the bishop.
>
> "I feel great hesitation about any program that unilaterally insists on fairness without concerning itself at the same time with increased employment opportunities particularly by American investment," he said.

Instead, he urged support for legislation recently adopted by the British Government.[7]

I was very upset, and issued the following statement: "It is not the first time in Irish history that the English Government was able to use an Irish bishop."[8]

This is the same Bishop Daly who, in 1983, had ordered the radio attack on our campaign against Shorts.

From the mid-1940s to the mid-1960s, Cahal Daly taught Moral Philosophy at Queen's University of Belfast – then a bastion of anti-Catholic discrimination. In all these years, he never opened his mouth against discrimination. What if Rev. Martin Luther King, Jr. had taught for twenty years in a discriminatory university, and never spoke in protest? Would he have any credibility as a spokesman on justice and peace? The first maxim of nonviolent resistance to injustice is that you can only teach it by example. You cannot turn a blind eye to injustice all your life, and then expect people to listen to you lecture them on how to respond to injustice.

When it was known that Cardinal Daly and three leaders of the main Protestant Churches in Northern Ireland were coming to the U.S. in February 1993, some feared that it was another anti-MacBride attempt. I felt it would not be – but only because President Clinton was on record for supporting the Principles. I felt that Irish Church leaders – who are very establishmentarian and somewhat obsessed by "respectability" – would now "cut their cloth to suit the fashion of the times," and not publicly denounce the MacBride Principles, which is what happened.

When Cardinal Daly and the other Church leaders were questioned in New York, *The Irish Echo* of February 12, 1993 quoted Daly as saying, "We are not opposed to the MacBride Principles here or at home."[9] Quite a backing-off from what he told *The Boston Globe* in 1989.

However, there seems to have been some dissembling going on in Cardinal Daly's response, as an American Bishop would unwittingly expose. In August 1993, Bishop Michael F. McAuliffe STD, Bishop of Jefferson City, Missouri, wrote to

John Carr, Secretary of the Department of Social Development and World Peace of the U.S. Catholic Conference: "the Cardinal indicated there were some others that could very well be added as part of those Principles … ."[10] Bishop McAuliffe, along with Bishop Anthony O'Connell of Knoxville, Tennessee had visited the Cardinal in Ireland during July. (O'Connell later had to resign because of a sex abuse scandal.) It was on that visit, according to Bishop McAuliffe, that the Cardinal had stated that he wanted to see the changes in the MacBride Principles.

Mr. Carr's office, as we shall see, had been very much involved in the controversy over a proposal to hold a conference on the MacBride Principles in Washington in the Fall of 1993. He had also been denying any attempt by the Catholic Church leaders either in Ireland or the United States to change the MacBride Principles.

And how had Bishop McAuliffe "unwittingly" exposed Cardinal Daly? Well – again through the grace of God – he had mailed his Carr-letter to me instead.

Ah, and some say there is no God!

I was used to people sending us copies of letters they have written to someone else. So I thought this was a case of some bishop sending me a copy of a letter he had written to the Catholic Conference. I had sent a copy of the letter I had written to John Carr to every Bishop in the U.S. It was only when I had re-read Bishop McAuliffe's letter that I realized it was not a copy, but rather that the Bishop had addressed the letter to John Carr at the address of the Irish National Caucus.

So doesn't providence work in a strange way? Here was a letter he clearly did not want me to see, but yet he had addressed it to my office. So that there would be no further delay with the letter, I very obligingly faxed it on to John Carr and faxed off my own letter to the good Bishop explaining his error.

I had never heard Bishops McAuliffe or O'Connell ever open their mouths about anti-Catholic discrimination in Northern Ireland. Yet they had the bloody nerve to interfere in the MacBride campaign. Did that happen accidentally? You bet it didn't. Someone had to recruit them. The question is who?

A final note on Daly. In 1979, after we had stopped American guns going to the RUC, and when the Caucus group was in Ireland, we met with the late Fr. Denis Faul. He had just come from a meeting with Daly, who was still Bishop of Down and Conor. Denis suggested that the Caucus should meet with Daly. I was not too interested, but out of respect for Denis, I agreed, and asked him to set it up. Denis got back to me with Daly's response: "It would not be good for the Church for me to meet with the Irish National Caucus." Not good for the Church? But it was okay for Irish Bishops to rotate priests, from parish to parish, who abused kids! That's the classic "Bishop's speak" – the spiritual narcissism and arrogance that has caved in the institutional church structures in Ireland.

I think it is pathetic that Ireland was inflicted with a Cardinal like Cathal Daly and a Taoiseach like Garret FitzGerald. Both of them personified what was wrong with Church and State.

U.S. Catholic Conference and Moderator Dunlop

The U.S. Catholic Conference (of Bishops) is in part the social arm of the Catholic Hierarchy. Its large headquarters in Washington has many departments – one of which is the Office of International Justice and Peace. This is the department, of course, that would deal with the Northern Ireland issue (on the rare occasions it had a mind to). Sadly, it had the same "establishment-elitist" attitude of all entrenched bureaucracies. On January 6, 1978, I met with that office. Afterwards I said, "It was just like being at the British Embassy. The Office of Justice and Peace has become the ecclesiastical arm of British propaganda."[11] As if to prove my point, the then Advisor on European Affairs – Edward Doherty, a layman, and British to his fingertips – wrote in a letter: "It is the Provos who are mainly responsible for the violence in Northern Ireland and this is recognized by every careful and impartial observer ... after due consultation with the Irish bishops, and in recognition of the efforts being made by the governments and church bodies directly concerned, we [the U.S. Catholic Conference] had concluded that there is no appropriate basis for public intervention in the problems of Northern Ireland, either by this conference, or any branch of the United States government ..."[12]

Thank God Bill Clinton was a Protestant because had he been guided by that Godless and immoral teaching of the Catholic Conference, he would never have intervened.

Do you think for one moment that the Office of International Justice and Peace would have released that document without first checking with the Irish Embassy? Indeed, you can be certain that the Irish Embassy approved (indeed, may have drafted) every word. To me – though the Irish Embassy would have denied it – it is the clearest and most frank expression of Irish Embassy policy of that time: "no appropriate basis for public intervention ... by this conference or any branch of the United States government"... And it shows clearly what we were up against.

As explained earlier, in August 1979 the Irish National Caucus led a successful campaign to have a ban put on the sale of U.S. weapons to the RUC. Well, later on, in January 1981, Archbishop Hickey of Washington and Bishop Thomas Kelly, Secretary General of the U.S. Catholic Conference, visited the White House to urge President Reagan to continue the ban on military aid to El Salvador.

I wrote to them, begging them also to urge President Reagan to continue the ban on the sale of U.S. weapons to the RUC. Archbishop Hickey responded to me saying, ".... Bishop Kelly and I will be in touch with our counterparts in Northern Ireland to seek their advice in this vexing question. Our intervention will depend on their response." And Bishop Kelly replied "... We have known of your position [on the RUC] for some time ... In the case of El Salvador, we have been encouraged to take what action we have taken by the local hierarchy. We have not, at this time, received such encouragement from the Irish hierarchy on the subject you have brought to our attention ..."[13]

By now you get my drift – dealing with these people was like dealing with the British Embassy. So you can imagine my surprise when I discovered, at the height of the MacBride campaign, a plot from these same folk to muscle in on our work – having never lifted a finger to help. Why would they do that? To enhance Mac Bride? The very opposite: to sabotage and neutralize it. Here's what happened.

Through a stroke of good fortune in May 1993, a letter from the Presbyterian Moderator, Rev. Dr. John Dunlop of Belfast, came into my possession. It made the astonishing revelation: "I have been advised that the Presbyterian Church USA and the United States Catholic Conference are prepared to convene a conference on fair employment and investment. I believe that such a conference, which would include a discussion about Mac Bride would be very helpful. Maybe an improved version of the Mac Bride Principles could command widespread support ... maybe even the name could be changed or modified to indicate that improvements have been made and at the same time move it from its explicitly partisan association ..."[14]

And, six days later, Josiah Beeman, Chair of the Northern Ireland Working Group of Presbyterian Church in the United States said in a letter (announcing the Conference) that one purpose of the Conference would be to raise "support for the Mac Bride Principles or a modified version of them that would eliminate contentious issues among supporters of fair employment."[15]

Well, you can imagine I was not going to take this lying down. So I released a blistering press release:

Is this the latest assault by the English Government against the Mac Bride Principles? These Church groups have never lifted a finger to support the Mac Bride Principles; indeed they either passively or actively opposed the Principles. Now they are going to have a conference about the Mac Bride Principles, with a view to changing the name and contents of the Principles.

Well, with all due respect, I think they have a bloody nerve and a colossal arrogance. Let me make it perfectly clear that no Church leader (Catholic or Protestant) or anybody else in Ireland or the United States has the right or authority to change one syllable – not one jot or tittle – of the

MacBride Principles.

If these Church groups have had their conscience pricked by the effective MacBride campaign and at long last want to oppose English Government discrimination in Northern Ireland, then I would welcome that. But surely a little bit of repentance – at least one *mea culpa* – would be in order from these Church people who, either passively or actively opposed the MacBride principles," McManus argued. "But instead of a *mea culpa*, they arrogantly call a conference to change the MacBride Principles – the one effective campaign against anti-Catholic discrimination in Northern Ireland."

I then did one of my massive mailings. The outside envelope carried the eye-catching warning: "Don't let the English Government use the Catholic Church against the MacBride Principles." I included a pre-written postcard the recipients could mail to their own Bishops. And I also wrote a very strong letter to each bishop in the U.S.: "It is beyond doubt that the English Government has often succeeded in using Church leaders in Ireland for its own oppressive purposes. It would be an enormous scandal if that tradition was transported across the Atlantic and that the Catholic Conference would become the latest tool of the English Government."[16]

Well, it scared the hell out of them, so to speak. You have never seen such scampering in all your life. The bishops became truly alarmed and immediately disassociated themselves from any anti-MacBride implication. All talk of a conference was dropped, even denied it had ever been planned. And in its place, the four main Churches in Ireland and their counterparts in the U.S. issued "A Call For Fair Employment and Investment in Northern Ireland." Not only that but they were forced to actually endorse the MacBride Principles: "Many Americans support the MacBride Principles, as amplified, as a good faith, nonviolent means to promote fair employment. We urge that any support of these amplified principles, which offer positive values and focus on fair employment, be joined with continued support for strong fair employment measures and an active commitment to investment and job creation ..."[17]

It was a remarkable turnaround. What started out as a covert and cynical effort to sabotage the Mac Bride Principles ended up as a ringing endorsement of them, by entities that, to say the least, were never too keen on them.

The Irish Government

The Irish Embassy in Washington was one of the very first to oppose the Mac Bride Principles. The Consul in New York actively lobbied against the Mac Bride Principles in Albany, New York, in 1986, much to the righteous anger of Paul O'Dwyer, the famed Mayo lawyer in New York.

Taoiseach Garret FitzGerald spelled out his attitude in a speech in Boston on May 3, 1985: "There is, however, a campaign under way which aims at discouraging American investment in Northern Ireland ... Those who pursue this campaign should know that they are inflicting injustice on both communities ... One can only wonder whether some of those who press for disinvestment do so as part of a calculated strategy which has as its goal the further weakening of the already strained Northern Ireland economy so that terrorism may have greater opportunities to flourish."[18]

I understandably condemned FitzGerald. He knew full well that the very first thing the Irish National Caucus said when it launched the Mac Bride Principles was that "they [the Principles] do not call for reverse discrimination, quotas or disinvestment." This mischievous statement by FitzGerald was used with abandon by the British government in the United States.

But here, again, Kevin Mc Namara puts a peculiar spin on my reaction to FitzGerald. In his book he writes: "FitzGerald is reported as saying that "new evidence" had caused him to drop the passage from his speech ... The Irish Consul-General in New York specifically informed the Comptroller of the decision to omit the passage. This did not prevent Mc Manus from declaring it to be: "The Big Lie. Vintage FitzGerald smear tactics. England has no better Friend than FitzGerald." It might be argued that these comments were "vintage" Mc Manus; to attribute to a political opponent words that he had not used, particularly when the lack of their use could be portrayed as a victory for Mc Manus' own campaign."[19]

Mc Namara is ridiculous when he says that because FitzGerald did not use that passage when he spoke, it did not matter. Nonsense. That passage had been widely disseminated in the media. Did FitzGerald ever officially withdraw it and apologize for it? FitzGerald, in effect, accused me (the Irish in Boston were very familiar with me and would have seen me as the main leader of the Mac Bride campaign) of "inflicting injustice on both communities ... so that terrorism may ... flourish." And yet, Mc Namara reshapes this to make FitzGerald the victim, and me the culprit. And he does that repeatedly in his book. Each time I stand up for Mac Bride, he sides with the governments and the establishment and tries to make me the villain (as we shall see later regarding my letter to Taoiseach Charles Haughey).

Finally on this, I remember the late, very just and honorable Kevin Boland, former TD and Minister, telling me that he was always shocked by the common tactic of government officials not saying at actual meetings what their press statements claimed.

However, imagine this delicious irony. Just eleven short years later, Taoiseach John Bruton in Washington was presented with a plaque "commemorating the inclusion of strong support in the Republican Party platform for the Mac Bride Fair Employment Principles." The presentation was done by presidential candidate Senator Bob Dole on behalf of the entire GOP (the "Grand Old Party", i.e. the Republican Party) leadership. According to a RNC (Republican National Committee) News Release, "Prime Minister Bruton thanked Mr. Dole and Republicans in Congress for ... the inclusion and endorsement of the Mac Bride Principles in their platform."[20] I was so elated I had to call my brother Frankie in Ireland, as he would be able to fully appreciate the incredible irony.

Charlie Haughey

I believe the most effective thing Charlie Haughey did

regarding Northern Ireland was his reversal of FitzGerald's policy on the MacBride Principles. In an address to the Dáil on April 7, 1986, Haughey said:

> I want to avail of this opportunity to state that I fully endorse the MacBride Principles. I welcome the efforts and initiative of concerned Americans who wish to see something done about the chronic discriminatory patterns in employment in Northern Ireland.
>
> The regrettable position is that fourteen years after the imposition of direct rule in Northern Ireland, the situation in most sectors of employment is as bad as it ever was. The purpose of the MacBride Principles is to ensure that if there is to be American investment, if there are to be American orders, the firms concerned will have to act fairly and in a non-discriminatory fashion in regard to employment.

When Haughey became Taoiseach, his government's position was that there was nothing "objectionable" to MacBride. However, it took a long time for Haughey's policy to be implemented by the Irish Embassy. On Seán MacBride's last trip to the United States, in April 1987, he spoke at the Eire Society dinner in Boston. He was accompanied by his son, Tiernan. The Irish Ambassador, Pádraic MacKernan, also attended the dinner, quite openly advising people that the MacBride Principles were a bad idea, and that they should follow John Hume's lead. Seán MacBride took the issue up with Haughey, writing to him on April 29, 1987: "... there is a general feeling among our leading supporters that our diplomatic and consular staff in the U.S. are using their influence to oppose the adoption of the MacBride Principles."[21] When Tiernan MacBride returned to Dublin, he complained to Haughey's people. They promised to force MacKernan to comply with Haughey's position, but it took a long time for that to happen.

Indeed, on February 11, 1988, I was forced to write this letter to Mr. Haughey – the very first time I ever thought it was worth writing to an Irish Taoiseach:

Dear Mr. Haughey,

Through the initiative of the Irish National Caucus, legislation on the Mac Bride Principles (Bill 7-394) has been introduced in the City Council of the District of Columbia.

You are on record as stating that you are not opposed to the Mac Bride Principles, and that you have not instructed any Irish Government official in the United States to campaign against them.

Because the Irish Embassy is in Washington, D.C., it will be particularly of interest to the Irish National Caucus to see if the Irish Embassy officials will campaign against the D.C. legislation on the Mac Bride Principles. We will be monitoring their activity very carefully.

We certainly hope that the Irish Embassy officials will not interfere with the D.C. legislation. Indeed, we will regard this as a test case.

Both before and after you were elected Taoiseach, Irish Government officials in the United States have actively campaigned against the Mac Bride Principles.

For example, on one of Sean Mac Bride's last visits to the U.S. to speak to the Eire Society (April 29, 1987), you were Taoiseach. The Irish Ambassador (then and now) Mr. Padraic Mac Kernan let it be known in conversation at the Eire society event that he was opposed to the Mac Bride Principles. One person told me that Mr. Mac Kernan vehemently expressed his opposition and declared his support of John Hume's position on the Mac Bride Principles.

Now that the great and illustrious Sean Mac Bride is dead, the Irish National Caucus is more determined than ever to promote the Mac Bride Principles in the United States. We see this as the most fitting memorial.

While he lived, there were many attempts to discredit the Mac Bride Principles by trying to discredit him.

And, I am ashamed to say, there is reason to suspect that this smear campaign was – in part – orchestrated by the Irish Embassy and Mr. John Hume M.P. S.D.L.P. The first shots in this anti-Mac Bride campaign were fired by U.S. Senator Daniel Patrick Moynihan (D-N.Y.) – who takes his cue on Irish matters from the Irish Embassy – when he spoke to a breakfast meeting of Irish-Americans and Irish-American labor leaders in Washington D.C. at the Sheraton-Carlton Hotel on May 7, 1985. When I challenged Senator Moynihan that he was misrepresenting the Mac Bride Principles, he retorted: "You tell your readers that Mac Bride was the Nobel Peace Prize Winner. Tell them he was, also, the Lenin Peace Prize Winner, and you don't get that for nothing."

It was a shocking and deliberate smear.

In follow-up conversations with his office, Senator Moynihan refused to retract his smear.

In August 1987, a Member of Congress visited Ireland on a fact-finding mission. He met with Mr. Seamus Mallon, M.P. S.D.L.P. Mr. Mallon told him that he had no real trouble with the Mac Bride Principles. His trouble was that Sean Mac Bride had been given and had accepted the Lenin Peace Prize. The attempted smear again.

A few weeks before Sean Mac Bride died, elected representatives from the State of Maine visited Ireland. They met with Mr. John Hume M.P. S.D.L.P. He told them that Sean Mac Bride had been senile for years, and that he was being exploited by the Mac Bride Principles. "He's an old man whom they prop up to say what they want him to say," said Mr. Hume.

I think you will agree that this is an outrageous pattern of vilification of one of Ireland's most illustrious sons. Coupled with the scurrilous British Press commentaries on Sean Mac Bride's death, it represents a deliberately orchestrated campaign.

Padraig Pearse predicted that an Irish patriot can be more powerful in death than in life. We are confident this will apply to Sean Mac Bride. He was deeply committed to and deeply interested in the progress of the Mac Bride Principles.

The Irish National Caucus is now more than ever dedicated

to the MacBride Principles. It is our earnest hope that you will immediately instruct all your officials in the United States to stop opposing the MacBride principles.

Thank you for your attention.

Sincerely,

Fr. Sean McManus

McNamara Distorts My Letter

Kevin McNamara again chooses to attack me for this letter in his book: "An intemperate letter from Fr. McManus to Haughey, included the old accusation that before and after Haughey's election [to his third term as Taoiseach, 1987 to 1992], 'Irish government officials in the United States have actively campaigned against the MacBride Principles.'"[22] It was not an "old accusation" but another example of the Embassy's opposition to MacBride. Then he – very usefully, indeed, and much to the credit of his research – makes public for the first time Ambassador McKernan's response as contained in the DFAMP (Department of Foreign Affairs. MacBride Papers) undated cable: "Although one can readily dismiss Fr. McManus's lurid assertions, at the same time there is a serious and unscrupulous intent behind them ... This is to try to intimidate Irish officials in the United States ... it is an attempt to intimidate the government. You have observed the minatory note struck in the letter when Fr. McManus says that the Caucus will be monitoring the activities of the Embassy." McNamara blithely continues: "The day to day work of the Embassy continued: monitoring the progress of the MacBride campaign ..."[23] So it was perfectly okay for the Embassy to monitor the MacBride campaign, but it was intimidatory and minatory for me to monitor theirs?

Yet McNamara does not describe the Ambassador's letter as intemperate, and he seems merrily oblivious to his own double standard, not to mention the Ambassador's. This is such a pity because Kevin McNamara has had a great record on Ireland, and it is truly puzzling that he can't seem to help himself: the "Brit-speak" holds him captive. For example, when I refer to Seán

MacBride's past, I call it heroic and noble – to McNamara it is "tempestuous."[24] It is as if he had his computer programmed to automatically enter a negative adjective before MacBride's name and mine.

What should have really upset the Ambassador was Senator Moynihan's attack on Seán MacBride. If Moynihan had accused a former British, Israeli or French foreign minister of being a Soviet agent or mole, their respective embassies would have created uproar. There was not one word of protest from the Irish Embassy. What does that reveal? After the meeting, I confronted him, demanded an apology, and told him that he had slandered a great man. He refused to apologize and walked off in a petulant huff. I refused to have any dealings with Moynihan's office from then on. By the way, this is how Moynihan histrionically ended his speech: "If the Soviets increase their subsidy to the Provisional IRA, think Lebanon."

The Irish Embassy's possible role in slandering Seán MacBride – and in their refusal to repudiate it – was similar to their role in blocking the Caucus' campaign to free the Birmingham Six. It was only in 1991, when Dermot Gallagher became Ambassador, that I noticed a change of attitude. Since that time, I have had nothing but respect for the Irish Ambassadors to Washington. I often wonder who really calls the shots in all these events – civil servants or Irish Taoisigh.

Teddy Kennedy

I always knew that Teddy Kennedy – with his good heart and right instincts – had to be most uncomfortable with being forced by John Hume and the Dublin government into a position of not supporting the MacBride Principles. And, sure enough, McNamara's book comes up with the evidence.

McNamara – in one of his most important revelations – explains:

The campaign outside Washington was being carefully watched by those on Capitol Hill, who felt that their position locally might be being undermined by the activities of the INC and the Ad Hoc Congressional Committee. Burke of the Irish Embassy reported a conversation that he had with a senior member of Senator Kennedy's office concerning the possibility of Kennedy introducing a bill into the Senate incorporating the MacBride Principles. The purpose was to pre-empt Representative Biaggi in the House or Senator De Concini in the Senate, both of whom were associated with the INC, and were thinking about introducing similar legislation. Burke cautioned against this course of action ... it would be perceived as a victory for the Ad Hoc ... and the INC. Burke's advocacy was successful. The idea of a Kennedy bill was quietly dropped.[25]

So there you have it: it was all about stopping the Irish National Caucus, and the Irish Embassy would use Kennedy – or any means necessary – to accomplish that.

But I was determined the Irish Embassy would not stop us. And no matter what the British Embassy tried, I was certainly not going to let them beat us, even though they had transferred, as McNamara's book reveals, "[Andrew] Henderson from the British consulate in New York to the embassy in Washington, to operate on a full-time basis to counteract the MacBride campaign;" and even though the Secretary of State for Northern Ireland, Sir Patrick Mayhew, approved that "Mr. Hume should be approached as a potential ally."[26]

I had earlier exposed that the British Embassy had brought in an MI5 agent to try and defeat us: "[President] Clinton was informed by a White House staffer that Father McManus had discovered ... a British intelligence MI5 agent used his embassy job to direct a campaign specifically against the MacBride Principles."[27]

I was not going to allow anyone to stop MacBride from becoming U.S. law – not even Bill Clinton, to whom I felt so deeply grateful for his magnificent work on the Irish peace process, and whom I see as Thomas Jefferson and Elvis Presley all rolled into one.

17

Forcing Clinton to Sign MacBride

The time is always right to do the right thing.
Martin Luther King, Jr.

Presidential candidate Bill Clinton made his pledge to support the MacBride Principles at the Irish-American Presidential Forum in New York City on April 5, 1992: "I like the Principles very much, I think they are a good thing, and if I were President, I would ask all state governments to take a look at adopting them. There's always that argument [that the Principles discourage investment] with this kind of thing, but I don't buy it. I see the MacBride Principles as a way of helping investment because it would help stabilize the Troubles."

After Clinton spoke, I remember telling a group of Irish reporters at the Forum that one of the most important effects of Clinton's promise would be to ensure that the new Irish Government did not revert to a position of opposing the MacBride Principles. Charlie Haughey had just ceased being Taoiseach, and I was concerned that his successor would revert to the position of the previous Irish government under Garret FitzGerald.

Because of my direct experience with how FitzGerald had

tried to sabotage Jimmy Carter's first pledge to the Irish National Caucus back on October 27, 1976, in Pittsburgh, I was especially concerned at how the new Taoiseach, Albert Reynolds, would react to Clinton's interest in the Irish issue. Reynolds welcomed Clinton's interest. And I knew it was the beginning of a new day. Because had Reynolds rebuffed Clinton, the way FitzGerald had rebuffed Carter, there would not have been an Irish Peace Process.

Surely there would now be plain sailing for Mac Bride? Well, in Washington, one learns there is no such thing. I had been pushing for a Federal/Congressional Bill on the Mac Bride Principles for some years now. In 1987 Congressman Fish (R-NY) – whom Irish Ambassador Sean Donlon had so disrespected over the Birmingham Six case – had introduced a Bill in the House (H.R. 725) and Senator Al D'Amato (R-NY) had introduced it in the Senate.[1]

But Congressman Lee Hamilton, Chairman of the House Subcommittee on Europe and the Middle East, would not schedule a hearing. He even told me there was not much interest in the Bill, despite the fact we had signed up almost a hundred co-sponsors.[2]

But it was not just Congressman Hamilton who was opposing us. Let me switch you back here to Kevin Mc Namara's book on the Mac Bride Principles. You saw earlier how the Irish Ambassador at that time, Padraic McKernan, had responded to my letter to Taoiseach Haughey. Well, in the same undated cable reply (which was his response to a letter of February 11, 1988, from the Department of Foreign Affairs (DFA) in Dublin) McKernan denied that the Irish Embassy was still conspiring against the Mac Bride Principles: "... Irish government officials have not campaigned and are not campaigning against the Mac Bride Principles."[3]

Here again Mc Namara reveals vital information hitherto unknown. (He had been given "unfettered access" to the files of the Irish government and Irish Embassy on the Mac Bride campaign.[4]) He reveals the Fish–D'Amato Bill was, indeed, of concern to the Irish Embassy: "The Ambassador, Padraic McKernan, wrote a private and confidential letter to Noel Dorr, the Secretary of the DFA, in which he conveyed the alleged concerns expressed by the Friends of Ireland and Tom Foley, the Majority Leader in the House of Representatives, at what they perceived as the shift in policy contained in Haughey's interview. They were concerned that two bills languishing in committee, Fish's in the House and D'Amato's in the senate, might now emerge. Both bills were very divisive."[5]

So here we go again! Were the Friends of Ireland really concerned or was it Ambassador McKernan? I had been well familiar with that tactic: the Irish Embassy would first wind up Members of Congress and then report to the Irish government that Members of Congress were "very concerned."

Lobbying Clinton on the National Mall

For years I have been doing my early morning, one-hour walk on the National Mall (the stunning, almost two-mile-long park that stretches from the Capitol Building to the Lincoln Memorial). On the morning of June 18, 1993, I was on the return stretch of my walk, facing the Capitol, plodding along and silently saying my rosary. I heard an unmistakable voice shout hello to someone on the Mall. I turn around, and there comes President Clinton, in shorts and a baseball cap, running at a pretty good clip, with a large retinue behind him, huffing and puffing. Now while my walk on the Mall is sacred time, how often does one get a chance to lobby the President of the United States?

"Bill," I shouted, "don't forget your Irish promises." He turned his head towards me as he kept going and said, "Don't worry." I then shouted as he sped away, "Keep supporting the Mac Bride Principles." He put his hand above his head and waved affirmatively. I continued saying the Fourth Joyful Mystery of the Holy Rosary, which the Baptist President had interrupted.

Later that day, Mayor Flynn of Boston telephoned me. "A good job of lobbying the President on the Mac Bride Principles,

Fr. Sean," he said. "How did you know that?" I asked. "The President called me and said, 'You know that Irish priest friend of yours? Well, he lobbied me on the Mall about the Mac Bride Principles.'" Clearly, according to Flynn, the President got a real kick out of it.

However, nice as that was, we were still not getting any real Congressional progress on the Mac Bride Principles. Nor would we, until the Democrats lost the House and Senate and Republicans took over in January 1995. Isn't that an extraordinary thing to say – especially when people in Ireland mostly associate the Irish issue with Catholic Democrats?

Chairman Gilman

For me, the Republican takeover meant one thing: the great Ben Gilman would be Chairman of the Foreign Affairs Committee (which would then be called the International Relations Committee). And, not just a Subcommittee but the full Committee. It was a perfect – although ironic – confluence of events. Bill Clinton in the White House, and Ben Gilman in the Chair of the House International Relations Committee.

With Ben as Chairman, I was now able to do in two minutes what I had not been able to do in twenty years. Immediately Ben told me I would get two hearings: one on the Mac Bride Principles and one on acceptable policing in Northern Ireland. My two top issues, just like that.

While two Irish Catholic Speakers – Tip O'Neill and Tom Foley – were in power, human rights hearings on Northern Ireland were banned. Yet when Newt Gingrich became Speaker, hearings were allowed. It took a Protestant Speaker and a Jewish Chairman to end the Congressional cover-up of British oppression of Catholics in Northern Ireland. For all time, that has to be a powerful ecumenical message for Irish-American Catholics. Their Church was silent, famous Irish Catholics were silent, even complicit. A Protestant and a Jew stood up to the British – broke the ban – and had hearings.

With Ben Gilman becoming Chairman, Congressman Chris Smith of New Jersey, became Chairman of the Human Rights Subcommittee. He would go on to hold eleven hearings on the Pat Finucane case and other human rights issues. Chris is the quintessential good guy – dedicated, courageous, and committed to human rights everywhere.

Ben told me to get him a list of witnesses for a Mac Bride Hearing, and told me to gird for battle because, although he could schedule a hearing, I had get the Committee members to vote for the Mac Bride Principles.

But first we had to have a Congressional Reception to celebrate Ben becoming Chairman. On January 26, 1995, the Irish National Caucus hosted an evening reception in Ben's new fiefdom – the huge and impressive House International Relations Committee Hearing Room. Forty Members of Congress and about two hundred local Irish-Americans attended. And in a sign of how completely things had changed for both Ben and me, the new Chairman of the Friends of Ireland, Congressman Jimmy Walsh, attended and expressed total solidarity with the Irish National Caucus and the Ad Hoc Congressional Committee for Irish Affairs. Chairman Gilman lavishly praised my work, which he said had been unfairly condemned by both the Irish and British governments, and by some big names in Congress "who should have known better." Then he officially announced that he was going to give "Fr. Mc Manus his long-sought prize: a hearing on the Mac Bride Principles."[6]

Congressional Hearing on Mac Bride

And so it came to pass. On March 15, 1995, I had my long-sought-for hearing. This despite the fact that the U.S. Ambassador to Ireland, Jean Kennedy Smith, had telephoned from Dublin to urgently beseech Chairman Gilman to call off the hearing.

The hearing would consider linking the Mac Bride Principles to the International Fund for Ireland (IFI).

Congressman Payne, the first speaker after Chairman

Gilman's introduction, quickly set the scene: "As an African American, I and eight other Members of the Congressional Black Caucus who are Congressional Friends of the Irish National Caucus can easily identify with the Catholic minority [in Northern Ireland] ... The Mac Bride Principles were modeled after the Sullivan Principles ... In the campaign for a free South Africa, we received a lot of help from Irish-Americans. For example, Fr. Sean Mc Manus, president of the Irish National Caucus, was the first white Catholic priest to go to jail overnight for protesting outside the South African Embassy."[7]

After that opening salvo, it was almost all downhill for the British government. The Clinton Administration attempted to bail them out. Assistant Secretary of State for European and Canadian Affairs, Richard Holbroke, speaking on behalf of President Clinton and responding to questions later submitted by Committee members, said: "While we support the Mac Bride Principles, the Administration sees no reason to promote additional legislation in the Congress. Federal enactment of the Mac Bride Principles would add reporting requirements on U.S. companies investing and operating in Northern Ireland. To put the Principles into specific legislation could have an inhibiting effect on the investment goals we seek."

Assistant Secretary of State for Legislative Affairs, Wendy R. Sherman, testified on behalf of the Clinton Administration at another hearing on May 15, 1995:

> We support and strongly prefer Mr. Hamilton's version of this. We believe that the amendment that Mr. Hamilton is offering [i.e. to delete mandatory linking of the Mac Bride Principles to the IFI] offers a constructive way forward to advance objectives that we all share. As Mr. Hamilton has appropriately pointed out, *senior levels of the Irish government have told Administration officials that linkage of the basic Mac Bride Principles to IFI funding will be controversial and could disrupt the White House Conference* [emphasis added], which is aimed at

increasing economic activity toward the disadvantaged and discriminated in Ireland.

As was mentioned, all the parties, Ambassador Jean Kennedy Smith and Ambassador Crowe both do not support the mandatory linkage through the IFI. We think it is quite important to advance the objectives and goals, but do not think it should be mandatory.

Certainly, the President absolutely, positively embraces the Mac Bride Principles completely, as does Mr. Hamilton's amendment. The only difference is whether it should or shall be mandatory. And I don't think anyone for a minute would think Ambassador Jean Kennedy Smith does not endorse and completely embrace the Mac Bride Principles or Ambassador Crowe or this Administration.

Chairman Gilman dismissed all that malarkey with: "Saying one supports the Mac Bride Principles without implementing them is like saying one supports the Ten Commandments as long as I don't have to implement them." He also dispensed with that old canard, beloved by the establishment and administrations, that although the idea was good, "the time was not right." Quoting Martin Luther King, Jr. he told the Clinton Administration, "It is always the right time to do the right thing."

Notice the words of Ms. Sherman that I place in emphases. They show that even then the Irish Embassy still opposed the Mac Bride Principles – seven long years after I wrote to Taoiseach Haughey, complaining about the Irish Embassy's obstructionism. Those words make nonsense out of Kevin Mc Namara's charge that I had raised "an old accusation."

We Win 32 to 8

Throughout the Hearing – whenever possible – I was grabbing every Member of the Committee urging them to vote for Mac Bride.

Remember, just six months previously, Congressman Hamilton

was the all-powerful Chairman who had been resisting me for years, trying to tell me there was no support for the MacBride Principles in the Committee. However, later that day when the Committee voted on the Hamilton Amendment, we beat him by thirty-two votes to eight. It was a sweet victory. All the members of the Democratic Minority panel in deference to Hamilton, now Ranking Member, prefaced their remarks with something like, "As much as I respect Mr. Hamilton, etc ... I cannot support his Amendment." When it came his turn, the usually unflappable Hamilton was visibly annoyed: "I could do with less respect and more support," he huffed at the Democrats. "I know what has happened here. The Irish National Caucus did its work on this Committee."

Later during the Hearing, I went up to Chairman Gilman (while Hamilton still sat on his left). "You have just been handed your diploma in lobbying," said Gilman – referring to Hamilton's bellyaching.

By the way, the Committee vote revealed an insight into how the "establishment" Irish media operates. When the results were announced, I glanced over at a reporter for a paper in Ireland. He could not hide his disappointment and displeasure at my victory.

Staffers on the Committee had long regarded him as a "spy for the Irish Embassy." At the end of the Hearing, I stood near him to test if he would ask me for a comment – as was surely warranted because I had pulled off an extraordinary victory, which any good, objective reporter would acknowledge. I waited, and waited. Not a thing. He never looked at me. There was no way, of course, I was going to let him off with his self censorship. So I strode over to him, as he was about to depart, and said: " [First name], aren't you going to ask me for a comment?" He shuffled around, tried to look professionable and sighed reluctantly, "Okay. What do you want to say?"

One simply cannot understand The Troubles if one does not realize the complicity of the Irish media. Large sections of this media acted as if they were departments of the Dublin Government. They bear huge responsibility and shame for their complicity.

On February 28, 1996, Ms. Sherman wrote as follows to Members of the House and Senate Conference, giving the "Administration's Position on Provisions in HR 1561": "The Administration opposes this provision ... Requiring compliance with the 'principles of economic justice', as defined in this provision would place an undue burden on small business and community development organizations ... We propose that all reference to the 'principles of economic justice' be deleted."

On April 11, 1996, Tony Lake, Assistant to the President for National Security Affairs, wrote to me. "Thank you for your letter about the legislation linking the Mac Bride Principles of fair employment to the funding for the International Fund for Ireland ... The President does not believe it would be useful to place conditions on the funding we provide to the International Fund for Ireland ..."

On April 12, 1996, President Clinton vetoed HR 1561.

Standing Up to President Clinton

I got eleven major Irish-American groups to co-sign a letter that I sent to President Clinton on April 19, 1996: "Because of our great gratitude for your crucial support of the Irish peace process, we've been reluctant to say anything up to now. But you cannot expect us to be silent as you continue to oppose one of our very top legislative issues. It is ironic that Senator Dole, the entire Republican leadership and the Republican National Committee are all supporting Congressional legislation on the Mac Bride Principles and you are opposing it. The peace process in Ireland cannot be separated from non-discrimination ... We are totally committed to both."

The letter was signed by the following organizations (in alphabetical order):

- John Finucane, President, American Ireland Education Fund
- Kathleen Holmes, Chairwoman, American Irish Congress

- Edward J. Wallace, National President, Ancient Order of Hibernians
- Larry Downes, Chairman, Brehon Law Society
- Mike Moroney, Secretary, Clan na Gael
- John D. Worral, President, Federation of Irish-American Societies of the Delaware Valley
- James V. Mullin, Coordinator, Irish-Action Coalition
- Fr. Sean McManus, President, Irish National Caucus
- Paul Doris, Chairman, Irish Northern Aid Committee
- Edmund Lynch, Chairman, Lawyers Alliance for Justice in Ireland
- Jean Forest, U.S. Coordinator, Voice of the Innocent

(Of the principal activist groups on the North, the Irish-American Unity Conference was the only organization that refused to sign on.)

The letter from the Irish-American leaders caused considerable attention, and put considerable pressure on President Clinton in the middle of an election.

Because of my deep gratitude for President Clinton's role in the Irish peace process, initiating that letter was one of the most difficult decisions I have ever made. I did not want to do it, yet I knew it would be a dereliction of duty not to. Behind the scenes, I had privately talked to White House officials and other key players in an effort to get the Administration to stop opposing the MacBride legislation. But I met with no success, and so I was reluctantly forced to go public. Some Irish-Americans condemned me for criticizing President Clinton. Maybe they did so because they lacked political self-confidence, or maybe it was because they did not have the experience of sitting for hours at hearings and listening to Clinton Administration officials opposing the MacBride legislation. Journalist Jimmy Breslin called to curse me out. In a tirade loaded with the F-word he berated me. "Clinton is the only president who has ever done so much for Ireland," he screamed. "Don't you think I know that, Jimmy," I replied. "Didn't I stress that in our statement." Uttering a few more expletives, he hung up on me.

But because I had stood up to President Clinton on principle (pun intended), I was later able to stand up for him with credibility. During his impeachment difficulty I wrote to every member of the House and Senate, telling them "Let those without sin, cast the first stone." Jimmy Breslin went on to write the most outrageous stuff against Clinton.

But whatever their reasons for opposing my standing up to Clinton, those Irish-Americans were ignoring a fundamental principle in political campaigning: when a political leader does the right thing on your issue, you praise him; when he does the wrong thing on your issue, you call him on it.

Just look at what the President's two most loyal constituencies – African Americans and the Labor Movement – do. When the President goes against them on basic issues they do not hesitate to criticize him publicly.

Indeed, when one very prominent Labor leader chastised me on the phone for criticizing President Clinton, I pointed to how Labor criticized him over NAFTA. He objected by saying, "But that was about jobs for our people." I replied, "And what do you think the Mac Bride Principles are about, but jobs for our people?" He had no answer to that.

There is another hard political reality in all of this. How could I go back to Members of Congress and campaign again for the Mac Bride Principles if I let the President roll us over without a murmur of protest? How could I expect Members of Congress – both Republican and Democrat – to fight for the Mac Bride Principles if I was not prepared to fight for them? By my silence I would be taking a dive and jeopardizing the integrity of the Mac Bride campaign.

Here again, Kevin Mc Namara's book on the Mac Bride Principles shows an inability to appreciate the dynamics of American politics. He asserts that my standing up to President Clinton "... was probably the most significant political error that he [Mc Manus] had made ... he shot himself in the foot."

Mc Namara was clearly misled, again, by Pat Doherty, whom he quotes as saying that I should not have stood up to Clinton, "despite this one difference" (i.e. Clinton's opposition to the Mac Bride Principles becoming U.S. law). However, "this one difference" would have in principle invalidated the entire Mac Bride campaign. If one accepted Clinton's argument against the Federal Mac Bride Bill, then one would have to accept the same argument against all state and city bills. Pat had absolutely no role in lobbying Congress on the Federal Mac Bride Bill. Indeed, his position – in effect, that I should have rolled over and sold out the Federal Mac Bride Bill – shows that he was not committed to Federal legislation – just as he was not at first committed to state and city legislation.

Despite his claim that I had shot myself in the foot, Mc Namara proceeds to prove that my strategy was very effective and successful. He writes: "The administration was caught unawares by the size of the storm ... There was no one better to orchestrate such an uproar than Mc Manus ... The strength of Mc Manus' attack ... forced the administration to consider making a gesture to placate the pro-Mac Bride Democrats ... The truth of the matter is that the President did not wish to go to Chicago ... without attempting to achieve a reconciliation with the Mac Bride campaign ... In an attempt to quell the controversy ... James Lyons (the U.S. observer to the IFI) wrote [to *The Irish Echo*, May 22, 1997] '... whether or not Congress sees fit to incorporate the principles ... in legislation, the Clinton administration and I ... will continue to see that these principles remain fully implemented in the International Fund for Ireland ... .'"

Then Mc Namara adds the clincher of all clinchers, delighting this Kinawleyman's heart: "Officials in the DED privately acknowledged that the UK government had lost the battle on Mac Bride. The UK Embassy in Washington immediately recognized that the Lyons letter was likely to encourage Mc Manus to press for legislation."[8]

In further evidence that our strategy was right, on August

24, 1996, President Clinton – in a move widely regarded as an attempt to defuse the Mac Bride controversy – issued a directive to the United States representative for the International Fund for Ireland, James Lyons:

> "In the 1996 Foreign Affairs Authorization Act (HR 1561) as passed by Congress, Section 1615 stated that U.S. contributions to the Fund 'should be used in a manner that effectively increases employment opportunities in communities with rates of unemployment higher than the local or urban average of unemployment in Northern Ireland. In addition, such contributions should be used to benefit individuals or entities which employ practices consistent with the principles of economic justice' as defined by the Act.
>
> "I vetoed HR 1561 for reasons entirely unrelated to the language in Section 1615. I am committed to equal opportunity and fair employment as necessary foundations for a just, peaceful, and prosperous future for all the people of both jurisdictions in Ireland. I therefore ask you, in discharging your duties under the Anglo-Irish Agreement Support Act of 1986, to ensure that the intent of Section 1651 of HR 1561 is carried out to the greatest extent possible."[9]

Ray O'Hanlon of *The Irish Echo* – the most professionally objective journalist I've ever known – summed it up this way, "Against the backdrop of the Democratic National Convention in Chicago, President Clinton has moved to mend damaged fences with Irish-American backers of the Mac Bride Principles." The Irish National Caucus put out a press release: "Caucus Welcomes President Back to Mac Bride Fold."[10] Remember, all this was happening in August 1996, with the Presidential elections scheduled for November 5, between President Clinton and Senator Bob Dole (R-KS).

Republican and Democratic Parties Endorse Mac Bride

On August 9, the Republican Party at their National Convention included support for the Mac Bride Principles in their party platform language. And on August 27, the Democratic National Convention also included the Mac Bride Principles in their platform. *The Irish Times* observed: The reference to the Mac Bride Principles could be seen as a mild criticism of British rule in Northern Ireland but it is also intended to mollify ... the Irish National Caucus."[11]

As I told Kevin Mc Namara in my review of his book, "For results like that, I would have shot myself in both feet".[12]

Let's take a moment to reflect on what had been achieved to date.

We had routed the Philistines on the Mac Bride Principles. Against all odds – the British government, the Irish government, John Hume, Tip O'Neill, Teddy Kennedy, etc., – we had taken the Mac Bride Principles from a simple press release on November 5, 1984, all across the United States, into the White House, to being endorsed by both the Democratic and Republican parties.

By any criterion, it was a stunning achievement. And it was done by the so-called "little people," the ordinary decent Irish-Americans, without big power or big money. Now, surely, we would get the Federal Mac Bride Bill passed into law?

But things were not as rosy as they appeared. Because, after the 1996 election, the Clinton Administration would again unbelievably oppose the Mac Bride Principles being attached to the International Fund for Ireland.

In 1997, Congressman Ben Gilman (R-NY) again attached the same Mac Bride language to the Foreign Policy Reform Act (HR 1486). On Wednesday April 30, 1997, HR 1486 was in Markup (when Committee Members can make amendments). I spoke with Rep. Lee Hamilton, former House International Relations Committee (HIRC) Chairman, at his seat in the Committee Room and asked him if he was still opposed to the Mac Bride legislation. He emphatically said he was. I asked him what form his opposition would take. He said he wasn't sure yet. He then asked me if the language was the same as last year. I told him it was. Then he said, "You know that it will never become law." I asked why. "Because the President is opposed to it," he replied, with great emphasis.

I then lobbied the other Democrats on the Committee and expressed concern that Hamilton was still opposing the Mac Bride legislation. Next I spoke to Barbara Larkin, Assistant Secretary of State for Legislative Affairs, in the Committee Room. She confirmed the Administration's continued opposition to linking the Mac Bride Principles to the IFI in the legislation. Later that day, I called Steve Kashkett, at the Irish desk of the State Department. He said the President's letter to Lyons did not represent a softening of the President's opposition to legislation linking the Mac Bride Principles to the IFI. I told him that Mary Ann Peterson, Director for European Affairs at the White House, was supposed to have said that President Clinton was no longer opposed to linking Mac Bride to the IFI. He expressed surprise and disbelief at that, and told me he would check it out and call me back.

On Thursday May 1, 1997, the Markup continued. I spoke to Barbara Larkin in the Committee Room. She said, "This is the man who knows all about Ireland," and introduced me to Michael Klosson, her assistant for legislative affairs. He told me that the Administration was opposed to legislation linking Mac Bride to the IFI for a two-fold reason: because the British Fair Employment laws made Mac Bride unnecessary; and because Mac Bride would place onerous burdens on recipients of the Fund.

On Friday May 2, 1997, at 4:40 p.m., Steve Kashkett called me back and told me he could find no indication that the President had changed his position, or that Mary Anne Peterson had ever said the President was no longer opposed to Congressional legislation linking the Mac Bride Principles to the IFI. The President, he said, was opposed to Congressional legislation linking Mac Bride to the IFI for the reasons stated last year. Those reasons still stand, and that is the position of President Clinton, Kashkett emphasized. However, despite Clinton's opposition, the House passed HR 1486 on March 27, 1998.

Mac Bride Becomes U.S. Law

Because the Mac Bride language was not contained in the Senate version of the Bill, the House and Senate Conference had to reconcile the two versions, (and not, of course, only on Mac Bride).

The reconciled Bill – now called the Omnibus Appropriations and Authorization Bill – was passed by the House on Tuesday evening, October 20, 1998, and by the Senate on Wednesday morning, October 21, 1998. Because the Omnibus Appropriations and Authorization Bill had bi-partisan support – and because the Administration wanted it – President Clinton signed it into law. He did not have the option of removing the Mac Bride section. It was either accept the whole Bill, or veto the whole Bill.

Although the Administration was adamantly opposed to the Mac Bride Principles being linked to the International Fund for Ireland, the Administration was forced to accept that link – and so were the British Embassy and the Irish Embassy.

Congressman Gilman took to the floor of the House of Representatives and declared: "I want to make a special note regarding Father Sean Mc Manus. No one has fought harder against discrimination in Northern Ireland. Father Sean single-handedly brought the Mac Bride fair employment principles to ... enactment."

Thus, because of the determined leadership of Congressman Ben Gilman, Chairman of the House International Relations Committee, and the Irish National Caucus, the Mac Bride Principles became U.S. law.

There is no other victory to match it in the history of Irish-American nationalism. John Devoy (1842–1928) would have been proud of us, and I dedicated this victory to him. His grave lies close to Seán Mac Bride's grave in Glasnevin Cemetery, Dublin. Each year I kneel and say an "Ave" there at the graves of my two Irish heroes.

18

"A Protestant Boy" on Capitol Hill

May the Lord in His mercy be kind to Belfast.
Maurice Craig

I arrived in America on October 2, 1972. And in one year and one week I had arranged my first Congressional Hearing on October 9, 1973 – at which my brother Frank and Ruairí Ó Brádaigh, President of Sinn Féin testified. Who would have thought that my latest (though maybe not my last) hearing would be for a hardy "Protestant boy" from Belfast?

In Northern Ireland parlance, "a Protestant boy" refers not to a child but to an adult, a hardy defender of the Unionist/Protestant cause.

The folk-song "The Protestant Boys." gives the flavor:

> The Protestant Boys are loyal and true
> Stout hearted in battle and stout handed too
> The Protestant Boys are true to the last
> And faithful and peaceful when danger has passed
> And Oh! they bear
> And proudly wear
> The colours that floated o'er many a fray
> Where cannons were flashing

And sabres were clashing
The Protestant Boys still carried the day ...

On October 22, 2009, before the same House Human Rights Subcommittee, I facilitated a hearing for Raymond McCord, Sr. – a staunch Unionist/Protestant, though never a paramilitary. I had been deeply touched by the compelling narrative of his heroic struggle to get justice for his son, Raymond Jr., murdered in 1997 near Belfast.

Because young Raymond's killers were part of a Protestant paramilitary group – and because some were police informers and British agents – the killers were protected, and their crime covered up by the Northern Ireland police and the British government.

Raymond Sr. embarked on a long quest for justice. His persistence persuaded Police Ombudsman Nuala O'Loan to launch an investigation that essentially vindicated his charges. Her report, "Operation Ballast," was published in 2007.[1] Still, despite that, nobody was arrested for the murder. Raymond then felt his only hope lay in the U.S. Congress.

I brought Raymond to Capitol Hill from May 3-15, 2009. We did a political blitz of Capitol Hill or, as one observer put it, "the priest and the Protestant took the Halls of Congress by storm." I introduced Raymond to many Members, especially Congressman Don Payne (D-NJ), Congressman Joe Crowley (D-NY), one of the co-chairmen of the Ad Hoc Congressional Committee for Irish Affairs, and Congressman Ritchie Neal, Chairman of the Friends of Ireland – all of whom treated Raymond with great respect and kindness. Then I brought him along to meet the Chairman of the Human Rights Subcommittee, Congressman Bill Delahunt (D-MA).

I began by saying: "Bill, for over thirty years I have been telling the Congress about how the British government covered up the murder of Catholics in Northern Ireland. But today I bring you a staunch Protestant from Belfast to tell you how the British government has covered up the murder of his son."

I then sat back and let Raymond do the talking. Within fifteen minutes, Congressman Delahunt promised a hearing.

Raymond could not believe it. That hardy boy – considered to have been one of the toughest street fighters in Belfast for the past forty years – was deeply moved by Delahunt's compassion and solidarity.

We took time out to meet with the Northern Ireland Bureau, which treated Raymond very nicely. But because justice and policing had not been devolved back to Northern Ireland, the Bureau could not deal with Raymond's case. They did, however, arrange for him to meet with the duly accredited spokesman at the British Embassy, Nic Hailey. Because of my own particular history with that Embassy, I excused myself from the meeting. However, I did drop Raymond off outside the Embassy.

McCord at British Embassy

I sat and watched him walk towards the massive building (the biggest Embassy in Washington, with over 600 employees) all by himself. A small man, with a slight limp that day – his knee was acting up. I watched as others passed him on the footpath, thinking how they would not have any idea of who he was ... and the huge mistake any young hood would have made trying to mug this hardy Protestant boy. I felt an overpowering sense of sadness as I watched Raymond enter the Embassy. I reflected on my own two past visits to the Embassy, on the arrests, and the nights in prison and thought how different it was for Raymond ... I was an Irish Catholic rebel, he a staunch Protestant Unionist.

For me, the British Embassy was the symbol of institutionalized violence, injustice and bigotry in Northern Ireland. But for Raymond, entering the British Embassy had to be a vastly different experience. It was his Embassy; his flag, the Union Jack, flew outside it; and his government operated it. Yet there he was, going in alone, to charge his Embassy with participating in the cover-up of the murder of his beloved Protestant and Unionist son.

I drove off, ruefully pondering how the British government

had used and abused the Protestants and Catholics of Northern Ireland. And yet I waited with optimism for Raymond's report when he came back. Because he had not just walked in from the street, but had his visit arranged by the Northern Ireland Bureau, and because we were so well into the peace process, I was expecting the British Embassy to give Raymond some sort of satisfaction and comfort (the word "closure" is over-used and besides, for the bereaved, there is no such thing). "Well, how did it go?" I asked Raymond the moment he walked back into the Caucus office. "Useless, a waste of time," was his answer. I was really disappointed and said so. "That's because you don't know the British government as well as I do, Sean," said Raymond.

What is wrong with that picture? I, a Kinawleyman, disappointed that the British were not more generous, and Raymond, a staunch Ulster Protestant telling me I was naïve. Raymond then issued a statement:

> I was low-keyed and respectful but Mr. Hailey never answered one question. He never even tried, maintaining almost virtual silence throughout the hour meeting. And when he did speak, it was to ask: Whom are you meeting on Capitol Hill? Do you think you are having any impact, and when are you going home? See here, I am an Ulsterman, a British citizen. The British Government and the Northern Ireland police colluded in the brutal murder of my son, Raymond Jr. I am given a fantastic reception on Capitol Hill. Then I go to my own Embassy in Washington, and I get nothing, absolutely nothing. Hailey's treatment of me is exactly what I get from his colleagues in the Northern Ireland Office in Belfast ... My treatment at the British Embassy illustrates and vindicates the need for my visit to Capitol Hill. It confirms my conviction that Congressional pressure in my son's case is my only hope ..."[2]

McCord Hearing

But Raymond would have the last word. On October 22, 2009, he had his Congressional hearing before the House Human Rights Subcommittee – and he gave the fight of his life. There was a stunned, sombre atmosphere as he recounted his son's murder, the collusion and the cover-up. And I knew that from then on, I would never have any difficulty convincing the Congress that the British can do bad things in Ireland.

But I was also deeply sad at how difficult it had to be for Mrs. McCord, young Raymond's mother, who had to listen to the retelling of the slaughter of her son. Raymond, Sr. somehow got through it all, with his voice breaking only once. Indeed, not only did he get through it – but also, very importantly, he kept to his allotted time. At hearings, the oral testimony is five minutes (to allow for other speakers and for question-and-answer time) with the written testimony – submitted for the record – being much longer. It is generally acceptable that the oral testimony can actually go a bit over five minutes, but witnesses abuse the privilege and courtesy of the Congress if they go over seven minutes. Raymond – a rough and ready working-class man – spoke for six and a half minutes – further earning the respect of the Subcommittee.

As I said, that may not be the last Congressional hearing I arrange, but I think it is fitting to bookend this story of my American struggle for Irish justice with the hearing at which my brother Frank testified on October 9, 1973 and the McCord Hearing, October 22, 2009. It gives new meaning to the famous phrase, "Observe the Sons of Ulster."[3] And maybe it beckons a new dawn.

Epilogue

Rem tene, verba sequentur
(Hold to the cause, the words will follow).
Cato the Elder[1]

Writing this book has been quite an experience: joyful, sorrowful, exciting, frustrating. But above all, it has been liberating to get all that stuff out of my head and onto paper. I knew I would not be content until I did so.

Furthermore, I was very aware if I did not write this book, nobody would – indeed, nobody could. Nobody – and certainly no Catholic priest – ever lobbied the U.S. Congress full-time and for as long as I have, with one mission: to maximize American pressure on the British government to end injustice in Northern Ireland.

Of course, one disadvantage of going through almost forty years of files is that it raises a lot of ghosts, and inevitably rakes up old issues one has put to rest. In retelling the story, and revisiting the evidence in cold print, I could feel the old righteous Kinawley anger bubbling up again – especially, it must be confessed, at the Dublin Government and the likes of Garret FitzGerald.

I should point out one thing here. For much of this book, I have referred to the "Dublin" government. However, because of my respect for the way Taoiseach Albert Reynolds bravely supported the peace process – and in deference to the person and office of President Mary McAleese – I no longer use that terminology. Instead, I use the term, Irish Government. As a Northerner, I was deeply encouraged when Mary McAleese became the Irish President. I saw it as a critical and integral part of the peace process. I have been proud of the way she has reached out to Northerners, especially the Protestants.

And, now, since the Irish Embassy and Consulates have ceased their campaigns to vilify and demonize me, I have no longer reason to be angry at them. Indeed, I am now able to appreciate the important work they do in support of the peace process. I am grateful that there are no more Sean Donlons and Carmel Heaneys trying to destroy me.

I had considered editing out "the old anger" but decided that would be unrealistic and unhistorical. Anger at injustice was an integral part, an ever-present dynamic of the Troubles – at least for those who were troubled by injustice. Furthermore, one cannot understand the Troubles if one does not understand the anger of Catholics at how they were treated by the British government, and how they were abandoned by the Irish government, with all the resulting feeling of powerlessness that entailed.

Now, of course, anger can lead to very bad things – spite, revenge and murder. That is why I use the term "righteous anger." My online dictionary says: "Righteous is similar in meaning to virtuous but also implies freedom from guilt or blame (i.e. righteous anger)." St. Thomas Aquinas tells us that anger used for revenge is bad, but good when used to "maintain justice."[2] God himself showed righteous anger at injustice. He told Moses, "I have observed the misery of my people; I have heard their cry on account of their taskmasters. Indeed, I know their sufferings, and I have come down to deliver them. (Exodus 3:7). God also tells us in Exodus that if we practice injustice His "anger will be aroused." (22:23). The Hebrew Prophets and Jesus Himself showed righteous anger. The Black Freedom Struggle in the United States would never have succeeded had Martin Luther King, Jr. not blazed with righteous anger at injustice. But when did Irish bishops show sustained righteous anger at British injustice?

I, long ago, came to the conviction that my righteous anger

could only be channeled through nonviolence. But (and this is something apparently often forgotten) "nonviolence" is only short for "nonviolent resistance". Many of the reports on the death of the late Cardinal Daly mentioned he was "committed to nonviolence." Well, whatever the cardinal was committed to, it certainly was not nonviolence. Unless you resist, you are not practicing nonviolence. If you close your eyes to injustice and violence – as so many Churchmen do – you are not being nonviolent: you are being cowardly, lazy and indifferent to human suffering. Instead of "staying out of politics" you are being complicit in the worst politics of all – political collaboration in oppression and injustice.

I have told my story. It is not the full story and it is certainly not the only story: many dedicated people in America were doing a lot of work of which I was not even aware, but they must give their own account. I feel it is a blessing from the Lord to have been able to do what I've done. Others might have done it better, but they did not, so I had to do it the best I could. In my haste to get the job done, I may have rubbed some people the wrong way, and for that I am sorry. But I always tried to treat people with kindness and respect.

Since I started writing this book, my large family has again been visited by death – but equally by the sure hope of eternal life. My lovely sister Celia in Enniskillen died from cancer on November 24, 2008, at the age of seventy-seven, and my indomitable brother Thomas, in Cornwall on the Hudson, New York, died on May 16, 2009, at the age of seventy-six, after a long battle with Alzheimer's.

I am hopeful for the future of Ireland – the whole island of Ireland. Even though, I think, we have still a long way to go. I believe "the Union" will die on the vine. The only way it can be saved is if the IRA came back into business. One of the great Irish ironies! But it is an irony I hope that patriotic young Irish men and women take heed of: no Irish person need be killed – or kill – for full Irish freedom.

There is one thing, however, that really concerns me about the present process: the digging-in of MI5. Instead of disengaging, they are building a massive infrastructure in Northern Ireland.

Their withdrawal would be far more important than that of the British Army (which, of course, is still there). The British Army has always been just the crude symbol of British rule in Ireland. How often were there pitched battles between the British Army and the IRA in the past forty years?

British control of Ireland has always essentially been a policing and intelligence operation. I believe acceptable policing will eventually be achieved. But even with the best of good faith, the police will have absolutely no control over MI5. And that shadowy organization can so easily manipulate the still deeply entrenched anti-Catholic sectarianism in the North.

However, I want to finish this book on an appreciative note. I am deeply grateful to former British Prime Minister, Tony Blair. He is the only British Prime Minister of whom I could ever think kindly. And God rest Mo Mowlam. She, more than anyone else, symbolized the sea change that was going to take place in Britain's attitude toward Ireland. When she saw me at an event in Washington, she came right over and said, "You're the MacBride Principles priest," and hugged me. Being hugged by a British Minister was definitely a new experience for me. And, of course, like all Irish-Americans, I will always be grateful to Bill and Hillary Clinton. Without them, there would not have been an Irish peace process. And I salute the leadership of Gerry Adams and Martin McGuiness. They pulled off the impossible. God bless them both.

From the bottom of my heart, I am grateful to all those dedicated and generous Irish-Americans who made my work possible. I could not have done a thing without them. They are the salt of the earth. Nor could I have done anything without some magnificent Members of Congress. I was always particularly moved by help from Members who were not Irish or Catholic. The entire Jewish American congressional delegation over the past forty years has been superb. There are too many Members to mention by name, but here are some of them: Lester Wolff (D-NY) 1965-1973; the already mentioned Dick Ottinger; Nita Lowey (D-NY); Elliott Engel (D-NY); Gary Ackerman (D-NY) former vice-chairman of the House Foreign Affairs Committee; Senator Chuck Schumer (D-NY); and, of course, the great Ben Gilman.

Don Payne (D-NJ), as I keep telling him, has been to Northern Ireland more often than I have! This African American Baptist lends the moral authority – and the insight – of Martin Luther King, Jr. to the Irish cause.

It gives me great ecumenical joy when Protestant Irish-American Members of Congress stand up for justice and peace in Ireland. Carolyn Maloney (D-NY) is a Presbyterian and a fervent Irish woman. As a member of New York City Council, she strongly backed the MacBride Principles, and takes great pride in having played a key role in naming a street after Joe Doherty when he was imprisoned in New York.

I expect great things from Congressman Russ Carnahan (D-MO) a Methodist, and an ardent Irishman, who is former Chairman of the Subcommittee on Human Rights.

The other ethnic group that has featured very significantly in my work are the Italian Americans. I have already mentioned Mario Biaggi who, despite massive opposition, stayed the course and backed me all the way. Former Speaker Nancy Pelosi is also Italian American. When she became Speaker, she did not follow Democrat Tip O'Neill's disgraceful ban on human rights hearings on Northern Ireland. Speaker Pelosi always invited me to her St. Patrick's Day Lunch – as, indeed, did Speaker Newt Gingrich (R-GA) and Speaker Denny Hastert (R-IL).

But I have to pay tribute to another great Italian lady – not a Member of Congress but my valued and trusted colleague in the Irish National Caucus – Barbara Flaherty. Barbara was first introduced to the Irish community in 1968 by her late husband, Martin, who was born and reared in Galway. Once – when I was singing the praises of Kinawley – he shot back: "The only good thing that ever came out of Kinawley was the road to Galway." He was a committed Irish patriot. After his death, Barbara wanted, in his honor, to devote more time to the Irish cause. Since then, she has played a key role in the Irish National Caucus – and in the production of this book. I can never adequately thank her for her help and counsel, and the friendship of her wonderful family.

Finally, let me conclude with a profession of faith, so to speak. After all these years, I still believe that God is the mystery at the center of all reality; that Jesus Christ is the Person at the center of all human history; that the Holy Spirit gathers us all into the Body of Christ – the Church, which is the Sacrament of Christ on earth. Throughout my long struggle, I have – despite my faults and failures – been sustained by faith and prayer and nourished by the Word of God and the Eucharist – the Bread of Life and the Cup of Eternal Salvation.

God bless America and God save Ireland.

Afterword to the American Edition

Changing My Sky, Not My Soul

"Caelum non animum mutant qui trans mare current."
(They change their sky but not their soul who cross the ocean.)
– Horace

On November 19, 2011, I held a launch of the Irish edition of this book at the Maine Irish Heritage Center. I was very impressed by what those fine people are doing.

They have preserved the "historic landmark that was formerly St. Dominic's Church, a hub of early Irish community in Maine." They kindly presented me with a copy of the book *They Change Their Sky: The Irish in Maine*.[1] I am indebted to this excellent collection of essays for the Horace quote, for which in turn that book credits Thomas Cahill's *How The Irish Saved Civilization*.[2]

Cahill says the Horace quote is, "a good maxim for all exiles, and in this context, a reminder of the constancy of the Irish personality."[3] (Daniel O'Connell, The Liberator, liked to use the Irish version of that proverb: "They change the climate, not their hearts, who leave their native shores."[4])

However, while crossing the Atlantic doesn't, and shouldn't, change one's soul, it does for sure change one's perspective – and not just geographically.

I am very conscious that I have changed my perspective. Growing up Catholic, and then being a member of a Religious

Order, I was always acutely aware of the "common good" – of the importance of community, and that the individual is not autonomous and separate from society.

But living in America has also taught me the importance of individual freedom and the right to privacy. That was not always appreciated in Britain and Ireland, where State and Church were too intrusive. And, of course, in England there is no separation between Church and State – the ultimate source of anti-Catholic sectarianism and bigotry, mandating that a Catholic cannot be Monarch.

I am consequently very grateful to America for giving me this perspective, which seems appropriate to mention in this Afterword before continuing with any update.

At the end of Chapter 18, I wrote that the McCord Hearing of October 22, 2009 might not be the last one I would be involved in. And, of course, it was not.

At the Speaker's St. Patrick's Day Lunch, 2010, I was speaking to Congressman Russ Carnahan (D-MO) who had recently succeeded Congressman Bill Delahunt (D-MA) as the Chairman of the House Human Rights Sub Committee. I urged him to hold a Hearing. He said he would love to. I told him there was a group of human rights people from Ireland in Washington at that moment with whom he should meet. He immediately called his office, changed his appointments for the following day, and asked me to bring the group to his office in the morning. I brought along the Northern Ireland Human Rights Consortium, represented by a number of young, very competent human rights activists, one of whom was Aideen Gilmore, Deputy Director, Committee for the Administration of Justice, along with Jane Winter of British Irish Rights Watch. I secured a commitment from Congressman Carnahan that, indeed, he would hold a Hearing.

On September 16, 2010, Chairman Carnahan held the Hearing. Aideen Gilmore was one of the witnesses along with John Finucane, Pat's youngest son.

Then in December 2010, Rita O'Hare, Sinn Fein Representative to the United States, brought the Ballymurphy

Massacre Committee to see me, seeking a Congressional Hearing on the British Army massacre in 1971. I promised I would do all in my power to help.

In January 2011, the Republicans took over power in the House of Representatives. Thus Congressman Carnahan lost the Chairmanship of the House Human Rights Subcommittee. However, his successor could not have been more perfect: the admirable Congressman Chris Smith (R-NJ), a veteran holder of Congressional Hearings on injustices in Northern Ireland. He would also assure Chairmanship of The Helsinki Commission, which could also hold Hearings.

I worked closely with Congressman Smith's excellent staff, earnestly promoting the cause of the Ballymurphy Massacre Committee. On March 16, 2011, Congressman Smith held his thirteenth Northern Ireland Hearing. John Teggart, Chairman of the Ballymurphy Massacre Committee gave excellent and very moving testimony. The eleven murdered victims of the British Army Massacre – including John's own father – would have been proud of his performance. And I was honored and humbled to have been able to help these noble Belfast families.

Ciaran Mc Airt testified on the Mc Gurk Bar bombing.[5]

In 2012 we focused on getting Mark Thompson, Relatives for Justice, Belfast, to testify. Oddly enough, Mark had never testified before Congress even though he has spent many years "in the trenches" doing very important work in exposing collusion and other forms of England's dirty war.

Again, we worked closely with Congressman Smith's excellent staff. And on March 21, 2012 the intrepid Congressman Smith held his fourteenth Hearing, with Mark Thompson being a witness – along with Mrs. Finucane, Christopher Stanley, British-Irish Watch, Dr. Patricia Lundy, University of Ulster and Brian Gormley, Director, Committee on the Administration of Justice.

So ... in 2009, 2010, 2011 and 2012 we have had Congressional Hearings on Human Rights in Northern Ireland. Tip O' Neill – who corruptly used his power to collude with the British Government and ban Human Rights Hearings on Northern Ireland – must be turning in his grave. And, please God, we will continue to have Congressional Hearings – because at the end of the day, the only thing the British Government fears is opinion on Capitol Hill.

In the Epilogue of the first edition I say that writing this book was quite an experience. Well, so has the launching and promotion.

The first edition of this book was published by Collins Press, Cork. We launched it on April 5, 2011, in Dublin Castle – formerly, and ironically, the center of British administration for the whole island of Ireland. When I walked into the Castle, the first person who bounded up to shake my hand was Raymond McCord: "We used to own this place, Sean," he chortled. My brother Frank would quip, "No wonder the Brits held on to it for so long" (referring to its splendor and magnificence).

I was truly taken aback that three hundred guests showed up for the book launch. Frankie and the organizing committee – one of whom was my cousin, John McKay – had done a superb job. A key member of the committee was Donal Donnelly, who previously had his own book launch in Dublin Castle for his "Prisoner 1080" – a wonderful account of his famous escape from Crumlin Road Jail, Belfast, in 1960. Donal had been, like my brother Patrick, in the 1956 IRA campaign. Indeed, there were a number of 1956 veterans at the book launch, and I was proud to see them all. Tom Cooper, Irish National Congress, provided key support.

The two speakers at the event were Bobby Ballagh, the famous artist and ardent Irishman, and Vincent Browne, the noted Dublin journalist and broadcaster. Browne, whose job is to give everyone a hard time, conceded: "[Fr. McManus] stood out against powerful forces in a fight for justice and fairness. I didn't always agree with the causes he supported but I admired his persistence, his courage, his relentlessness. And admiration that one person, almost alone, could make such impact on public policy in the United States."

During the proceedings, the Collins Press photographer assembled different people outside in the Castle yard to be photographed with me. The process seemed to last forever, and I find it hard to keep smiling all the time. At one point, as I turned round to my right, from shaking some well wisher's hand, I noticed that the photographer had placed a small grey haired man in position to be photographed with me. I immediately recognized him. I loudly asked: "Was this man dragooned into the photo?" He replied, shaking my hand, "Not at all, Father. I am proud to be here. Congratulations on your Memoirs."

It was the eminent Michael D. Higgins, whose sense of social justice and independence of mind I had always admired. He was running for President of Ireland and would be elected on October 27, 2011 ... And there he stood proudly holding my book for the cameras. He stayed for the entire event, listening to the speeches with great interest.

I was especially pleased and honored that my old friend and fervent Irish patriot Derek Warfield and his Young Wolfe Tones performed for the event.

Next, I had the book launch in Belfast, which was sponsored by Mairtin O'Muilleoir, publisher of the *Irish Echo*, and hosted by Mark Thompson and Clara Reilly, Relatives for Justice.

Then it was onto Bellaghy, where Oliver Hughes hosted me at the Wolfe Tone's GAA. Deputy First Minister, Martin Mc Guinness, had planned to attend the book launch in Bellaghy, but at the last minute he had to cancel. However, he graciously telephoned me before the event to apologize.

Next it was back to my home turf. My brother Frankie and his Organizing Committee assembled a large crowd at the Enniskillen Library. The well-known Peter Quinn, former president of the GAA, was the speaker. I was honored that Michelle Gildernew, MP for Fermanagh and S. Tyrone, attended the book launch, and spoke warmly and supportively.

I was deeply touched by the enthusiasm and support at all three book launches in Ireland. It was a wonderful experience.

Then it was back to Washington. We had the Capitol Hill book launch on May 1, 2011. The indefatigable Barbara Flaherty ran the show and since then has been the prime promoter of my book – demonstrating remarkable devotion to the success of the project. She has played a key and central role in all the book launches: Boston, New York City; the Ladies and Men's AOH

New York State Convention, Pearl River, NY; Woodlawn, Bronx, NY; Philadelphia, PA; Seattle, WA; Portland, ME; Cleveland, OH; Greensboro, NC; Greenville, SC; Los Angeles and San Francisco, CA – with more to come.

Barbara, now Executive Vice President of the Irish National Caucus, generously remarks: "Working on the project is a labor of love. It is a truly joyful experience." Indeed, she maintains the book will be made into a movie!

Over the years, I had to cut back on speaking around the country, so the book tour has given me an opportunity to see a lot of people I had not seen in a long time, as well as meeting new faces. It was heartening to see that Irish-Americans are still as nice as I discovered them to be when I first came to America in 1972, and that they still care deeply about justice and peace in Ireland. I am so proud of them.

I am particularly grateful to the Ladies AOH and the AOH for all their support. They very graciously and generously provided me with a platform all across the U.S. to promote my book. Mary Hogan, National Secretary of the LAOH, has become a most enthusiastic promoter of my book. She has done excellent work in spreading the word. Mary says: "Fr. Mc Manus' book is a blessing to the LAOH. It is educational and inspiring – and full of spiritual insights into how working for justice is at the heart of the Gospel and the teaching of the Catholic Church."

National AOH Vice-President, Brendan Moore, says: "We are proud to provide a platform for Fr. Mc Manus' book, which is the perfect tool for promoting the Irish Cause." This is especially meaningful to me because Brendan is a distinguished and dedicated campaigner for Irish justice. [Note: In July 2012, Mary was elected LAOH National Vice President, and Brendan was elected AOH National President].

Sean Pender of New Jersey – National Chairman of the key AOH committee, Freedom for All Ireland Committee – is also a strong backer of the book. Sean has become a real force in the AOH, and has a keen appreciation of the importance of Congressional action. He and I work closely together in pushing for Congressional scrutiny on key issues like collusion and other forms of British Government assassination in Northern Ireland.

Dan Dennehy, National Chairman of the AOH Immigration Committee, is also a key leader. He has shown impressive commitment to Irish immigrants in general, and especially to the case of "the Deportees" – those who fell through the cracks of the Clinton initiative that gave permanent status to those who had to flee Ireland to escape from The Troubles. Malachy McAllister and Matt Morrison are two of the better known cases.

Another key player on immigration issues is Mayo-born Ciaran Staunton with whom I'm proud to work. Ciaran, a brother-in-law of Publisher Niall O'Dowd, played a vital role with Niall in facilitating Sinn Fein's dramatic and successful entrance onto the American scene.

Owen Rodgers, a proud native of County Tyrone, has been a strong, dependable ally for many years. He specializes in providing forums for important Irish issues, and has twice hosted my book-launches in New York City.

The Irish American Unity Conference, under the current leadership of Tom Burke, has been very supportive of my book. I work closely with the president of their Washington Chapter, Peter Kissel, who is doing excellent work on cases such as The Ballymurphy Massacre.

I am very gratified by the American response to my book. And now with this American edition, I believe the response will be even greater. I have been particularly struck by the number of people who have told me they have read my book twice – some even three and five times. That has to be pleasing to any author. Perhaps the most fulsome praise of all came from the great Bill Flynn, Chairman Emeritus, Mutual of America and Chairman, National Committee on American Foreign Policy. He telephoned to tell me he was profoundly moved by reading my book, saying, "Your book's authenticity is its crowning glory."

Forty years ago I came to America. I based my work on three principles:

1. A Catholic principle, spelled out in official Church teaching:

"Action on behalf of justice ... [is] a constitutive dimension to the preaching of the Gospel ..." (Justice in the World. Synod of Bishops. 1971).

2. An American principle: Respect for international human rights is an integral part of American foreign policy.

3. An Irish National Caucus principle: U.S. dollars should not subsidize anti-Catholic discrimination in Northern Ireland (the genesis of the Mac Bride Principles).

These principles are still as valid as they ever were. And the work must continue.

I wrote this book – over and above the reasons already given – to provide Irish-Americans with a tool to replenish, reinvigorate and recharge the Irish cause in America. I hope I have succeeded because we still have a long way to go, and it is imperative that we keep America involved in standing up for justice and peace in Ireland. That remains the key, and is now as important as ever. And I pledge that the Irish National Caucus will stay the course ... until Ireland, too, has the right to be One Nation under God, indivisible, with liberty and justice for all.

I believe now more than ever before the words of Fr. Haring, previously quoted: "If strength and resolve to become witnesses to justice, peace and nonviolence do not flow from our Eucharistic celebrations, then we must fearfully and sadly conclude that far too many priestly and lay Christian vocations are not sufficiently authentic."

I have stressed throughout this book that struggling for justice is at the very heart of the Judeo-Christian faith. To me, it is also the essence of being authentically Irish.

God bless America and God save Ireland.

This is where American Edition ended. What follows is the new text of The Holy Land Edition.

Holy Land Principles

The Holy Land

Over the years various groups have approached me about a Mac Bride Principles-type campaign for their homeland or cause. For example, one black man visited me from London asking my advice about a Mac Bride-type campaign for Blacks in England. I willingly helped him.

I really don't know if anything much resulted from those approaches.

However, in August 2012, I was approached by a group of Americans concerned about the hiring practices of American companies in The Holy Land. They asked for my assistance. I replied: "How could I say no? If I believe that the Mac Bride Principles are good for Holy Land number two (Ireland!), how could I be opposed to the same principle – and Principles – being applied in Holy Land number one? How could anyone? My fervent belief is that American principles should follow American investment everywhere, in every country, no exception."

Then these concerned citizens urged me to visit The Holy Land. I agreed and we began discussions on creating and initiating The Holy Land Principles.

I knew I would be deeply moved to be in the land where my Lord and Savior, Jesus Christ, was born, reared, died, rose again for my sins, and the sins of all mankind, making us heirs to eternal life. And deeply conscious, too, that this land is sacred to Jews and Muslims alike. That, despite the obvious theological differences, only served to deepen my awareness of our common humanity. As Dr. Martin Luther King, Jr. said: "We are all caught in an inescapable network of mutuality, tied into a single garment of destiny. Whatever affects one directly, affects all indirectly. We are made to live together because of the interrelated structure of reality… This is the way our universe is structured, this is its interrelated quality. We aren't going to have peace on Earth until we recognize this basic fact of the interrelated structure of all reality."[1]

Not for Me to Expound

This is not the place, nor am I the person, to expound on the sad history of this land.

Furthermore, this not a political treatise on the Holy Land, but rather part of my Memoirs.

However, for the sake of the narrative, it is important for the reader to have some concept, some mental image of the background, otherwise their mind goes blank and their eyes glaze over. I think many people find it hard to capture a picture of the Israeli-Palestine issue. I will try to briefly present the issue without being caught up in the political controversy in any partisan or unfair way.

It appears to me that that the following is a fair and objective postulation of the problem: "The conflict between Palestinian Arabs and Jews is a modern phenomenon, which began around the turn of the 20th century... Until 1948, the area that both groups claimed was known internationally as Palestine. But following the war of 1948-49, this land was divided into three parts: the state of Israel, the West Bank (of the Jordan River) and the Gaza Strip. ... Jewish claims to this land are based on the biblical promise to Abraham and his descendants, on the fact that this was the historical site of the Jewish kingdom of Israel (which was destroyed by the Roman Empire [CE 70]), and on Jews' need for a haven from European anti-Semitism. Palestinian Arabs' claims to the land are based on continuous residence in the country for hundreds of years, and the fact that they represented the demographic majority. They reject the notion that a biblical-era kingdom constitutes the basis for a valid modern claim. If Arabs engage the biblical argument at all, they maintain that since Abraham's son Ishmael is the forefather of the Arabs, then God's promise of the land to the children of Abraham includes Arabs as well. They do not believe that they should forfeit their land to compensate Jews for Europe's crimes against them."[2]

Zionism

The Holy Land's problem that began "at the turn of the 20th century" has a longer history and deeper roots in European anti-

Where is Palestine?

The Institute for Middle East Understanding (IMEU)
SEP 28, 2011
Institute for Middle East Understanding (IMEU)
Tel: (718) 514-9662. E-mail: info@imeu.net
315 Bleecker Street, Suite 171. New York, NY 10014

Palestine is at the eastern end of the Mediterranean Sea, and forms a land bridge connecting the continents of Africa and Asia. One of the longest continuously inhabited areas of the world, Palestine has been recognized as a distinct geographical region since the Greek and Roman eras. (The name derives from the Philistines, a sea-faring people who invaded and settled the area in ancient times. The Arabic name for the country is still Filasteen.)

More recently, Palestine has been used to refer to the Occupied West Bank and Gaza Strip, areas administered by the Palestinian Authority. However, these territories represent less than a quarter of former Palestine.

The modern boundaries of Palestine were drawn by the British, following their conquest of the region from the Ottoman Turks during World War I. Against the explicit wishes of the native Palestinian Arabs, the British were granted a "mandate" over Palestine after the war ("mandates" were granted by the League of Nations to Britain and France over former Ottoman provinces to assist their peoples toward eventual national independence). Originally the mandate included what is today the Hashemite Kingdom of Jordan, but the British split off Jordan for autonomous governance in 1921. The British ruled Palestine directly through an appointed High Commissioner from the end of World War I to 1948. The terms "Historic Palestine" or "Mandate Palestine" are
continues

Semitism. The development of Zionism as a solution began to take shape in Russia after the assassination of Tsar Alexander II in 1881.

While Enlightenment ideals of legal equality (Jews and non-Jews) had spread from Napoleon's France (1791) through the Ottoman Empire (1839), they had not reached Russia by the time of the assassination of Tsar Alexander II (1881), which resulted in harsh laws against Jews (the May Laws). A Jewish physician in Odessa, Leo Pinsker, sought equal rights for Jews, but concluded the solution was to flee Russia. In 1882, he wrote *Auto-Emancipation*, which argued for Jewish separation and return to Zion, resulting in a series of Jewish immigrations from Russia to Palestine (backed by Baron Edmund de Rothschild).[3]

This "Lovers of Zion" project was secular in nature, believing freedom from legal discrimination was only possible in a separate Jewish homeland. This movement became known as Zionism. In 1897, Theodor Herzl, an Austro-Hungarian Jew, established the World Zionist Organization, which had as its objective, "a national home for the Jewish people." (It puts things in perspective to be aware that the Zionists considered Argentina, Uganda, and even Texas as possible sites for their national home.) Some argue that this is another example of White European colonialism, which believed it had a right to claim other parts of the world, settling it with its own people. But to be successful, Zionism would need the support of a major power, and the world's expert in colonialism. (No marks for guessing who.) Until the monstrous rise of Hitlerism, Zionism was a minority movement in Judaism. Indeed, most Orthodox Jews strongly opposed Zionism regarding it as a heretical, secular doctrine. For Orthodox Jews, only God should be bringing all Jews back to the Promised Land.

Ottoman records of 1878 show that there were 462,465 subjects in the area, and only 15,011 were Jews (3.5%). Additionally, there were 10,000 more Palestinian Jews with foreign citizenship. By 1914, as Russian and European settlers arrived, Palestine's Jewish population had risen to 8% (60,000 Jewish, 683,000 Arab) due to recent settlers.

Where is Palestine? *continued*

sometimes used to denote this entity, which was about the size of Vermont.

The mandate ended on May 14, 1948, when British troops withdrew from Palestine. The previous November 29, the United Nations General Assembly had recommended the partition of Palestine into two states, one Jewish and one Arab, with an internationalized status for Jerusalem. Civil war broke out almost immediately. Better-armed and trained Jewish forces began to expand out of the areas allocated to the Jewish state, pushing many Palestinians into exile.

By the time of Israel's declaration of independence the day after British withdrawal, on May 15, 1948, hundreds of thousands of Palestinians had fled their homes. When armistice agreements were concluded in 1949, Israeli military forces controlled 78% of Mandate Palestine. The remaining 22 percent, comprised of the West Bank and Gaza Strip, fell under Jordanian and Egyptian administrations, respectively.

Britain's Nefarious Role

World War I had now allied Western Europe and Russia against the Ottomans and Germany. In 1917 Britain was desperate for funding to support its war effort, and feared the collapse of its alliance with Russia because of The Revolution. Britain issued The Balfour Declaration a few weeks later, expressing support for a Jewish homeland in Palestine.

Some argue The Declaration, in part, was intended to persuade some of Russia's new leaders, with Jewish backgrounds, to remain Allies in the war effort. The Declaration was issued to Baron Walter Rothschild, of the Rothschild banking dynasty, to help secure wartime funding, and for transmission to the Zionist Federation of Great Britain and Ireland. Thus, Britain became a principal supporter of the Zionist project.

Britain, in typical fashion, made contradictory promises to the Arabs and Jews.

Britain promised the Arabs an independent state if they supported Britain during World War I. (Remember Peter O'Toole in *Lawrence of Arabia*?)

The Irish reader of this book will not be surprised by the nefarious role Britain played in this tragic situation. Renowned Jewish historian, Ilan Pappe says: "But nowhere in its [British] Empire did Albion demonstrate such perfidious behavior."[4]

Albion is, of course, the ancient name for England, which for centuries has been nicknamed Perfidious Albion.

The fundamental moral point here is that Britain had absolutely no right to assign Palestine to anyone.

The Ottoman forces in Jerusalem surrendered to British Field Marshal Allenby in 1917 and in 1918. Palestine was occupied by the Allies under Allenby. Then the British continued to rule Palestine until May 15, 1948.

The 1922 British census shows that there was a total population of 757,182 of which 83,290 were Jews (11%). Despite protests from the local population, immigration continued, and by 1931 the census shows that the total population was 1.03 million, of which 175,006 were Jews (17%). This unrestrained immigration (regarded by Arabs as European and white, not just Jewish) increased the Jewish population to almost 30%, and led to nationwide strikes, and the largely non-violent Arab Revolt of 1936-39. In response, Britain at last accepted restrictions upon immigration though the White Paper, approved in 1939.

By 1947 the Jews still owned no more than 6% of the land.

UN Partitions Palestine

Despite sub-committee reports that the plan was not within the UN's jurisdiction, and after delays in voting – to allow time for bribes, intimidation, and pressure upon smaller countries from the major powers – the UN voted on November 29, 1947, to follow the British plan to partition Palestine. Without the consent of the governed in Palestine, it gave 56% of Palestine to the Jewish people: "The injustice was as striking then as it appears now, and yet, it was hardly commented on at the time by any of the leading Western newspapers then covering Palestine: the Jews, who owned less than 6% of the total land area of Palestine and constituted no more than a third of the population, were handed more than half of its overall territory. Within the borders of their UN-proposed state, they owned only 11% of the land, and were a minority in every district."[5]

1947–1949 War

The organization "Jews for Justice" summarizes this war thus:

"By the end of the war, Israel had conquered 78% of Palestine; three-quarters of a million Palestinians had been made refugees; over 500 towns and villages had been obliterated; and a new map was drawn, in which every city, river and hillock received a new, Hebrew name, as all vestiges of the Palestinian culture were to be erased."[6]

Indeed, former Israeli Prime Minister Golda Meir declared, "There is no such thing as a Palestinian."[7] Very reminiscent of the Lord Chief Justice who declared in the 18th Century: "The laws of Ireland did not presume a Roman Catholic to exist," or Maggie Thatcher's imperial rant (1981), "Northern Ireland is as British as Finchley."

It is important to stress here that Jewish forces had already expelled a quarter of a million Palestinians before Britain departed on May 15, 1948. That refutes the false myth that the Palestinians voluntarily fled their homes when the Arab armies entered Palestine on May 15 to protect them from the Jewish forces.

After the 1967 war (Six Day War), Israel occupied the remaining 22% of Palestine – The West Bank and the Gaza Strip. The West Bank (which encompasses the heart of the Biblical Land of Israel – Judea and Samaria) is about the size of Delaware, and the Gaza Strip is about twice as large as Washington, D.C.

Remember, the entire area of Palestine is only 10,000 square

Delegation at Dome of the Rock, Islamic shrine in Jerusalem. Author standing at right.

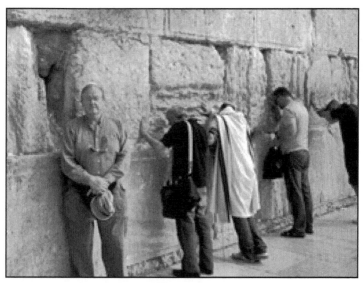

Author wears yarmulke at Wailing Wall.

Author with Fr. Elias M. Odeh and Archdeacon Samuel Barhoum.

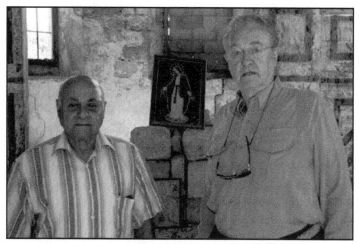

Author with caretaker Khalil Asi in Greek Orthodox Church destroyed in 1948.

*Author
with Daher
Nassar.*

Author harvesting olives.

*Author
clearly
was not
the first
Irishman
at the Tent
of Nations!*

You are now entering Free Deheisheh.

Author with Cindy Corrie, mother of Rachael.

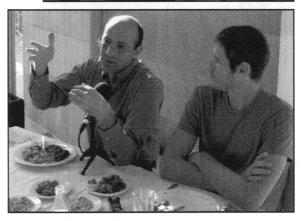

Rev. Mitri Raheb and Mike Daly, IFPB.

miles – about the size of the state of Maryland. (Today the population of Israel is 7,848,800 (80% Jewish); the West Bank is 2,622,544; and the Gaza Strip is 1,710,257.)

The Nakba

Since 1948, at least 800,000 Palestinians were forced to flee, their homes destroyed and their land confiscated. These "Refugees" are at the heart of the Israeli-Palestinian conflict.

Palestinians refer to this violent expulsion as The Nakba (The Disaster) in much the same was as the Irish refer to The Famine (not that I am saying the two events are exactly the same). The Nakba is a powerful, evocative and haunting word. The policy of Transfer (expulsion) of non-Jews was discussed at the turn of the 20th century. It was explicitly planned for as early as 1937 by the establishment of a "Transfer Committee," and was fully implemented in 1948 and 1967. Some, indeed, fear that the ongoing illegal settlements are part of the historic pattern: settlements first, expulsions later.[8]

As a condition for entry into the United Nations, Israel accepted Resolution 194, which called for the right of return of Palestinian refugees to their previous homes, and compensation for losses. But Israel has never honored this obligation.

Again, Jews for Justice in the Middle East sums it up: "There are two primary issues at the core of this continuing conflict. First, there is the inevitably destabilizing effect of trying to maintain an ethnically preferential state, particularly when it is largely of foreign origin. The original population of what is now Israel was 96% Muslim and Christian, yet these refugees are prohibited from returning to their homes in the self-described Jewish state (and those within Israel are subjected to systematic discrimination).

Second, Israel's continued military occupation and confiscation of privately owned land in the West Bank, and control over Gaza are extremely oppressive, with Palestinians having minimal control over their lives."[9]

Pappe describes Israelis policy as taking over "as much of Palestine as possible with as few Palestinians as possible."[10] That will strike any Irish person as being remarkably like what the

British Government and the Unionist/Protestants did when Ireland was partitioned by the 1920 Government of Ireland Act. They not only partitioned Ireland, but excluded counties Donegal, Cavan and Monaghan from "Northern Ireland" because there were too many Catholics there. So they "took over as much of the Province of Ulster as possible with as few Catholics as possible."

That is why in the 1970s and 1980s, Catholics often referred to themselves as "the Palestinians of Western Europe" – because everyone abandoned them.

I can now hear the Jews say: " Yeah, tell us about abandonment! We were abandoned for centuries by the entire world. And although we were not a threat to Germany, we did not have any Army, the monster Hitler slaughtered us by the millions, and the world was silent – Britain, America – nobody stood up for us."

When we speak of evocative words, there is no word more powerful and overwhelming than Holocaust.

I fully understand why Jews worldwide adapted the motto, "Never Again." And I am very aware of the violence that Israel has suffered since the foundation of the State. That must be condemned unequivocally – as do the fanatical threats to exterminate Israel.

Israeli journalist and author Boas Evron adds the caveat here: "The true guarantee against ideologically-based extermination is not military power and sovereignty but the eradication of ideologies which remove any human group from the family of humanity."[11]

The Catholic and feminist theologian Rosemary Reuther has a cautionary observation in this regard: "There is a tortured reasoning … which seems to suggest that Christians should not speak out in criticism of Israel until there are a substantial number of Israelis and Western Jews doing so. This is an odd moral principle. Is it not mostly a strategy for saving oneself from attack as an "anti-Semite"? ... Would one really wait to criticize American or White South African racism until there was a majority of white Americans or white South Africans doing so?[12]

When I finally forced myself to visit the Holocaust Museum here in Washington, I wept like a baby at the absolute horror of it all. My grief was compounded by guilt because I felt deeply ashamed of the past, long history of Catholic anti-Semitism: how the Catholic Church helped to spread anti-Semitism all over the world, spread it even by some of its great saints and preachers. When The Reformation came along, Protestantism was just as bad. Martin Luther was a virulent anti-Semite.

I am further conflicted over this entire issue because the Jewish Members of Congress are totally supportive of my work for justice in Northern Ireland. The great Congressman Ben Gilman made it possible for me to get Congress to pass the Mac Bride Principles into U.S. law in 1998. I would be deeply distressed if Congressman Gilman felt I have been ungrateful or unfair. I have huge respect for Jewish-Americans, and feel a deep bond with them.

Still, one surely must believe that justice for the Palestinians is possible without being unfair to the Jews, and vice versa. Surely it ought to be possible for people of good will to address the issue without being accused of being anti-Semitic or anti-Palestinian. The old Irish joke about The Troubles comes to mind: A man was challenged in Belfast. He held up his hands, explaining he was a Jew. "But are you a Catholic Jew or a Protestant Jew?" was the next demand.

I hope I am not commanded to answer if I'm a Jewish Catholic or a Muslim Catholic!

My Visit to The Holy Land

I travelled to The Holy Land on October 22. I had planned to visit The West Bank for two weeks and then go to Gaza for one week. But, unfortunately, I had to cancel Gaza because of travel illness. This was an awful disappointment to me. I was part of a Delegation from Interfaith Peace-Builders (IFPB), based in Washington, D.C., and which describes itself in these words:

"Interfaith Peace-Builders fosters a network of informed and active individuals who understand the Israeli-Palestinian conflict and the United States' political, military, and economic role in it. To build and nurture such a network, we lead delegations of people from diverse backgrounds to Israel/Palestine. These delegations emphasize listening to and learning from those immersed in the reality of the conflict, and advancing the work of Israelis and Palestinians committed to nonviolent struggle and peace with justice."[13]

I was honored, humbled and inspired to be included in this Delegation, composed of 32 remarkable men and women, young and old. The Delegation was led by four extraordinary leaders: Mike Daly, from Boston, IFPB Program Coordinator; Andy Clarno, assistant professor of Sociology and African American Studies, at the University of Illinois; Hanan Idilbi, a young Palestinian-American woman; and Cindy Corrie, mother of Rachel, a 23-year-old American peace activist who was crushed to death by an Israeli bulldozer on 16 March 2003 in Gaza.

The IFPB is a really special organization that does courageous and heroic work.

Simultaneously, there was a large African Heritage Delegation with whom we shared the same hotel. Needless to say, these African-Americans brought to the issue that extra-special perspective, gained from their own Black Freedom Struggle.

One of the most notable members of the African American Heritage Delegation, Aaron Dixon, strode up to me and said: "I have always been in solidarity with the Irish struggle for freedom."

Aaron is a former Black Panther who has just published his Memoirs, *My People are Rising*.[14] This is a book people in Ireland will love. Aaron is an impressive man with the quiet stillness of one who has been through a long struggle.

Later on he issued this statement: "I was pleased to meet Fr. Mc Manus in Palestine pursuing our mutual struggle for justice. I greatly appreciate that Fr. Mc Manus was the first white Catholic priest arrested at the South African Embassy back in 1984, protesting Apartheid. The Black, the Palestinian and the Irish cause are one – basic justice and equality."

Our Delegation was based in Jerusalem. We visited The Holy Sites in the city – Jewish, Christian and Muslim. We travelled to the following areas: Bethlehem, Deheisheh, Sderot, Nazareth, Jenin, Akka, Tel Aviv, Hebron, Ramallah, Nabi Saleh and At Tuwani.

We Did Not Come from Rocks

"We did not come from rocks," my most gracious host said with great intensity in his home in the beautiful city of Akka, situated on the Haifa Bay in western Galilee. His response came when I double-checked his family having legal documents proving they owned land stolen from him by the government. This was a constant and profound grievance I heard over and over again.

"They drove us out, killed our families, destroyed our villages, grabbed our land, never compensated us and will not allow us to return."

It's not the Irish speaking about England's colonialism but the Palestinians speaking about the official and illegal policy of the State of Israel.

And it is not just a case of their being driven out of the country: there is another technique of expulsion that the Irish will immediately recognize, if not by the name but by practice: "Internal Displaced Person (IDP): person who left his/her place of origin but did not cross an international border." (Definition by BADIL Resource Center for Palestinian Residency & Refugee Rights, Bethlehem.)

Think of the brutal Dictator Oliver Cromwell – the self-styled Puritan Moses – (1599-1658), and his policy: "To Hell or to Connaught." The Irish had to face death or flee to the poorest, western province of Ireland – while Cromwell simultaneously perpetrated a massive transfer of land from Irish hands to English hands ... And, of course, he did it because God told him to.

Poor God, the things He's blamed for.

Daher Nassar is a gracious, determined man who has struggled to stop his olive farm from being grabbed. The farm called "Tent of Nations" is a couple of miles from Bethlehem. His family has legally owned it since 1916. Every dirty trick in the book is used against him, legal, official and paramilitary. They have even tried to bribe him to sell his land. This noble son of Palestine replies: "The land is like my mother. And I won't sell my mother."

The illegal Settlements increasingly encircle Daher (the State of Israel is forbidden by international law from building settlements in occupied territory). The United Nations, the United States, etc., all condemn the Settlements, but the State of Israel keeps building them, often thousands of homes.

Daher told our Delegation that one day young armed thugs approached him demanding to know why he was "on their land." Daher told them that time after time he had won in court proving it was his land. "I have the papers," he defiantly told them. "But we have the papers from God," they shouted.

That is the thuggery that many fundamentalist American Protestants are supporting in the name of God. And a most remarkable aspect of all of this is that a number of the Zionists involved in the land grabbing are American atheists – Jews who do not believe in God. So they are saying: "We don't believe in God, but He gave us the land – and therefore, we can steal it from the Palestinians, Muslim or Christian."

Again, shades of Northern Ireland.

When the British Government partitioned Ireland in 1920, the pro-British Unionists/Loyalists set up the new artificial entity to be, in effect, a "Protestant State for a Protestant people."[15] Nothing too surprising in that since England itself is a sectarian State, in which there is no separation of Church and State. Obviously, when a Protestant State is set up, Catholics better look out.

What happens when a self-defined Jewish State is set up on the land of Palestine? Well, inevitably, Palestinians – Muslims and Christians – better look out because by definition they are going to be treated as different, unequal and, de facto as inferior.

Consider these basic facts, presented by the aforementioned BADIL:

1948

- More than 500 Palestinian villages were depopulated and later destroyed to prevent the return of the refugees.
- In the districts of Jaffa, Ramla and Bir Saba not one Palestinian village was left standing.
- Approximately 750,000 Palestinian refugees were displaced beyond the borders of the new state to West Bank, Gaza Strip, Jordan, Lebanon, Syria, Iraq and beyond.

PALESTINIAN LOSS OF LAND 1946 TO 2010

BADIL Resource
Center for Palestinian
Residency & Refugee
Rights.

Email: info@badil.org

Web: www.badil.org

1948-1967

• In 1948, 85% of Palestinians living in what is now the state of Israel became refugees.

• 130,000 Palestinians remained in the areas of Palestine that became the state of Israel. Around 40,000 of these were internally displaced. Israel refused to allow these IDPs [Internal Displaced Person] to return to their homes and villages.

Ongoing Displacement 1948-1967

Population transfer and internal displacement

1967

• Over 400,000 Palestinians, approximately 35% of the Palestinian population of the West Bank, eastern Jerusalem, and Gaza Strip, were forcibly expelled.

Please remember we are not talking about Cromwell in the 1600s. This is the reality of modern day Israel. And yet – as was constantly pointed out to the Delegation by worn down but resilient Palestinians – it does not seem to matter whether there is a U.S. Republican President or a Democratic President – the Palestinians are still treated as inferior in their own land. Just as it was a wrong for America to have "a hands off policy" on the North of Ireland because it was under England's rule, so, too, is it wrong for America to have the same policy towards the oppression of Palestinians. I believe that in time America will be deeply embarrassed by the role it has played.

"Before the Zionists came, Palestinian Jews, Palestinian Christians and Palestinian Muslims lived in peace – before the Zionists turned a religion into a State."

Was the speaker a Palestinian militant – a revolutionary jihadist? Hardly.

It was the Venerable Samuel Barhoum, Archdeacon of the Episcopal Diocese of Jerusalem, speaking to our Delegation. He and his Palestinian wife spoke movingly about discrimination and the denial of rights, not just of Muslims but Christians as well. Then in a lovely display of ecumenism, the local Catholic priest Fr. Elias

M. Odeh of the Latin Parish joined the discussion. Speaking truth to power was all too real to him and his family. His brother Alex (April 4, 1944 – October 11, 1985) was killed in a bombing as he opened the door of his office in Santa Ana, California. Alex was Westcoast regional director of the American-Arab Anti-Discrimination Committee (ADC), founded by former U.S. Senator Jim Aboureszk (D-SD) whom I have the honor of knowing. Indeed, I was arrested with him at the South African Embassy protesting Apartheid.

Despite a reward of one million dollars for information leading to arrest and conviction, no arrests have been made for Alex's assassination. The media has, however, reported that the FBI identified members of the Jewish Defense League (JDL) as suspects. None have ever been charged, but some have fled to Israel.

I was very touched when Fr. Elias spoke so lovingly about Our Lady of Palestine – to this mostly Protestant Delegation! And, there and then, I decided that from now on I would pray to The Blessed Mother under that title. With all due respect to the titles of "Our Lady of Fatima" and "Our Lady of Knock" that title has a wonderful resonance, historicity and meaningfulness to it."

Fr. Elias appealed to our Delegation to inform Americans that Palestinian Christians are also oppressed. Later we had a timely example of this. We had a meeting with Reverend Mitri Raheb, the Palestinian Pastor of the The Evangelical Lutheran Christmas Church in Bethlehem. We were shocked when he told us that he had to cancel a lecture in Jerusalem the day before because the Israeli Government would not give him a permit to travel because he speaks out against occupation. That is the type of religious persecution fundamentalist American Protestants are supporting! Can you imagine the furor there would be if an American Protestant Pastor were not allowed to travel in the United States to give a lecture?

These dedicated Christian pastors reflect the spirit of the famous 2009 document issued by all the Christian Churches in Palestine, "Kairos Palestine – a moment of truth":

"We, a group of Christian Palestinians, after prayer, reflection and an exchange of opinion, cry out from within the suffering in our country, under the Israeli occupation, with a cry of hope in the absence of all hope, a cry full of prayer and faith in a God ever vigilant, in God's divine providence for all the inhabitants of this land. Inspired by the mystery of God's love for all, the mystery of God's divine presence in the history of all peoples and, in a particular way, in the history of our country, we proclaim our word based on our Christian faith and our sense of Palestinian belonging – a word of faith, hope and love....

... the reality is one of Israeli occupation of Palestinian territories, deprivation of our freedom and all that results from this situation:

The separation wall erected on Palestinian territory, a large part of which has been confiscated for this purpose, has turned our towns and villages into prisons, separating them from one another, making them dispersed and divided cantons. Gaza, especially after the cruel war Israel launched against it during December 2008 and January 2009, continues to live in inhuman conditions, under permanent blockade and cut off from the other Palestinian territories.

Israeli settlements ravage our land in the name of God and in the name of force, controlling our natural resources, including water and agricultural land, thus depriving hundreds of thousands of Palestinians, and constituting an obstacle to any political solution.[16]"

It is important to be aware of the response that fine statement received from Kairos USA, in their own noteworthy and profoundly Christian confession of solidarity:

"We have forgotten the difference between a theology that supports the policies and institutional structures of oppression and a theology that, in response to history and human affairs, stands boldly with the widow, the orphan, the poor and the dispossessed. In our churches, political activities and personal interactions we have adopted the use of words that uphold rather than challenge injustice. We have accepted a notion of justice that is defined by the powerful and is equated with "security" and "law and order." Declaring ourselves committed to nonviolence, we have condemned the resistance of the oppressed while legitimizing the use of overwhelming force by the powerful. We have called for reconciliation in the form of dialoguqe and mutual understanding while overseeing the continuation and advancement of the oppressive conditions that breed continued conflict and violence."[17]

Welcome to Muslim West Belfast

The comparisons between British oppression of Catholics in Northern Ireland and mistreatment of Palestinians continue to be inescapable. When we got off the bus in the Deheisheh refugee camp near Bethlehem, the co-leader of our intrepid band, Mike Daly, called out to me, "Come over here, Sean. You will be interested to see this." And there before my very eyes was the sign painted on a wall: "YOU ARE NOW ENTERING FREE DEHEISHEH" – in clear imitation of the famous sign: "YOU ARE NOW ENTERING FREE DERRY."

Walking through this camp (now no longer composed of tents but replaced with terrible cement tenements I used to see in Glasgow) was like going through West Belfast at the height of The Troubles in the 70s and 80s with murals on the walls commemorating resistance fighters and defiant slogans. I turned to Mike and said, "Welcome to Muslim West Belfast."

We visited the Palestinian Youth Action Center for Community Development for a talk by the Director, Naji Odah. He used the same word as I use in the title of this book, "struggle": "We keep struggling. Nobody can give you freedom; you have to earn it." His son gave us a conducted tour through the alleys and poor streets of the camp. And later his wife Suheir gave an impassioned, compelling talk in their home. Again, I was reminded so much of the Irish struggle. Here was a family totally committed to the struggle for justice and freedom – fearless, impressive and authentic. Like in Ireland, oppression has only made this family stronger and more invincible.

Some of my colleagues in the Irish National Caucus kept telling me, "Sean, don't go forgetting the Irish cause." That will never happen. Anyway, they needn't have worried as it is impossible to forget the Irish cause while studying oppression in Palestine.

To Kibbutz or Not Kibbutz

I had often wondered about the idea of the Kibbutz – a sort of utopian, collective, community, initially inspired by a mixture of Marxism and Zionism, and started in Palestine in the early 1900s. Kibbutzim in the early days were largely based on agriculture but naturally that has changed over the years. Also, over the years, some have become privatized. In the beginning Kibbutzim was secular, some being called "monasteries without God." In 1946, the first religious kibbutz was formed.

We went to two Kibbutzim. In one, an American-born Jewish woman explained the movement. She described herself as liberal, pro-Palestinian rights. And even though seventy rockets had been fired into her area from nearby Gaza, she was most forgiving. It was very touching when she let her fear slip out, and admitted she feared the destruction of the Jews.

I was sorry I missed one meeting with a New Jersey-born Spokesperson for the Settlements (the illegal occupation of land – always built on the high ground, heavily armed and into which the Palestinians cannot enter).

To gain a different perspective, one day I withdrew from the Delegation and spent hours praying at the Wailing Wall and in the Armenian Catholic Patriarchate in Adoration of The Blessed Sacrament … Again, justice-connections – the Armenian Genocide during World War I when the Ottoman Government exterminated about a million and a half Armenians.

I was grateful for all the opportunity I had to pray during the trip – with Jews, Catholics and Muslims.

Destroyed Churches

One area that moved me to the core – apart from all the obvious Catholic sites – was the destroyed village of Bassa, destroyed in 1948. There we saw the remains of a Greek Orthodox Church and a Catholic Church, which the Israeli government will not allow to be restored. A local Palestinian Catholic, Khalil Asi, serves as the voluntary caretaker. Khalil, at his own expense, put on a door to the Greek Orthodox Church, which is in better condition than the Catholic church.

I was deeply touched to see that inside the Greek Orthodox Church, Khalil had erected a sketching of Our Blessed Lady (the Mother of Jesus). I instinctively dropped to my knees in prayer. I felt that surely this good man was doing his bit to heal the most deplorable split of all – that between the Catholic Church and the Greek Orthodox Church – dating back to 1054.

Khalil with deep sadness recounted how the local Kibbutzim had used both Churches to house their animals. ... Again, for me, a reminder of Oliver Cromwell who stabled his troopers' horses in St. Patrick's Cathedral, Dublin, in 1649.

I went to Sunday Mass in the Church of the Annunciation, and that was truly a profound experience. I must confess I was reduced to tears by the profundity of the moment. The Holy Land does have that effect. Time and time again I got choked up and tried to hide it from the others in the Delegation.

A few days earlier, I was trying to visit the same church, but got caught at the wrong end of the building. In the town square, a group of Muslim men were praying. I went over to a bench where three young guys were sitting, waiting their turn to pray on the mat. I asked them if it would be alright to join them. They graciously said yes. After the prayers, the leader of the group – a meticulously well dressed 70-year-old man – came to me and said: "You are welcome," in that special way that I love to hear. When I told him I was a Catholic priest, he embraced me, then when I told him I was from Washington, he said: "Tell the Americans we are not terrorists. We are good people who want to be treated with equality and respect in our own country."

On my way back to the bus, I thought it was so immensely sad that a good, decent man like that had to appeal for understanding. What an awful sin the West has committed against the Palestinians. And this realization pounded over me like a mighty Atlantic wave: how religion has been used to tear God's people – all His people – asunder. What evil we have wrought in His Holy Name!

I got on the bus, pretended I was sleeping and prayed all the way back to the hotel that The Holy One of Israel (not to be confused with the modern State of Israel) would forgive me my own sins, and all the sins we commit against Him and our brothers and sisters.

Here might be an appropriate place to quote a modern prophetic Jewish voice. Mark Braverman, a Jewish American has written – more like poured out – a wrenching book on the mistakes of Zionism and the State of Israel, *Fatal Embrace*: "I would argue that a just political settlement cannot be achieved as long as the Jews of Israel and their supporters in North America are operating from the position of being the light to the nations, God's special treasure, and a nation of priests. The natural outcome of such an attitude is that Jews will feel they deserve the land more than the Palestinians. They already have taken an unfair portion. The Palestinians already have compromised repeatedly, at each pass giving up more territory, more control, and more resources. The facts on the ground today represent a stupendous set of losses for the Palestinians: forested hilltops and fertile valleys have been replaced with cities of stone (for Jews only). Restricted roads now crisscross Palestinian byways. Checkpoints are destroying their commerce, hampering their opportunities for education and disrupting their personal lives. The separation wall [the 430-mile long barrier that separates Israel and the West Bank] has turned Palestine into a giant prison ... The root cause is the Zionist project to establish Jewish sovereignty over Palestine. This is the fundamental fact that created the settlers, that built the wall, and that drives the conflict. This is the fact that underlies the whole project that has put 100 years of Jewish settlement at risk, created 4.5 million regional refugees, and subjugates 4 million Palestinians today."[18]

The eminent Hebrew Scripture (Old Testament) scholar Mark Brueggemann says: "Mark Braverman has written a courageous, evocative book that merits close attention and continued pondering."[19]

Holy Land Principles

While I had to give essential background on The Holy Land, I do not want to confuse the issue or misdirect the reader

Because here's the real point about the Principles: The MacBride Principles never asked the huge ethnically diverse United States to take a position on any solution in Ireland – a United Ireland, England out off Ireland, an Independent Northern Ireland, etc., etc. Indeed, that issue was only introduced when some wanted to change the subject, obfuscate the issue and escape responsibility. The Principles are not about foreign policy, not about telling the British Government or any party in Northern Ireland what to do. The Principles ARE ONLY about making sure U.S. investment dollars do not subsidize discrimination in Northern Ireland.

In the very same way, the Holy Land Principles are not about foreign policy – but about American principles (fairness and nondiscrimination in employment) following American investment in the Holy Land. The Principles are about American investors in the 573 American companies doing business in The Holy Land.

Fairness and nondiscrimination in employment is the issue and the only issue for the Principles. Anything else simply destroys the inherent power of the Principles. I have been amazed over the years why some folk, even the bright and well-intentioned, failed to "get it."

"But what about a United Ireland, what about kicking England out off Ireland, what about the IRA, what about the Unionist/Protestant paramilitaries, what about Dublin neglecting The North, what about ... ?" They would go on and on. "Nothing to do with The Principles," I would patiently (and sometimes not too patiently) answer.

Indeed, ironically, my own lack of expertise in the Middle East will help to keep me "on message." I do not need – nor want – to get into all the intricacies of a very complicated political issue. When I need it, I can turn to a lot of knowledgeable people. My experience in initiating, launching and pursuing the Mac Bride Principles is what counts here.

Holy Land Principles Launched

I launched Holy Land Principles on International Human Rights Day, December 10, 2012, just as I did the Mac Bride Principles on

November 5, 1984. And I did it with the same abiding commitment to justice and nonviolence – and the same deep conviction that these Principles can do untold good for equality and fairness in The Holy Land. Also, we have established Holy Land Principles, Inc. – a nonprofit organization to promote the Principles.

Irrespective of how Americans view the problem there, surely all Americans of goodwill can agree that American investment dollars should not subsidize discrimination in The Holy Land – that American principles should follow American investment … Surely no American company, nor anyone else, can argue that Catholics in Northern Ireland deserve these Principles but Palestinians do not. (See list of Holy Land Principles on next two pages.)

The basic strategy of the campaign is to persuade all the 573 U.S. companies in The Holy Land to sign the Principles. They sign by agreeing in writing "to make all lawful efforts to implement the Fair Employment Practices embodied in the Holy Land Principles in their operations in The Holy Land" – the very same language used by companies signing the Mac Bride Principles.

1. The campaign for the Holy Land Principles will be conducted through Shareholder's Resolution and through public education.

2. This book with a personalized letter will be sent to the CEOs of all 573 companies – plus their Investor Relations Contact – doing business in The Holy Land (Israel/Palestine, The West Bank, The Gaza Strip and East Jerusalem). The letter urges them to sign the Principles.

3. This book with a personalized letter will be sent to all Members of Congress, House and Senate, urging support for the Principles. The book will also be sent to all key media personnel.

4. An extensive Direct Mail campaign will be conducted to prospective supporters – Americans of good-faith, especially Irish-Americans, Arab-Americans and the faith and social-justice communities.

We are confident that fair-minded Americans will rally to the Holy Land Principles, just as they did to the Mac Bride Principles.

God bless America and God save Ireland and The Holy Land.

Holy Land Principles
American principles following American investment

A Corporate Code of Conduct for
U.S. Companies in The Holy Land

American companies have a responsibility to maximize the profits of their shareholders. And shareholders have the right and responsibility to insist that their profits are earned through ethical corporate practices – that they avoid discrimination based on racial, ethnic or religious identity.

Moreover, ethical investment not only benefits society but also creates stronger and more sustainable profits for their shareholders.

In the tradition of the Sullivan Principles (South Africa) and the MacBride Principles (Northern Ireland), the Holy Land Principles seek to ensure that American dollars do not support discrimination, human rights abuses, or violations of international law in The Holy Land (Israel/Palestine, The West Bank, The Gaza Strip and East Jerusalem). The Principles do not call for disinvestment, divestment or reverse discrimination.

Responsible corporate conduct is especially urgent today because of the deprivations and sufferings caused by the conflict.

By endorsing the Holy Land Principles, corporations will enhance America's security as people in the Middle East see that American companies support equality and fairness for all.

The Principles call on American companies conducting business in the Holy Land to:

1. Adhere to equal and fair employment practices in hiring, compensation, training, professional education, advancement and governance without discrimination based on racial, ethnic or religious identity.

2. Identify underrepresented employee groups and initiate active recruitment efforts to increase the number of underrepresented employees to a level proportional to their representation in society.

3. Make every reasonable effort to ensure that all employees have the ability to easily, openly and equally travel to and access corporate facilities.

4. Maintain a work environment that is respectful of all racial, ethnic and religious groups.

5. Work with governmental and community authorities, and support local initiatives to eliminate disparities among racial, ethnic and religious groups in government spending on education, training, access to health care and housing.

6. Not make military service a precondition or qualification for employment for any position, other than those positions that specifically require such experience, for the fulfillment of an employee's particular responsibilities.

7. Not accept subsidies, tax incentives or other benefits that lead to the direct advantage of one racial, ethnic or religious group over another.

8. Appoint staff to monitor, oversee, set timetables, and publicly report on their progress in implementing the Holy Land Principles.

APPENDIX A
How many Palestinian refugees are there?
The Institute for Middle East Understanding (IMEU)
SEP 28, 2011

Reliable figures on the Palestinian refugee and displaced population are hard to find, as there is no centralized agency or institution charged with maintaining this information, and there is no uniform definition of a Palestinian refugee.

The United Nations Relief and Works Agency (UNRWA) administers the only registration system for Palestinian refugees, but it only includes those displaced in 1948 (and their descendants) who are in need of assistance and located in UNRWA areas of operation – West Bank, Gaza Strip, Jordan, Lebanon, and Syria. BADIL, a Palestinian non-governmental organization, estimated that there were more than 7.2 million Palestinian refugees and displaced persons at the end of 2005. (report)

This includes Palestinian refugees displaced in 1948 and registered for assistance with the UNRWA (4.3 million); Palestinian refugees displaced in 1948 but not registered for assistance (1.7 million); Palestinian refugees displaced for the first time in 1967 (834,000); 1948 internally displaced Palestinians (355,000); and, 1967 internally displaced Palestinians (57,000).

APPENDIX B
What are the Occupied Territories?
The Institute for Middle East Understanding (IMEU)
SEP 28, 2011

The Occupied Territories are the West Bank, East Jerusalem, the Gaza Strip, and the Golan Heights. "Occupied Palestinian Territories" or simply "Palestinian territories" is sometimes used to refer to the West Bank, East Jerusalem and the Gaza Strip, excluding the (Syrian) Golan Heights.

On June 5, 1967, Israel launched what it claimed to be a preemptive attack on Egypt, citing Egypt's announced closure of the Straits of Tiran (the opening from the Gulf of Aqaba to the Red Sea) to Israeli shipping, and other provocations. Israeli military and political leaders later admitted that they had not, in fact, genuinely feared attack, and had no doubt about Israel's vast military superiority over its neighbors.

By the time fighting ended six days later, Israel had seized Egypt's Sinai Peninsula, the Gaza Strip (which had been under Egyptian administration since 1948), the West Bank (which had been under Jordanian rule since 1948), and Syria's Golan Heights. (The Sinai Peninsula was returned to Egypt after the 1979 peace treaty between Egypt and Israel.)

"Occupation" is a legal status in international law, not just a description of the forceful means by which Israel has controlled the territories it seized in 1967. Although Israeli diplomats contest the designation of the territories as "occupied," and describe them as merely "administered" by Israel, there is no such status in international law.

All competent legal authorities – including the International Court of Justice, the United Nations Security Council and Israel's own Supreme Court – recognize the Gaza Strip, West Bank, and Golan Heights as occupied territories.

International law imposes obligations and limitations

on the actions of an occupying power, and the Charter of the United Nations bars acquisition of territory by war. Thus Israel has never had any legal rights of sovereignty over any of the lands it took in 1967, and never had any right to settle its own citizens there.

The Gaza Strip continues to be "occupied" notwithstanding Israel's withdrawal of settlers and redeployment of troops outside the Strip in 2005. Effective control is the measure of "occupation" in international law, and Israel clearly continues to control the coast, borders and airspace of the Strip, claims the right to reinvade at will, and provides Gazans their water, electricity, and other vital services.

APPENDIX C
Discrimination Against Palestinian Citizens of Israel
The Institute for Middle East Understanding (IMEU)
SEP 28, 2011

Racism & Discrimination Against
Palestinian Citizens of Israel

Palestinian citizens of Israel are those Palestinians who remained behind in what became the state of Israel following the Nakba (1947-9), or "catastrophe," when approximately 725,000 Palestinians were expelled from their homes and land by Zionist forces in order to make way for a Jewish-majority state.

Between 1948 (when Israel declared independence) and 1966, Palestinians living in Israel were granted no political rights and were subject to Israeli military rule. After 1966, they were granted the right to vote and other civil rights, but to this day they continue to suffer from widespread, systematic and institutionalized discrimination affecting everything from land ownership and employment opportunities to family reunification rights. Today, there are approximately 1.2 million Palestinian citizens of Israel, about 20% of the population.

Institutionalized Discrimination

There are more than 30 laws that discriminate against Palestinian citizens of Israel. directly or indirectly, based solely on their ethnicity, rendering them second or third class citizens in their own homeland.

93% of the land in Israel is owned either by the state or by quasi-governmental agencies, such as the Jewish National Fund, that discriminate against non-Jews. Palestinian citizens of Israel face significant legal obstacles in gaining access to this land for agriculture, residence, or commercial development.

More than seventy Palestinian villages and communities

in Israel, some of which pre-date the establishment of the state, are unrecognized by the government, receive no services, and are not even listed on official maps. Many other towns with a majority Palestinian population lack basic services and receive significantly less government funding than do majority-Jewish towns.

Since Israel's founding in 1948, more than 600 Jewish municipalities have been established, while not a single new Arab town or community has been recognized by the state.

Israeli government resources are disproportionately directed to Jews and not to Arabs, one factor in causing the Palestinians of Israel to suffer the lowest living standards in Israeli society by all socio-economic indicators.

Government funding for Arab schools is far below that of Jewish schools. According to data published in 2004, the government provides three times as much funding to Jewish students than it does to Arab students.

According to the 2009 US State Department International Religious Freedom Report, "Many of the national and municipal policies in Jerusalem were designed to limit or diminish the non-Jewish population of Jerusalem."

In the Spring of 2011, Jerusalem city councilman Yakir Segev stated: "We will not allow residents of the eastern [occupied Palestinian] part of the city to build as much as they need... At the end of the day, however politically incorrect it may be to say, we will also look at the demographic situation in Jerusalem to make sure that in another 20 years we don't wake up in an Arab city."

The Nationality and Entry into Israel Law prevents Palestinians from the occupied territories who are married to Palestinian citizens of Israel from gaining residency or citizenship status. The law forces thousands of Palestinian citizens of Israel to either leave Israel or live apart from their families.

In October 2010, the Knesset approved a bill allowing

smaller Israeli towns to reject residents who do not suit "the community's fundamental outlook", based on sex, religion, and socioeconomic status. Critics slammed the move as an attempt to allow Jewish towns to keep Arabs and other non-Jews out.

The so-called "Nakba Bill" bans state funding for groups that commemorate the tragedy that befell Palestinians during Israel's creation in 1948, when approx. 725,000 Palestinian Arabs were ethnically cleansed to make way for a Jewish majority state.

The British Mandate-era Land (Acquisition for Public Purposes) Ordinance law allows the Finance Minster to confiscate land for "public purposes." The state has used this law extensively, in conjunction with other laws such as the Land Acquisition Law and the Absentees' Property Law, to confiscate Palestinian land in Israel. A new amendment, which was adopted in February 2010, confirms state ownership of land confiscated under this law, even where it has not been used to serve the original confiscation purpose. The amendment was designed to prevent Arab citizens from submitting lawsuits to reclaim confiscated land.

Over the entirety of its 63-year existence, there has been a period of only about one year (1966-1967) that Israel did not rule over large numbers of Palestinians to whom it granted no political rights.

Former Israeli prime ministers Ehud Barak and Ehud Olmert have both warned that a continuation of the occupation will lead to Israel becoming an "apartheid" state. Barak stated: "As long as in this territory west of the Jordan river there is only one political entity called Israel it is going to be either non-Jewish, or non-democratic... If this bloc of millions of Palestinians cannot vote, that will be an apartheid state."

Archbishop Desmond Tutu and Nelson Mandela, heroes of the struggle against apartheid in South Africa, have both compared Israel's treatment of Palestinians to apartheid.

Today, there is a virtual caste system within the territories that Israel controls between the Jordan River and Mediterranean Sea, with Israeli Jews at the top and Muslim and Christian Palestinians in the occupied territories at the bottom. In between are Palestinians with Israeli citizenship and Palestinian residents of occupied East Jerusalem.

APPENDIX D
GAZA
The Institute for Middle East Understanding (IMEU)
SEP 28, 2011

Why is Israel's siege of Gaza illegal under international law?

As an occupying power that exercises effective control over Gaza, Israel has legal obligations to the residents of the occupied territory under the Fourth Geneva Convention, including the general duty to protect civilians under its control, and the specific duty to allow adequate access to food and medical supplies. Israel's siege of Gaza, including its land and sea blockade, violates these duties of protection by denying Gazan Palestinian civilians access to adequate amounts of the most basic food and medical supplies, not to mention a host of other supplies necessary for rebuilding after the destruction wrought by Israel's overwhelming destruction of Gaza's infrastructure in its 2009 attacks. Israel's violation of its duties, extensively documented by international organizations, ultimately amounts to the collective punishment of 1.5 million civilians, in violation of Article 33 of the Fourth Geneva Convention. The International Committee of the Red Cross, a UN fact-finding mission into Israel's attack on the 2010 Gaza flotilla, and a UN panel of five independent Special Rapporteurs have all found the siege to be in violation of international law.

Why does the international community continue to consider Israel an occupying power in Gaza?

Israel's claim that its occupation of Gaza ended with its 2005 withdrawal of troops and settlers from the Strip is an attempt to absolve itself of responsibility for Gazan civilians. Israel's continued control of Gaza's territorial waters, its airspace, the flow of people and goods through its land borders, and its continued ground and air incursions into the territory, verify that it exercises the "effective control" necessary to qualify as a foreign occupying power under the Fourth Geneva Convention. This has been acknowledged by the United Nations, the United States, Amnesty International, Human Rights Watch, and others.

Noam Chomsky: My Visit to Gaza, the World's Largest Open-Air Prison
November 9, 2012

Even a single night in jail is enough to give a taste of what it means to be under the total control of some external force.

And it hardly takes more than a day in Gaza to appreciate what it must be like to try to survive in the world's largest open-air prison, where some 1.5 million people on a roughly 140-square-mile strip of land are subject to random terror and arbitrary punishment, with no purpose other than to humiliate and degrade.

Such cruelty is to ensure that Palestinian hopes for a decent future will be crushed, and that the overwhelming global support for a diplomatic settlement granting basic human rights will be nullified. ...

Punishment of Gazans became still more severe in January 2006, when they committed a major crime: They voted the "wrong way" in the first free election in the Arab world, electing Hamas. ...

A visitor to Gaza can't help feeling disgust at the obscenity of the occupation, compounded with guilt, because it is within our power to bring the suffering to an end and allow the Samidin to enjoy the lives of peace and dignity that they deserve."

Jewish writer Noam Chomsky is emeritus professor of linguistics and philosophy at the Massachusetts Institute of Technology in Cambridge, Mass.

APPENDIX E
Catholic Bishops Demand Israel End Occupation of Palestinian Land
Huffington Post. November 10, 2012

VATICAN CITY — Bishops from the Middle East who were summoned to Rome by the pope demanded Saturday that Israel accept U.N. resolutions calling for an end to its "occupation" of Arab lands.

In a final joint communique, the bishops also told Israel it shouldn't use the Bible to justify "injustices" against the Palestinians.

The bishops issued the statement at the close of their two-week meeting, called by Pope Benedict XVI to discuss the plight of Christians in the Middle East amid a major exodus of the faithful from the birthplace of Christianity.

The Catholic Church has long been a minority in the largely Muslim region but its presence is shrinking further as a result of war, conflict, discrimination and economic problems.

During the meeting, several bishops blamed the Israeli-Palestinian conflict for spurring the flight – a position echoed in their final paper. While the bishops condemned terrorism and anti-Semitism, they laid much of the blame for the conflict squarely on Israel.

They listed the "occupation" of Palestinian lands, Israel's separation barrier with the West Bank, its military checkpoints, political prisoners, demolition of homes and disturbance of Palestinians' socio-economic lives as factors that have made life increasingly difficult for Palestinians.

They said they had "reflected" on the suffering and insecurity in which Israelis live and on the status of Jerusalem, a city holy to Christians, Jews and Muslims.

"We are anxious about the unilateral initiatives that threaten its composition and risk to change its demographic balance," they said.

They called on the international community to apply U.N. Security Council resolutions adopted in 1967, which called on Israel to withdraw from Arab land conquered in the Six-Day War that year.

"The Palestinian people will thus have an independent and sovereign homeland where they can live with dignity and security," they said, while Israel will be able to enjoy peace and security.

APPENDIX F
The Inequality Report:
The Palestinian Arab Minority in Israel. March 2011
(EXTRACT)
ADALAH – THE LEGAL CENTER FOR ARAB
MINORITY RIGHTS IN ISRAEL
94 Yaffa Street, PO Box 8921, Haifa 31090, Israel
Tel: +972 4 950 1610 – Fax: +972 4 950 3140
Email: adalah@adalah.org. Website: www.adalah.org

Introduction

Inequality in Israel takes many forms. Some of the major fault-lines that divide Israeli society, creating relatively privileged and deprived groups, are (Ashkenazim) versus (Mizrahim); men versus women; Israel-born Jews (Sabar) versus new immigrants (Olim); Orthodox versus secular Jews; rural versus urban dwellers; rich versus poor; left-wing versus right-wing supporters; and gay versus straight people. This report focuses on inequalities between Jewish citizens of Israel – the majority – and Palestinian Arab citizens of Israel, a national, non-immigrant minority living in its historical homeland.[1]

Today, Palestinian citizens of the state comprise 20% of the total population, numbering almost 1.2 million people.[2] They remained in their homeland following the establishment of the State of Israel in 1948, becoming an involuntary minority. A part of the Palestinian people who currently live in the West Bank, the Gaza Strip and the Diaspora, they belong to three religious communities: Muslim (82%), Christian (9.5%) and Druze (8.5%).[3] Their status under international human rights instruments to which Israel is a State party is that of a national, ethnic, linguistic and religious minority.

However, despite this status, the Palestinian minority is not declared as a national minority in the Basic Laws of Israel. In 1948, Israel was established as a Jewish state. The definition of Israel as "the Jewish State" or "the State of the Jewish People" makes inequality a practical, political and ideological reality for Palestinian citizens of Israel, who are marginalized and discriminated against by the state on the basis of their national belonging and religious affiliation as non-Jews. They are frequently and increasingly viewed as a "fifth column" as a result of their Palestinian identity and national, religious, ethnic and cultural ties to their fellow Palestinians in the Occupied Palestinian Territory (OPT) and surrounding Arab and Muslim states, a number of which are considered "enemy states" by Israel.[4] Furthermore, this perception is not restricted to the state authorities: according to the Israel Democracy Institute, in 2010 53% of the Jewish public maintained that the state was entitled to encourage Arabs to emigrate from Israel.[5]

Numerous groups of Palestinian citizens of Israel face "compound discrimination" or multiple forms of discrimination on the basis of both their national belonging and their membership in one or more distinct subgroups. For instance, Arab women in Israel face discrimination as members of the Arab minority and as women, and Arab Bedouin face an additional layer of institutional and social discrimination. Some individuals are subjected to multiple forms of discrimination, for instance disabled female Arab Bedouin children living in the unrecognized villages in the Naqab (Negev), referred to by the state as "illegally constructed villages" or "illegal settlements". With regard to certain marginalized groups, Israel has some of the world's most forward-thinking and progressive laws and policies. Israel's Knesset, for example, has legislated strong anti-discrimination legislation and legal protections for women and disabled persons.[6] However, the same has not been done for the Palestinian minority in Israel. As a result, Palestinians who are also members of other marginalized groups do not receive the full benefit of such protections. Moreover, according to a recent poll, just 51% of Jewish citizens of

Israel support full equality in rights between Jewish and Arab citizens of Israel.[7] The same attitude prevails among Jewish youth, with 49.5% of Jewish 15- to 18-year-olds responding negatively, in a poll carried out in 2010, to the question of whether Arab citizens should be granted rights equal to those of Jews.[8]

This report details some of the main legal, political and policy structures that institutionalize discrimination against the Palestinian minority in Israel, and entrench inequalities between Palestinian and Jewish citizens. It provides indicators of inequalities, including official state data, and explains how specific laws and policies work to exclude the Palestinian minority from state resources and services, as well as the structures of power. It further demonstrates how the State of Israel, as an ethnocracy or "ethnic nation-state", is systematically failing to adopt effective measures to redress the gaps that exist between the Palestinian minority and the Jewish majority and, moreover, how, by privileging Jewish citizens in many fields, the state actively preserves and even widens these gaps. Finally, the report reflects on the impact of inequality on the Palestinian minority in Israel and its ramifications for the state as a whole.

This report is part of a project on inequality. In addition to the report, Adalah has produced three videos on the subject of inequality in Israel. The first of these videos, Targeted Citizen, surveys discrimination against Palestinian citizens of Israel.[9] The second and third videos focus on case studies of discrimination in land and planning rights and in employment rights, and considers the effect of these inequalities on Israeli society as a whole.

The report is organized into chapters and includes a section on "Main Findings". The following subjects relating to inequalities between Palestinian and Jewish citizens of Israel are surveyed:

• The legal framework of inequality

- Citizenship rights
- Income/poverty
- Redistribution of resources and social welfare
- Employment

Main Findings

- Economic assets: land
- Educational access/attainment
- The Arabic language
- Health
- Political participation

The legal framework of inequality

- Inequalities between Arab and Jewish citizens of Israel span all fields of public life and have persisted over time. Direct and indirect discrimination against Palestinian citizens of Israel is ingrained in the legal system and in governmental practice.

- The right to equality and freedom from discrimination is not explicitly enshrined in Israeli law as a constitutional right, nor is it protected by statute. While Supreme Court justices have interpreted *The Basic Law: Human Dignity and Liberty* as comprising the principle of equality, this fundamental right is currently protected by judicial interpretation alone.

- The definition of the State of Israel as a Jewish state makes inequality and discrimination against Palestinian citizens of Israel a reality and a political project. The pairing of "Jewish" and "democratic" both codifies discrimination against non-Jewish citizens and impedes the realization of full equality.

- Numerous groups of Palestinian citizens of Israel face "compound discrimination" or multiple forms of discrimination on the basis of both their national belonging as Arabs/Palestinians and their membership in one or more other distinct subgroups, such as women, the disabled and the elderly.

• More than 30 main laws discriminate, directly or indirectly, against Palestinian citizens of Israel, and the current government coalition has proposed a flood of new racist and discriminatory bills which are at various stages in the legislative process.

Citizenship rights

• Palestinian citizens of Israel are afforded differential and unequal treatment under Israeli law in the field of citizenship rights. The most important immigration and nationality laws – including the Law of Return (1950) and the Citizenship Law (1952) – privilege Jews and Jewish immigration.

• If the spouse of a Palestinian citizen of Israel is a Palestinian resident of the OPT, it has been virtually impossible for him or her to gain residency or citizenship status in Israel since May 2002. This ban on family unification is totally disproportionate to the alleged security reasons cited by Israel to justify it; rather, it is motivated by the state's desire to maintain a Jewish demographic majority.

• A new law makes it possible to strip Israeli citizenship for various reasons related to alleged "disloyalty" to the state or "breach of trust", indirectly targeting the citizenship rights of Palestinian citizens. Several attempts to pass additional laws that grant the authority to revoke citizenship and impose further loyalty oaths are currently pending in the Knesset.

Income/poverty

• Arab families are greatly over-represented among Israel's poor: over half of Arab families in Israel are classified as poor, compared to an average poverty rate of one-fifth among all families in Israel. Arab towns and villages are heavily over-represented in the lowest socio-economic rankings, and the unrecognized Arab Bedouin villages in the Naqab are the poorest communities in the state.

• Gaps in income and poverty rates are directly related to institutional discrimination against Arab citizens in Israel.

Redistribution of resources and social welfare

• Although the right to equality demands that states take positive steps to bridge the gaps between the various population groups, the State of Israel actively seeks to promote and direct resources to Jewish citizens as a privileged majority within the "Jewish State". In many policy areas, including the designation of "National Priority Areas" and the use of the military-service criterion to allocate resources, the state actively preserves and perpetuates inequalities between Arab and Jewish citizens of Israel.

• The state has consistently failed to take adequate and effective action to address the phenomenon of absolute and relative poverty among the Arab minority in Israel. Where it has initiated development programs targeting the Arab minority, such as the "Multi-Year Plan", the state has tended to implement them partially, gradually, or not at all.

• Direct state policy measures to reduce poverty disproportionately target Jewish citizens, with the result that poverty rates have fallen far more sharply among Jewish citizens than among their Arab counterparts, and inequalities have consequently persisted.

Employment

• Palestinian citizens of Israel often face discrimination in work opportunities, pay and conditions, both because of the inadequate implementation of equal-opportunity legislation and because of entrenched structural barriers, which particularly affect women, and include poor or non-existent public transportation, a lack of industrial zones, and a shortage of state-run daycare centers. Palestinian citizens are also excluded from the labor force by the use of the military-service criterion as a condition for acceptance for employment, often when there is no connection between the nature of the work and military experience.

- Unemployment rates remain significantly higher among Arab than among Jewish citizens, and the rate of labor-force participation among Palestinian women citizens of Israel, at just about 20%, is among the lowest in the world.
- Palestinian citizens of Israel in general, and women in particular, continue to be sorely underrepresented in the civil service, the largest employer in Israel (in total, Arabs constitute just around 6% of all civil service employees), despite affirmative-action legislation stipulating fair representation for the Arab minority and for women.
- The lack of development and investment in Arab towns and villages inside Israel and the unexploited or under-exploited human resources of the members of the Palestinian minority inhibit the growth of the Israeli economy. The lost potential to Israel's economy has been estimated at around US$8 billion per year by the Organisation for Economic Co-operation and Development (OECD).

Economic assets: land
- In continuation of a pattern that was established with the founding of the state in 1948, Palestinian citizens of Israel continue to be deprived of access and use of the land under long-standing and more recent land laws and policies. Furthermore, new measures – including a new land reform law from 2009 and an amendment to the Land Ordinance from February 2010 – aim at confirming state ownership of land confiscated from Palestinians in perpetuity and blocking Palestinian restitution claims.
- Admissions committees operate in around 700 agricultural and community towns and filter out Arab applicants, on the basis of their "social unsuitability", from future residency in these towns. The operation of admissions committees contributes to the institutionalization of racially-segregated towns and villages throughout the state and perpetuates unequal access to the land.
- The Jewish National Fund (JNF) – a body with quasi-state authority that operates solely for the interests of

the Jewish people and controls 13% of the land in the state – continues to wield decisive influence over land policy in Israel, having been allocated six of a total of 13 members of the newly-established Land Authority Council.

• Arab towns and villages in Israel suffer from severe over crowding, with Arab municipalities exercising jurisdiction over only 2.5% of the total area of the state. Since 1948, the State of Israel has established approximately 600 Jewish municipalities, whereas no new Arab village, town or city has ever been built.

• While the Arab Bedouin population in the Naqab stands at around 170,000 persons, or 14% of the total population in the Naqab, the combined areas of the government-planned and newly-recognized Arab Bedouin towns and villages in the Naqab account for just 0.9% of the land in the district.

• Israel is currently intensifying its efforts to forcibly evacuate the unrecognized villages in the Naqab (referred to as "illegal clusters"), including by demolishing entire villages, as recently witnessed in the repeated demolition of the village of Al-Araqib. In pursuing this policy, the state has rejected the option of affording recognition to these villages, many of which predate the establishment of Israel. Between 75,000 and 90,000 Arab Bedouin live in the unrecognized villages in the Naqab, whom the state characterizes as "trespassers on state land."

Educational access/attainment

• The Ministry of Education retains centralized control over the form and substance of the curriculum for Arab schools, with few Arab educators wieldingdecision-makingauthority.TheStateEducationLawsetseducational objectives for state schools that emphasize Jewish history and culture.

• The current under-investment in Arab schools in Israel threatens to sustain the gaps between the Jewish majority and the Arab minority in the future. Since Arab children account for 25% of all children in Israel, the unequal investment in their education and development can be expected to act as a major brake on the Israeli economy in the coming generation.

• State funding to Arab schools in Israel falls far behind that provided to Jewish schools. According to official state data published in 2004, the state provides three times as much funding to Jewish students as to Arab pupils. This underfunding is reflected in many areas, including relatively large class sizes and poor infrastructure and facilities.

• There are few elementary schools in the unrecognized Arab Bedouin villages in the Naqab, severely overcrowded and poorly-equipped, and not a single high school. Despite a settlement reached by the state with Adalah to establish the first high school in the unrecognized village of Abu Tulul by 1 September 2009, no school has yet been opened.

• Arab students are dramatically underrepresented in Israel's universities and other institutes of higher education. Arab academics constitute only about 1.2% of all tenured and tenure-track positions in Israeli universities, leaving Arab citizens marginalized in the production of knowledge in society.

• The Ministry of Education's policies actually act to entrench the gaps between Arab and Jewish school children, since special programs to assist academically weak or gifted children, such as the "Shahar" academic enrichment programs, are disproportionately awarded to Jewish schools.

The Arabic language

While Arabic is an official language in Israel, there is clear inequality in the opportunities granted to Arabic-speakers as compared to Hebrew-speakers to enjoy and use their language in official and public fora. In practice, the status of Arabic is vastly inferior to that of Hebrew in terms of the resources dedicated to its use, despite Israel's duty under international human rights law to protect the language rights of the Arab national minority in Israel.

Health

• Arab citizens of Israel can expect to live shorter lives than Jewish citizens (about four years less) and face significantly higher mortality rates, particularly after the age of 60. The rate of infant mortality among Palestinian citizens is approximately double that among Jewish citizens, and higher still among the Arab Bedouin population in the Naqab (Negev), where it reaches more than 15 per 1,000 live births.

• While Israeli law provides that equitable, high-quality health services should be provided to all residents of Israel, various barriers – including the lack of clinics and hospitals in Arab towns and villages and limitations on mobility – mean that Palestinian citizens are frequently unable to exercise their right to the highest sustainable standard of health.

• The health situation is most critical in the unrecognized Arab Bedouin villages in the Naqab, where health services are either limited or non- existent. The inadequate provision of health services in the unrecognized villages is a deliberate policy of neglect on the part of the state, which is seeking to evacuate them and relocate their residents, in part by creating intolerable conditions.

Political participation

• Palestinians citizens have unequal access and lower levels of participation than Jewish citizens in all spheres of public life and decision-making, from the judiciary, the legislature, and government to the civil service. As a result, they have limited access to decision-making processes and centers of power, and a diminished ability to redress inequality and discrimination.

• Recent election cycles have witnessed attempts by the Attorney General (2003) and right-wing political parties and MKs to disqualify Arab parties and MKs from the Knesset, aimed at severely limiting the Palestinian political voice in the legislature. In 2003 and 2009, the Israeli Supreme Court overturned decisions of the Central Elections Committee to disqualify Arab political parties and Arab leaders from participating in the national elections.

• The Arab voice has become increasingly delegitimized in the Israeli political and legislative process: according to recent polls around one-third of Jewish citizens agree that Arab citizens should be denied the rights to vote and to be elected to the Knesset, and more than half of Jewish teenagers would deprive Arabs of the right to be elected to the Knesset.

• The criminal justice system is regularly used as a means of delegitimizing political acts and expression by Palestinian citizens of Israel, including their elected political leadership. Several Arab MKs have been indicted or had parliamentary privileges revoked for legitimate political activities and speech that falls within the scope of their work as elected representatives.

• A series of Israeli laws institute a range of restrictions on freedom of movement, freedom of speech, and access to the political system, including ideological limitations on the platforms of political parties and severe restrictions on travel by MKs to Arab states classified as "enemy states". Such laws are used predominantly to curb the political freedoms of Palestinian citizens and their elected representatives and are steadily shrinking the space for political action available to them.

• The police routinely use force and arrest against Arab demonstrators as a deterrent in order to silence voices of protest. Anti-war protestors against the Israeli military operation "Cast Lead" in Gaza – mainly Arab citizens, including many minors – were subjected to serious police violence. They further encountered disproportionate and systematic mass arrests, primarily on the pretext of their mere presence at the scene.

• Until today, ten years after the fact, no police officer,

commander or political leader has been held accountable for the killings of 13 unarmed Palestinian citizens of Israel in October 2000 during demonstrations staged against Israel's brutal policies in the OPT.

• Years of deliberate discrimination, unequal citizenship and a limited voice in the political system have left Palestinian citizens of Israel with a sense of vulnerability, marginalization, insecurity, and distrust of and alienation from the state. Consistently lower voter turn-out rates among Palestinian citizens are one result: in the 2009 elections, the voter turn-out rate was 64.7% overall and 53% among Arab voters.

• By approaching the Arab minority in Israel as a "fifth column" to be controlled and contained, at times employing state violence and draconian legal measures against them, Israel is ultimately undermining the emergence of genuine stability and a culture of respect for democracy, good governance and human rights norms. It also risks relegating issues of human rights to "threats" to security and sovereignty, to be dealt with by the state.

[1] The report will not discuss gaps between the various religious subgroups that exist within the Palestinian minority (Muslim, Christian and Druze) except where the Israeli official data are broken down according to these groups. Where the relevant data are available, however, they do include a gender breakdown.

[2] Israeli Central Bureau of Statistics (CBS), Statistical Abstract of Israel 2009, No. 60, Tables 2.2, 2.8, 2.10. This figure does not include the Arab population of occupied East Jerusalem or the occupied Golan Heights.

[3] Ibid.

[4] Although not specifically defined as "enemy states" in legislation, they are treated as such by a number of laws that restrict relations and contacts between Israel and a number

of countries, all of which are Arab and/or Muslim states. For example, The Citizenship and Entry into Israel Law (2003) prohibits family unification in Israel between Israeli citizens and non-Jewish spouses from Syria, Lebanon, Iraq and Iran. The law imposes a similar ban on spouses from the Gaza Strip, in addition to harsh restrictions on family unification between Israeli citizens and Palestinian West Bank residents. A 2008 amendment to The Citizenship Law (1952) allows the revocation of the citizenship of Israeli citizens who acquire citizenship or permanent residency in Iran, Afghanistan, Lebanon, Libya, Sudan, Syria, Iraq, Pakistan, Yemen or Gaza. The Prevention of Infiltration (Offences and Jurisdiction) Law (1954) makes it a criminal offence to leave Israel and knowingly and illegally enter Lebanon, Syria, Egypt, Jordan, Saudi Arabia, Iraq, Yemen Iran or the OPT, and for nationals of Lebanon, Egypt, Syria, Saudi Arabia, Jordan, Iraq and Yemen, as well as a resident or visitor to these countries or to the OPT, to enter Israel knowingly and illegally.

[5]Israel Democracy Institute, Auditing Israeli Democracy – 2010, (English), v, available at: http://www.idi.org.il/PublicationsCatalog/Documents/Book_7114/madad_2010_eng_abstract. pdf

[6]The Women's Equal Rights Law (1951) and The Equal Rights for People with Disabilities Law (1998).

[7]Israel Democracy Institute, Auditing Israeli Democracy – 2010, (English), viii.

[8]Poll commissioned by the Maagar Mochot research institute, reported in Or Kashti, "Poll: Half of Israeli high schoolers oppose equal rights for Arabs," Haaretz (English edition), 11 March 2010.

[9]Documentary filmmaker Rachel Leah Jones directed the three videos for Adalah. To view the videos, please visit: http://www.adalah.org/eng/video.php

APPENDIX G
Speaking Frankly about Israel and Palestine

Jimmy Carter was the 39th president of the United States.
His newest book is "Palestine: Peace Not Apartheid,"
published last month.
Jimmy Carter
Los Angeles Times. December 8, 2006

I signed a contract with Simon & Schuster two years
ago to write a book about the Middle East, based on my
personal observations as the Carter Center monitored three
elections in Palestine and on my consultations with Israeli
political leaders and peace activists.

We covered every Palestinian community in 1996, 2005
and 2006, when Yasser Arafat and later Mahmoud Abbas
were elected president and members of parliament were
chosen. The elections were almost flawless, and turnout
was very high – except in East Jerusalem, where, under
severe Israeli restraints, only about 2% of registered voters
managed to cast ballots.

The many controversial issues concerning Palestine
and the path to peace for Israel are intensely debated among
Israelis and throughout other nations – but not in the United
States. For the last 30 years, I have witnessed and experienced
the severe restraints on any free and balanced discussion
of the facts. This reluctance to criticize any policies of the
Israeli government is because of the extraordinary lobbying
efforts of the American-Israel Political Action Committee
and the absence of any significant contrary voices.

It would be almost politically suicidal for members of
Congress to espouse a balanced position between Israel and
Palestine, to suggest that Israel comply with international
law or to speak in defense of justice or human rights for
Palestinians. Very few would ever deign to visit the
Palestinian cities of Ramallah, Nablus, Hebron, Gaza City

or even Bethlehem and talk to the beleaguered residents. What is even more difficult to comprehend is why the editorial pages of the major newspapers and magazines in the United States exercise similar self-restraint, quite contrary to private assessments expressed quite forcefully by their correspondents in the Holy Land.

With some degree of reluctance and some uncertainty about the reception my book would receive, I used maps, text and documents to describe the situation accurately and to analyze the only possible path to peace: Israelis and Palestinians living side by side within their own internationally recognized boundaries. These options are consistent with key U.N. resolutions supported by the U.S. and Israel, official American policy since 1967, agreements consummated by Israeli leaders and their governments in 1978 and 1993 (for which they earned Nobel Peace Prizes), the Arab League's offer to recognize Israel in 2002 and the International Quartet's "Roadmap for Peace," which has been accepted by the PLO and largely rejected by Israel.

The book is devoted to circumstances and events in Palestine and not in Israel, where democracy prevails and citizens live together and are legally guaranteed equal status.

Although I have spent only a week or so on a book tour so far, it is already possible to judge public and media reaction. Sales are brisk, and I have had interesting interviews on TV, including "Larry King Live," "Hardball," "Meet the Press," "The NewsHour With Jim Lehrer," the "Charlie Rose" show, C-SPAN and others. But I have seen few news stories in major newspapers about what I have written.

Book reviews in the mainstream media have been written mostly by representatives of Jewish organizations who would be unlikely to visit the occupied territories, and their primary criticism is that the book is anti-Israel. Two members of Congress have been publicly critical. Incoming House Speaker Nancy Pelosi for instance, issued a statement (before the book was published) saying that "he does not speak for the Democratic Party on Israel." Some reviews posted on Amazon.com call me "anti-Semitic," and others accuse the book of "lies" and "distortions." A former Carter Center fellow has taken issue with it, and Alan Dershowitz called the book's title "indecent."

Out in the real world, however, the response has been overwhelmingly positive. I've signed books in five stores, with more than 1,000 buyers at each site. I've had one negative remark – that I should be tried for treason – and one caller on C-SPAN said that I was an anti-Semite. My most troubling experience has been the rejection of my offers to speak, for free, about the book on university campuses with high Jewish enrollment and to answer questions from students and professors. I have been most encouraged by prominent Jewish citizens and members of Congress who have thanked me privately for presenting the facts and some new ideas.

The book describes the abominable oppression and persecution in the occupied Palestinian territories, with a rigid system of required passes and strict segregation between Palestine's citizens and Jewish settlers in the West Bank. An enormous imprisonment wall is now under construction, snaking through what is left of Palestine to encompass more and more land for Israeli settlers. In many ways, this is more oppressive than what blacks lived under in South Africa during apartheid. I have made it clear that the motivation is not racism but the desire of a minority of Israelis to confiscate and colonize choice sites in Palestine, and then to forcefully suppress any objections from the displaced citizens. Obviously, I condemn any acts of terrorism or violence against innocent civilians, and I present information about the terrible casualties on both sides.

The ultimate purpose of my book is to present facts about the Middle East that are largely unknown in America, to precipitate discussion and to help restart peace talks (now absent for six years) that can lead to permanent peace for

Israel and its neighbors. Another hope is that Jews and other Americans who share this same goal might be motivated to express their views, even publicly, and perhaps in concert. I would be glad to help with that effort.

APPENDIX H
Palestine: A question of refugee rights
BADIL - Resource Center for Palestinian Residency and Refugee Rights, Karkafa St., PO Box 728, Bethlehem, West Bank, Palestine.

This paper will illustrate very briefly why it is indispensable to understand the issue of Palestinian refugees in order to understand the overall situation in Palestine and Israel:

First, because of the total number of Palestinian refugees – almost 70 percent of the Palestinian people are forcibly displaced persons: refugees and/or Internally Displaced Persons. Additionally, nearly every Palestinian family consists of members who have been forcibly displaced.

Second, and most importantly, the general situation is one of forcible displacement. The Zionist Movement, and later Israel, had and still has no interest in simply creating a system of domination of one "racial" group over another. Israel's aim was, and still is, not to exploit the indigenous workforce or simply to limit their political and social participation. Rather, the intention was to establish a homogeneous Zionist-Jewish state predominantly for Jewish people.

This was apparent from the early years of the Zionist Movement, illustrated by the fact that Israel has hitherto no defined borders. As explained by Golda Meir, "The borders are determined by where Jews live, not where there is a line on a map."[1] This statement, in combination with Ben-Gurion's famous writings in 1937, "[that] the compulsory transfer of the Arabs from the valleys of the projected Jewish state could give us something which we never had... We have to stick to this conclusion the same way we grabbed the Balfour Declaration, more than that, the same way we grabbed at Zionism itself,"[2] offers endless possibilities for transferring Palestinians out and implanting Jewish settlers into the territory.

This process of forcible population transfer started prior to 1948, and is still ongoing today in the form of the overall policy of 'silent' transfer. This displacement is silent in the sense that Israel carries it out while trying to avoid international attention, displacing small numbers of people on a weekly basis. It is to be distinguished from the more overt transfer achieved under the veneer of warfare in 1948. The Israeli policy of silent transfer is evident in the State's laws, policies and practices. Israel uses its power to discriminate, expropriate and ultimately effect the forcible displacement of the indigenous non-Jewish population from the area of Mandate Palestine (historic Palestine).

Therefore, this Israeli policy is not limited to the Palestinians living in the Occupied Palestinian Territory (OPT), but it is also targeting Palestinians residing on the Israeli side of the "1949 Armistice Line" as well as those living in forced exile. Indeed, Israel's treatment of non-Jewish Palestinians throughout Israel and the OPT constitutes an overall discriminatory regime aimed at controlling the maximum amount of land with the minimum amount of indigenous Palestinians residing on it. The main components of that structure discriminate against Palestinians in areas such as nationality, citizenship, residency rights and land ownership. This system was originally applied in 1948 in order to dominate and dispossess all forcibly displaced Palestinians, including the 150,000 who were able to remain within the borders of the "1949 Armistice Line" and later became Palestinian citizens of Israel. After the occupation of the remaining part of Mandate Palestine by Israeli forces in 1967, this territory became subjected to the same Israeli regime.

Therefore, when discussing the situation in Palestine, one has to bear in mind that the issues involved, in particular, circulate around the question of already existing Palestinian refugees and prevention of future forcible displacement.

[1]Noam Chomsky, "Middle East Diplomacy: Continuities and Changes", Z *Magazine* (December 1991).
[2]Nur Masalha, Expulsion of the Palestinians: the concept of "transfer" in Zionist political thought, 1882-1948 (Institute for Palestine Studies 1992), p. 210.

References

Introduction

1. The four letters – CSsR – that follow a Redemptorist's name represent the Congregation's official Latin name: *Congregatio Sanctissimi Redemptoris* (The Congregation of the Most Holy Redeemer). They are more popularly known as the Redemptorists: "A society of missionary priests [and Brothers] founded by St. Alphonsus Maria Liguori, 9 Nov., 1732, at Scala, near Amalfi, Italy, for the purpose of laboring among the neglected country people in the neighborhood of Naples. The Redemptorists are essentially and by their specific vocation a missionary society." (Catholic Encyclopedia, www.newadvent.org/cathen/12683a.htm). JMJA stand for Jesus, Mary, Joseph and Alphonsus. Fr. Shepherd was the Provincial, the superior, with total power, of the London Province of Redemptorists, which was then comprised of England, Scotland, Wales, and a Vice-Province of South Africa. Since that time South Africa has become its own independent Province.
2. The full poem can be read on www.irishnationalcaucus.org.
3. "With malice toward none, with charity for all, with firmness in the right as God gives us to see the right, let us strive on to finish the work we are in; to bind up the nation's wounds; to care for him who shall have borne the battle, and for his widow and his orphan – to do all which may achieve and cherish a just and lasting peace, among ourselves, and with all nations." Abraham Lincoln's Second Inaugural Address, March 4, 1865.
4. "Action on behalf of justice and participation in the transformation of the world fully appear to us as a constitutive dimension of the preaching of the Gospel, or in other words, of the church's mission for the redemption of the human race and its liberation from every oppressive situation." Justice in the World. Number 6. Synod of Bishops. Rome, November 30, 1971. www.osjspm.org/majordoc_ justicia_in_mundo_offical_test.aspx
5. There was one splendid exception, one American Bishop who was not scared to take a stand against Britain's oppression in Ireland: my good

friend, the late Bishop Thomas Drury of Corpus Christi, Texas. The late Bishop Mark Hurley of Santa Rosa and the late Cardinal O'Connor of New York were fairly outspoken but were not in the same league as Bishop Drury, a native of Gurteen, County Sligo.

6. Social Gospel: "Christian faith practiced as a call not just to personal conversion but to social reform." *New Oxford American Dictionary*

Chapter 1: Bonny Banks of Lough Erne

1. St. Naile was a contemporary of St. Columcille (AD 521–597). He became the second abbot on Devenish Island on Lower Lough Erne, just north of Enniskillen. Devenish is one of the finest monastic sites in Ireland, first established in the sixth century. The site is dominated by a round tower thought to date from the twelfth century (see www.kinawleyparish.com).

2. The Big Snow of '47 (www.irishidentity.com/extras/weather/stories/snow.htm).

3. Kinawley Parish Bulletin, July 29, 1984.

4. Nicholas Christopher Michael Ring (October 12, 1920 – March 2, 1979), better known as Christy Ring, was a famous Cork hurler. He is generally regarded as one of the greatest hurlers in the history of the game.

5. *Eucharistic Doctors: A Theological History*. Owen F. Cummings. p.98. Paulist Press New York. 2005

6. Frank McCourt, *Angela's Ashes* (Scribner, New York, 1996), p. 1. When I told Frank that an elderly lady in Kinawley had read *Angela's Ashes* five times he was so touched he wrote her a lovely letter. Later when I was coming out of Kinawley chapel after saying Mass, there was that wonderful lady, since deceased, waiting to thank me for putting Frank McCourt in touch with her. I asked her if she had told the *Fermanagh Herald* about the letter but she responded with great dignity: "No, that's between Frank McCourt and me." And then added with obvious pride, "But I will leave it in my will."

7. *A Monk Swimming* (1998). A memoir by Malachy McCourt. Wheeler Publishing. 1998

Chapter 2: The Day Celia Was Married and Patrick Was Killed

1. Patrick Mc Manus. *United Irishman*. August 1958.

2. J. Bowyer Bell, *The Secret Army: the IRA, 1916–1970* (John Day Company, New York, 1970), p. 309, footnote 14.

3. In 1953, Rocky Marciano defended his world heavyweight title against Jersey Joe Walcott, knocking him out in the first round with his deadly uppercut. The previous year, Marciano had taken the title from Jersey Joe.

Chapter 3: The Call

1. Bayard Rustin (March 17, 1912 – August 24, 1987) was an American civil rights activist and principal organizer of the 1963 March on Washington for Jobs and Freedom. He counseled Martin Luther King, Jr. on the techniques of nonviolent resistance.

Chapter 4: Kinnoull and Hawkstone Years

1. Karl Barth (May 10, 1886 – December 10, 1968) (pronounced "Bart") was an eminent Swiss Reformed theologian, one of the most important Christian thinkers of the twentieth century. Even Pope Pius XII described him as the most important theologian since Thomas Aquinas.
2. Hawkstone Hall is an early eighteenth-century Georgian mansion set in extensive parkland in Shropshire, England. It now serves the Church as an international center for spiritual renewal.
3. Richard P. McBrien (ed.), *Encyclopedia of Catholicism* (HarperCollins, New York, 1995), p. 1,254.
4. Thomas F. O'Meara, O.P., *A Theologian's Journey,* (Paulist Press, New York, 2002), p. 25.
5. McBrien, *ibid.,* pp. 1,254–1,255.
6. Fergus Kerr, *Twentieth-Century Catholic Theologians* (Blackwell Publishing, Malden, MA., 2007) pp. 4–5.
7. "This decree of condemnation may be found in *Acta Sanctae Sedis* (5th ed., Rome, 1872–1911), V (1911), 389." Fr. William D'Arcy, O.F.M. Conv., *The Fenian Movement in the United States: 1858–1886.* (The Catholic University of America Press, Washington, D.C., 1947), p. 329.
8. From "Flower of Scotland" (1974) by the Scottish folk group, The Corries. It celebrates the victory of the Scots, led by King Robert the Bruce over the King of England, Edward II, at the Battle of Bannockburn, 1314. It has become the unofficial Scottish Anthem for rugby and soccer events.

    "O flower of Scotland
    When will we see your like again
    That fought and died for
    Your wee bit hill and glen
    And stood against him
    Proud Edward's army
    And sent him homeward
    Tae think again

9. Seán Mac Stíofáin, *Memoirs of a Revolutionary* (R. & R. Clark Ltd, Edinburgh, 1975), p. 4.

Chapter 5: The Troubles Come Back to Haunt

1. "But just when I thought I was out, they pull me back in." Michael Corleone in *Godfather III* (Mario Puzo and Francis Ford Coppola, 1990).
2. Michael Farrell, *Arming the Protestants: The Formation of the Ulster Special Constabulary and the Royal Ulster Constabulary, 1929–27* (Brandon Books, Kerry, 1983).
3. "Enniskillen Anti-Internment Meeting." Letters to the Editor, *Fermanagh Herald*, Saturday, August 21, 1971.
4. J. M. Synge, *Playboy of the Western World* (J. W. Luce, Boston, 1911).
5. Henry David Thoreau's essay "On the Duty of Civil Disobedience."1849.
6. "The Devlin made me do it." *The Big Issue*.
7. Letter from Birmingham Jail. April 16, 1963. Penn University, African Studies Center (www.upenn.edu).

Chapter 6: Bound for America

1. Bernard Haring, *Priesthood Imperiled* (Triumph Books, Chicago, 1989), pp. 146–147.
2. Thomas Merton, *Passivity and Abuse of Authority* (The McCall Publishing Company, New York, 1968), pp. 128–133.
3. Raymond Arsenault, *Freedom Riders* (Oxford University Press, Oxford, 2006), p. 419.

Chapter 7: Formation of Irish National Caucus

1. Joseph E. Thompson, *American Policy and Northern Ireland: A Saga of Peacebuilding* (Praeger, Westport, Connecticut, 2001), p. 38.
2. Frank McManus statement, June 6, 2008.
3. Jack Holland, *The American Connection*. (Viking Penguin, New York, 1987), p. 117. Two later books repeat Holland's error: Andrew J. Wilson, *Irish-America and the Ulster Conflict 1968–1995* (The Catholic University of America, Washington, DC, 1995), p. 99 and Joseph E. Thompson, *American Policy and Northern Ireland: A Saga of Peacebuilding* (Praeger, Westport, Connecticut, 2001), p. 51. This latter book seems to confuse the formation of the Irish National Caucus with its later endorsement by many different Irish-American organizations.
4. Statement issued by Jack Keane to the author in a telephone interview on Friday, May 30, 2008, 7.30 p.m.

Chapter 8: Caucus Baptized in Blood at British Embassy

1. "Stickies" and "Pinheads": after the 1969–70 IRA split, which led to the emergence of the Provisional IRA, the Official IRA used a type of Easter

Lily with a self-adhesive backing. This led to them being branded as the "Stickies." The Provisionals retained the traditional paper-and-pin Easter lily and thus became known as the "Pinheads," a nickname which has not lasted.

2. Jack is one of the very few in the Washington area from that time who has stayed the course, and is still active in the struggle for Irish justice.

3. The following account is largely based on contemporaneous notes I made and on a report I wrote at that time.

4. "Embassy Protest Held By An Unlikely Band." Carl Schoettler, *Baltimore Sun,* Saturday April 27, 1974.

Chapter 9: All the News That's Fit to Print – Or Not

1. "Papacy at the crossroads." John Organ, *Sunday Telegraph,* January 4, 1976.

2. "Irish-American Group Aired Issue In Vatican." Carl Schoettler. *Baltimore Evening Sun*, Friday, December 26, 1975; "Irish Caucus Delegation Well Received," *The National Hibernian Digest*, January–February 1976; "Jackson's bid to scoop the Irish," *Irish Post* (London), January 24, 1976.

Chapter 10: The Caucus and Jimmy Carter

1. Joseph E. Thompson, *American Policy and Northern Ireland: A Saga of Peacebuilding* (Praeger, Westport, Connecticut, 2001), p. 38.

2. "Boston, Where it Began, Salutes the English Queen." *The New York Times*, July 12, 1976.

3. Telegram from Al Stern, September 8, 1976. INC files.

4. "The peanut and the shamrock," the *Guardian,* Friday, October 29, 1976.

5. *Boston Globe*, Monday April 18, 1977.

6. Tim Pat Coogan, *A Memoir*, (Weidenfeld & Nicolson, London, 2008), p. 198.

7. "Irish priest denies forcing Carter remark in talk here." National Catholic News Service, week of November 17, 1976.

8. "The one about Jimmy & the Irish." Jack Anderson with Les Whitten, *Daily News*, Tuesday, November 16, 1976.

9. Paul O'Dwyer's letter to Jimmy Carter. INC files.

10. "President's hearty welcome in Massachusetts shows strength of popular support." *The Times*, March 18, 1977.

11. White House mailgram from Stephen Aiello, special assistant to the President for Ethnic Affairs, April 2, 1980. INC files

12. "Fr. McManus Meets Carter in White House." *Fermanagh Herald*, June 14, 1980.

13. Professor Paul Power, "The United States and Northern Ireland: the Carter Initiative and its Aftermath", (paper presented at annual meeting of American Committee for Irish Studies, University of Delaware, April 24-26, 1980).
14. Joseph E. Thompson, *American Policy and Northern Ireland: A Saga of Peacebuilding* (Praeger, Westport, Connecticut, 2001), p. 38.
15. "President Carter States Policy on Northern Ireland" (Department of State Bulletin, 77, September 26, 1977).
16. "The Carter Initiative: How the Caucus got their Man." John Kelly, *The Sunday Press* (Dublin), September 4, 1977.
17. "Irish Caucus cued Carter: McManus." *The Irish Times*, August 31, 1977.

Chapter 11: The Long Knives of the Irish Government

1. Letter from INC member, INC files.
2. *The New York Times*, Sunday March 20, 1977.
3. "Dublin players get warning on U.S. tour." *The Irish Press*, Thursday April 21, 1997.
4. "GAA tour of United States is on." Paddy Downey, *The Irish Times*, Saturday April 23, 1977.
5. "Hub priest denies he backs IRA." David Nyhan, *Boston Globe*, April 18, 1977.
6. "Ireland putting heat on me," says priest, David Nyhan, *Boston Globe*, May 19, 1977.
7. "Hub priest charges Irish consul with 'dirty trick.'" *Boston Herald American*, Friday May 20, 1977.
8. "Consul accused of 'dirty tricks.'" *Irish Post*, Saturday June 11, 1977.
9. *The Evangelist*, Diocese of Albany, NY, Thursday, June 9, 1977.
10. Letter of Charles H. Gibbons, Jr. to editor of *Boston Globe*, June 3, 1977. INC files.
11. "Priest hits at bishops over silence on North." *The Irish Press*, December 30, 1976.
12. "Court Tells Writer to Name Informant." *The New York Times*, Sunday April 29, 1979.
13. "Reveal the Name or go to Jail." Russell Warren Howe, *Washington Journalism Review*, January/February 1991.
14. "Lobby ... gaining support in Congress." *The New York Times*, September 21, 1979.
15. "Formation of Ad Hoc Committee for Irish Affairs." INC press release, September 27, 1977. See also "Kinawley-born Rev. Sean McManus Chairs Press Conference in Washington," *Fermanagh Herald*, November

19, 1977; "Irish Get Ear of Congress," *Irish News* (Belfast), Thursday, September 29, 1977;. "U.S. Committee to Consider Injustice," *The Irish Times*, Thursday, September 29, 1977.

16. "Irish Priest Blasts U.S. Hierarchy." Religious News Service, September 28, 1977.

17. "The Irish National Caucus," Editorials, National Hibernian Digest, September-October 1983.

18. *The Irish Times*, June 29, 1978.

19. "Northern Ireland: A Role for the United States?" Report by two members of the Committee on the Judiciary (Ninety-fifth Congress, U.S. Government Printing Press), p. vii.

20. *Ibid.*, p. 219.

21. "Provisionals Disown U.S. Caucus Man." *The Irish Press*, September 27, 1978.

22. INC press release, October 18, 1977; "Caucus to Boycott Provisionals." *The Irish Times*, October 19, 1978.

Chapter 12: Move to Washington

1. Joseph E. Thompson, *American Policy and Northern Ireland: A Saga of Peacebuilding* (Praeger, Westport, Connecticut, 2001), p. 38.

2. "Blaney elated at FF choice." Sean Cronin, *The Irish Times*, Saturday, December 8, 1979.

3. "Irish Caucus in the Corridors of Power." *The Irish Times,* September 4, 1979.

4. "The American Connection ... the men behind the mounting anti-British chorus in Congress." *Belfast Telegraph*, May 16, 1979.

5. "A Shift on Ulster." Ken Hartnett, *Boston Globe,* March 17, 1979.

6. Garret FitzGerald, *All in a Life: An Autobiography*, (Macmillan, London 1991), p. 348.

7. Fr. William D'Arcy, OFM Conv., *The Fenian Movement in the United States: 1858–1886* (The Catholic University of America Press, Washington, D.C., 1947), p. 364.

8. Sean Donlon's letter to Congressman Fish, November 6, 1979, copy in INC files.

9. "Irish Drop Plans to Replace Envoy." Leonard Downie, Jr., *The Washington Post*, July 9, 1980.

10. "Birmingham Six Case 'discredited' ". *The Irish Press*, Monday, November 4, 1985.

11. "FitzGerald Calls on Haughey to Reject IRA 'Front' Groups." Geraldine Kennedy, *The Irish Times*, July 21, 1980.

12. "FitzGerald Asked for Condemnation." *The Irish Times,* July 28, 1980.

13. FitzGerald, *ibid.,* p. 350.
14. "Report from Capitol Hill: As if Congress Were Not Already Splintered." *U.S. News and World Report,* February 4, 1980.
15. "What's a Boycott Between Friends?" *The New York Times,* May 28, 1980.
16. "The Donlon Affair: Irish May Replace Envoy to U.S. in Policy Shift on Northern Ireland." Leonard Downie, Jr. and Virginia Hamill, *The Washington Post,* July 8, 1980.
17. "US is reviewing RUC arms sales." *The Irish Press,* August 3, 1979.
18. Letter of State Department Counselor Matthew Nimetz to Mario Biaggi and twenty-eight other members, June 15, 1979.
19. "No Guns for Violating Irish Rights: Letter on Arms Sale to Britain." Mario Biaggi, *The New York Times,* Saturday, June 7, 1980.
20. "Paisley's Visa is Revoked by US." *Boston Globe,* Tuesday, December 22, 1981.
21. "Kennedy, O'Neill ask U.S. to bar Paisley." *Boston Globe,* Wednesday, December 9, 1981.
22. "Taking the Bob Out of Bob Jones U[niversity] – Christian Institution Readies For the Next Generation." Peter Carlson, *The Washington Post,* Thursday, May 5, 2005.
23. Statement, May 30, 1981, INC files.

Chapter 13: The Old Sow that Eats Its Own Farrow

1. Horace, Roman poet, 65 BC – 8 BC.
2. James Joyce, *Portrait of the Artist as a Young Man* (Modern Library, New York, 1928), p. 238.
3. "Provos Fall Out with Caucus Priest." *Sunday World,* March 21, 1982.
4. The Fenian Movement in the United States 1858-1886. p. 218. The Catholic University of America. Washington, DC 1947.
5. Interview with Gerry Adams, *Hibernia Review,* October 1979.
6. David Lynch, *Radical Politics in Modern Ireland: the Irish Socialist Republican Party, 1896–1904* (Irish Academic Press, Dublin, 2005), p. 2.
7. "Washington Caucus," editorial, the *Irish People,* October 18, 1980.
8. "Banished Priest Who Has Ear of All America's Top Politicians." John Cassidy, *Sunday World,* March 18, 2007.
9. Telephone conversation on Sunday January 24, 2010.
10. Joseph E. Thompson, *American Policy and Northern Ireland: A Saga of Peacebuilding* (Praeger, Westport, Connecticut, 2001), p. 55.
11. They Change Their Sky, p. 23. University of Maine Press. 2002.
12. "Ford Admits Plot to Rewrite MacBride Principles." INC press release,

August 29, 1990.

13. "MacBride Campaign Takes Harrisburg by Storm." INC press release, September 20, 1989.

14. "Caucus Leader Grand Marshall in Harrisburg." INC press release, March 12, 1990.

15. Letter of Mary Pat Clarke, President, Baltimore City Council, August 9, 1993, INC files.

16. "Funeral Guns Mute Ministerial Offensive," David Blundy, *The Sunday Times*, July 12, 1981.

Chapter 14: Capitol Hill Struggle

1. Frederick Douglass, American Abolitionist, lecturer, author and slave, 1817–1895. The quote is from a "West India Emancipation" speech he gave on August 3, 1857 at Canandaigua, New York, on the twenty-third anniversary of the event.

2. "Growing Interest in NI." Vincent Browne, *Evening Herald*, August 3, 1979.

3. Joseph E. Thompson, *American Policy and Northern Ireland: A Saga of Peacebuilding* (Praeger, Westport, Connecticut, 2001), p. 80.

4. *Ibid.*, p. 80.

5. *Ibid.*, p. 84.

6. *Ibid.*, p. 229.

7. Kevin McNamara, *The MacBride Principles: Irish-America Strikes Back* (Liverpool University Press, 2009), p. 15.

8. *Ibid.*, p. 15.

9. "Kennedy, Donnelly Unveil Visa Proposal: Sen. Edward M. Kennedy and Rep. Brian J. Donnelly yesterday introduced legislation to increase annually by 50,000 the number of visas available to people from Ireland, Italy, some other Western European countries and Canada who wish to immigrate to the United States. Charging that the present system discriminates against countries ..." *Boston Globe*, August 7, 1987.

10. The Sunningdale Agreement, signed on December 9, 1973, led to the establishment of a cross-community, power-sharing Executive to govern Northern Ireland. The Agreement collapsed six months later because of strenuous opposition from Unionists and Loyalists.

11. "The Status of the North: It's not F.F. Policy." Vincent Browne, *Sunday Independent*, January 29, 1978.

12. "Departure of Two Top O'Neill Aides Marks Loss Of Key Participants in Shaping House Agenda." Al Hunt, *The Wall Street Journal*, December 9, 1985.

13. "Irish Politics." Jack Anderson and Les Whitten, *New York Daily News*,

October 21, 1977.

14. "White House Policy." Jack Anderson, *The Washington Post*, June 17, 1978.

15. "Carter Pressured on Northern Ireland." Jack Anderson, *Detroit Free Press*, October 29, 1978.

16. Joseph E. Thompson, *American Policy and Northern Ireland: A Saga of Peacebuilding* (Praeger, Westport, Connecticut, 2001), p. 57.

17. "Tip O'Neill," *Irish-America*, October 1986.

18. "The Anglo-Irish Agreement Support Act of September 19, 1986 (P.L. 99–415) authorized U.S. contributions to an international fund for economic development projects in Northern Ireland and the Republic of Ireland ... This is the first time the U.S. Government has ever given economic aid to this region," CRS Issue Brief, Northern Ireland and the Republic of Ireland: U.S. Foreign Assistance Facts, October 6, 1989.

19. T. S. Elliot. *Murder in the Cathedral*, (Harcourt, Brace and Company, Florida, 1935).

20. "Irish-American Leader Seeks Roadblocks in Aid to Ireland." *New Hampshire Sunday News* (the Sunday edition of the *Union Leader*), March 9, 1986. Of course, I wanted conditions, not "roadblocks" – but Tom Gorey did not write the headline.

21. "The most helpful ally Ireland has ever had in Washington." Garret FitzGerald, *The Irish Times*, January 8, 1994.

22. "The Government Strikes Back." Kate O'Callaghan, *Irish Voice*, May 6, 1989.

23. *Ibid*.

24. "Angry Words at Ireland Fund Hearing." Sean Cronin, *The Irish Times*, April 26, 1989.

25. "This Week They Said." *The Irish Times*, May 20, 1989.

26. INC press release, August 5, 1985. Biden's quote from stenographic transcript of hearing on August 5, 1985 before Senate Committee on Foreign Affairs, p. 34.

27. "Britain and Irish in Battle on Capitol Hill." Simon Hoggart, *Observer*, September 15, 1985.

28. "When Irish Eyes Are Frowning." *The Washington Post* National Weekly Edition, October 7, 1985.

29. "Attacking an IRA Refuge." Christopher Hitchens, *Spectator*, October 5, 1985.

30. "Battling Extradition Treaty." David Blundy, *The Sunday Times*, August 11, 1985.

31. "Treaty Stalled." John Robinson, *Boston Globe*, October 23, 1985.

32. "Caucus Blocks Anti-IRA Move." Niall O'Dowd, *The Sunday Press*, July 21, 1985.

33. "Delay in Extradition Law Irks Thatcher." Fergus Pyle, *The Irish Times*, April 28, 1986.

34. Senator Hatch correspondence, INC files.

Chapter 15: The MacBride Principles: Genesis and History

1. "An Army of Principles Will Penetrate Where an Army of Soldiers Cannot." Thomas Paine, *Agrarian Justice*. Pamphlet was written in 1775, published in 1797.

2. The Sullivan Principles are a corporate code of conduct developed by the African American preacher Rev. Leon Sullivan in 1977 for U.S. companies doing business in South Africa to protest against apartheid.

3. "Caucus in Jobs Blacklist Move: Americans Probe Workers' Religions." *Sunday News*, July 29, 1979.

4. "Irish Caucus Investigates American Firms." *The Irish Times*, July 30, 1979.

5. "Investigating Behaviour of American Firms." *The Irish Press*, July 28, 1978.

6. "Investigating Alleged Discrimination." *Belfast Telegraph*, July 28, 1979.

7. "MacBride to head new Irish Caucus group." *The Irish Times*, August 4, 1979.

8. "Sean MacBride Heads Caucus Liaison Group." *Irish World*, September 15, 1979.

9. INC press release, November 4, 1983, INC files.

10. "Irish Embassy Move Angers U.S. Groups." *The Irish Press*, November 4, 1983.

11. "Americans in Ulster Maelstrom." *Daily Telegraph*, August 18, 1983.

12. "Anti-British to the hilt." *News Letter* (Belfast), August 18, 1983.

13. "Rancid Bigot." *Daily Express* (UK), August 18, 1983.

14. Cardinal Ó Fiaich's mailgram, April 22, 1987, INC files.

15. "Eccles Not Paid." *Sunday News*, April 2, 1989.

16. Kevin McNamara, *The MacBride Principles: Irish-America Strikes Back* (Liverpool University Press, 2009), pp. 103–104.

17. "FEA Man's Firm Lashed Over Bias." *Sunday World* (Dublin), June 3, 1990.

18. "Aer Lingus Covers up for Shorts." INC press release, June 30, 1983.

19. Congressman Shannon's letter, September 2, 1983, INC files.

20. "MacBride Principles Spell Kiss of Death." Paddy Devlin, *Sunday World*, May 11, 1986.
21. "The MacBride Principles a Sham." Paddy Devlin, *Sunday World*, June 7, 1987.
22. "Caucus Proposes New Initiative to Stop Discrimination in Northern Ireland." *Irish Echo* (New York), November 10, 1984.
23. "New U.S. Company code endangers NI investment." Michael Farrell, *Sunday Tribune*, November 4, 1984. Of course, Farrell did not write the headline, and he was one of the first journalists in Ireland to immediately realize the importance of our initiative.
24. "Albanese urges bias bill on U.S. firms in Ulster." *New York Daily News*, January 2, 1985.
25. "Fr. McManus Press Conference." *Irish Echo*, January 2, 1985.
26. "Investment Pressure for NI Catholic Rights." *Chief Leader*, January 11, 1985.
27. "Pension Fund Proposal." Tricia Gallagher, *Catholic New York*, February 7, 1985.
28. "New York Threat of Ulster Shares Boycott." Will Ellsworth-Jones, *The Times*, January 6, 1985.
29. "US bill on North Bias by Companies." Niall O'Dowd, *The Irish Press*, January 4, 1985.
30. "Koch & Goldin Oppose Ulster Investment Ban." *New York Daily News*, January 4, 1985.
31. "Of pension fund investments," from Patrick Campbell's column, "Campbell's Scoop," in *The Irish Echo*, January 19, 1985.
32. "Investment in Ulster Opposed." Jesus Rangel, *The New York Times*, January 4, 1985.
33. "Goldin visit to NI." *New York Daily News*, June 25, 1985.
34. "Goldin's Irish Tenor is Way Off Key." *New York Daily News*, July 19, 1985.
35. "Unfair to Ulster." *The New York Times*, July 5, 1985.
36. "Goldin and Northern Ireland." *New York Post*, June 27, 1985.
37. "Economic Influence Suggested for Ulster." *The Sunday Republican*, February 3, 1985.
38. State Representative Tom Gallagher's letter to the author, October 1, 1985, INC files.
39. Tiernan MacBride's letter to the author, January 25, 1988, INC files.
40. Caitriona Lawlor's letter to Ken Bertsch, June 28, 1993, INC files.
41. Kevin McNamara, *The MacBride Principles: Irish-America Strikes Back* (Liverpool University Press, 2009), p. 27.
42. *Ibid.*, p. 24.

43. "Agonizing over a few principles." Mary Holland, *The Irish Times*, Wednesday, October 7, 1987.
44. Mary Holland's letter, November 15, 1987, INC files.
45. "Doherty's Way. NYC Aims to Keep Investments Ethical." Peter McDermott, *Irish Echo*, November 12, 2008.
46. Ray MacManais, *The Road From Ardoyne: The Making of a President* (Brandon Press, Dingle, 2004), p. 153.

Chapter 16: Anti-MacBride Campaign

1. N. E. Sheinwald's letter to Tom Donahue, Secretary-Treasurer, AFL-CIO, March 1, 1985.
2. Kevin McNamara, *The MacBride Principles: Irish-America Strikes Back* (Liverpool University Press, 2009), p. 89.
3. *Sunday Life* (Belfast), March 22, 1992.
4. "Ulster Leader Assails American Supporters of MacBride Plan." *The Boston Sunday Globe,* March 8, 1987.
5. "Principles that Burden." *Boston Globe* editorial, March 11, 1987.
6 "Ex-IRA Leader Fights for Jobs." *Boston Globe*, April 25, 1987.
7. "Bishop Opposes Jobs Measures." *Boston Globe*, November 25, 1989.
8. "Bishop Daly Questioned on MacBride." *Irish Voice*, December 9, 1989.
9. "Daly Denies He's Opposed to MacBride." *Irish Echo*, February 12-23, 1993.
10. Bishop McAuliffe's letter to John Carr, August 3, 1993, INC files.
11. INC and Office of Justice and Peace Meeting, INC press release, January 6, 1978, INC files.
12. Letter to Caucus member, dated October 17, 1979. Edward Doherty writing on the official stationery of the United States Catholic Conference, INC files.
13. Archbishop Hickey's letter to the author, February 6, 1981; Bishop Kelly's letter to the author, January 29, 1981, INC files.
14. Moderator Dunlop's letter to Sister Regina, May 14, 1993; letter of Josiah Beeman, Chair of the Northern Ireland Working Group of Presbyterian Church in the United States, to Sister Regina, INC files.
15. "Proposed Church Conference on MacBride Principles Provokes Questions, Suspicions." INC press release, May 26, 1993, INC files.
16. Author's letter to all U.S. Catholic Bishops, May 26, 1993, INC files.
17. "A Call For Fair Employment and Investment in Northern Ireland," statement issued by the four main Churches, January 14, 1993.
18. "The Path to Peace," remarks by An Taoiseach, Dr. Garret FitzGerald, Kennedy Library, Boston, May 3, 1985.
19. *Ibid.*, p. 131.

20. "Dole, GOP Congressional Leaders Meet With Irish Prime Minister." RNC News Release, September 11, 1996.
21. *Ibid.*, p. 150.
22. *Ibid.*, p. 131.
23. *Ibid.*, p. 159.
24. *Ibid.*, p. 160.
25. *Ibid.*, p. 23.
26. *Ibid.*, p. 141.
27. *Ibid.*, pp. 124–125.

Chapter 17: Forcing Clinton to Sign MacBride

1. "Andrews Backs MacBride Principles." September 30–October 6, 1992, *Irish Echo*
2. H.R. 725: "To provide for adherence with the MacBride Principles by United States persons doing business in Northern Ireland. Sponsor: Rep. Fish, Hamilton, Jr. [NY-21] (introduced 1/31/1989). Cosponsors (97). Latest Major Action: 5/5/1989. Referred to House subcommittee. Status: Referred to the Subcommittee on Rules of the House.
SUMMARY AS OF: 1/31/1989 – Introduced.

   Northern Ireland Fair Employment Practices Act – Prohibits an article from being imported into the United States from Northern Ireland unless documentation is presented at the time of entry indicating that the enterprise which manufactured or assembled such article complied at the time of manufacture with certain fair employment principles (such as freedom from religious discrimination). Bases such principles on the MacBride Principles, a nine-point set of guidelines for fair employment in Northern Ireland.

   Requires any U.S. person who has a branch or office in Northern Ireland or who controls an enterprise in Northern Ireland in which more than 20 people are employed to insure implementation of such employment principles and compliance with this Act ..."
3. Congressman Lee Hamilton's letter to the author, August 14, 1987, INC files.
4. Kevin McNamara, *The MacBride Principles: Irish-America Strikes Back* (Liverpool University Press, 2009), p. 159.
5. *Ibid.*, p. viii.
6. "Capitol Hill Reception Huge Success: Gilman Announces MacBride Hearing." INC press release, January 27, 1995, INC files.
7. Hearing before House International Relations Committee, March 15, 1995. (US Government Printing Office, Washington, 1995), p. 2.
8. *Ibid.*, pp. 74–79.

9. "Clinton Bids to Quell Storm Over MacBride." Ray O'Hanlon, *Irish Echo,* August 28 – September 3, 1996.
10. "Caucus Welcomes Clinton Back to MacBride Fold." INC press release, August 28, 1996, INC files.
11. "Democratic platform renews support for NI peace moves.", Joe Carroll, *The Irish Times,* August 27, 1996.
12. Author's reviews of Kevin McNamara's book: *The MacBride Principles: Irish-America Fights Back,* INC website (www.irishnationalcaucus.org).

Chapter 18: "A Protestant Boy" on Capitol Hill

1. "Operation Ballast, A Report on the Police Ombudsman's investigation into matters surrounding the death of Raymond McCord Jr." by Nuala O'Loan, 2007.
2. "McCord at British Embassy: Deep Disappointment, Thursday, May 14, 2009, INC press release, INC files.
3. *Observe the Sons of Ulster Marching Towards the Somme* is, perhaps, one of Frank McGuinness' most respected plays.

Epilogue

1. Cato, Marcus Porcius (234–149 BC), Roman statesman, orator and writer; known as Cato the Elder.
2. St. Thomas Aquinas, *Summa Theologica,* 11-11, 158, 1 and 3.

Afterword

1. *They Change Their Sky: The Irish in Maine.* Edited by Michael C. Connolly, The University of Maine, 2004.
2. *How the Irish Saved Civilization.* Thomas Cahill, Anchor Books, New York, 1995.
3. *Ibid.,* p. 193.
4. *American Slavery: Irish Freedom.* Angela F. Murphy. p. 158. Louisiana State University Press, 2010.
5. On Saturday, December 4, 1971, loyalists from the Ulster Volunteer Force (U.V.F.), under the control of the British military, planted a no-warning bomb on the doorstep of a family-run bar in north Belfast … killing 15 people. However, the security forces deliberately lied, claiming it was an IRA bomb that had exploded prematurely as it was being constructed inside the bar. Ciaran MacAirt's grandmother, Kathleen Irvine, was one of fifteen people killed. www.themcgurksbarmassacre.com

Holy Land Principles

1. King, Jr., Martin Luther, *A Christmas Sermon for Peace*. (December 24, 1967).
2. Benin, Joel and Lisa Hajjar, *Primer on Palestine, Israel and the Arab-Israeli Conflict*. October 2000. "www.merip.org"
3. Rothschild, Lionel Walter, 2nd Baron Rothschild, Baron de Rothschild FRS1868 – 1937), a scion of the Rothschild family, was a British banker, politician, and zoologist.
4. Pappe, Ilan, *The Ethnic Cleansing of Palestine*, (One World Publications, Oxford. 2006.) p. 124.
5. Ibid., p. 34.
6. *A Synopsis of the Israel/Palestine Conflict*. p. 2. August 2012. "www.ifamericansknew.org"
7. Ibid., p. 2.
8. Pappe, Ilan, I (*One World Publications*, Oxford. 2006.) p. 62.
9. A Synopsis of the Israel/Palestine Conflict. August 2012. "www.ifamericansknew.org"
10. Pappe, Ilan, *The Ethnic Cleansing of Palestine*. p. 251.
11. Evron, Boas, *The Holocaust: Learning the Wrong Lessons*. 1981 Essay.
12. Ruether, Rosemary, I. Quoted in Mark Braverman's, *Fatal Embrace*. Beaufort Books. 2010. P169.
13. Mission Statement "http:/ifpb.org"
14. Dixon, Aaron, *My People are Rising*. Haymarket Books, Chicago, Illinois. 2012
15. The first Prime Minister of Northern Ireland, James Craig, stated in parliament, "All I boast of is that we are a Protestant Parliament and a Protestant State." April 24, 1934.
16. *Kairos Palestine*: a moment of truth. kairospalestine.ps
17. Call to Action: U.S. Response to the Kairos Palestine Document.
18. Mark Braverman, *Fatal Embrace*. p. 217. Beaufort Books. New York. 2010.
19. Ibid.

The Carn Lintel by Patrick Maguire
(Thoughts on a visit to Carn with American cousins. August 20, 2002)

Tired and hungry fields, receding, as the gorse reclaims its space,
Our ancestral tracks have vanished, footprints faded beyond trace.
Vengeful bramble, angry briar, that for long were held at bay,
Boldly colonize the meadow where my mother trampled hay.

Where the spud proliferated, with the cabbage and the corn,
Greedy rushes are competing with the thistle and the thorn.
And the path up to the bogland purple heather now conceals
Where, in sunshine, neighbours ambled with their donkeys and their
    creels.

Scalloped thatch has long since fallen on this little house that's died.
Still the naked walls are standing … sadly … strangely dignified.
Now the chimney lies in rubble, choking up the cold fireplace,
And a rusty crook's protruding from the ruins of the brace.

Nettles, tall as were my uncles, stretch up from the strewn floor
And yet, the stubborn lintel sullenly protects the door.
Persevering through the decades, resolutely standing fast,
Tireless, it maintains the portal; guards this entrance to our past.

Underneath its rugged toughness life was played across the years.
Here were scenes of hope and heartache; joy and laughter; anguished
    tears.
Here were cameos enacted in a drama of the strife
Of a family for survival - in the tragedy of life.

O'er this threshold, worn and weathered, once a girl was borne, with
    pride,
By a young man – my grandfather – celebrating his new bride.
Was that moment lost, I wonder; had it gone beyond recall,
When, by hand, my sister led him, in his dotage, lest he'd fall?

In the years intervening, sons and daughters travelled through;
Maggie, Celia, Katie, Alice, Terence, James, Pat, Felix, Hugh.
From beneath this guardian lintel, each first looked upon the world.
Back through here they ran for refuge, as their early lives unfurled.

Hence they went as carefree youngsters; off to school… to church…
to dance;
Later, forth to work and marriage, and to fight a war in France.
Here the ceilidhers were greeted, welcome of a winter's night.
(Others came, though uninvited, black and tanned, at dawn's first
light.)

Round this doorway neighbors huddled; men came in, with voices
low,
Muttered, "Sorry for your trouble", on an August evening, long ago.
So the family decremented, till but one was left to cope,
With the cross of aged parents and the withering of hope.

Then the long and lonely winters, in the turf and tilley light;
One alone where there'd been many, in the cold and silent night.
Till the solitude and shadows sapped, at last, the will to try
And the fire was raked forever and the house was left to die.

Now, some forty years later, ruined; derelict; and yet
There remains a sense of life here; this is not a place of death.
What has pulled us here together, some who've never met before?
What has drawn us from the distance back to this, our common core?

Are there threads we are unaware of; bonds we do not comprehend?
Links that cross the generations and our simple thoughts transcend?
Is there something here of others; those who left long, long ago?
Susan, Catherine and Bessie; Jemmy, Terry, Hugh and Joe?

Underneath this granite lintel they too passed in younger days;
Travelled tracks that are no longer; moved along those mountain
ways.
Here they loved and laughed together, whispered secrets, hopes and
fears,
In the days before New Zealand; long before the Boston years.

Yes, the golden thatch has perished; stones, once white, are hushed
and grey.
Now the stacks of weeds and briars stand instead of turf and hay.
While we have spread across the world, nature has regained its space
But, beneath this Carn Lintel, here we have yet a sense of place.

Index

Irish National Caucus

Ireland, too, has the right to be one nation, under God, indivisible with liberty and justice for all.

THE IRISH LOBBY – The Irish National Caucus (INC) is the Irish lobby on Capitol Hill, Washington, D.C. It is a human rights organization dedicated to getting the United States to stand up for justice and peace in Ireland.

NONPROFIT – The Irish National Caucus is a nonprofit organization (registered in Washington, D.C., 1978). It is 501(c)(4). The INC's sister organization, the Irish Peace Foundation, is recognized by the I.R.S. as being eligible to receive tax-deductible contributions under Internal Revenue Code Section 501(c)(3).

NONVIOLENT – The Irish National Caucus is nonviolent, nonpartisan and nonsectarian. It has no foreign principal and does not support, morally or financially, any group or party in any part of Ireland. It does not send money to Ireland. All its funds are raised and spent in the United States.

HISTORIC VISION – The Irish National Caucus was the first organization in history to open and maintain headquarters on Capitol Hill to lobby for justice and peace in Ireland. That fact alone tells you a lot about the vision and purpose of the Irish National Caucus – not to mention its determination and ability.

OUTSTANDING RECORD – The Irish National Caucus initiated the formation of the Ad Hoc Congressional Committee for Irish Affairs, which over 100 Members of Congress have joined.

MAC BRIDE PRINCIPLES – The Irish National Caucus in 1984 initiated, proposed, and launched the Mac Bride Principles – a fair employment code of conduct for U.S. companies doing business in Northern Ireland. Named after the late, great Sean Mac Bride of Ireland, the Principles have already proven to be the most effective campaign ever against anti-Catholic discrimination in Northern Ireland. The Principles – which do not call for disinvestment, quotas or reverse discrimination – were passed into law in 18 states, numerous cities, and became U.S. law in October 1998.

Tel (202) 544-0568 · Fax (202) 488-7537
support@irishnationalcaucus.org · Website: irishnationalcaucus.org